China's Holy Mountain

China's Holy Mountain

An Illustrated Journey into the Heart of Buddhism

Christoph Baumer

I.B. TAURIS

LONDON · NEW YORK

Published in 2011 by I.B.Tauris & Co Ltd
6 Salem Road, London W2 4BU
175 Fifth Avenue, New York NY 10010
www.ibtauris.com

Distributed in the United States and Canada Exclusively by Palgrave Macmillan,
175 Fifth Avenue, New York NY 10010

First published in 2008 in Germany by Pedro Detjen Verlag, Hamburg under the
title: *Wutai Shan – Mittelpunkt des chinesischen Buddhismus. Klöster und Pilger am
heiligsten Berg Chinas*
Copyright © 2008 Christoph Baumer
This translation published by arrangement with Pedro Detjen Verlag, Hamburg

Translated by Miranda Bennett
Photographs © Christoph Baumer 2008, 2011

ISBN: 978 1 84885 700 1

A full CIP record for this book is available from the British Library
A full CIP record is available from the Library of Congress

Library of Congress Catalog Card Number: available

Designed by Christopher Bromley

Printed and bound in China.

Endpapers illustration: Hand-tinted woodblock print on linen in sino-mongol
style from *c.* 1846, produced at Wutai Shan. 118 x 165 cm. Rubin Museum of Art,
New York.

Contents

Glossary and abbreviations

The words in **bold** have a separate glossary entry.

Amitabha (Chinese: Amituofo) Buddha of light who rules
over the paradise of **Sukhavati.**

Ananda (Chinese: Anan) the favourite pupil of **Shakyamuni.**

arhat (Chinese: luohan) one who has achieved
enlightenment.

Avalokiteshvara (Chinese: **Guanyin**) the **bodhisattva** of
compassion.

BCE before the common (or current) era (i.e. before the
present), equivalent to 'Before Christ'.

Bodhidharma (Chinese: Putidamo) Founder and spiritual
father of Chan Buddhism.

bodhisattvas (Chinese: pusa) 'enlightened beings' who
strive for enlightenment on the path of perfect virtue
but promise to forgo entry into nirvana until all living
beings are likewise enlightened.

Buddha-nature idea prevalent in **Mahayana** Buddhism
that all sentient beings have the potential to achieve
enlightenment and thus become like the Buddha.

Chan Buddhism known in the West by its Japanese name,
Zen: its central tenet is that the nature of all living
things is fundamentally good and that enlightment can
be reached by a 'correct' daily life.

CE common or current era (i.e. the present), equivalent to
'A.D.', 'Anno Domini'.

chakravartins (Chinese: zhuanlun) universal rulers of the
world who supported Buddhism, likenesses of Buddha
on earth.

Confucianism a Chinese ethical, quasi-religious teaching
based on the philosophy of Confucius. It deals with the
morally right code of conduct, the right social relations
and the ideal state.

Daoism one of the three religions that have most influenced
China, alongside **Confucianism** and Buddhism. Most
associated with the philosopher **Laozi**. Its central ideas
relate to cosmology, universal energy or Qi, patterns of
change, and divination, veneration of ancestors, and
immortality, as well as the perfection of body and soul.

dharma Buddhist concept that has several possible
meanings, including: the cosmic law governing
rebirths; the eternal teaching; ethical norms; observable
phenomena; mental content, an idea; in **Hinayana**, an
element of existence.

Dharmaguptaka One of the 18 schools of early Buddhism.

Guanyin (Pusa) in China, the bodhisattva of compassion;
usually represented as female and originated as
Avalokiteshvara.

Han Chinese largest ethnic group in China, making up
over 90% of the population.

Han Dynasty China's second imperial dynasty after the
Qin. It lasted from 202 BCE–220 CE and was succeeded
by the 'three kingdoms': Wei, Shu Han and Wu.

Hinayana (Chinese: Xiaosheng) (also known as
Theravada). The form of Buddhism that developed after
the death of **Shakyamuni**. The doctrine of Hinayana
understood itself as a pragmatic guide to individual
deliverance from the cycle of rebirth, called Samsara.
Unlike **Mahayana** Buddhism, Hinayana considers that
every individual human being must find his or her own
path to salvation and travel it alone.

Laozi Semi-legendary philosopher who is believed to have
written one of the foundation texts of **Daoism**, the *Dao
De Jing*. He is said to have been an elder contemporary
of Confucius, placing him in the sixth century BCE.

luohan *see* **arhat.**

Mahayana (Chinese: Dasheng) One of the two main
branches of Buddhism today. The name means
'the wide path' and it refers to the journey to seek
enlightenment. Unlike **Hinayana** Buddhism, however,
Mahayana does not expect believers to do the journey
alone but with the aid of merciful **bodhisattvas.**

Mahakashyapa (Chinese: Dajiaye) one of the two main
disciples of **Shakyamuni.**

Maitreya (Chinese: Milefo) the coming or future Buddha;
a **bodhisattva** who will achieve full enlightenment and
will succeed **Shakyamuni.**

mandala a design often found in Buddhist artworks. It is
usually a combination of circular and square patterns
and has complex imagery representing aspects of the
Buddhist worldview.

mandorla roughly almond-shaped aureole surrounding
the figure of the Buddha in carvings and sculptures.

Manjushri (Chinese: Wenshu Pusa) the **bodhisattva**
of wisdom.

Middle Kingdom term often used in the West as
synonymous with China, as a translation of the
Mandarin Chinese word for the country: 'Zhongguo',
meaning middle or central (Zhong) land (guo).

Milefo *see* **Maitreya.**

nirvana the state in which one transcends the cycle
of reincarnation, marked by the extinction of all
desires, suffering and the bonds of existence, and the
attainment of enlightenment.

pusa *see* **bodhisattvas.**

Piluzhenafo (Sanskrit: Vairocana) The transcendent or
primordial buddha; often statues of him are pure white.

sangha (Chinese: heseng) the Buddhist religious
community.

Shakyamuni spiritual teacher who founded Buddhism in
the late sixth/early fifth century BCE. He is also called
'Gautama'.

stupa dome-shaped Buddhist shrine.

Sukhavati (Chinese: Xifang jile shijie) paradise ruled over
by the Buddha Amitabha. Its name means 'pure land'.

sutra canonical Buddhist scripture.

Theravada *see* **Hinayana.**

Vairocana *see* **Piluzhenafo.**

Vajrayana a further development of **Mahayana**. Vajrayana
arose in India at the start of the seventh century as a
reaction against the increasing intellectualism within
Mahayana.

Vimalakirti an enlightened layman who is supposed to
have written a sutra named after him.

Vinayapitaka monastic rules for Buddhist clergy.

Wenshu Pusa *see* **Manjushri.**

中國五臺山大顯通寺

前言

位于中国五台山中心的显通寺是中国最古老和最重要的佛教圣地之。 五台山是大智菩萨文殊的道场。

据传说公元六十四年汉明帝梦见一个会飞的金人， 他的大臣将此金人释为佛。 三年以后两个印度僧人带着佛经来到当时中国的首都洛阳。 明帝亲自召见了他们， 以后下令在洛阳和五台山分别修建了白马寺和大孚灵鹫寺两座佛庙， 后来大孚灵鹫寺又改称显通寺。明朝（一三六八年至一六四四年）传下来的称著《清凉山之旧志》的五台山志记载，显通寺建于北魏孝文帝时代（公元四百七十一年至四百九十九年）。按此计算显通寺至少也有一千五百年的历史了。

现今仍拥有五十多座佛教寺庙的五台山不但是中国重要的佛教朝圣地，同时也是对佛教在中国延续的最好证明 。 五台山作为抗日（一九三七年至一九四五年）和后来抗击国民党（一九四五年至一九四九年）的一个红军根据地， 在中国二十世纪的政治上也占有重要的地位。五台山同供汉，藏佛教两派， 这也是它独有的特色。

我非常高兴克利斯托夫·包默博士编著了这么一本全新的关于五台山圣地的重要著作。 他遍访了该地区所有的佛教寺庙， 并作了详细的纪录。 我希望通过此书可以鼓励更多的欧洲人同美国人去五台山观览。

中国山西省五台山显通寺
静行法师

二零零七年五月

地址：山西省五臺縣臺懷鎮大顯通寺

電話：0350－6545988　　　　傳真：0350－6545414　　　　郵編：035515

Foreword

The Buddhist Xiantong Si Monastery in the heart of the Wutai Shan Mountains is one of the oldest and most important Buddhist institutions in China. We believe the Five Terrace Mountain is the spiritual home of Wenshu Pusa, the bodhisattva of wisdom.

According to legend, in the year 64 Emperor Han Mingdi dreamed of a golden man, whom his ministers interpreted to be the Buddha. Three years later two Indian monks arrived in the Chinese capital Luoyang, bearing Buddhist texts. Emperor Mingdi welcomed them and then had two monasteries built, Beima Si in the capital Luoyang and Xiantong Monastery on Wutai Shan; at the time the monastery was called Da Fu Ling Jiu Si. The chronicle of Wutai Shan called *The History of Qing Liang Shan* from the Ming Dynasty (1368–1644) reports that Emperor Xiaowendi (ruled 471–99) of the northern Wei dynasty founded the monastery. The monastery is thus at least 1,500 years old.

The sacred mountain of Wutai Shan, with its more than 50 extant monasteries, is not only China's most important Buddhist pilgrimage site; it is also the best evidence for the continuity of Buddhism in China. The region of the Wutai Mountains likewise played an important political role in the twentieth century, as it served as headquarters for part of the Red Army first during the war against the Japanese invaders (1937–45) and then against the Nationalists (1945–9). The mountain is also unique because Han Chinese and Tibetan monasteries have flourished there side by side.

I am extraordinarily pleased that Dr Christoph Baumer has written this new and important book about the sacred mountain of Wutai Shan. He has visited and documented all the Buddhist monasteries in the region. I hope the book will inspire many people from Europe and America to visit Wutai Shan in the future.

Monk Fan, Abbot of Xiantong Monastery,
Wutai Shan, Shanxi Province, China.

Introduction

Buddha Shakyamuni said to Bodhisattva Maitreya: 'If you, Maitreya, are able to attain anuttara-samyak-sambodhi [enlightenment], then all living beings should likewise be able to attain it. Why? Because all living beings in truth bear the marks of bodhi [Buddha-nature].'

—Vimalakirti Sutra[1]

In this quotation from the *Vimalakirti Sutra* (Chinese: *Weimojie Jing*), which appeared in India around the year 100 CE and was first translated into Chinese in 188 CE, we find exemplified the foundational idea of Chinese Buddhism, particularly Chan Buddhism, which is known in the West by its Japanese name, Zen: the nature of all living things is fundamentally good, despite the evident suffering in this world. Since every living thing carries within itself the kernel of the Buddha-nature, it can potentially experience enlightenment (Chinese: Wu). In contrast to Indian Buddhism, which posits in the end that one must escape this existence, experienced as suffering, through 'entrance' into nirvana, Chinese Buddhism emphasises the possibility and necessity of recognising and awakening one's own slumbering Buddha-nature. By giving the Buddhist message this optimistic perspective, Chan succeeded in adapting the essentially pessimistic worldview of Indian Buddhism to Chinese thought.

While in Indian thought, change and the multifariousness of phenomena resulting from that change are understood as illusions, Chinese thought has always affirmed the principle of change as the foundation of all things.[2] Change and variety are not illusions that ought somehow to be overcome, but rather they are the very nature of all things. It is no coincidence that the oldest and best-known classic book of China, the *Yi Jing* from the epoch of the later Western Zhou (1122–771 BCE), is called the *Book of Changes*. As a pure white lotus blossom can grow in a turbid swamp, the ever-present Buddha-nature can bloom in every person, including unbelievers and even criminals. One of the spiritual founders of Chan, called Dao Sheng (*c.* 360–434 CE), shocked the Buddhist 'monks' establishment' of China, which was still marked by Indian Buddhism, with his radically new conviction that enlightenment consists in the realisation of the positive forces of our nature; that is, our slumbering Buddha-nature, and not in release from an inherently bad nature. This new focus corresponded to the definition of the Chinese word for religion, zong jiao, which basically means education or instruction (jiao) in returning to the origin (zong) – in other words, to one's own Buddha-nature.

Four statues of Buddha Shijiafo (Sanskrit Shakyamuni), facing the four directions, in a lotus blossom. The eight wooden petals can be opened and closed using a crank mechanism. Hall of the Revelation of Buddha, Luohou Si Monastery.

The monastery village of Taihuai, the main town of Wutai Shan, under the northern terrace. From the front right to the rear left, the pagoda of Tayuan Si and the great monasteries of Xiantong Si and Pusading Si can be seen.

Dao Sheng's message was revolutionary, even anarchic, in two ways. First, he broke down the then strongly hierarchical social order by asserting that living beings, including beggars and slaves, possess the Buddha-nature and could experience enlightenment. Thereby Dao Sheng endowed every person with existential worth, apart from lineage or social rank, and returned to them the autonomy that Buddha Shakyamuni had originally taught in rejecting the Vedic determinism then accepted. For Shakyamuni, every person was responsible for his own 'redemption'.

The so-called Lesser Vehicle of Hinayana, which stands more closely to the original teaching of Shakyamuni, required the individual believer to travel alone on the narrow path of redemption, while the 'wide path' of the Great Vehicle, called Mahayana, which arose in the first century CE, promised people the help of merciful bodhisattvas. Bodhisattvas are enlightened beings who have postponed entrance into nirvana as long as living beings still await redemption. They swear to delay their own redemption until all living things have been saved. This more accessible teaching led to the Buddhist doctrine of Jingtu, today the most widely held in China, according to which it is sufficient to call fervently on the name of Buddha Amitabha in order to be reborn in his pure land Sukhavati.[3]

Dao Sheng went still one step further and emphasised that one can experience enlightenment suddenly and completely; that is, not necessarily only as the long-drawn-out result of one or more meritorious lives. Expressed figuratively, he interpreted life as a pilgrimage to one's own Buddha-nature. As a result, the Buddhist establishment, associated in central China with the nobility, attacked Dao Sheng and expelled him.[4] Despite his exile, Dao Sheng had set the course for Buddhism in China, about three centuries after its introduction into the Middle Kingdom. It was the moment of birth for Chinese Buddhism.

The oldest, most significant, and only international Buddhist pilgrimage site in China is Wutai Shan in the northern Chinese province of Shanxi, lying about 350 km southwest of Beijing. It serves as the 'Mecca of Chinese Buddhism', to which Mongols, Tibetans, Koreans and Japanese also make pilgrimages. But in contrast to the pilgrimage destinations of Semitic-monotheistic religions, which are buildings or gravesites – in the cases of Christianity and Islam, connected to the religion's founder, his disciples, or his successors, e.g., Bethlehem, Santiago de Compostela, Mecca, or the grave of Imam Hussein in Kerbala, Iraq – Chinese pilgrimage sites, whether Buddhist or Daoist, are features of the natural world, specifically mountains. In spite of a distinctive ancestor cult, no gravesites in China are sacred, since veneration of ancestors is a family or clan matter, nothing more. The Chinese Buddhist or Daoist encounters the divine in nature, as unspoiled as possible. For that reason, in China we speak mostly of extended pilgrimages, in contrast to shorter, more easily accomplished journeys.

In Indian Buddhism a profane landscape was sacralised only by a historical event, by becoming a station in the life of Buddha Shakyamuni, such as his birthplace Lumbini; the site of his enlightenment, Bodhgaya; or that of his first preaching, Sarnath. Chinese Buddhism and Daoism, however, perceive the sacred in nature itself; the object of veneration is not separate from the landscape but is a special part of nature itself, principally a mountain. Sacred mountains are the residences of gods, bodhisattvas or Daoist immortals. Mountains support heaven; they provide a bridge, accessible to human beings, to a supernatural sphere. By making a pilgrimage to a sacred mountain, believers hope to encounter the deity residing there. That such a mountain is venerated not only as the home of a deity but is also considered holy in and of itself is indicated by the Chinese term for pilgrimage, chao shan jinxiang. Chao shan means 'to show respect to a mountain', and jinxiang 'to bring incense [to the deity]'.[5] Monasteries erected in a mountainous landscape are only of secondary sacral significance, since they are consecrated first by the mountain itself. Because in the Dao-Buddhist conception of the world every manmade structure represents an infringement of the harmony of nature, architects made a great effort to conform monasteries and temples to the landscape.[6] Architecture and nature should stand not as opposites but rather in a harmonious relationship with one another.

Wutai Shan, whose northern peak is, at 3,058 m, the highest mountain in northern China, rises just a few kilometres south of the inner Great Wall, which from the Chinese perspective separates the civilised world of China from the world of the barbarians. Thus Wutai Shan forms a spiritual

bulwark for China on its perpetually threatened northern border. The significance of Wutai Shan for Chinese Buddhism can be seen in the tradition that its most venerable monastery, Xiantong Si, is the second-oldest Buddhist monastery in all of China. (The word si means monastery.) The first monastery, Beima Si, is said to have been founded in the year 67 CE in the then-capital city of Luoyang, and Xiantong just one year later.[7] Although this early founding date belongs in the realm of legend, it is possible that the first three monasteries on Wutai Shan had been founded by the end of the fifth century. Ironically it was the non-Chinese 'barbarian' emperor Xiaowendi (ruled 471–99), from the dynasty of the northern Wei (386–534), who descended from a nomadic people of Mongolian origin, who established the three monasteries, Xiantong, Qingliang and Foguang, and gave early Chinese Buddhism important impetus. Shortly thereafter the first

The bodhisattva Wenshu Pusa (Manjushri) on his lion and another bodhisattva. Jin Dynasty (1115–1234). Hall of Wenshu Pusa, Foguang Si.

One of the five slender bronze pagodas in front of the Bronze Hall of Xiantong Si.

Abbess Shi Chang Long speaks
in front of the Great Hall about
the coming ceremony of the
symbolic washing of Shijiafo at his
birthday celebration in Baiyun Si.

translation of the *Avatamsaka Sutra* indicated that, according to Shakyamuni, the next revelation of the teaching would take place on Wutai Shan.[8]

Wutai Shan achieved even greater significance when the Indian monk Bodhiruci (Chinese: Putiliuzhi, 672–727) recorded in 710 that at the end of the effectiveness of Buddha Shakyamuni's cycle of teaching, Buddhist teaching would be proclaimed anew by Bodhisattva Manjushri (Chinese: Wenshu Pusa) on the Five Terrace Mountain in northern China.[9] In this way, within Buddhist cosmology, the Chinese borderland moved to the centre of Buddhist sacred history. Henceforth Wutai Shan served as the sole authentic site for proclamation of Buddhist teaching, where believers could have unmediated contact with a merciful bodhisattva. In light of the apparent decline of Buddhism in India as of the sixth and seventh centuries, China became the only source of new Buddhist revelation.

The pilgrimage centre has experienced a chequered history. During the heyday of the Tang Dynasty (618–907), Wutai Shan was home to about 360 monasteries, and before the Communist takeover in October 1949, 100 of these remained. From this time on pilgrims and visitors were forbidden access to Wutai Shan, and later the so-called Cultural Revolution (1966–76) wreaked havoc here, as in all of China, and left behind a chaotic scene of senseless destruction.

According to official reports, the most important monasteries in the centre of Wutai Shan withstood this act of cultural barbarism, and there were said to be 58 monasteries and temples again active in 1993.[10] When I visited Wutai Shan for the first time that year, this number seemed to me too high.

In 2006 and 2007, during two extended visits, I paid Wutai Shan my respects like a traditional pilgrim and explored all its monasteries, shrines and hermits' caves. Earlier I had undertaken Buddhist pilgrimages to sacred landscapes in

Tibet. These pilgrimages took the form of circum-ambulations of a particular mountain, such as Mount Kailash and Kongpo Bönri, or a lake like Dangra Tso. These pilgrimages followed a prescribed route. The distinctive topography of Wutai Shan requires another type of pilgrimage; it is not circular but rather star-shaped. As so often in Chinese, the name expresses the defining characteristic of the object, as it means Five (Wu) Terrace (Tai) Mountain (Shan). The five plateau-like peaks mark out the inner Wutai Shan region, which is less than 800 km² in extent. The region's centre is considered to be not the middle peak but rather the Xiantong Si Monastery in the heart of the monastery town of Taihuai.

The Five Terrace Mountain resembles a gigantic, three-dimensional mandala. Unlike the traditional mandala, in which the meditating person moves spiritually from the periphery to the centre, pilgrims advance directly to the centre, from which they stream out in all directions to visit the five terraces and their sacred sites. I encountered a total of 68 monasteries and shrines, of which 63 were active; at two there stood only a sporadically visited pagoda, two had been destroyed, and in the case of one other monastery rebuilding had only just begun.

In a broader sense, the outer flanks of the five terraces and their foothills also belong to Wutai Shan; they form the outer region with an area of approximately 6,500 km². Here I investigated and documented 12 monasteries of art historical significance; today most of them are museums.

In this book I want to take readers on a virtual pilgrimage to Wutai Shan. After overviews of the historical and spiritual context as well as of the most prominent schools of Chinese Buddhism, all the monasteries, shrines and caves of Wutai Shan will be considered. The fascination of Wutai Shan lies partly in the fact that in post-Communist China an almost 2,000-year-old tradition is awaking to new life. People of varied backgrounds come together here. There are simple farmers from the province of Shanxi, *nouveau riche* merchants from Beijing, Shanghai or Shenzen, Communist Party functionaries, uniformed groups from Japan and Korea, Mongolian nomads and Tibetan pilgrims, who, in the most extreme cases, journey on foot from their homelands, thousands of kilometres distant, and within the inner region measure out the paths to the monasteries and terraces with their own bodies. For them a pilgrimage from Tibet to Wutai Shan lasts years; they demonstrate Dao Sheng's insight that our life resembles a continuous pilgrimage to our own true nature. Before a statue of Manjushri all pilgrims are equal, and likewise during the exhausting climb up to a mountain temple.

This book also shows that the heart of a culture lies in its spiritual convictions and religions, which resist all governmental repression. The atheistic delusion mandated by the state until the end of the twentieth century has long since capitulated in China, Tibet and the Soviet Union, as Chinese and Tibetan Buddhism, Orthodox Christianity and Islam awoke to new life in those countries. Force can command everything except thoughts, feelings and desires.

Tibetan monks at the ritual in honour of the patron and meditation deity Weilowa Jingang (Vajrabhairava) in Guangren Si.

The spiritual and historical context

Most Chinese 'wear a Confucian crown, a Daoist robe, and a pair of Buddhist sandals.'

—Chinese saying [1]

The uniqueness of Chinese culture lies in its extraordinary endurance and longevity within the same geographic space in which Emperor Qin Shi Huangdi defined national unity in 221 BCE. China's history has been textually documented for more than 3,000 years and is attested to archaeologically for a period of 6,000 to 7,000 years. Older civilisations are known, but they have long since collapsed. The early civilisations of the Indus Valley and Mesopotamia disappeared millennia ago, as did the pharaonic culture of Egypt. The Roman Empire is also long gone.

Until the beginning of the twentieth century, external influences were able to shape Chinese culture only minimally, with the exception of Buddhism from India. Buddhism was not absorbed by the traditional spiritual environment of China but was rather appropriated at various times by Chinese thought. In this way new cultural syntheses developed, differing significantly from earlier versions. Outstanding examples of such syntheses include the rationalist neo-Confucianism that emerged in the eleventh and twelfth centuries, the 'School of

Mind' and the idealistic neo-Confucian 'School of Spirit' of Wang Yangming (1472–1529). Foreign peoples, however, who conquered and ruled parts or all of China, were without exception absorbed and assimilated into Chinese culture. This fact is all the more astonishing considering that the Chinese empire – or at least its northern half – was ruled by non-Chinese 'barbarians' from Mongolia and Manchuria for nearly 1,000 years after imperial unification in 221 BCE. until the revolution of 1911. The history of China also teaches that the Great Wall, which grew out of various partial walls over 2,000 years ago, offered protection from the attacks of nomadic horsemen only when the empire was strong and the Chinese armies attacked the peoples advancing from the north on the other side of the wall. Thus the Great Wall functioned less as a defensive bulwark than as a base for military offensives. Without sufficient troops it was a paper tiger. The widespread opinion that the Great Wall is an expression of a supposedly arch-Chinese instinct for defensiveness and isolation is a myth.

Wenshu Pusa (Manjushri) stands before the seated Milefo (Buddha Maitreya). Hall of the Buddhas of the Three Ages, Zunsheng Si.

In China the principles of Feng Shui ascribe to incense a function of purifying the vital energy Qi; purifying power is attributed to its fragrance in Buddhism as well. Shuxiang Si.

The term 'Chinese' has been applied in different ways. In a political sense it refers to a feature within the Chinese state; in this way one speaks of Chinese citizens or the Chinese army, regardless of whether the people are Chinese in the ethnic sense. But with regard to ethnicity, China is hardly homogeneous. Although the Han make up about 91% of the total population, China counts 55 officially recognised minorities, who are spread across two-thirds of the country. The terms 'Chinese culture' and 'Chinese Buddhism' are used in an ethnically defined way. By Chinese culture we mean the culture created primarily by Han Chinese in the region between the Huang He (Yellow River) and the Yangtze in today's central China. Discoveries made at the end of the twentieth century in Sichuan at Sanxingdui, Baodun and Jinsha show, however, that the cradle of Chinese culture should be sought not just in central China but also south of the Yangtze. We consider Chinese Buddhism to encompass those schools founded

within the cultural realm of the Han Chinese by Han monks. This is distinct from Tibetan Buddhism, although the latter was actually present in China at times from the thirteenth century on.

In Mandarin Chinese, the word for 'China' is 'Zhongguo', meaning middle or central (Zhong) land (guo). In the West the term 'Middle Kingdom' has often been cited as evidence of the cultural ethnocentricity of China, but this is not the case. During the 'Spring and Autumn Period' (770–475 BCE), Zhongguo referred to the central states along the Yellow River, distinct from those on the periphery. A millennium later, during the division of China into a northern region ruled by proto-Mongols and Tibetans and a southern region ruled by the Han (316–581 CE) the term took on another meaning, as it now argued for its own political legitimacy. And so the Northern Wei, for instance, renamed themselves Zhongguo and the rival southern dynasty Yi or 'barbarians'. The latter, however, characterised the Northern Wei as Lu, 'criminals'. Under the Tang (618–907) the term

'Zhongguo' included all peoples belonging to the empire, irrespective of their ethnic affiliation. In today's People's Republic the word also refers to all the regions and peoples within the national borders.

Origins of China's cultural development

On both sides of the lower reaches of the Huang He an elaborate cult of the dead emerged at least 6,000 years ago in the prehistoric period. It included lavish burial chambers, grave goods, animal and human sacrifices, funeral feasts and prophecies. For these one held the shoulder blade of a deer, an ox, or a sheep, or the plastron of a tortoise in a fire and interpreted the cracks in the bones caused by the heat. This style of divination, called scapulomancy, is still practised today among Mongolian peoples. In any case, the prehistoric people of central China believed in life after death and began to venerate their ancestors – one of the kernels of Chinese social culture.

Compared to other early civilisations, in China the historical fog began to lift only relatively late and slowly, in the twenty-first century BCE. After the presumably historical Xia Dynasty (twenty-first to sixteenth centuries BCE) there followed in northern and central China the historical Shang Dynasty (sixteenth century to 1122 BCE) and in the southern province of Sichuan the culture of Shu (c. twentieth to ninth centuries BCE), discovered only in the late twentieth century, which existed in several stages and culminated in the culture of Sanxingdui. Here in 1986 archaeologists found two sacrifice pits with bronze artifacts from 1300 to 1000 BCE. These included spectacular and monumental figures and masks with protruding eyes, made from bronze and gold leaf. They are radically different from the bronze artifacts of the Shang period, which consist of weapons, vessels with abstract masks, and instruments.

Whether the two sacrificial pits of Sanxingdui were connected with a grave is unknown.[2]

Regarding culture and beliefs at the time of Shang Dynasty, two sources provide information: gravesites and inscriptions on bronze vessels, the plastrons of tortoises or shoulder blades. The earliest Chinese script, which emerged in the thirteenth century BCE, supported divination. Knowledge of it was reserved for priest-scribes of both sexes, who practised the art of divination only in service to the rulers. During divination the script served to establish the connection to the deities and spirits being invoked. The script had a purely sacral function and was not available to the general public. Only when the official oracle was abolished and scapulomancy declined in significance around the eighth century BCE did the Chinese script change from an exclusive, magical instrument of communication into a generally accessible, rational means of communication and the transmission of knowledge.[3] Secularisation of writing had already begun earlier, however, as the priests of the oracle wrote down not only the questions asked to the deities but also their 'answers' and the resulting decisions of the rulers. In this way soothsayers served also as court historians.

The gravesites of the Shang Dynasty, richly appointed with ritual objects such as bronze vessels, jade, and mussel shells, and provided as well with animal and human sacrifices, belonged to members of the ruling clan. They hoped to live just as luxurious a lifestyle in the afterlife as they enjoyed in this life. The living regularly brought sacrifices to the idolised ancestors. Thanks to the oracular bones described above, we know they ascribed healing powers to them and beseeched them to act as intercessors and advocates for their descendants with powerful deities such as the nature gods who sent rain or granted good health. This principle of pragmatic, even mercantile reciprocity is still found today in Chinese folk religion: one offers sacrifices to particular ancestors or local deities and expects a tangible return, such as a good harvest, healing, or the end to an epidemic. Should the anticipated results routinely fail to appear, people turn away from them toward other ancestors and spirits. Religious sacrifice to the ancestors is in fact bartering. At the peak of the hierarchically ordered pyramid of ancestors, spirits, and gods stands the highest god, Shangdi, whose name means 'higher, superior (Shang) god (Di)'. Human beings rarely turn directly to him; they implore lower gods and ancestors to discern his will and intercede for supplicants.

The veneration of heaven

Around the year 1122 BCE the dynasty of the Western Zhou (c. 1122–770 BCE) split off from the Shang Dynasty. The work known as the *Bamboo Annals*, which dates from the early third century BCE, gives a date of c. 1050 BCE for the split, indicating that it may have occurred over several decades. The Zhou reorganised central China as a feudal state with hundreds of small city-states under royal administration, which was led by members of the royal family and allied clans. The king was both the chief feudal lord and highest priest in the cult of the ancestors. The king regularly brought royal sacrifices to the ancestors and especially to the highest god and forefather Tian, heaven, who had taken the place of Shangdi. The king was considered the 'son of heaven' who had the 'mandate of heaven' to rule the people wisely and justly on his behalf. As long as the king obeyed the prophecies of heaven, peace and prosperity would prevail. But if he was corrupt, negligent or cruel, famine or natural disasters would occur as heavenly warnings. Thus the king was dependent on soothsayers, since only they could discern the mind and will of Tian.

If the king persisted in his misconduct, he forfeited his heavenly mandate and the people were permitted to revolt. This theory of the divine mandate from heaven served to legitimate the dynasty, and the idea was developed further by the philosophers Confucius (551–479 BCE) and Mengzi (c. 372–289 BCE). Mengzi in particular emphasised the right of the people to rebel in the case of poor administration by the king; his theory posited an early version of the social contract, which J.J. Rousseau developed fully two millennia later in 1758. For Mengzi the king was subject to a heavenly duty to rule properly, according to moral principles. If he violated his duty, the people had the right to demand back and use the natural freedoms they had ceded to the state, such as the use of force.

In 771 BCE the dynasty lost the mandate of heaven, when King Yu fell in battle against invading nomadic horsemen; at the same time the feudal lords gained power. The subsequent era of the Eastern Zhou (770–256 BCE) was marked by a military process of consolidating power in a few kingdoms, but also by a period of creative philosophy. On the political level, during the Spring and Autumn Period (770–475 BCE) the families of the nobility lost control of the increasingly powerful client states, the leadership and administration of which was now frequently delegated by the rulers to skilled ministers and functionaries. In place of a feudal structure monopolised by noble families, there arose a state apparatus based on personal loyalty and competence. The king of the Eastern Zhou now had only a ceremonial function to maintain the cult of the ancestors, whose former practice of human sacrifice was abolished. In the subsequent Warring States Period (475–221 BCE) the conflict over supreme power in northern and central China intensified. As of 403 BCE only seven kingdoms still wrestled for dominance, and their administrative structures and standing armies became increasingly professionalised.

Two horsemen at battle in a presumably Daoist portrayal. Sandstone decoration on the Hall of the Four Heavenly Guardians of the Buddhist monastery of Youguo Si.

In the fourth century BCE two seminal reforms took place. First, in 307 BCE the kingdom of Zhou, north of the Yellow River – whose territory also included the modern province of Shanxi – adopted the military techniques and weaponry of the proto-Mongolian nomadic cavalry, using their style of fighting on horseback, armed with bows and arrows. This change paid off handsomely, and Zhao gained decisive victories in the north over the Xiongnu, a proto-Turko–Mongolian people, which a century later grew into China's strongest rival.[4] Thanks to this new method of warfare, Shanxi and thus Wutai Shan remained in Chinese hands. Still more important were the four reforms of the Legalist[5] and minister Shang Yang (c. 390–338 BCE) in the small kingdom of Qin in today's Shaanxi Province. Unlike the Confucians, he considered virtue and morality to be unsuitable means of rule and created a tightly controlled system of administrative functionaries, who enforced strict application of the law. He persuaded the king of Qin to establish a new nobility, entry into which could only be gained by outstanding service to the state or by military service. At the same time he encouraged farming and fishing and doubled the tax burden on single and childless men. The anticipated rapid increase in population was to revive agriculture and above all ensure a steady supply of soldiers. The reforms bore fruit in the long run. Prince Zheng of Qin (ruled 247–221 BCE) succeeded in eliminating his rivals one after another and, in 221 BCE, in uniting China politically for the first time. The victorious Zheng adopted the name Qin Shihuangdi (ruled 221–210 BCE), meaning the 'first (Shi) exalted (Huang) supreme being (Di) of Qin'.

The Hundred Schools of Thought

He who by respect for the Spirits keeps them
at a distance, may be termed wise.

—Confucius[6]

The age of the Eastern Zhou was not only marked by enormous political and social agitation but was also philosophically the most creative and productive period in all of Chinese intellectual history. With the exception of Buddhism, every significant philosophical strain in Chinese culture flowered in this period, which is rightfully called the 'Hundred Schools of Thought' (551–213 BCE). This fundamental reorientation of Chinese thought was initiated by the collapse of the Western Zhou Dynasty in 770 BCE and the subsequent splintering of the kingdom into about 30 warring city-states. Not only had the Zhou lost the mandate of heaven; the gods had likewise failed in their obligation to protect the land and the people. Since none of the small states was able to dominate, no one could receive a new mandate of heaven and draw on the patronage of new, effective gods. The dynasty of the Eastern Zhou maintained cultic legitimacy to carry out state sacrifices but was powerless. Conversely, the most powerful princes, who overran all of China, lacked any religious legitimacy. For this reason, in the sixth century BCE philosophers turned away from the obviously useless gods and spirits and began a rational discourse on the nature of human beings, ethical norms, social structures and governance.

Confucius and the belief in morality and education

The most important and influential philosopher was Confucius (551–479 BCE). He initially

Shijiafo (Buddha Shakyamuni, left) and Confucius in the syncretic monastery of Xuankong Si, Heng Shan Bei.

held a low-ranking government office in the state of Lu, in today's eastern Chinese province of Shandong, and then tried in vain to offer his services as an advisor to the princes of neighbouring states. Returning to Lu, he worked in *c.* 499 BCE in the Ministry of Public Works before becoming Minister of Justice a year later. He must have quickly determined that his influence on the government was only slight; he resigned and left his homeland. He gathered a few students with the goal of shaping their character in such a way that they would one day achieve high political office and renew from within the state employing them.

Confucius brought about a Copernican shift, which was just as radical as that of the European Enlightenment. Rather than considering the human being only in relation to ancestors, spirits and gods, as had been done up to that point, he consistently moved the individual into the centre of his worldview. Confucius asked first about the code of conduct of a noble and humane person; secondly about those social relationships appropriate for the ideal noble person; and thirdly about the nature of a state that would create the conditions for realisation of the ideal person and ideal social relationships. A millennium later Confucius's ethical norms would compel important adaptations of Indian Buddhism. Confucius was a moralist and theorist of the state; he considered metaphysics superfluous, and religious rituals interested him only insofar as they encouraged virtuous living. In his book *The Analects* he maintains pragmatically:

[The student] Zilu asked how one should serve ghosts and spirits. The Master said, 'Since you haven't learnt to serve men, how can you serve ghosts?' [When Zilu continued,] 'May I ask about the nature of death?' the Master answered, 'Since you don't know about the living, how are you to know about the dead?'[7]

Confucius abhorred the use of force and brutish violence. He believed that society and the state should be governed by moral rules rather than by laws and punishment. His optimism was based on the conviction that human beings were capable of learning, and their imperfect nature could be improved through educational measures. Virtue and ethical conduct were learned, not innate. Insofar as he taught that true nobility was not a matter of inheritance but rather of character and willingness to learn, and that all human beings could attain this nobility, he was revolutionary.

Confucius saw in the patriarchal structure of the family the cornerstone of a harmonious society. The relationships within the family should be governed by respect for the head of the family, 'filial piety', love for older brothers, and reciprocal loyalty. Within this context Confucius considered the ancestor cult and its accompanying rituals useful because they offered occasions to praise the forefathers' virtues as worthy of

emulation. Confucius did not believe in gods but considered belief in them to be useful insofar as it encouraged people to behave well because they hoped to be rewarded for virtuous conduct and feared being punished for misdeeds.

Confucius applied the model of virtuous and harmonious family relations, in which each member accepted his naturally assigned place, to society and the state. If the relationships within families, as well as those among families and clans, are harmonious, society will function harmoniously, provided that the rulers and the ruled are governed by the same values as the family; that is, reciprocal loyalty, respect for superiors, goodwill toward subordinates, morality, humaneness and willingness to learn. More than two millennia before Immanuel Kant's 'categorical imperative', Confucius summed up his teaching as follows:

When a student asked him, 'is there any single saying that one can act upon all day and every day?' The Master said, 'Perhaps the saying about consideration: "Never do to others what you would not like them to do to you".'[8]

We must note, however, that Confucius in no way aspired to the equality of humanity or even an egalitarian social structure but rather a hierarchically ordered society with patriarchal governance. Confucius said in this regard, 'Let the prince be a prince, the minister a minister, the father a father and the son a son'.[9] But he made great demands of the prince, believing he should provide his subordinates with a visible example of ethical conduct. Confucius taught princes and ministers: 'Once a man has contrived to put himself aright, he will find no difficulty at all in filling any government post. But if he cannot put himself aright, how can he hope to succeed in putting others right?'[10] Consequently he denied rulers the right to compensate for their

The names of deceased relatives hang in a special side chapel of Shuxiang Si Monastery.

own moral failings with legal severity. Baron Gi Kang asked the master regarding governance,

Suppose I were to slay those who have not the Way in order to help on those who have the Way, what would you think of it? Master K'ung replied saying, 'You are there to rule, not to slay. If you desire what is good, the people will at once be good. The essence of the gentleman is that of wind: the essence of small people is that of grass. And when a wind passes over the grass, it cannot choose but bend.' The Master continued, 'If the ruler himself is upright, all will go well even though he does not give orders. But if he himself is not upright, even though he gives orders, they will not be obeyed.'[11]

Confucius had to concede, however, that in a turbulent time such as his a benevolent government, operating on moral principles, could only be built on the foundation of military power.

Confucius spoke less of human rights than of human obligations. Broadly speaking, the accent in his social teachings lies on the duties of the individual to support harmonious relations within the family, society and state, while modern Western human rights theory emphasises the duties of state and society to the benefit of the individual. Insofar as the Confucian model still characterises the philosophy of state and society in China and, to a lesser degree, Korea, it is not surprising that international talks on human rights have degenerated into a 'dialogue of the deaf', with misunderstandings on both sides.

In this consistent emphasis on norms of ethical conduct to ensure a harmonious society we find the weakness of Confucianism as well. It makes no allowance for the individual's irrational hopes, fears and quest for meaning. There are fears of death and hopes for an afterlife to follow, as well as incomprehension in the face of injustice and senseless suffering. Between the fourth and sixth centuries CE, at a time when northern and

central China were almost constantly afflicted by war, these gaps were quickly filled by Buddhism, with its revolutionary new ideas. These were the promise of deliverance from suffering – be it in nirvana or in the paradise of a Buddha; the hope of help from compassionate bodhisattvas; the possibility, through entry into a monastery, to lead a meaningful life or at least to escape material hardship; and the doctrine of karma, of cause and effect, recompense in one's next incarnation for good or evil deeds. This doctrine made it possible to 'explain' why a slave was a slave or a cripple a cripple, why wars claimed thousands of victims and, in general, why life seemed so unjust: everything was a function of past deeds. As will be explained in the next chapter, Chinese Buddhism not only offered individuals a meaningful worldview; it was also able to react creatively and flexibly to threatening critiques on the part of Confucian policymakers within the Chinese state apparatus.[12]

With his two central ideas – that the human being is capable of learning and that the state should be governed by moral principles – Confucius established two basic pillars of Chinese thought. During the following three centuries all philosophers had to grapple, whether directly or indirectly, with these two axes of thought. The first dealt with the nature of the human being, the second with the governmental organisation of society. The nature of humanity was deemed to be either fundamentally good or fundamentally bad. From this it was determined that society had to be governed either by moral principles or by strong laws and strict punishments. With the exception of the Daoists, however, no school of thought addressed the existential needs and fears of the individual and none whatsoever broached the subject of the question of the meaning of suffering and 'unjust' fate. Buddhism would later discover the immense field of personal and existential desires lying fallow.

Mengzi and the goodness of human nature

The moral philosopher Mengzi (*c.* 372–289 BCE) was a close follower of Confucius; he developed his teachings further and argued against his opponents, such as adherents of the 'universal love' of Mozi and the early Daoists. He replied to Mozi's address by saying that the command of undifferentiated, universal love weakened and negated the special, natural feelings and duties between parents and children. This close relationship between parental love and filial piety provided the cornerstone for the construction of a harmonious society. Thanks to Mengzi's efforts, Confucianism was elevated to the state religion under the Han Dynasty (202 BCE–220 CE). Mengzi had a positive image of humanity; he was convinced that the nature of the human being was fundamentally good, as all people were born with 'seeds of heaven'. This nature, good in itself, could, however, be corrupted by evil tendencies or wither away as a result of terrible life circumstances such as war and poverty. With this optimistic view of humanity, Mengzi paved the way for the Buddhist monk and spiritual father of Chan, Dao Sheng (*c.* 360–434), who preached the Buddha-nature dwelling within every person.

Based on this axiom, Mengzi expected that a good government would cultivate people's good nature through instruction and moderate educational measures, systematically improve their living conditions, relieve their tax burden, and forgo wars of aggression. It was incumbent upon the government to ensure such harmony in society that it conformed to the harmony of heaven. As has already been mentioned, Mengzi granted the people the right of rebellion if the ruler was unwilling or unable to secure prosperity and peace in his kingdom. On account of this right given to the people, Mengzi always seemed suspect to authoritarian emperors, and his work was banned.

Mozi and the state-mandated universal love of humanity

Like Mengzi and Confucius, Mozi (*c.* 479–381 BCE) was an 'itinerant philosopher', who travelled from state to state and tried to persuade the princes there to accept his ideas. In contrast to Mengzi, Mozi's view of human nature was pessimistic, as he believed that the unsocialised person recklessly sought only his personal, short-term gain, like a 'wild animal'. But in diametric opposition to the Legalists, who advocated strict laws and harsh punishments as the only effective means of socialisation, Mozi saw the remedy in state-supervised, all-encompassing charity and mutual aid. Mozi assumed that before 'heaven' all people were equal and equally worthy of love, since differences in social status or wealth were artificially created by human beings. Because all people were equal before divine heaven, he judged differences in human love, whether in relationships among family members, friends, or neighbours, to be the source of injustice and cause of all evil. In this respect he anticipated an aspect of the universalist ethics of Buddhism, according to which each life is equally valuable, though his motivation was entirely different.

Mozi preached an all-encompassing, non-discriminating love of humanity not out of romantic sentimentalism but rather because he considered it very useful. This close link between universal love of humanity and social utility stands as Mozi's innovation. He taught,

When one regards other states as he does his own and other families as his own and other people as himself, then the princes will love each other and not make war, and heads of families will be friends, and people will love and not harm each other. ... Misery, dissatisfaction, and hate will no longer appear in the world.[13]

For Mozi everyone was responsible for everyone else's welfare and obliged to help others. Mozi's utilitarian love applied horizontally, between 'common' people, and also vertically, between princes and subjects, parents and children. But, unlike Mengzi, Mozi denied the people the right to rebel against a bad ruler.

Mozi's utilitarianism went so far as to reject all impractical activities and expenses, such as elaborate rituals, music, art, banquets, etc. Religious aspects of life were also subject to the primacy of utility. 'If one could induce all the people in the kingdom to believe that gods and spirits were in the position to reward virtue and punish vice, how could there be disorder in the kingdom?'[14] Whether the gods and spirits actually exist is immaterial; what counts and is of use is that people hope for their rewards and fear their punishments.

Despite all the talk of love of humanity, a clear propensity for totalitarianism in Mozi's thought ought not be overlooked. Since he did not share Confucius's belief in a fundamental human ability to learn and in the possibility of improving a person's character, he posited the total control of the person by the state and society. Such comprehensive control of individuals, who may not revolt in the face of bad government, may be interpreted as the precursor to an all-powerful intelligence service and an attendant system of informants. The universal love of humanity carried with it the threat of governmental sanctions.

The Legalists and the rule of law

In the fourth century BCE the old feudal system in central China had long since collapsed, and the seven remaining kingdoms and duchies fought relentlessly for predominance. At the same time the kingdoms to the north, west and south were expanding into regions inhabited

The 'military emperor' Guandi, venerated in both Daoism and Buddhism, was originally a famous historical commander at the time of the Eastern Han Dynasty (25–220 CE). Lateral shrine, Xiantong Si.

Watchtowers of the Great Wall on the
outer northern flank of Wutai Shan.

not by Han but by 'barbarians'. Therefore belief in the old moral values so prized by Confucius, in unwritten ethical laws, was obsolete. In their place emerged penal law. The legalists were more political theorists than philosophers, and since they considered humans by nature egotistical, greedy and barely educable, they advocated the regulation of society by strict laws. In the ideal case, all people, including the ruler, were subordinate to the law. The law must rule, and kings, dukes and ministers may only use and administer it.

The Legalist and minister Shang Yang (*c.* 390–338 BCE) was the first to demonstrate the effectiveness of a government run according to legalistic principles. Shang Yang was radical, as he considered the ethical teachings of Confucius and Mozi to be worthless and dangerous, so he had Confucius's books burned in the duchy of Qin, foreshadowing the general *auto-da-fe* of 213 BCE. He demanded of the ruler and his ministers that they be just as ruthless, unbiased and impersonal as the law itself: 'When virtuous people are in charge, transgressions remain hidden; but when wicked people lead, criminals are punished. ... Rule by good-hearted people leads to anarchy and dissolution; rule by evil people leads to order and strength.'

Shang advocated not only the universality of law but also the principle of 'zero tolerance':

In the meting out of punishment, a minor crime should be treated the same as a serious one, for if this does not happen, minor crimes will never stop and as a consequence bring about serious crimes. Conversely, if the smallest offence is taken seriously, all penalties will eventually cease.[15]

A century later it would be shown that an excessively rigorous Legalism, which took ruthless advantage of the powerlessness of the individual, in practice soon led to rebellion.

Less radical than Shang Yeng was the philosopher and Legalist Xun Kuang (*c.* 313 or 298–220 BCE), who was also called Xunzi, 'Master Xun'. Although he was also convinced of the egotistical and aggressive nature of humanity, which 'exhibited envy and hatred from the moment of birth', he believed in the Confucian tradition that the human person was to a certain degree capable of education and growth. Nevertheless, he agreed with the rest of the Legalists that the state must be led by a strong central government that paid attention to strict enforcement of the law. One of his students was the genial and ruthless Li Si, who organised the new government of China, unified for the first time, according to strict Legalist principles.

In contrast to the other Legalists, Xun Kuang addressed epistemological and religious questions as well. He interpreted the sky, Tian, no longer as a kind of sentient being with a relationship to humanity, but rather as the inscrutable essence and nature of the universe, thus shifting the sky in the direction of the cosmic Dao. Xun Kuang was a sceptic and he disdained the belief of the uneducated in gods, spirits and ancestors. But he recognised the utility of religious rituals such as burial rites and veneration of ancestors, since these represented practical means of expression for human feelings. Religious activities have a value that is purely social, not objective. With this distinction, Xun Kuang laid the theoretical foundation for a distinction between an elite, philosophical approach to religion and an uncritical folk religion.

Han Feizi (died 233 BCE) and Li Si (*c.* 280–209 BCE) were both students of Xun Kuang. In 246 Li Si entered service as a chancellor to Prince Zheng (ruled 247–221 BCE) of Qin, the future Emperor Qin Shihuangdi (ruled 221–210 BCE). When his erstwhile colleague Han Feizi arrived in the court of Qin in 234 BCE, Li Si feared this potential rival, who made a strong impression on

Prince Zheng, and drove Han Feizi, by means of a plot, to suicide. Like Shang Yang, Han Feizi spurned the moral teachings of Confucius and Mozi and further developed Legalist political theory. In light of the innate depravity of human nature, the state could govern the people only by means of strict law and draconian punishment. Taking governmental utilitarianism to its conclusion, he advocated the maximum strengthening of the state through the development of a professional administration, the expansion of military power, and the promotion of agriculture. Conversely, unproductive groups, for instance, philosophers of a rival school, should be banned and persecuted – a measure Li Si soon put into effect.

As chancellor, Li Si implemented the political theory of his unfortunate rival Han Feizi consistently and without remorse. In 221 BCE he asserted Qin's economic and military power, thus enabling Prince Zheng to unite China under his sole rule. The emperor and his chancellor divided the new empire into 36 provinces and separated the civil authority from the military. Each province was presided over by both a civil and a military governor, who were overseen by a supervisor. Even then the civil governor enjoyed precedence over his military colleague, an arrangement that remained a constant in Chinese history into the twenty-first century. Since in the Legalist view, all people were equal before the law, it was obvious for Li Si to take this central idea of universal equality further. He standardised not only laws and punishments but also weights and measures, currency, script, the length of wagon axles, and even thought. In 213 BCE Li Si forbade under threat of death the discussion of Confucian books and principles and ordered the nationwide burning of all books, with the exception of Legalist works and those dealing with medicine, agriculture or divination. When Confucian scholars protested this destruction of cultural heritage, he had 460 of them buried

alive. A cultural catastrophe threatened China, all the more so when the imperial state archives went up in flames during the unrest following Qin Shihuangdi's death. The dynasty collapsed only seven years later in 206 BCE, which allowed the surviving philosophers and scholars to record their knowledge from memory.

The short-lived Qin Dynasty (221–206 BCE) foundered not only because of its inhumanly strict Legalism but also because of its indiscriminate spending of economic and human resources on huge construction projects. Among these were the consolidation of individual defensive fortifications into the Great Wall, the construction of a system of roads to provide a postal service and enable the rapid movement of troops, the creation of navigable waterways, and, not least, the erection of monumental above- and below-ground palace complexes. The burial site of Emperor Qin Shihuangdi was nothing less than a subterranean city of the dead, of which the world-famous Terracotta Army was but the guard of the grave itself. For each of these building projects, hundreds of thousands of men had to work like slaves, often dying in the process. For this reason, shortly after the death of the emperor and the simultaneous onset of court intrigue, farmers' uprisings and local rebellions broke out, bringing down the dynasty in 206 BCE.

The construction of the imperial burial site showed, however, that even in the rationally governed state of Qin, or in any case for its emperor, magical-religious thinking prevailed. One believed in a smooth transition between life and death and hoped for the continuation of life after death. One imagined that the world of the dead was a reflection of the world of the living, in which the emperor would continue in his reign. Since both worlds were similarly structured, the dead would have the same needs as the living. Thus the imperial grave was constructed as an underground palace complex, symbolically

Palace architecture of northern
China in the twelfth century,
mural from the year 1167.
Wenshu Hall, Yan Shan Si.

The Daoist temple of Bixia Si
on the sacred mountain of Tai
Shan, Song Dynasty (960–1279).
The most important Chinese
emperors, including Qin
Shihuangdi (ruled 221–210 BCE),
Han Wudi (ruled 141–87 BCE),
Kangxi (ruled 1661–1722), and
Qianlong (ruled 1736–95), made
offerings on the peak of Tai Shan.

China's first emperor makes a pilgrimage to a sacred mountain

Qin Shihuangdi not only ordered enormous construction projects in his new empire; he also observed them with his own eyes. In 219 BCE, during an inspection trip to the east in what is now the province of Shandong, he climbed Mount Tai Shan, to show his respect to both the mountain and heaven; he is the first emperor whose pilgrimage to a sacred mountain is historically verifiable. As mentioned in the introduction to this book, the Chinese word for pilgrimage means in effect 'to show respect to a mountain'. The renowned historian Sima Qian (*c.* 145–90 BCE) reported that the emperor sought to demonstrate his legitimacy by celebrating two very solemn and rare sacrificial rituals called Feng and Shan, which were addressed to heaven and earth. An inscription chiselled into the mountain commemorates the imperial pilgrimage. Dozens of emperors and princes followed this example, into the eighteenth century. Sima Qian noted, however, that hard rain and strong winds stopped the Qin emperor during his ascent of Tai Shan, and he, as well as his entourage, had to seek shelter under a large tree. Confucian scholars interpreted this meteorological disturbance as an inauspicious omen, in which the heavens denied the emperor the legitimacy of the Feng and Shan rituals and thus of his rule.[16]

That Qin Shihuangdi chose Tai Shan, 1,545 m above sea level, was no coincidence, as the mountain had been since prehistoric times the holiest mountain in China. The *Shujing*, the 'Classic of History', written in the fifth or fourth century BCE, tells of the legendary Emperor Shun (ruled *c.* 2255–2206 BCE) that every five years he 'showed his respect and brought sacrifices' to the four mountains that formed the borders of his empire – that is, he made a pilgrimage. But only Tai Shan belongs to both these four mountains and to the five sacred Daoist mountains.[17] At that time, mountains were venerated for several reasons. First, mountains, which rose high and steep out of the plains, seemed to be meteorological regulators, since moisture and clouds regularly accumulated on them during certain seasons, triggering rain; and the ability to forecast rain is of course of great significance in agrarian societies. Secondly, mountains served not only as pillars of heaven but also as the residence of the gods, spirits and Daoist immortals, where chosen pilgrims could encounter them. Certain mountains were also revered as deities in themselves, likened hierarchically to imperial ministers. When the emperor climbed such a mountain, he symbolically subordinated it and demonstrated his rule over the mountains marking out his realm; at the same time, he received the mandate of heaven.

equipped with functionaries, servants and armed soldiers, as well as horses, carriages, clothing and food. But instead of sacrificing humans and animals, as was done in the time of the Shang and the Western Zhou, the dead were given such things made of painted clay or bronze. Such grave gifts were not only much more humane; they were also more appropriate images of the world of the living than were corpses.

Daoism and non-action

Along with Confucianism and Buddhism, Daoism belongs to the three religions, called San Jiao, that have decisively influenced China. The Chinese language distinguishes between two types of Daoism: philosophical Daoism or Daojia, based on the texts of Laozi and Zhuangzi (fourth to third centuries BCE), and religious Daoism or Daojiao, out of which a Daoist folk religion later developed. Although the Daoist religion Daojiao first crystallised out of various streams of thought only during the Han Dynasty (202 BCE–220 CE), its ideas go back to the time of the Shang (sixteenth century BCE to 1122 BCE) and Western Zhou (1122–771 BCE). These are ideas of cosmology, universal energy or Qi, patterns of change, and divination, veneration of ancestors, and immortality, as well as the perfection of body and soul.

Two philosophers are closely associated with early Daoism, representing two quite different lifestyles. The first is Laozi, who is shrouded in legend and whose name means 'old (Lao) master (zi)'; myths about him cannot be untangled from facts. Tradition holds that he was an elder contemporary of Confucius, placing him in the sixth century BCE. But Sima Qian (c. 145–90 BCE) was already expressing doubt about his historicity. The book *Dao De Jing* is ascribed to him. Its name means the guide (Jing) to the principle,

Laozi (*c.* sixth century BCE).
Xuankong Si, Heng Shan Bei.

the way (Dao), and virtue, strength (Te), and it is honoured as the canonical text of all strains of Daoism. It is presumed to have been written in the late fourth and early third century BCE. The philosophy of the *Dao De Jing* is diametrically opposed to that of Confucianism, as it condemns every form of control of individuals and society as unnatural. The *Dao De Jing* conveys a spirit of quietism, which accords with the life of a hermit, devoted to peace of mind and non-action.

The second Daoist patriarch is Zhuangzi, who in the mid-fourth century BCE composed the *Nanhua Zhenjing*, the 'True Classic of Southern Florescence', whose first seven chapters are attributed to him. He also rejected Confucian moralism as useless and destructive activism, which spoils the perfect course of nature. He interpreted Confucian moral teachings, with their conventions and rituals, as imprisoning human beings by false principles and misguided state control of the inherently good individual. Zhuangzi was a sceptic and advocated a certain romanticism in the form of a return to an idyllic and pure nature. Zhuangzi's bitter critique of civilisation and glorification of virgin nature decisively marked the Chinese worldview and art of painting. Not even Buddhism could extinguish this influence, and it is striking how often Buddhist monasteries in China were intentionally built in idyllic locations. Although Buddhism devalued the phenomenal world as an illusion, many Chinese Buddhist teachers prized attractive landscapes as conducive to the enlightenment of the mind. The Chinese master Nenghai (1886–1967) explained in 1936,

Beauty is an impediment only when we desire its exclusive possession. But the contemplation of natural loveliness – mountains, forests, waterfalls, and the right contemplation of works of art do not excite any longings for hampering possessions, or any lusts. Rather they reflect the silent, shining perfection of Nirvana.[18]

Zhuangzi's epistemological approach, which consisted of a rhetorically brilliant combination of scepticism, a provocative inclination toward paradox, and humour, left its traces in Chan Buddhism. Zhuangzi's aphorisms are precursors to the gong'an (Japanese: koan) of Chan (Zen), those questions and sayings that on a superficially logical level seem nonsensical but convey on another level a deeper truth.

The term 'Dao' was known long before the *Dao De Jing*. It originally meant 'way', then basically 'principle' or 'method', and, for Confucius, 'the morally proper form of action'. In the *Dao De Jing* the Dao takes on a metaphysical sense, as it denotes the cosmic principle and the primordial unity, comprising both being and non-being. Since it 'is' an absolute opposed to all opposites, it cannot be captured conceptually. For this reason Laozi and Zhuangzi caution that 'the Dao of which one can speak is not the Dao'.[19] From this first principle and its vital energy emerged the universe of being and non-being; these are the two poles that put the world into a perpetual state of flux. As can be seen in nature, a process of constant change underlies the world. This process is not chaotic but rather is governed by an unchanging principle. This is the law of the balance of opposites.

In this instance the author of the *Dao De Jing* harks back to the older book, relied on by Confucius, the *Yi Jing* or *Book of Changes*. The eternal change of all existence emerges out of the equally constant change of the two polar primeval energies. These are the principle of the creative, active, light, masculine, called yang, and the receptive, passive, dark, feminine of the yin. In the familiar symbol of the taiji the white yang and the black yin are united in one circle and divided from each other by a mirror-image 'S', and within the yang a black dot and within the yin a white dot denote the inexorable interpenetration of the two principles. According to the *Yi Jing*, every phenomenon arises from a particular combination of yang and yin. Since the changes of yang and yin occur according to the balancing of opposites based on the Dao, Laozi concludes that human beings should not disturb by wilful interference this natural equilibrium and the corresponding course of all existence.

Thus Daoist ethics teach that the human being should orient himself to the Dao. The wise man understands that all existence changes and follows his own way, his Dao. Since all manifestations of existence and their changes develop 'of themselves' from, and order themselves according to, the universal Dao, it is ethically correct not to intervene in this natural spontaneity. The main idea of Daoist ethics, especially those of Zhuangzi, is the principle called Wuwei, meaning 'non (wu) action (wei)'. Wuwei does not mean total passivity, but rather such action as occurs spontaneously in harmony with the Dao. This attitude is described by the paradoxical expression 'Wei Wuwei', 'action through non-action'. The will and actions of the human being should be integrated into the Dao of natural events; they should be as supple as water and avoid the unproductive severity of inflexible moralism or blind voluntarism. The wise man does not through his actions impose upon phenomena, including his fellow human beings, artificial values such as moral principles or rituals but instead his actions are in accord with the principles of nature; that is, of the Dao. Instead of interfering with or struggling against the operations of the Dao in order to fulfil his own desires or assert his own principles, the Daoist wise man acts with equanimity toward earthly goods such as wealth or social status and conforms to the course of the Dao. Beginning in the fourth century, Buddhists criticised this ethic of natural spontaneity and non-action as immoral opportunism and irresponsible fatalism.

According to the nature mysticism of Zhuangzi, the world rests in peace and harmony as long as its development follows only the natural laws of the Dao; disorder and war emerge only from the aggressive intrusion of human will into natural processes. 'True human beings ... did not forget their origin'; that is, the cosmic Dao, of which they are part. 'They did not interfere through their own consciousness [their own values] with the Dao and did not seek to come to nature's aid with their humanity [through their own will].'[20] In philosophical Daoism the wise man put the Dao into practice through a certain mindset and particular attention to the natural laws determined by the Dao. As will be explained later, in religious Daoism, various methods, such as meditation techniques, breathing techniques, visualisation, alchemy, magic and rituals, supplant the philosophical approach.[21]

Applied to the state, the Daoist maxim of Wuwei implies a city-state with a little-educated and thus unassuming populace and a ruler who prefers to remain in the background. He enacts few laws, abstains from pomp to avoid the envy of his neighbours, forgoes wars of expansion, and levies few taxes. But within Daoist nature mysticism, which rejects 'artificially' created moral value systems and conventions and distrusts social hierarchies, there slumbers a rebellious, even somewhat anarchistic potential, which was released in times of social distress, such as at the end of the second century during the uprisings of the Yellow Turbans and the Five Bushels of Rice.[22] This early philosophical Daoism eventually foreshadowed Buddhist Chan in two essential respects. First, it granted all people a share in the cosmic Dao, which corresponds to the Buddha-nature inherent in all living things. Secondly, the claim of 'action through non-action' requires that the human being can recognise spontaneously and directly the natural course of the Dao, which anticipates the possibility, posited by Chan, of spontaneous and complete enlightenment.[23]

On the left side of the image, Laozi, riding an ox, leaves his country after foreseeing the increasing corruption of the state. At Louguantai, about 70 km west of Xian, the astrologer Yin Xi is said to have stopped him and asked him to write down his knowledge (centre of image). Laozi wrote the *Dao De Jing* and then rode off to the west. Sandstone relief sculpture on the Hall of the Four Heavenly Guardians at the Buddhist monastery of Youguo Si.

It was these specifically Chinese schools of thought, Daoism and Mengzi, that shifted the discourse of Buddhism from the metaphysical and epistemological plane predominant in India to the level of ontology and psychology, and made possible the development of an independent Chinese Buddhism. This in turn decisively shaped the evolution of Buddhism in Korea and Japan.

Confucianism as state ideology

If any of the princes or governors discovers a man of talent and virtue under his jurisdiction, he should personally invite him to serve the government. An official who knows a virtuous man within his jurisdiction and chooses not to report it shall lose his position.

—Emperor Gaodi (ruled 202–195 BCE)[24]

After the fall of the Qin Dynasty in 206 BCE, the rebel leader Liu Bang, who was of humble origins, succeeded in uniting all of China under his rule. In 202 BCE he declared himself Emperor Gaodi (ruled 202–195 BCE) of the Han Dynasty (202 BCE–220 CE), adopting most of the reforms and institution of the preceding Qin establishment. In terms of foreign affairs, the first 60 years of the new dynasty were marked by pressure from the proto-Mongolian Xiongnu, who regularly overran the northern border during their raids and even threatened the capital city of Chang'an (Xian). The early Han emperors had to purchase short-lived periods of peace with costly tribute payments of gold, silk and princesses. Emperor Wudi (141–87 BCE) was the first to counter the ongoing border attacks with an offensive strategy. He forced the Xiongnu back into the Gobi Desert and shifted the northwest border almost 2,000 km west to Ferghana (now in eastern Uzbekistan

Classically dressed deities and
dignitaries from the pantheon of
Buddhist folk religion. Great Hall,
Gong Zhu Si, mural in the style of
the eleventh/twelfth century from
the Ming Dynasty (1368–1644).

and western Kyrgyzstan); at the same time he initiated diplomatic missions to Central Asia. This expansion had far-reaching consequences, as it opened up direct trade routes with the West and with India. Not only did goods move in both directions along these Silk Roads; they were also travelled by Buddhist missionaries to China from India and Central Asia, beginning in the first or second century CE. It was this initial contact of China with India and Central Asia that enabled or at least made easier the spread of Buddhism.

The edict of Emperor Gaodi cited above, from the year 196 BCE, heralded the rehabilitation of Confucianism. Emperor Wendi (ruled 180–157 BCE) systemised Gaodi's recruitment of educated and virtuous candidates for civil service through the introduction of state examinations based on knowledge of Confucian works. Simultaneously he ordered the search for books that had been lost during the *auto-da-fe* of 213 BCE. Thirty years later Emperor Wudi declared the Five Classics of Confucius the official canon of state education and the topic of the state examinations. The path to an administrative career and to power followed the course of a successfully completed classical education in the state Confucian academy.[25]

Emperor Wudi further cemented the pre-eminence of Confucianism by elevating it to the state religion. The philosophical groundwork for this was laid by the philosopher Dong Zhongshu (*c.* 179–104 BCE), who combined Confucian thought with older ideas. He proceeded from the ten universal principles: heaven, earth, human being, yang, yin and the five elements – fire, earth, water, wood and metal. Dong adopted the idea of Xun Kuang, according to which heaven creates all things, the earth nourishes all things, and the human being, through virtuous deeds, completes and perfects all things, as heaven intended. Heaven created human beings so that they could develop and ensure social and political order and thus actualise its intentions.

The ruler had at his disposal the mandate of heaven to bring together the three spheres and lead the people. The Chinese character wang, 'king', expresses this integrated function, as it consists of a vertical line drawing together three horizontal lines. The ruler holds the mandate of heaven in order that he may govern the people entrusted to him in such a way that they can fulfil the duty of heaven. The ruler is responsible for both the material well-being of his subjects and their civilising 'upbringing' in the matters of virtuous living, knowledge of rituals, and music.

Since Dong Zhongshu was convinced that the cosmos was an interconnected system of relationships, in which heaven, humanity and its institutions, and natural phenomena, were all bound up together, he believed that heaven reacted to human wrongdoing and poor governance with punishments in the form of natural disasters or epidemics. Ongoing crises meant that heaven had revoked its mandate from the ruler. The idea of a heavenly mandate for the emperor was a double-edged sword that proved fatal to the Han Dynasty at the end of the second century CE.

In order that the legitimacy provided by the mandate of heaven should be made visible, Emperor Wudi took an active part in the performance of special ceremonies and rituals of sacrifice. Four groups of deities and spirits should be distinguished as objects of official sacrifice ceremonies. In the first group of natural forces, heaven and earth enjoy the greatest honour, followed by celestial bodies as well as high mountains and wide rivers. Like Qin Shihuangdi, Emperor Wudi made a pilgrimage in 110 BCE to Mount Tai Shan to carry out there the Feng and Shan ritual, which was reserved for the emperor, and to confirm his mandate from heaven.[26] The second group of gods consisted of the regional titular deities of the empire, the third of the god of wealth and the god of wheat, and the fourth encompassed the ancestors, of which the ancestors of the emperor and Confucius stood out. In this way the modest teacher Confucius was transformed into the 'holy' patron saint of China and the administrative caste.

The peculiarity of the Chinese state cult consisted in the fact that it was not really a living religion at all. In contrast to other state religions – such as Zoroastrianism in Achaemenid Iran, Christianity in Byzantium, or Islam in the Abbasid Caliphate – which were shared by a majority of the population, the Confucian state cult had little relation to Daoism, Buddhism or neo-Confucianism. In the end it consisted of empty rituals, imitations of ancient ceremonies that were intended only to demonstrate the legitimacy of the ruling dynasty. The function-aries and the emperor were free to render homage to other deities in private. Insofar as Confucianism valued external behaviour above all, and Buddhism emphasised the proper orientation of the mind, the two worldviews could exist side by side, as long as a spirit of mutual respect prevailed. It is remarkable that institution of the heavenly commissioned emperor, embedded in the Confucian state religion, proved to be so robust that, prior to the proclamation of the republic in 1912, no rebellion thought to change the system but rather simply replaced the ruler and the dynasty.

The imperial reorganisation so success-fully implemented by the early Han emperors had a fundamental weakness: the question of imperial succession remained unregulated. Because the emperor had available not only an official empress, whom he could demote, but also dozens of concubines of various ranks, his personal court resembled a nest of scorpions in which the empress, the concubines, their sons, their wider families and the eunuchs, engaged in perpetual power struggles. Only too often, empresses and concubines murdered sons-in-law

who threatened their own offspring, sometimes by having them poison one another. Emperors were also the victims of murder by young, ambitious concubines. Or the emperor's widow appointed a small child emperor, in order to rule in his place. Thus in each case of the fall of a Chinese dynasty, court intrigue played a decisive role, from the Western Han (202 BCE–9 CE) to the Qing (1644–1911). After two irresponsible and dissolute emperors, as well as a 12-year-old child, the mandate of heaven for the Liu family of Western Han was considered to have ceased. The regent Wang Man (ruled 9–23 CE) usurped power and put an end to the dynasty of the Western Han. But his ambitious reform programme, in particular the attempt to redistribute farmland and ban the slave trade, failed; he fell victim to a group of rebels. Wang Man was succeeded by the Eastern Han Dynasty (25–220 CE).

Daoism becomes a religion

The history of the Eastern Han Dynasty (25–220 CE) followed a course similar to that of the Western Han (202 BCE–9 CE). After a devastating civil war with millions of victims, the Middle Kingdom experienced an economic revival, the reconquest of the Central Asian colonies, the re-establishment of trade with the West, military victories over the Xiongnu, and important develop-ments such as the invention of the seismograph, the refinement of paper from a crude packing material into a fine writing material, and the formulation of a lunar calendar still used today.[27] The first indications of the loss of authority of the emperor and government institutions in favour of the eunuch cliques and relatives of the concubines appeared as early as the end of the first century CE. A disastrous earthquake in 151 and plague of locusts two years later, which led to severe famine, were interpreted as proof of

Daoist monk on the peak of the sacred mountain Wudang Shan, Tian Zhu Feng Monastery. The flute-playing practised by Daoist monks serves to refine the spirit.

an impending loss of the mandate of heaven. At the same time individual landholders and eunuchs gathered up enormous estates and wealth, forcing farmers into suffering and slavery. This dire turn of events formed the backdrop for the origin of the first two Daoist churches, which displayed strongly messianic traits.

The first founder of a Daoist organisation was Zhang Daoling (died 156), who in 142 established the church Tianshi Dao, the 'Way of the Celestial Masters'. At that time Laozi instructed him in a vision to preach the true law of Zhengyi, to put to an end the chaotic circumstances prevailing under the Eastern Han, and to establish the rule of the Three Pure Heavens. Zhang Daoling saw himself as the representative of the divine Laozi,

who should found a lawful and egalitarian state, governed by Daoist principles. Upon his death he assigned the title of Celestial Master to his son, Zhang Heng, and Zhang Heng passed it on to his grandson Zhang Lu in 179. These first three Celestial Masters were active in Sichuan and reformed the folk religion found there. They acted as healers and explained illnesses as the result of the sins of the sick or of their ancestors. They instructed the sick to confess publicly and show remorse, as well as to atone for their sins with works of public good such as the construction of roads or bridges. The path to salvation was open to all, as long as they repented of their sins, followed the moral law, participated in the required ceremonies, believed in the Dao, and swore loyalty to the Celestial Master. In return the Celestial Master and his priests conveyed to the faithful in the course of their initiation the names of gods upon whom they could call. These names were written down, and believers carried the record of the names with them like an amulet, which also served as a pass into heaven at the time of their death. The new movement was also called the 'Way of the Five Bushels of Rice', Wudoumi Dao, after the tax of five bushels of rice paid by all adherents.

The three Zhangs had a strong practical orientation, as they wanted to establish an ideal society in a perfect state; their goal was the realisation of the Daoist paradise in the here and now. In this essential regard the early Tianshi Dao sect differed sharply from the later esoteric and alchemistic movements, which sought individual immortality and distanced themselves as much as possible from politics and social engagement. Zhang Lu (ruled c. 190–220) put their vision into practice and founded in 190 the city-state Hanzhong on the border between the provinces of Shaanxi and Sichuan. Zhang Lu established throughout Hanzhong state-sponsored hostels, in which travellers found free meals and lodging. This independent Daoist state held its own for 25 years, but had to surrender in 215 to the next-to-last imperial chancellor and

Three Daoist immortals, from from left to right: Shou embodies longevity; Lu, good health; and Fu, happiness. Puhua Si.

The patron goddess of infants, Alidi (Hariti), and her heavenly entourage. In China Alidi resembles female Daoist deities. Before she was converted by Buddha Shakyamuni, she was a child-eating monster, so she is also called Guizi Mushen, 'demonic mother goddess'. Mural from 1167. Wenshu Hall, Yan Shan Si.

warlord Cao Cao (155–220). Cao Cao recognised Zhang Lu and his successors as leaders of the Daoists, and in 220 Zhang Lu legitimated Cao Cao's son Cao Pi as the sole rightful emperor, the first ruler of the new imperial Wei Dynasty. The Five Bushels of Rice movement became the predominant religion in the state of Wei, where the Daoist high clergy held jurisdiction.

The second Daoist messianic movement was founded by Zhang Jiao, together with his brothers Zhang Bao and Zhang Liang in 175 in eastern China. Like the Celestial Masters, Zhang Jiao acted as a healer and invoked the Daoist book *Taiping Jing*, which Zhang Jiao's master, Yü Zhi, had bequeathed to Emperor Shundi (ruled 125–144). This book taught the Daoist cosmology and the correspondence between heaven and human beings, according to which every earthly event had a parallel event in the heavenly realm, or the former would be determined by the latter. Thus the *Taiping Jing* opened for its adherents the possibility to become immortal, and it condemned the exploitation of the rural population.[28] For this reason the movement of the Zhang brothers was called Taiping Dao, with Taiping meaning both 'great peace' and 'great equality'.

In 184 the Zhang brothers called for the Taiping Rebellion against the moribund Han Dynasty, an event that became known as the Yellow Turban Rebellion.[29] Although General He Jin succeeded that same year in defeating the army of the Yellow Turbans and killing the three Zhang brothers, the rebellion remained a threat until 205. Afterwards many adherents of Taiping converted to the Tianshi Dao, out of which emerged the church of Zhengyi Daoism, still in existence today. The second large organisation, Quanzhen Daoism, appeared in the twelfth century. While the Zhengyi sect retained many original Daoist elements and magical practices and allowed its priests to marry, the priests of the Quanzhen School lived celibately. Quanzhen Daoism strongly resembled Buddhism, since it adopted from the latter practically its entire dogma, the structure of its scripture, the ideas of heaven and hell, the system of monasticism, and many rituals.

In northern China the organisation of the Celestial Masters – which, beginning in the fourth century, was often hostile to Buddhism – was influential for centuries. Daoist counsellors were significant participants in all three of the first great persecutions of Buddhism in 446, 574–77 and 843–45. South of the Yangtze, however, esoteric strands of Daoism developed, which sought means of physical immortality. At that time in China the focus was on ancestor spirits and there was little concept of an eternal soul. For this reason, related doctrines in Daoism attracted great interest. All esoteric efforts had as their goal to return to the human body, by means of alchemical processes, its original purity and vigour. The exponents of external alchemy, who stood in the tradition of the exorcists, charlatans and soothsayers – called fangshi – not only employed breathing techniques, diets and sexual practices, but also tried to create special elixirs and pills, containing, among other substances, mercury, gold and cinnabar. Many Daoists, who sought from these elixirs the promise of immortality or at least long life, died of mercury poisoning, as did a few emperors. Ironically, the Daoist emperor Wuzong (ruled 840–46), who in the years 843

to 845 carried out the worst persecution of Buddhism, suffered such a death from poisoning a year later. Adherents of internal alchemy, by contrast, sought to regenerate their bodies by means of meditation and breathing techniques.

With time Daoism developed a complex pantheon, as well as its own liturgy. Both served as formal frameworks for many schools of thought, countless local deities, spirits and demons, as well as various regional cults. Common to all forms of Daoist belief are the three highest gods, the Three Pure Ones. These are Yuanshi Tianzun, 'the Universally Honoured One of Origin'; Lingbao Tianzun, 'the Universally Honoured One of Divinities and Treasures'; and Daode Tianzun, also called Taishang Laojun, 'the Universally Honoured One of Dao and Virtues', more precisely 'the highest Lord Lao', the deified Laozi. In the tenth century the Jade Emperor Yudi supplanted Yuanshi Tianzun. The Jade Emperor – in ancient China jade was a symbol of long life and immortality – ruled over heaven and earth as an ideal emperor ought to rule the Middle Kingdom. In the Daoist pantheon

The Daoist monk Piyunzi, whose civilian name was Song Defang, lies on a stone bed as if he, like Buddha Shakyamuni, were entering nirvana. The portrayal accords with the tendency of Daoism to adopt figurative forms from Buddhism. In the thirteenth century Piyunzi collected and compared Daoist classics, which he issued as a corpus. In 1295 he returned to Mount Long Shan, which lies a few kilometres south of the capital of Shanxi, Taiyuan, in order to secure immortality there [Siren: Chinese Sculpture, Vol. II, p. 75]. Long Shan Caves, Yuan Dynasty (1271–1368).

Ritual cairn, decorated with two yellow cloths, on the central terrace of Wutai Shan.

and settled for the title King of Wei, which encompassed northern China to the Yangtze, excluding Sichuan, his son Cao Pi, upon the death of his father, forced the abdication of the last Han emperor and declared himself emperor of Wei under the name Wendi. In the following year in Sichuan the warlord Liu Bei proclaimed himself emperor of Shu Han, and in 222 Sun Quan did the same as ruler of Wu in southwest China. The Three Kingdoms period (220–280) had begun, as had, simultaneously, the splintering of China, which, with the exception of a fragile, nominal unity from 280 to 316, would last more than three and a half centuries until 581.

With the collapse of the Han Dynasty, Confucianism also fell into a deep crisis. It lost all credibility, since it was unable as the state-supported ideology to prevent the breakup of the empire. The loss of imperial unity meant the total loss of legitimacy for Confucianism. Members of the scholarly and administrative classes turned away from it and looked for alternative systems of thought, whether from the ancient philosophers of the period of the One Hundred Schools or from new approaches. For Buddhism, which to this point had gained only a weak and spotty foothold in China, there now opened up an unparalleled chance to speak to both the indigenous upper classes and the masses. This opportunity was greatly enhanced at the start of the fourth century by an invasion of non-Chinese peoples from the north and east, who founded their own empires in northern China. These 'barbarian' rulers distrusted Han Chinese ideologies and religions, so Buddhism from India appeared particularly attractive to them as a potential new imperial religion.

the heavenly world is a reflection of the earthly world: there a strictly hierarchical order prevailed, with a clear division of labour, in which every deity under its superior deity and according to its designated function is responsible for a segment of the earthly world. In both Daoism and Dao-Buddhist folk religion the pantheon is a mirror image of the state administration. The all-too-human gods behave like temperamental, greedy and corrupt functionaries who can be bribed with prayers and sacrifices. Relationships with such deities lack all transcendence, since they resemble commerce at a carnival or in an office. Laypeople can only hope to achieve unmediated contact with the divine by going on especially sacred pilgrimages such as that to Wutai Shan.

In the last two decades of the Eastern Han Dynasty Cao Cao was the strongman of China. While he maintained a façade of loyalty to the puppet-emperor Xiandi (ruled 189–220)

The spread of Buddhism to China

Emperor Mingdi [ruled 57–75] dreamed one night of a golden man with an aureole of light, whose brilliance shined from his brow to the throne room of the palace. When he asked his ministers about the identity of this deity, the astrologer Fuyi replied that in India there lived a sage called 'Buddha', who had achieved enlightenment. The emperor then sent eighteen delegates to India, where they met [the Buddhist scholars] Kasyapamatanga and Dharmaratna and entered the capital city Luoyang in the year 67. They carried the sutras on a white horse, so the emperor had the Beima [white horse] Temple built.

—Foreword to The Sutra in Forty-Two Sections[1]

Challenges of the early Chinese Buddhist scholars

When Buddhist texts and missionaries reached China in the first century CE, Buddhism could look back on around 500 years of history. During the first centuries of Buddhism's expansion into China, an intense dialogue was underway in its homeland between the strain of Hinayana and that of Mahayana, both of which claimed to be guardian of the true teaching of Buddha.[2] After the second council, the so-called Schism Council, which took place in 380 BCE, 100 years after Buddha's death, there was no longer such a thing as Buddhism as a monolithic doctrine. For the Chinese monks, who mastered Sanskrit only at the end of the fourth century CE and were then able to read the Buddhist sutras in the original, understanding of the doctrine was made still more difficult by the fact that they faced partially inaccurate translations of individual sutras, traditions and legends, which had either been interpreted differently by different Indian schools of thought or, in the case of the later sutras

of the Mahayana, were not recognised by their Hinayana opponents. The Chinese were simply not aware that Hinayana and Mahayana were two very different sects, which fought against one another in India and were each split into numerous subgroups. Chinese monks were confronted with an extremely heterogeneous doctrine, whose cultural context was unknown to them and whose texts in parts directly contradicted themselves despite purporting to be the Buddha's own words.

It was this extraordinarily difficult set of circumstances that motivated Chinese monks at the end of the fourth century to travel to India to acquire original texts and study at the Buddhist universities there. The dramatically varied doctrinal opinions inspired the Chinese masters to meld various strains into new syntheses, to interpret self-contradictory texts historically as stages in a long process, and, analogous to the sutras of the Indian Mahayana, to compose their own sutras, which answered specifically Chinese questions.[3] In this way independent schools of Chinese Buddhism appeared; China can claim to be, after India, the second cradle

The future buddha Milefo (Maitreya). The almost life-size bronze statue was perhaps manufactured on Wutai Shan in the second quarter of the fifth century. The facial expression and drape of the monastic garment reveal the influence of Gandhara and Central Asia. Metropolitan Museum of Art, New York.

of Buddhism, after which, more than half a millennium later, Tibet became the third.

The development of Indian Buddhism

The teaching of Buddha Shakyamuni (c. 563–483 BCE) emerged as an alternative, accessible to all people, to the three religious paths to salvation then found in India.[4] It retained, however, the fundamental premise of every religion of salvation, that the world is fundamentally evil and life is in need of redemption, as well as the ideas of karma; that is, personal recompense for all deeds, and rebirth. Shakyamuni expanded the concept of karma, however, to include the intention behind an act, since even an intention not carried out in deed affected karma. Buddha rejected as methods of salvation both the extreme mortification of the ascetics and the philosophical path of the Upanishads, as well as pedantic obedience to Vedic rituals with their bloody animal sacrifices, as taught by the Brahman caste. His teaching, understood as a guide to self-redemption, devalued the gods of the day and resembled a twilight of the gods. By addressing not only the Brahman caste but all people, beyond the bounds of caste, Shakyamuni laid the cornerstone for a universal, missionary religion.

Shakyamuni outlined his doctrine of salvation in the Four Noble Truths: life is suffering; suffering is caused by the desire for existence and sensual pleasure; this suffering can be overcome by neutralising this desire; and the way to this is the Noble Eightfold Path. Buddha's path to salvation placed responsibility for continued existence in each person's own hands; the path consisted of mental understanding, spiritual discipline and right action. Buddha's teaching is clearly oriented to the next world, as its primary goal was not concrete change of this world but

rather the correct perception of it in order to escape it forever by breaking free of the chains of rebirth. As in all religions of salvation, the value of this life was reduced to a function of the process of redemption, which contradicted the traditional, optimistic Chinese view of the world.

The first planned missionary efforts were undertaken by the Indian emperor Ashoka (ruled c. 268–232 BCE), of the Maurya Dynasty, who not only sought to govern his empire according to Buddhist principles such as renunciation of violence and aid to the weak and the sick; he also sent Buddhist delegations to Sri Lanka, Kashmir and Gandhara, to the Graeco-Bactrian Kingdom and the Himalayan states, as well as to the Seleucid Empire, which stretched from eastern Iran to Syria, to the Ptolemies of Egypt, the Antigonids of Greece, and perhaps also to China. A legend originating in China tells that Emperor Ashoka exhumed the relics of Buddha Shakyamuni and divided them among 84,000 stupa-shaped reliquaries. He sent 19 such reliquaries to China, one of which was kept in the great white pagoda of the Tayuan Monastery on Wutai Shan.[5] In the second century BCE Buddhism spread into the Hellenistic world, as shown by the conversion of the Indo-Greek king Menander I (ruled c. 155–130 BCE), who ruled over the southern half of Bactria, which included the modern states of northern Pakistan, southern Afghanistan, and Kashmir. Buddhism had presumably already gained a foothold there a century earlier. Early in the first century CE, Buddha's teaching reached Parthia in modern Turkmenistan and Sogdia in today's Uzbekistan.

Following the Maurya emperors, the Indo-Greek and the Indo-Scythian rulers, the Kushan (c. 30–375 CE) also supported Buddhism. The Kushan originally came from northwestern China, where they were called the Yüezhi, and were of Indo-European descent. In its heyday, their empire extended from central India to Sogdia

Shijiafo (Buddha Shakyamuni) in the Great Hall of the monastery of Zhenhai Si. His left hand holds a begging bowl, the right makes the gesture of the dispensing of favour (varadamudra).

to the northwest and to the Tarim Basin to the northeast. Even though King Kanishka I (ruled *c.* 127–47) was personally more a Zoroastrian than a Buddhist, he allegedly convened the Fourth Buddhist Council in Kashmir and had minted gold coins with the image of a standing Buddha Shakyamuni and the Greek caption *ΒΟΔΔΟ* (Buddha).[6] These coins are one of the first figurative representations of the Buddha, who until this time had been portrayed only symbolically, by, for instance, his footprint, a column of fire, an empty throne, the Wheel of Dharma or his stupa. As will be discussed

later, the figurative representation of the Buddha played a role that cannot be overstated in the spread of Buddhism in China, especially among the illiterate general public. At the start of the first century CE Buddhism crossed the mountains of Pamir and Karakorum and during that century reached the kingdom of Kucha on the northern edge of the Tarim Basin, as well as the kingdom of Khotan on its southern edge in the second century; at the time of Kanishka both kingdoms belonged to the cultural sphere of influence of the Kushan. Buddhism stood at the gates of China.

The great stupa of Tayuan Si, which – according to tradition – is said to hold a relic of Buddha Shakyamuni given by the Indian emperor Ashoka in the third century BCE.

Hinayana and Mahayana, the Lesser Vehicle and the Great Vehicle

The term Hinayana (Chinese: Xiaosheng) was coined by representatives of Mahayana (Chinese: Dasheng) in a pejorative sense, since they placed the domain of their Great Vehicle (Mahayana) above that of the original teaching, the Lesser Vehicle (Hinayana). For this reason adherents of earlier Buddhism reject the term and call their school Theravada, School of the Elders, although Theravada was only one of at least 18 Hinayana schools. Theravada is, however, the only strain of Hinayana still existing today; it is found in Sri Lanka, Southeast Asia, scattered in India and in the southwestern Chinese province of Yunnan. The doctrine of Hinayana understood itself as a pragmatic guide to individual deliverance from the cycle of rebirth, called Samsara. Every individual human being must find his or her own path to salvation and travel it alone, so Hinayana monasteries are not communities of mutually supportive confreres but rather a collection of solitary individuals. Hinayana rejects philosophical speculation as a hindrance and considers earthly suffering, which it aims to escape, real, and regards the Buddha as a historical man, not as a transcendental essence or as a god. Hinayana accepts only the canon of Buddhist scripture written in the third century BCE, the Tripitaka (Chinese: Sanzang), the so-called Three Baskets. This encompasses the Vinaya-Pitaka (Chinese: Lü), the monastic rules for monks and nuns; the Sutra-Pitaka (Chinese: Jing), the teachings of the Buddha and his closest students; and the Adhidharma-Pitaka (Chinese: Lun), a compendium of Buddhist psychology and philosophy.[7] The narrow path of renunciation to nirvana (Chinese: niepan) can be followed only by monks and nuns who have freed themselves of all worldly attachments; it is not open to the laity. Laypeople can only support monks and nuns by feeding and clothing them; enlightenment is denied to them. The ideal to be reached is the arhat (Chinese: luohan), the venerable, who has with his own power developed himself to such an extent that at death he goes immediately to nirvana.

When after a few centuries the monastic community degenerated into hairsplitting over the correct interpretation of Buddha's words and neglected its social duties, opposition arose to this monopolisation of Buddhism as the exclusive sphere of monks. Around the start of the first century CE Mahayana emerged, calling itself the Great Vehicle, since it presented the possibility of salvation not only to monks and nuns but to all people. Lay believers could also, thanks to the help of compassionate Buddhas and bodhisattvas, reach nirvana, or at least paradise as a precursor.

The pre-eminent instance of the new direction of Mahayana is the *Vimalakirti Sutra*, in which the rich merchant Vimalakirti not only exceeds in wisdom 500 students of the Buddha and all the bodhisattvas but also teaches them that laypeople can achieve enlightenment just as well as monks, since all people partake in the Buddha-nature. The sutra can also be understood as a glorification of lay believers and a condemnation of idle and greedy monks. The sutra, which was translated into Chinese as early as 188, was exceedingly popular in China, since the layman Vimalakirti also corresponded to the ideal of a reclusive Confucian scholar. In the figure of Vimalakirti, world-renouncing, almost asocial Buddhism and Confucianism, which emphasised the significance of social values, could be reconciled.

In order not to damage the reputation of Buddha, whose original teachings the adherents of Mahayana had expanded, they argued that he had not only preached publicly but also had given selected students special instruction, which had been kept secret up to that time. They called the generally accessible teachings the First Turning of the Wheel of Dharma, which corresponded to Hinayana, while the teachings that were only now becoming known were ascribed to the Second Turning of the Wheel of Dharma.

The Mahayana movement not only developed complex philosophical systems; it also moved into the foreground for a large majority of ordinary believers the figure of the male or female bodhisattva. Bodhisattvas, whose Sanskrit name means 'enlightened beings', are called 'pusa' in Chinese. They strive for enlightenment on the path of perfect virtue but promise to forgo entry into nirvana until all living beings are likewise enlightened. Bodhisattvas are merciful and compassionate, as they actively help other living beings, taking their sufferings upon them and, at the same time, confer upon them their own merit with its effect on karma. Thus the broad road of faith was opened even to people who could not or did not want to follow the narrow path of monastic renunciation. It was enough to call on the aid of helpful bodhisattvas and fulfil one's own religious and moral obligations. In this way Mahayana Buddhism, which one could also call 'Buddhism of the bodhisattvas', became more accessible to the general populace; by abandoning the elitist requirements of a path to salvation open only to monks and nuns, it mutated into a genuine folk religion.

Hinayana in fact also used the term 'bodhisattva' but limited it to earlier lives of the historical Buddha as they were specified in the 547 legends of the *Jataka*, and to the future Buddha Maitreya. Belief in the coming Buddha Maitreya, already widespread in Hinayana, built a bridge to the ideas of the future found in Mahayana.

Mahayana, by contrast, recognised many bodhisattvas, both earthly and transcendental. Earthly bodhisattvas are currently living people, who distinguish themselves by particular compassion and extraordinary helpfulness; they strive for enlightenment in order to be better able to help their fellow human beings. Transcendental bodhisattvas are celestial enlightened beings who, for altruistic reasons, forgo nirvana until all living beings are saved. Of the Eight Great Bodhisattvas, the following are especially popular in China: Manjushri (Chinese: Wenshu Pusa), the bodhisattva of wisdom, who resides on Wutai Shan and serves as the bodhisattva of China par excellence. The most popular is Avalokiteshvara (Guanyin Pusa), the bodhisattva of universal compassion, who in China beginning around the tenth century was also portrayed in female form. The full Chinese name is actually Guanshiyin, but the syllable 'shi' has been omitted since the seventh century, since it appeared in the personal name of Emperor Li Shimin (Taizong, ruled 626–49) and was therefore taboo.[8] Other important pusas are Maitreya (Milefo), the loving future Buddha; Samantabhadra (Puxian Pusa), the universal virtue and patron of teachers of Buddhism; and Ksitigarbha (Dizang Pusa), who assists the dead in the underworld and rescues sinners in hell. To these is added Mahasthamaprapta (Dashizi Pusa), who embodies the wisdom of Buddha Amitabha. Since each bodhisattva distinguishes itself through a particular attribute, they may be understood as personifications of abstract concepts.

In contrast to the merciful bodhisattvas, Mahayana sharply criticised the arhats for attending only to their own personal development and detaching themselves from the world. This attitude displayed not only egotism but also a fear of human weaknesses and attachments. In the famous instruction of Vimalakirti a goddess appears and admonishes the arhats as follows: 'Just as evil spirits are able to take advantage of a person who is beset by fear, so because you disciples are fearful of the cycle

A Chinese artist painted this thanka (scroll) on linen around 1900 in a monastery on Wutai Shan. In 1909 the Finnish linguist G.J. Ramstedt bought it, along with 62 additional thankas from Wutai Shan, in Urga (Ulaan Baatar), Mongolia [Halén: Mirrors of the Void, p. 4]. The thanka shows the luohan Damotolo (Dharmatala), a manifestation of Guanyin and originally a layman who served the 16 luohans and who brought forth a tiger from his right knee, in order to better protect them. In front of Damotolo sits Amituofo (Buddha Amitabha), whom the luohan invoked daily. Damotolo was endlessly wise and carries on his back the books of the Dharma. Damotolo's legend later became entwined with the historical Chinese pilgrim monk Xuanzang and with Korean tiger mythology. Finland National Museum, Helsinki.

The Indian philosopher Nagarjuna
(Chinese: Lungsuzixi, second/
third century) was one of the
most important co-founders of
Mahayana Buddhism. According
to legend, Nagarjuna received the
Prajnaparamita scriptures from the
nagas, dragon-like snake-beings.
The Buddha himself is said to have
given these sophisticated texts to
the nagas for safekeeping, until
the time was ripe for their release.
Nagarjuna's connection to the
nagas is preserved in his name,
which means 'snake arjuna'; it
is also shown in the widespread
depiction in which snakes tower
behind his head. Linen scroll
from Wutai Shan, *c.* 1900, Finland
National Museum, Helsinki.

of birth and death, the senses of form, sound, smell, taste, and touch are able to take advantage of you.'[9] Precisely because monks and nuns eschew the worldly, they cannot overcome it. The layman Vimalakirti addressed the arhats,

> *The lotus does not grow on the upland plain; the lotus grows in the mud and mire of a damp low-lying place. ... If you plant seeds in the sky, they will never grow. ... If you do not descend into the vast ocean, you can never acquire a priceless pearl. In the same way, if you do not enter the great sea of earthly desires, you can never acquire the treasure of comprehensive wisdom.*

The layman Vimalakirti also advised the bodhisattva Manjushri, when visiting someone who is ill, 'tell him about the impermanence of the body, but do not tell him to despise or turn away from the body'.[10]

At another point Vimalakirti warned the bodhisattvas against the avoidance of the earthly and bodily: 'To become infatuated with the taste of meditation is the bondage of the bodhisattva. To be born in this world as a form of expedient means is the liberation of the bodhisattva.' In a reversal of the hierarchies in place up to this time, according to which monks instruct the laity, the merchant Vimalakirti formulates the ideal for which the bodhisattvas should strive: 'The bodhisattva is like this [the sun]. Though he is born in an impure Buddha land, he does this so he can convert living beings. He does not mix with or share its stupidity and darkness. He merely wipes out the darkness of earthly desires that besets living beings.'[11]

The two strains differ with regard to the idea of Buddhas as well: while Hinayana recognises the existence of only one Buddha per era, in Mahayana there are innumerable transcendental Buddhas, who can appear in three forms. The starting point for this new concept was the disturbing question of whether the Buddha was gone forever after his entrance into nirvana and thus inaccessible to human beings. According to the 'Teaching of the Three Bodies', Trikaya (Chinese: Sanshen), the term Dharmakaya, the 'dharma body', refers to the absolute, transcendent reality of the Buddha, and Samboghakaya, the 'body of enjoyment', the Buddha's ultimate manifestations, as they appear in paradises and the bodhisattvas. Especially popular in China were the 'paradises' of the 'Pure Land' Tushita of Buddha Maitreya (Chinese: Milefo) and, beginning in the sixth century, the 'Pure Land' Sukhavati of Buddha Amitabha (Chinese: Amituofo). Both Pure Lands served as a kind of waystation on the path to nirvana, as the next and final rebirth would lead inevitably to enlightenment.[12] Finally, the 'transformation body' Nirmanakaya refers to the material form of a Buddha who tarries on earth to help people on the path to enlightenment.

To the left stands Shakyamuni's student Dajiaye (Mahakashyapa), to the right Milefo (Maitreya) sits enthroned. Murals and statues in the style of the eleventh/twelfth century from the Ming Dynasty (1368–1644). Great Hall, Gong Zhu Si.

Eight luohans stand against the western wall of the Great Hall in Baiyun Si.

Yüezhi and Central Asian translators in China

The first Buddhist missionaries and translators came from the west via the Silk Roads to central China. When precisely Buddhism gained a foothold in China is debated. Traditions holding that Ashoka's delegates reached the court of Emperor Qin Shihuangdi (ruled 221–210 BCE) or that Emperor Wudi's (ruled 141–87 BCE) ambassador Zhang Qian, who lived among the Xiongnu and in Ferghana from 138 to 126 BCE, brought Buddhist teachings to the Chinese court, are legends, as is probably the report that the defeated king of the Xiongnu, called Kun Xieh, gave a gold Buddha statue to the victorious Chinese general Ho in 120 BCE.[13] The foreword to the *Sutra in Forty-two Sections*, cited at the start of this chapter and often mentioned in literature, is also of a legendary nature. This tradition is important for Wutai Shan, however, insofar as a stone stele near the Yuanzhao Monastery there reports that two Buddhist missionaries from India, Kasyapamatanga (Chinese: Jiaye Moteng) and Dharmaratna (Chinese: Zhufalan), who, according to Emperor Mingdi's dream, reached the capital city of Luoyang in the year 67, founded in the following year the second-oldest monastery in China, called Xiantong, on Wutai Shan.[14]

Historically documented, on the other hand, is the practically contemporaneous reference to a Buddhist community in the chronicle of the Eastern Han. In 65 CE a half-brother of Emperor Mingdi, Prince Ying of Zhou, which encompassed the modern eastern Chinese provinces of Shangdong and Jiangsu, made use of an amnesty. He offered a specific number of balls of silk as atonement for his lack of loyalty, upon which his imperial half-brother gave the following edict:

There is no reason to doubt the loyalty of Ying, who observed a three-month fast out of reverence for the [Daoist] Yellow Emperor, Laozi, and Buddha. ... Since he repents, he should be given back his ransom, so that he can provide a rich banquet for the Upasakas (Buddhist lay adherents) and Sramanas (monks).[15]

The decree is the first reference to a Buddhist community in China with a temple, lay believers, and most likely foreign monks. This community must have existed for a time before the year 65. The text indicates, however, that Buddha was venerated within a Daoist context. When Prince Ying committed high treason five years later, the emperor banished him to south of the Yangtze, where he took his entire court and probably began to spread Buddhism.

A chronicle of the Later Han then said that Emperor Huandi (ruled 146–68) made sacrifices to Laozi and Buddha simultaneously in his palace in the then capital, Luoyang, in 166. Presumably in this case Buddha was understood as an additional Daoist god. The same chronicle reported that in 193 in the eastern Chinese province today called Jiangsu, the warlord Zhai Yung built a large, stupa-shaped Buddhist temple, where up to 5,000 people, whom he had relieved of taxation and compulsory labour, read and studied Buddhist texts. Zhai Yung also had a statue of Buddha made out of gilded bronze, which was clothed in silk brocade. At the ceremony of 'the washing of the Buddha', presumably held annually, he offered over 10,000 people wine and food.[16] This is the earliest evidence of a large public monastery in China, a statue of Buddha, and the ceremony of the washing of the Buddha, which is still performed today at the celebration of the birthday of Buddha Shakyamuni.

When it is mentioned that indigenous Chinese read Buddhist texts in Zhai Yung's temple, this implies that Chinese translations were available. In fact, from the mid-second century a Buddhist translation centre existed in the capital city,

The wealthy merchant and Buddhist lay scholar Vimalakirti resembled the Chinese ideal of a Confucian private scholar. Mural from the eighth century in Cave 103 in Mogao, Dunhuang.

Luoyang. The earliest leading translators came from Central Asia and northwestern India; they were Yüezhi, Parthians or Sogdians and travelled to China along the Silk Roads. The most important were the Parthian An Shi Kao (from *c.* 148), who translated sutras from the Sarvastivada School of Hinayana; his Parthian student An Xuan (from *c.* 181), who, with the help of Yan Fotiao, the first known Han Chinese monk, translated into Chinese the texts of the Mahayana; and the Yüezhi Lokaksema (Chinese: Zhi Loujiachan), who beginning in 167 also translated Mahayana texts. Lokaksema's students Zhi Liang and Zhi Yao continued the translation work of their teacher in Luoyang. Other translators from that time from Sogdia and northwestern India, as well as indigenous Han Chinese, are also known by name.[17] In summary, it can be seen that at the end of the Eastern Han Dynasty there were two great Buddhist centres, Luoyang and the eastern Chinese provinces of Shangdong and Jiangsu.[18]

These translators worked from texts that were written not in Sanskrit but rather in Gandhari. Gandhari was a north-western Prakrit spoken in northwestern India and belonged to the many local Indian vernaculars called Prakrit which were spoken from the sixth century BCE to the tenth century CE. The Sanskrit name 'Buddha' was rendered by the translators as Fo, which was written with a combination of the characters for 'man' and 'not'.[19] In this way it was indicated that Fo had overcome the boundaries of the human and achieved enlightenment.

The translators faced great difficulties. For one, Chinese vocabulary lacked terms to precisely express complex Buddhist content, so the translators had to rely on Daoist words. This led to misunderstandings and reinforced the impression that persisted among non-Buddhists until the end of the fourth century that Buddhism was merely another strand of Daoism, Buddha was a sage like Laozi, and the bodhisattvas were a kind of Daoist

Shijiafo (Buddha Shakyamuni) between his students Anan (Ananda, left) and Dajiaye (Mahakashyapa, right), twelfth century. Main hall of Hongfu Si.

immortals. Additionally, the translators did not
have a complete doctrine but rather individual
texts from the mutually contradictory schools
of Hinayana and Mahayana; at the start of the
fourth century there were already about 300 texts.

Over the course of the third century leading
Chinese monastic scholars became ever more
aware that there were irreconcilable contradictions between the ideas of Hinayana and those
of Mahayana. This intolerable situation led Zhu
Shixing in the year 260 to travel west on a Silk
Road – the first Chinese monk to do so. He
reached the kingdom of Khotan, where Buddhism
had flourished since the first century CE and
which fell one century later in the cultural sphere
of influence of northern India. Although in the
third century Hinayana was presumably still
dominant in Khotan, Mahayana experienced
a significant upsurge there. As one of my own
archaeological discoveries attests, Mahayana
enjoyed royal support before 263 in the kingdom
of Shan Shan, to the east of Khotan.[20] Zhu Shixing
reported tensions between the two currents, as
the Hinayana monks of Khotan were said to have
tried to prevent him from sending to Luoyang
a scroll he acquired of the Sanskrit *Pancavim-
satis-Prajnaparamita Sutra in 25,000 Verses*, an
important Mahayana sutra.[21] They claimed that
the sutra was un-Buddhist and filled with the
spirit of Brahman Hinduism – an argument that
is understandable from the Hinayana perspective.
For in Hinayana Buddha Shakyamuni is the only
teacher and healer of his era, so only his teachings
are genuine and the faithful should venerate
him alone. Belief in a multitude of buddhas and
bodhisattvas was nothing but polytheism. In
addition, after entrance into nirvana, a buddha
was entirely inaccessible to human beings;
he continues to act on earth only through his
teachings and his relics. Despite the resistance
of the Hinayana monks, Zhu Shixing's student

Buddha Shakyamuni between his
favourite students Anan (Ananda)
and Dajiaye (Mahakashyapa).
Section of one of the five bronze
pagodas of Xiantong Si.

Fazhao succeeded in 282 in getting the sutra
translated into Chinese in the capital Luoyang.

In the same period in which Buddhism was
experiencing a strong upsurge in northern China,
on account of good relations with Central Asia
and India, the Yüezhi Dharmaraksa (Chinese:
Zhu Fahu, 230–c. 313), who came from Dunhuang,
translated two other important Mahayana
scriptures. The first was the sutra *Lalita Vistara*,
a biography of Buddha Shakyamuni written
from the perspective of early Mahayana, and the
second was the central sutra *Saddharmapundarika*,
called the *Lotus Sutra* for short, which was
composed first in a local dialect of Central Asia
or northern India and only later, for reasons of
prestige, translated into Sanskrit.[22] It teaches not
only that the transcendental, absolute essence
of Buddha manifests itself in innumerable

earthly buddhas and bodhisattvas, but also that every living being takes part in that essence.

A century later, the most famous of all the translators, Kumarajiva (Chinese: Jiumoluoshi, 344–413), who came from Kucha on a Silk Road, produced new, clearer translations. He not only rejected any use of Daoist terminology but also first compared several Sanskrit versions of the same text and had his translations checked by monks and translated back into Sanskrit. These new translations, which have remained useful into the present day, pertained to the *Vimalakirti Sutra*, the *Amitabha Sutra*, the *Lotus Sutra*, and the *Prajnaparamita Sutra in 25,000 Verses*, whose name means 'perfect (paramita) wisdom (prajna)'. He also translated the *Diamond Sutra (Vajracchedika Prajnaparamita)*.

At the same time his rival Buddhabhadra (Chinese: Fotuo Batuluo, 359–429), who came from Kashmir, translated the *Avatamsaka Sutra* (Chinese: *Huayan*), which was highly influential in China and whose name means 'Flower Ornament Sutra'; it provided the foundation for the school of Chinese Buddhism of the same

The Chinese invention of paper and later woodblock printing contributed significantly to the rapid spread of Buddhism in China. Watercolour-tinted drawing. Museum of Yunju Si.

name.[23] The sutra, which was composed around the end of the fourth century in Central Asia, not only emphasised the permeation of all living things by the Buddha-nature – even dragons could recognise and realise their Buddha-nature – but also described in its last chapter the spiritual development toward enlightenment as a lifelong pilgrimage. It is, moreover, the first text to suggest that the bodhisattva of wisdom, Wenshu Pusa, lives on Wutai Shan, called here the 'clear and cool mountain', and expounds his teaching there.[24] These lines form the theoretical background against which Wutai Shan developed into the most sacred and important pilgrimage site of Chinese Buddhism.[25] A few decades earlier the Chinese Daoan (312–85) had carried out some important translations, as he worked on the translation of and commentary on not only texts on Buddhist praxis and meditation but also on monastic rules, which had until then been neglected by translators. Still more important, he took up the translations of Hinayana scriptures by An Shi Kao and assiduously cultivated the translation of texts from the Sarvastivada School, an intermediate strand between Hinayana and Mahayana.

These translations not only laid the groundwork for the ten most important schools of Chinese Buddhism but also revealed the fundamental differences between Hinayana and Mahayana, as well as their numerous subgroups. So many different and mutually contradictory ideas, which all claimed to faithfully express the words and intentions of Buddha! Which doctrines really accorded with Buddha's beliefs and with his final and definitive intent? Since these ideas often contradicted one another, surely some had to be wrong and some right, but how was it possible to decide? In contrast to Western thought, which tends to proceed analytically, Chinese thought tends toward synthesis. Instead of the Chinese schools fighting with

Guanyin Pusa (Avalokiteshvara),
bodhisattva of universal compassion.
Wenshu Pusa Hall, Shuxiang Si.

The future buddha Milefo (Maitreya), whose right hand is supported by Miji Jingang (Vajrapani). Cave 13, Yungang, created 470–94.

one another and accusing each other of heresy, they sought ways to explain the disparate ideas within a holistic system of thought.

The solution worked out by the monk Zhiyi (538–97), founder of the Mahayana school Tiantai, involves aligning the different teachings of Buddha with his various periods of instruction and their different audiences. Zhiyi explained that the individual sutras differ from one another because Buddha Shakyamuni adapted his teachings to the moral and spiritual level of his listeners. Zhiyi divided Buddha's time of teaching into five periods: in his first, three-week period, immediately following his enlightenment, Buddha taught the philosophically demanding *Avatamsaka Sutra*, although his listeners at the time did not understand it, particularly its non-dualistic

central verse, according to which the universe is the manifestation of the absolute. For this reason, for the next 12 years Buddha proclaimed only easily understood parts of his teaching, such as the Four Noble Truths and the Eightfold Path; that is, the teachings of Hinayana. In the third, eight-year period he taught the simpler doctrines of Mahayana, such as the ideal of the bodhisattva and the universal Buddha-nature, which also permeated the inanimate plant world. In the fourth, 22-year-long phase, he taught the various *Prajnaparamita Sutras* on existence and the emptiness of every being, and in the final, eight-year instructional period he proclaimed the *Lotus Sutra* and the non-existence of opposites. In Zhiyi's model all contradictions among the sutras reveal themselves to be myopic and illusory,

(Left) Puxian Pusa (Samantabhadra)
rides his six-tusked white
elephant. Great Hall, Baiyun Si.

(Right) Wenshu Pusa (Manjushri)
rides his green lion, which
stands on lotus blossoms.
Great Hall, Baiyun Si.

comparable to the perspective of a frog sitting on the bottom of a well, unable to see over the edge.

A similar Buddhist doctrine developing along a timeline was formulated a century after that of the Tiantai School by the Huayan School, founded by Dushun (557–640) and Fazang (643–712). Their arrangement, which sought a synthesis of all sutras and all Chinese schools, likewise consisted of five parts: first the initial period of Hinayana, second the foundational teachings of Mahayana and the *Prajnaparamita Sutras*, third the teaching of Tiantai, fourth the possibility, elaborated by Chan, of a sudden and complete enlightenment, and fifth the insight of the *Huayan Sutra* (*Avatamsaka*) that all phenomena would interpenetrate one another.

Revolutionary aspects of Buddhism

When Confucianism lost its state-supporting function with the fall of the Han Dynasty, its politically motivated metaphysics of the emperor's intermediary role between heaven and earth became obsolete as well. Many Confucian scholars perceived this sea change as a release from the chains of a prudish and parochial political doctrine and opened themselves, if only privately, to Daoism and fundamental ontological questions about the nature and origin of existence and other topics. These speculations, which deliberately excluded socio-political subjects and avoided any reference to material reality, were called Qingtan ('pure conversations'), and the conclusions, incomprehensible to outsiders, as Xuanxue ('dark teachings').[26] Even if the 'pure conversations' were nothing more than the intellectual gymnastics of wealthy and idle Confucians, they prepared an excellent foundation for a debate with the complex ontology of the Indian Nagarjuna (second/third century CE), one of the most important thinkers of Mahayana Buddhism.

When the Xiongnu, advancing to the south from Mongolia, reduced to rubble the two capital cities of the Han Chinese dynasty of the Western Jin (265–316), Luoyang in 311 and Chang'an five years later, they brought an end to Han Chinese sovereignty north of the Yangtze for almost three centuries. Most well-to-do Confucians and nobles – both groups adherents of the 'dark teachings' – fled to southern China, where they soon converted to Buddhism. In this way there emerged among the aristocracy south of the Yangtze an intellectual, elitist Buddhism, which was at best limited to the study of texts and often served wealthy and influential monks and nuns as an excuse for ruthless exploitation of the rural population. Buddhism developed very differently north of the Yangtze, where on the one hand it was elevated to the state religion of 'barbarian' dynasties from Mongolia and on the other it appealed to the impoverished general populace as their only source of hope.

Daoism for its part reacted with irritation at the increasingly apparent fact that Buddhism was a fully independent doctrine that displayed superficial points of contact with it only because of poor translations. It tried to absorb the new doctrine as a simplified variation of 'true' Daoism. The memorandum mentioned above from 166 from the annals of the Eastern Han states 'that some people say Laozi went to the [western] land of the barbarians and there became the Buddha'.[27] Additional texts, such as Laozi's *Later Writings*, *Hua Hu Jing*, say that Laozi went to India in order to teach the Indian barbarians there Buddhism, a simplified version of Daoism.

The Chinese Buddhists struck back and accused the religious Daoists of plagiarism, which did apply in many regards, since they not only adopted from Buddhism its central ideas, religious institutions, and pantheon, but also did not shy away from copying Buddhist sutras verbatim and simply replacing the word 'Buddha' with the name 'Laozi'.[28]

The Buddhists finally won out only after about 1,000 years of polemics, when Kublai Khan (ruled 1271–94) decided in 1281 that, with the exception of the *Dao De Jing*, all texts ascribed to Laozi, including the *Hua Hu Jing*, should be burned, together with the blocks used to print them.[29]

But Buddhism was entirely different from a watered down type of Daosim, offering instead, especially in the traditional context of China, revolutionary new approaches to thought. The rapid success of Buddhism in China can be attributed not least to the fact that, in contrast to Confucianism and Daoism, it offered solutions to all three fundamental questions of philosophy. These are: 'What can I observe and know?'; 'What can I expect in this life and, above all, in the afterlife?'; and 'How should I act?' Confucianism addressed only the third question and completely neglected the second; Daoism likewise concentrated on the third problem and touched selectively on the second, insofar as it proclaimed bodily immortality or strived energetically for the realisation of a social utopia.

Buddhism, by contrast, offered answers to the first question, which occupied primarily intellectual circles, with the epistemology highly developed in Mahayana and a complex ontology, and it also commented extensively on the second topic, which interested the general public in particular.[30] Although it developed no political philosophy, its ethics largely answered the third question.

Apart from its contemporary, religious Daoism, the approach of the Buddhist religion of salvation was radically new for China, as it presumed that the world was so evil that nothing remained to do but to save human beings from it. Here lies the fundamental difference between Indian and traditional, non-Buddhist Chinese thought: for Indian thought and for Mahayana Buddhism above all, the permanent changeability of all beings is evidence that all existence is only the temporary result of a cause and thus is an illusion, lacking its own substance. If the human being wants to escape from this world of illusions, he must give up all natural and especially all social attachments. For Chinese thought, however, variation and change are not evil but rather the basic preconditions for all existence. Neither the world nor the human being needs salvation; the work of one's life consists in developing and nurturing the optimal natural and social attachments.

For the general public the revolutionary element of Buddhism was that it demolished the prevailing fatalistic concept of society. This worldview, shaped by Confucianism, did not ask why certain people were born as nobles and others as beggars or cripples, and whether these 'natural' differences were 'just', nor did it address the question of whether unfortunate destinies could be changed or avoided. Just as heaven and the head were by nature above and earth and the feet were below, there was a natural social order – how could the feet ever lay claim to the highest place? The traditional Chinese worldview accorded with a society ruled by nobles and with impermeable social classes.

With the concept of karma, individual recompense for past 'good' and 'bad' actions and intentions, Buddhism not only provided an easily understood explanatory model for natural and social differences but also opened up the prospect of an almost predictably improved future, whether in the form of a better rebirth on earth or in the paradise of a merciful Buddha or entrance into the bliss of nirvana. Looked at from a metaphysical standpoint, an unfathomable, morally indifferent Dao was replaced by a supernatural, incorruptible, and impersonal justice, which operated according to moral principles known to all. The faithful Buddhist was no longer the victim of a rigid system but rather had the possibility himself to shape his future fate. In light of karma, every person was equal, be he emperor, soldier, farmer, or beggar.

Shihou Wenshu Pusa (Bodhisattva Manjushri) rides his blue-green lion, whose paws stand on lotus blossoms, on Wutai Shan. The bodhisattva holds a sceptre, called ruyi. Four standing bodhisattvas surround him, in front on the left stands the young pilgrim Shancai, to the right the king of Udayana holds the lion with rope. In the background three of the five terraces of Wutai Shan are recognisable, and in front to the left Wenshu Pusa, in the form of an old man, converses with the Indian monk Buddhapala (Fotuoboli), who made pilgrimages to Wutai Shan in 676 and 683. Inscriptions incorporated into the landscape describe monasteries, a few of which still exist today, such as Jinge Si, on the right side of the picture near the foot of the outer bodhisattva, and, across from it, Zhulin Si. Silk scroll of unknown origin and date, probably eleventh century, acquired by Paul Pelliot in Dunhuang. Musée Guimet, Paris [Giès: Les arts de l'Asie centrale, Vol. II, p. 284]

The Wheel of Life in the Tian Wang Hall of Guangren Si. The Wheel of Becoming, called Shilun in Chinese (Sanskrit Bhavacakra) illustrates the cycle of rebirths and is held by the ferocious demon of death. Outside of the wheel are portrayed, in the upper left, Guanyin, and in the upper right, Shijiafo (Buddha Shakyamuni). In the centre of the wheel the three passions that keep the process of rebirth in motion are portrayed in the form of animals, with the dove symbolising greed; the snake, hatred; and the pig, ignorance. In the next ring karmic decline is shown on the right and karmic ascent on the left. The six sections of the next, broad ring present the six possible realms of existence, in which living beings are incarnated, depending on karma. After the highest section of the gods there follow clockwise the human beings, the hungry ghosts, those being punished in the ice and fire hells, the animals, and the titans. In the outer ring 12 scenes symbolise the 12 factors that lead to rebirth.

In this way Buddhism answered the question of a potential afterlife, which keenly interested people, especially during times of war – such as the period beginning in 311 with the invasion of the Xiongnu into northern China. Still more important, the Buddhist doctrine of salvation addressed all people, even poor farmers, day labourers and slaves. Finally, the concept of personal karma supplanted earlier ideas of clan guilt or punishment for misdeeds committed by one's ancestors.

Also contributing to Buddhism's success was the fact that it offered women new roles and opportunities for development. In traditional China, shaped by Confucianism, women were limited to the roles of wife, mother, daughter or daughter-in-law. But Buddhism opened to them fundamentally new alternatives outside the family structure, whether in convents or in lay organisations. In the convent women were given not only the possibility of a certain social advancement and independence from their families but also the prospect of learning to read and write.

In the context of the idea of karma, early Chinese Buddhists had to change the original understanding of a 'perishable soul' to that of an 'immortal soul'. All the Buddhist schools of India considered all perceptible and visible beings to be transitory, the temporary result of a cause, whose efficacy will inevitably cease at a certain time, so Buddhism, unlike Hindu beliefs, strictly denies the existence of an unchanging self or, more precisely, an immortal soul. It recognises only an unstable agglomeration of the five aggregates: the material body, the feelings, perceptions, tendencies, and consciousness. Thus the question naturally arises: what will be reborn?

To this question, the Buddha replies that at death the five aggregates break apart, but, because of karma, they must lead to an effect. For this reason a new living thing would inherit the karma, but it is neither the same as, nor different from, the deceased. He compared this paradox to

the image of a river, which yesterday flowed by a particular place, for instance, a bridge. Today beside the bridge it maintains the same form and existence, although not a single drop of water that was there yesterday is there today.[31] It was, however, the claim of a 'true self' and an 'immortal soul', put forth by early Chinese scholar-monks – and really a serious heresy in the eyes of Indian Buddhism – that inspired Dao Sheng (c. 360–434) to attribute to all people an indestructible Buddha-nature. To recognise this hidden Buddha-nature in oneself was the work of each person. On this point as well Dao Sheng departed radically from the original teaching of Buddha, as he understood life not as a struggle to escape from an existence full of suffering, which amounted to a negative motivation, but rather as the realisation of the highest awareness and the greatest happiness, as the pilgrimage to the cosmic self, to Buddha. This approach not only lent life a strongly positive orientation but also granted all people, regardless of their social rank, a divine worth. Dao Sheng's term 'Buddha-nature' differs from the comparable Indian term 'buddhata' insofar as it does not refer to an original ontological kernel but rather to the fulfilment of something potentially achievable. To support this interpretation Dao Sheng invoked the *Mahaparinirvana Sutra*, a collection of writings preserved only in Chinese, which attributed to Buddha an immortal self and understood nirvana as eternal bliss and purity.[32]

Likewise foreign to Chinese thought was the Buddhist claim of a universal ethics, which was not limited to members of one's own tribe or clan, but rather applied to all people, even all living beings. The Buddhist emphasis on compassion for all one's fellow human beings and a general love of humankind was alien, as the claims of the Mohism of Mozi, which sound similar, grew out of a different, purely utilitarian motivation.[33] Just how differently the Buddhist command to love others

played out can be seen in one of its extremes. Since it was ostensibly possible to transfer one's own merit to others, in isolated cases monks chose the path of self-mutilation or even self-immolation, in order to transfer the merit accumulated thereby to other, suffering people.[34]

Still more surprising for China was the fact that Buddhism not only was a new religious worldview but also led to an entirely new social organisation: communities of world-renouncing monks and nuns, called sangha (Chinese: heseng). These nuns and monks conformed to the ideal of the early Christian monk, Evagrius Ponticus (345–99), who lived a solitary life in Egypt: 'Monks and nuns are separated from all and bound to all.'[35] This idea of celibate people

who refuse to perform familial and social tasks and operate outside the rigid code of conduct of an ideal Confucian society represented to the Chinese upper class, to whom the idea of monasticism was completely foreign, the height of social parasitism. This point was seized upon by the biting critique of a reinvigorated Confucianism, which got a lift from the fact that Buddhist monasteries very quickly became refuges for conscientious objectors, those fleeing compulsory labour, runaway slaves, wanted criminals, and bandits. The tax-exempt monasteries also served wealthy families as a means to evade taxes by transferring all their assets to a relative who had entered a private monastery. The monk or nun then reverted the tax-free

The future Buddha Milefo (Maitreya), the transcendental Buddha Piluzhenafo (Vairocana), and the past Buddha Randengfo (Dipankara), from left to right. Wanfo Ge Monastery.

The Tathagata Buddha Ajiu Rulai
(Akshobhya), twelfth century.
Main hall of Hongfu Si.

money to the family. This kind of unintentional abetting of tax evasion was on several occasions the undoing of a monastic community.

Finally, the many representational cult figures were novel for China. The visual portrayal of the manifold Buddhas, bodhisattvas and other deities offered the mostly illiterate general population the possibility of easy access to divine sources of hope, whether in the form of statues, portable illustrated scrolls or painted murals. The visual arts, developed to perfection in Buddhism, contributed strongly to its rapid spread and enabled the emergence of popular piety, which is exemplified by the school of Jingtu.[36]

The critique of the Confucians

Although the Confucian state cult lost a great deal of its prestige with the fall of the Han Dynasty, it was able to maintain itself in the northern Chinese state of Wei (220–65), which considered itself heir to the Han. The dynastic founder Cao Cao (155–220) had, at the time he ruled over parts of eastern China in the name of the collapsed Han Dynasty, already forbidden all shamanistic folk rituals, which were not sanctioned by the Confucian canon. The second emperor of Wei, Mingdi (227–39), affirmed in an edict in 233 that only Confucian rituals and those honouring mountains and rivers could be performed.[37] Confucian scholars and functionaries soon developed a series of anti-Buddhist arguments, which remained the same until the revolution of 1911. They may be summarised in six categories:[38]

1. Buddhism is a foreign, 'barbarian' religion, which is inferior to Chinese culture. This general argument sparked two local persecutions of Buddhists in the southern Chinese kingdom of Wu between 258 and 280.[39]

Tibetan monk at the top of the 108-step stairway of Pusading Si. In the background is the great pagoda of Tayuan Si.

2. The axioms of Buddhist doctrine, such as the concepts of individual karma, rebirths, Buddhas and bodhisattvas, etc., are unverifiable fantasies.

3. Buddhist rituals are useless and merely a squandering of money and labour. The monks strike fear and terror into uneducated people with their threatened hells and lull them into passivity with promised paradises.

4. Buddhism undermines the authority of the state, since monks refuse to render homage to the emperor and monastic communities claim complete autonomy for themselves. Furthermore, it grants sanctuary to antisocial people such as tax dodgers, debtors, runaway serfs, shirkers of military duty or compulsory labour, deserters, thugs and criminals, which not only damages the economic basis of the state and jeopardises agriculture but also threatens internal and external security. The

countless monasteries and bronze statues would also needlessly consume important raw materials. For this reason, beginning in the fourth century, emperors and kings – whose orientation toward Buddhism was either not fundamentally hostile or even friendly – issued writs to limit the number of monks and nuns.[40] They ordered that monks and nuns could take final vows only after successfully completing entrance examinations, which entitled them to receive the mandatory certification. An upper limit on the number of monks and monasteries was set for each city and province, and itinerant monks were forbidden.

5. The Buddhist monastic ideal was highly antisocial and unethical, since it required a celibate life and the relinquishment of familial and social ties. This contradicted the paradigm of the family that produces offspring, filial piety, the veneration of ancestors, and social responsibility. For the same reason Confucian scholars condemned the Buddhist practice of pilgrimage because it led the faithful to abdicate their familial and social duties, threatening the social order. For Confucians Buddhist pilgrimages amounted to anarchist activity.

6. Still worse, the Buddhist delusion of a world-renouncing monastic ideal led unbalanced people to self-mutilation or even self-immola-tion, which represented for Confucians and Daoists an egregious sacrilege, since for both worldviews the integrity of the body was one of the greatest goods. The morbid practice of self-immolation, which is explained in the *Lotus Sutra*, among other works, is a form of self-sacrifice that is rare but typical of Chinese Mahayana Buddhism. The first historical verifiable self-immolation occurred in 396 CE; the practice continued into the late

twentieth century, when the self-immolation of Vietnamese monks protesting against the Vietnam War caused a great furore.[41]

The Chinese Buddhists were flexible enough to take these critiques seriously and to adapt themselves accordingly, above all when the emperor commanded it. As for the charge of being a non-Chinese religion, this 'foreignness' emerged as a great advantage under the 'Barbarian Dynasties' that ruled China for three centuries, so there was no need for action.[42] Here and there Buddhist apologists reversed the thesis presented by the Confucians that Buddha was an embodiment of Laozi adapted for the barbarians, with the equally absurd claim that Laozi and Confucius were students or embodiments of Buddha. Regarding the second and third allegations, of being an empirically unverifiable and useless error, they gave little opinion, since holding unverifiable ideas is the essence of every religion. As for the fourth

This woman is burning special joss paper, so that it can be used by her deceased relatives.

critique, Buddhist monks had to concede in part and acknowledge the emperor's authority. Moreover, during the dynasty of the Northern Wei (386–534), monks close to the emperors certified that they were the earthly embodiments of the Buddha or 'chakravartins' (Chinese: zhuanlun), universal rulers of the world who supported Buddhism, likenesses of Buddha on earth.[43] Later representatives of the Chinese esoteric Buddhism called Mi Zong even recognised individual emperors of the Yuan Dynasty (1271–1368) and the Qing Dynasty (1644–1911) as embodiments of the bodhisattva of wisdom, Manjushri.[44]

However, the failure of the Buddhists to understand that they needed to relinquish their envy-inspiring grandiosity, excessive tax-free wealth, extensive landholdings and countless slaves provoked in the years 843–45 the worst anti-Buddhist persecution in Chinese history, apart from the Cultural Revolution. In China, philosophical Buddhism, grounded in the study of scripture, never recovered from this blow.[45]

Chinese Buddhism tried particularly hard to rebut the charge that it lacked social morality and to appropriate the traditional Chinese values of starting families, filial piety, and ancestor veneration. In this regard, the *Vimalakirti Sutra*, so popular in China, portrayed the prosperous, married head of the family, Vimalakirti, as the perfect Buddhist and simultaneously implied that monasticism was not the only, ideal path to enlightenment. That Buddhism in northern China approved of the key Confucian value of filial piety can be seen, for instance, in the numerous inscriptions in the Buddhist cave temples of Yungang near Datong and of Longmen near Luoyang. In these inscriptions laypeople, monks and nuns beseech Buddha to grant their deceased parents commendable rebirths in a Buddhist paradise.[46] Such individual cases consolidated themselves in the sixth century into the Festival of the Hungry Ghosts, which for lay believers is one of the most important holidays of the Chinese calendar.

The 'Festival of the Hungry Ghosts'

With Zhongyuan Jie, the 'Festival of the Hungry Ghosts', Chinese Buddhism established a ceremonial occasion for the lay faithful that accorded with the traditional Chinese values of veneration of parents and ancestors and laid to rest Confucian accusations on this front. This festival, beginning on the fifteenth day of the seventh lunar month, which was celebrated for the first time in 538 and remains very popular, is nothing other than the reconceptualisation of Confucian content in a Buddhist form. Its foundation is provided by the *Ullambana Sutra* (Chinese: *Yulanpen Jing*), which most likely emerged in China. In it Buddha Shakyamuni instructs his student Mahamaudgalyayana how he can help his deceased mother, who was reborn as a hungry ghost. The world of the hungry ghosts is one of the lowest possible levels of existence, where people who distinguished themselves in their earthly lives by greed and ruthlessness are punished with eternal hunger and thirst. Their throats are as thin as a needle, so they can take in no food; and every morsel they place in their mouths turns to a burning coal. Buddha teaches his student that only the collective spiritual power of the monastic community can help his mother, and he directs him to offer the monastic community flowers, food, incense, candles, etc., so that they might pray for a speedy and better rebirth for his mother.

The world of the wraiths and the hungry ghosts (top) and the fire and ice hells (bottom). Tian Wang Hall, Guangren Si.

Finally Buddha advises all believers in the finest Confucian spirit:

Those disciples of the Buddha who cultivate filial conduct should in thought after thought, constantly recall their present fathers and mothers when making offerings, as well as the fathers and mothers of seven lives past. Every year, on the fifteenth day of the seventh month, they should always, out of filial compassion, recall their parents who bore them and those of seven lives past, and for their sakes perform the offering of the Ullambana basin to the Buddha and the Sangha and thus repay the loving kindness of the parents who raised and nourished them.[47]

In time the sacrifice was no longer offered to the monastic community but instead directly to the dead, and it was believed that the food presented would feed not only the hungry ghosts but also all of one's ancestors. The festival of the ancestors coincided with 'Buddha's joyful day', which celebrates the end of a three-month period of meditation. Today believers still pile food and clothing on special altars in the temples, and they burn joss paper, which they believe can serve as money for their ancestors.

The 'Festival of the Hungry Ghosts' is a good example of how Chinese Buddhism was able to adapt itself to traditional values of Chinese society. When in the spring of 2007 I asked a very well-educated monk of the Chan monastery Bishan on Wutai Shan whether such an ancestor ritual, which was closer to Daoist or Confucian rituals, was compatible with Buddhist teaching, he opined pragmatically,

For people's development, what is meaningful is their conduct and their spiritual attitude, since these factors concern community life and effect karma, but not whether their simple faith agrees with complex Buddhist axioms. If such a festival encourages loving respect for bodily parents and fore-fathers and instils in the faithful loving interaction with their fellow human beings, it is compatible with the Buddha's command to respect life and to live the virtues of mercy and helpfulness. Secondly, the festival is a good opportunity for us to welcome Daoists and followers of Confucius. And thirdly, every world religion must make efforts toward a certain acculturation in order to succeed in foreign cultures. This is true for Buddhism as for Islam or Christianity. A good example is your successful Jesuit mission at the time of Emperor Kangxi (ruled 1661–1722), which won hundreds of thousands of Chinese for the Christians because they allowed converts to continue to practise the Confucian ancestor rituals. But when popes (Clement XI in 1704 and Benedict XIV in 1742 and 1744) forbade this acculturation (called accommodation), this roused the anger of the authorities and the mission failed.

Chan monks of the monastery of
Xiantong Si pray by request between
the 9th and 16th days of the fourth
lunar month for the welfare of
deceased souls, as is done during
the 'Feast of the Hungry Ghosts'.

'Barbarian Emperors' elevate Buddhism to the state religion

Religion, politics and art

The three kingdoms that succeeded the Eastern Han in 220 and 222 – Wei in the north, Shu Han in the southwest, and Wu in the southeast – were unable to stop the collapse of the central institutions; political power lay with noble clans of estate holders, who maintained private armies. After the Wei succeeded in 263 in conquering their southern neighbour, the Shu Han, a more powerful clan seized power in a coup and founded the dynasty of the Western Jin (265–316). In 280, by means of the conquest of the Wu, the new dynasty re-established the unity of China, but this fell apart only 30 years later with the invasion of the Turko–Mongolian people of Xiongnu. In 311 they conquered Luoyang and in 316 Chang'an, which led to a division of China, as well as of Buddhism, north of the Yangtze River, lasting nearly three centuries. In the north, non-Chinese ruled, and there developed a Buddhism that cooperated with these 'barbarians', which simultaneously gained rapid acceptance among

the people. In the south, however, there arose the 'Six Dynasties' (317–589); power lay in the hands of powerful clans that constantly formed and reformed alliances among themselves.[1]

Aristocratic Buddhism in southern China

In the south Buddhism found favour especially among the lower nobility and also came to enjoy generous state support, e.g., from Emperor Xiaowudi (ruled 373–96) of the Eastern Jin Dynasty (317–420), who in 381 took the five solemn vows of the laity. These consist of forbidding killing, stealing, extramarital sexual conduct, lying, and consuming alcohol. The last of these vows did not, however, did not stop the emperor in the final years of his life from neglecting the affairs of state on account of his alcoholism. Another generous sponsor was Emperor Liang Wudi (ruled 502–49). Although he re-established the Confucian system of training functionaries, he was a devout Buddhist

A monk calls the monastery of Xiantong Si to morning devotions with a drumroll at 4:45 a.m.

and outlawed the traditional animal sacrifices during ancestor rituals. He entered a Buddhist monastery three times, in order to force his ministers to pay an enormous ransom for him.

In the fifth century tax-exempt Buddhist monasteries succeeded in amassing large landholdings in the south, whose inhabitants had to pay taxes to them, and immense wealth, which they invested profitably in the form of credit extended to princes and merchants. Although Buddha Shakyamuni taught and lived a life of poverty and humility, and monastic rules forbade the ownership of private property, apart from a few items to meet one's daily needs, abbots and abbesses, as well as monks and nuns who lived at court, pursued an opulent lifestyle. A minister of Emperor Xiaowudi stated in a memorandum,

Monks and nuns crowd together and, though relying on (the prestige associated with) their religious dress, they are yet unable to observe even the most elementary rules of the five commandments, let alone the (more) detailed and subtle (rules for the monastic life) ... [They], by robbing the common people, build stupas and convents on a large scale, resorting to ostentation and extravagance, but all to no valid purpose.[2]

Aristocratic Buddhism lacked seriousness in religious practice and the critical study of scripture. Scholarly monks copied the fantastical 'pure conversations' of the 'dark teaching' and made almost no effort to create new, text-critical translations of Buddhist scripture.

The community of Buddhist monasteries developed here into a state within the state that was not only fully autonomous from an economic point of view but was also outside the control of the secular jurisdiction. For this reason rulers tried repeatedly to regulate the number of monks. An early example is the edict

released around the year 400 by the powerful warlord Huan Xuan (369–404), who tried unsuccessfully to found his own dynasty in 403. He ordered that all monks and nuns be laicised if they did not meet the following three conditions:

1. They are capable of reading, preaching, and commenting on Buddhist scripture.

2. They live permanently in a recognised monastery and strictly obey the monastic rule.

3. Or, if they live as hermits in the mountains, they have no contact with the people.[3]

Folk Buddhism and state religion in northern China

The north of China experienced a much more turbulent time than did the south, since it was overrun in the fourth century by Mongol, Turkish, Tungusian (Manchurian), proto-Tibetan and eastern Tibetan nomadic horsemen. They founded a whole kaleidoscope of 16 short-lived states, which engaged in internecine warfare, so the period is called the Era of the Sixteen Kingdoms. From 316 to 581 the Han Chinese of northern China were ruled by those foreign peoples whom they had for centuries regarded as barbarians. Two of these 'barbarian kingdoms', however – those of the Later Zhao and the Northern Wei – were of decisive importance for the development of Buddhism; the Northern Wei also initiated the development of Buddhist sculpture and founded the first monasteries on Wutai Shan. The invading nomadic cavalries first caused great damage, destroying early Buddhist artworks and scriptures, but many of these 'barbarian rulers' quickly discovered the political value of a universal religion. This allowed Buddhism in northern China to revive rapidly as both a popular and a state religion.

The missionary and magician Fotudeng converts a Turko-Mongol people

The cornerstone of the rapid expansion of Buddhism north of the Yangtze lies with the Central Asian-born Hinayana monk Fotudeng (c. 232–348), who is said to have reached Luoyang only at the advanced age of 78. He experienced the destruction of the capital by the Xiongnu and was witness to the unimaginable cruelty toward the defenceless civilians and the vanquished enemies, whom the Xiongnu buried alive. He realised that if he could stop the foreign warlords from brutally butchering innocent civilians, Buddhism would find great favour with the beleaguered people. For this reason he affiliated himself with the notorious Xiongnu general Shile (died 333), who named himself king of Zhao in 319 and emperor of the short-lived dynasty of the Later Zhao (330–50) in 330. Not only was Fotudeng a charismatic preacher, he also had clairvoyant abilities. He was able to predict the outcome of an impending battle every time, and he served Shile as a valuable military advisor. Fotudeng used his strong position to persuade the tyrant that he could rule his new empire more effectively if he won the hearts of his subjects by ruling with clemency than if he terrorised them.

Thanks to his magical powers, Fotudeng also gained the trust of the succeeding emperor, Shihu (ruled 334–49), and served him as a personal adviser. The most decisive breakthrough came when Minister Wang Tu warned Emperor Shihu that no Chinese emperor could tolerate the spread of Buddha's teaching, since he was 'a foreign god'. Wang Tu's recommendation yielded the opposite result, however, from what the minister intended. Shihu recalled his Mongol heritage and proclaimed the following edict:

Tu's argument is that Buddha is a deity of foreign lands and is not one whom it is proper for the emperor and the Chinese to worship. We were born out of the marches, and though We are unworthy We have complied with Our appointed destiny and govern the Chinese as their prince. ... Buddha being a barbarian god is the very one we should worship. ... As for I, the Chao, and the myriad barbarians, if there are those who abandon their unauthorised worship and take pleasure in worshipping Buddha, We hereby permit all of them to become adherents.[4]

Shihu recognised that a universal state religion that addressed all people of all ethnicities would help to unite his empire and that Buddhism was growing in popularity among the people. Since the Xiongnu represented only a vanishingly small minority in northern China, they were mistrustful of all Chinese, so the emperor consciously adopted a non-Chinese religion. He also prized the magical powers of Fotudeng and his students and hoped that the Buddhist monks, who had to separate themselves from their families upon taking their vows, would become reliable public servants, since they depended on his favour.

Fotudeng not only prevented northern China's two most powerful warlords of the first four decades of the fourth century from committing senseless carnage; he also founded 893 temples, gave monks a rudimentary monastic rule, and established Buddhism as a widespread popular religion, in contrast to the situation in the south, where it was a matter for the nobility. Buddhist sculpture also developed further during Fotudeng's time, as we gather from the earliest dated gilded Buddha figure in China, from the year 338.[5]

The Northern Wei and the cave temples of Yungang

For the development of Buddhism in China, the dynasty of the Northern Wei (386–534) was still more important than that of the Later Zhao, since for the first time a strong and truly stable dynasty supported Buddhism and encouraged its visual presence in the form of massive cave temples and stone sculptures. It was no coincidence that the dynasty's founders were not Chinese but rather 'barbarians'; they belonged to the Mongol–Manchurian people called the Tuoba, a clan of the federation of the Xianbei. The first ruler, Daowudi (ruled 386–409), founded his empire in 386 and chose Shengle (Shiling Gol), in today's Inner Mongolia, as his capital, which he relocated 12 years later to Pingcheng, now known as Datong, in the north of Shanxi Province. He was also the first to introduce an office, under his authority, of an overseer of all monks and nuns, who was responsible for all Buddhist affairs throughout the empire. The first officeholder was the monk Faguo (in office 396–98), who not only ordered the construction of the first Buddhist monastery of Pingcheng but also advanced the ground-breaking theory that the ruling Tuoba emperor was a tathagata (Chinese: rulai), an incarnation of the Buddha. Faguo chose this bold axiom to resolve a serious dilemma. On the one hand, Daowudi insisted that the monks recognise his secular authority, but on the other, Buddhist scriptures emphasise that a monk should bend his knee to neither parents nor kings. Faguo argued, 'As he [the emperor] is the Tathāgata of the present time, the śramanas should pay him all homage. ... I am not bowing before the emperor, I am just paying homage to the Buddha'.[6]

After the second emperor, Mingyuandi (ruled 409–23), who died as a consequence of 'life-lengthening' Daoist pills, Emperor Taiwudi (ruled 423–52) succeeded in 439 in uniting all of northern China, including the border city of Dunhuang which lay far to the west, under his rule and bringing to an end the period of the Sixteen Kingdoms. Taiwudi was a Daoist, who elevated Daoism to the state religion in 442 and for whom the rapidly growing wealth of Buddhist institutions was a thorn in the side. When, three years later, evidence emerged that several monasteries of Chang'an were involved in a rebellion, he followed the advice of his Confucian minister Cui Hao and his Daoist adviser Ku and proclaimed the following radical edict: 'all stupas, paintings, and foreign sutras are to be beaten down and burned utterly; the śramanas without distinction of age are to be executed'.[7] Presumably the initiator of this comprehensive persecution, Minister Cui Hao, wanted a further sinicisation; that is, the adaptation of the Tuoba to traditional Han Chinese culture, a process with which Buddhism interfered. This persecution led in northern China to the loss of almost all Buddhist art objects and many translations. It was the first of five anti-Buddhist persecutions. The next four took place in the years 574–77, 843–45, 955 and 1966–76, with the third and fifth affecting all of China. The final persecution, during the Cultural Revolution, targeted all cultural assets, not just Buddhist ones. Also during the Taiping Rebellion of 1850 to 1864 hundreds of monasteries in southern China went up in flames. Remarkably, many small, portable bronze figures escaped the waves of destruction of 574–77 and 843–45, as Japanese pilgrim monks, who had visited China, had taken the statues home to Japan with them.

The fifth Tuoba emperor, Wenchengdi (ruled 452–65), was a Buddhist, however; when he ascended the throne he lifted the anti-Buddhist edict and began one of the greatest Buddhist art projects. In 460 he appointed the monk Tanyao as overseer of all monks, an office Tanyao held until c. 484. Tanyao resolved to revive Buddhism by means of an indestructible visible sign. After

The past buddha Randengfo (Dipankara) to the right in Cave 19 and the 14 m-tall, seated present buddha Shijiafo (Shakyamuni) to the left in Cave 20 of Yungang, c. 460–70 CE. The front wall of Cave 20 and the side of Cave 19 collapsed in the tenth century.

Taiwudi's persecution destroyed artworks made of wood and metal, he chose a less easily damaged material: stone. He recommended to the emperor that he have five great cave temples hewn out of the stone of Mount Wuzhou, near the then capital Pingcheng. Tanyao selected this location because he saw in Mount Wuzhou great similarities to the sacred mountain of Indian Buddhism, Gridhrakuta, the 'hill of vultures', where Buddha Shakyamuni is said to have preached the *Lotus Sutra*. In this regard he drew upon the descriptions of the Chinese pilgrim monk Faxian (337–422), who travelled in India between *c.* 401 and 411.[8] Its resemblance to the Hill of Vultures also inspired the building of the earliest monasteries on Wutai Shan.

The excavation of a mountain for a religious purpose follows the tradition, already widespread in India, of Buddhist cave temples. This in turn referred to the monastic hermitages in mountain caves from the early period of Buddhism. The cave temples also have a highly symbolic significance. As the faithful enter the cave through a narrow, dark passage, they leave the earthly world with all its imperfections and enter a mystical zone. At the end of the ever-darker corridor they encounter the great Buddha statue and confront the image of the divinity, so that the visit to the temple takes on the character of a cathartic rebirth. The practice of carving enormous artificial cave temples out of rock followed the spread of Buddhism from India, first to Bactria; then in 344 or 366 CE to Dunhuang, the first Buddhist pilgrimage site in China; and towards the end of the fourth century along a Silk Road further east to the caves of Bingling Si in Gansu.[9]

To atone for the persecutions of his grandfather Wenchengdi agreed to the construction of the first five cave temples, the so-called 'grottoes of Tanyao', and had them carved out of the stone from 460 to 470. They are so huge that the entire cave temple complex is called Yungang

Shiku, 'cloud-ridge stone caves'. In these caves, numbered 16–20, the gigantic figure of Buddha is enthroned. Like other emperors of China, the rulers of the Northern Wei supported Buddhism not least in order to have themselves celebrated as manifestations or representatives of Buddha. It is said that the five stone buddhas bear the faces of the first five Tuoba emperors. In this way the structure enabled the veneration of ancestors, and the faithful who venerated the Buddha could at the same time render homage to the emperors. For the faithful the cave temples, with their stone buddhas up to 17 metres high, were the ultimate proof that Buddhism was eternal and indestructible. Since the monastic rules of the time banned monks from manual labour, Tanyao provided them with prisoners of war, converted slaves and criminals to work as farm labourers; communities that were called 'Buddha households'.[10]

The second phase of construction lasted from 470 to 494 and included caves 1 and 2, as well as 5–13. The colossal buddhas yielded in part to smaller figures. Thus, one finds in a few caves a central pillar with a rectangular shape, which brings together the floor with the ceiling; that is, like the world tree, it symbolically unites earth with heaven. On each side of the column is a large niche out of which is carved a buddha figure; relief sculptures of scenes from Buddha's life adorn the walls. This arrangement is also borrowed from the Buddhist cave temples of India where, in Ajanta for example, in the rear section of the cave there stands a stone stupa with a buddha figure carved into a niche. Today pilgrims still walk reverentially around these pillars, in a clockwise direction, as they complete a ritual circumambulation of individual shrines and altars on Wutai Shan and sacred mountains in Tibet such as Mount Kailash. However, the cave temples of Yungang were built mainly to increase the merit of the emperors, rather than to provide the people with a publicly accessible place of reflection.

A bodhisattva in Cave 18.
Yungang, carved 460–70.

A wheel between two gazelles
was one of the earliest symbols of
Buddha and his teaching. It refers
to Buddha's first sermon in the deer
park of Sarnath. Railing at Wanghai
Monastery, eastern terrace Dongtai.

The second period of construction ended in 494 when the seventh Tuoba emperor, Xiaowendi (ruled 471–99), who is also said to have founded the three monasteries Foguang Si, Xiantong Si, and Qingliang Si on Wutai Shan, moved the capital to Luoyang. He did this in order to move the political centre of his empire closer to the geographic centre of China, since he planned (but never carried out) a conquest of southern China. For this reason the remaining grottoes were commissioned not by emperors but by governors, generals, functionaries and private citizens. The third stage of construction ended in 524. In Luoyang the Tuoba continued the construction of cave temples in the monumental style, which the Tang Dynasty (618–907) brought to a brilliant conclusion.

The next emperor, Xuanwudi (ruled 499–515), proclaimed Buddhism the state religion of northern China. He was a fervent Buddhist who publicly commented on the sutras, as did his successor Emperor Xiaoming (ruled 510–28). But Xiaoming was weak, and when he tried to limit the political influence of his mother Hu, she promptly had him poisoned. The empire now became increasingly unstable, with six emperors in as many years. It eventually splintered into the regional dynasty of the Eastern Wei (534–50), which was followed by the dynasty of the Northern Qi (550–77), and that of the Western Wei (535–56), which was succeeded by the Northern Zhou (557–81). Although these dynasties were short-lived, they played an important role for the development of Buddhist sculpture. On the other hand, Buddhist art suffered a terrible blow under the Northern Zhou when Emperor Wudi (ruled 561–78) elevated Confucianism to the only permissible state religion and triggered the second persecution, which lasted from 574 to 577: temples were destroyed, metal statues melted down, wooden statues and sutras burned, and confiscated possessions divided up among the nobility. The overthrow of the Northern Zhou

soon thereafter by the founder of the Sui Dynasty (581–618), Emperor Wendi (ruled 581–604), saved Buddhism from an even worse crisis.

In 589 Emperor Wendi united all of China again for the first time since 316. He standardised the currency, encouraged agriculture, restored the Great Wall, and built the Great Canal, which linked the Yangtze with the Yellow River and Hangzhou in the south with Luoyang and today's Beijing in the north. Although he reorganised the state according to Confucian principles, he strongly supported Buddhism. He used it and its distinctive art purposefully as a unifying cultural force to renew China's culture on a national level. For this reason he converted to Buddhism and declared himself the chakravartin, the lawful Buddhist world ruler. In the Buddhist worldview a chakravartin rules according to religious and ethical principles; he provides peace and security and alleviates poverty.

The devastating war against the Korean kingdom of Koguryo, lost by Wendi's son and successor Yangdi (ruled 605–18), in which more than two million Chinese soldiers fell, led to severe unrest in the Middle Kingdom. Li Yuan, governor of Taiyuan, Shanxi Province, took advantage of this in 617 and hoisted the flag of rebellion with the help of his battle-hardened sons. A year later he declared himself the first emperor of the Tang Dynasty (618–907) and took the name Gaozu (ruled 618–26). In 626 his second-eldest son Li Shimin murdered two of his brothers, one of them the crown prince, and Gaozu abdicated in favour of his violent son, who adopted the official imperial and temple name Taizong (626–49).

The period of the Tang Dynasty stands as the zenith of Chinese cultural history. Although the Tang emperors further refined the system of Confucian state examinations, considered themselves descendants of Laozi, and supported Daoism accordingly, Buddhism experienced an unparalleled florescence until the mid-ninth century. The regime was quite stable, apart from the usurpation by Empress Wu Zetian (ruled 690, de facto from 660, to 705) and the rebellion of the Sogdian general An Lushan from 755 to 763. However, the Tang emperors were able to quell An Lushan's rebellion only thanks to military aid from the Turkic Uighurs, so they had a dependent relationship with the militarily superior Uighurs until 840. When the Kyrgyz from southern Siberia destroyed the Uighur Empire in what is now Mongolia, Emperor Wuzong (ruled 840–46) expelled them and at the same time targeted all 'foreign' religions. He struck the first blow against the Manichaeans, who had been supported by the Manichaean Uighur rulers, then against the Christian Nestorians and the Zoroastrians, and finally, between 843 and 845, against the Buddhists. Not least for economic reasons, Wuzong ordered the destruction of 4,600 Buddhist monasteries and 40,000 temples, the confiscation of their lands, the melting down of their metal statues, and the burning of sutras, as well as the forced return of 260,000 monks and nuns to status of tax-paying laity.[11] Ironically, Emperor Wuzong died from taking Daoist pills that were supposed to have granted him immortality. Although Wuzong's successor Xuanzong II (ruled 846–59) rescinded the anti-Buddhist edicts as soon as he ascended to the throne, only the two anti-intellectual schools, Jingtu and Chan, which considered the study of scripture inessential and were not dependent on it, survived. By contrast, the hermeneutical and philosophical schools such as Tiantai or Huayan practically died out; their most important writings are known in part only because of Japanese translations. The esoteric school of Mi Zong, for its part, has benefited since Kublai Khan from the sponsorship of the similar Tibetan Buddhism.

The final decades of the Tang Dynasty were similar to those of the Han Dynasty. The central government's authority was collapsing amid court intrigues fuelled by eunuchs and concubines, leaving it too weak to deal with natural disasters such as the floods of 858 and the crop failures of 873. In 875 the outlaw leader Huang Chao led a national uprising, which culminated in 879 with a massacre at Guangzhou, where up to 100,000 foreign merchants were murdered, and in 880 with the sacking of Luoyang and Chang'an. Although imperial army commanders were able to defeat Huang Chao in 884, the days of the Tang Dynasty were numbered, and in the south individual provincial governors began declaring themselves independent. In 907 the Tang Dynasty finally collapsed, leading to a new division of China: in the north there arose the Five Dynasties (907–60), and in the south the Ten Kingdoms (897–979). The reunification of China came about only under the Mongol emperor Kublai Khan (ruled 1271–94) in 1279, after nearly four centuries of division.[12]

The development of Buddhist sculpture before the Sui Dynasty

Like early Christian art, early Buddhist art refrained from figurative representations of Buddha Shakyamuni.[13] He was portrayed visually by means of a symbol that designated an important event in his life. Thus a tree was an emblem of Buddha's enlightenment, which took place under a tree; a wheel, the setting in motion of the Wheel of Dharma; or a stupa, his entrance into nirvana. Only Shakyamuni's earlier incarnations, as they were handed down in the Jataka tales, were portrayed figuratively. Around the start of the first century CE, however, Mahayana introduced the idea of many buddhas, which are differentiated from one another by their nirmanakaya or created bodies, and innumerable, likewise embodied

The 56.4 m-tall, bell-shaped stupa Tayuan Si, done in the Tibetan style, is said to have been built in 1301 by the Nepalese painter and architect Aniko (1245–1306) and restored in 1407 by the Fifth Karmapa.

bodhisattvas. This multitude of new 'divine' figures cried out for representational portrayals, in order to bring the faithful closer to them. Both the veneration and the commissioning and producing of images were considered meritorious.

It was no coincidence that the first statues of buddhas and bodhisattvas appeared in Gandhara, the southwestern portion of the former kingdom of Bactria, for Bactria was a land of two cultures that had become closely intertwined: the Greek and the Indian. The first human Buddha figures appeared in the first century CE, strongly influenced by the idealised bodies of Greek sculpture and showing influences from Iran. Buddha appeared in a peaceful state, whether sitting in meditation or standing to teach; the mind is turned inward. The art of Gandhara represents the union of the wisdom of Buddha with the classical Hellenistic aesthetic. A few decades later, in Mathura in northern India, a second artistic tradition arose. In the school of Mathura Buddha appears stronger, more athletic and ready for action. The two approaches soon came to resemble each other and there developed an independent Buddhist aesthetic that was able to adapt to its environment, be it China, Korea, or Japan, and yet remain distinctive.

Both the school of Gandhara and that of Mathura followed the expansion of Buddhism into Central Asia and along the route of the Silk Roads to China. Examples of early Buddhist sculpture crafted from clay, stucco, stone or wood and influenced by both schools can be found in many ruins in the Tarim Basin in far northwestern China, which belonged to China's sphere of influence from the end of the second century BCE until 791, with some interruptions. Buddhist monasteries appeared here in the second century CE, and since the 1890s Buddhist statues and murals from the second to the seventh centuries have been discovered in the ruins of old monastery sites, for instance on the southern Silk Road of the Tarim Basin in Rawak, Karadong, Endere, Miran, and Loulan, and along in the northern Silk Road in Tumshuq, Duldur Aqur and Kizil.[14]

As for China itself, chronicles report at least two Buddhist statues from the second century CE.[15] Among the oldest surviving depictions of Buddha from the turn of the second century are the standing and seated buddha figures carved out of rock at Kungwang Shan in Jiangsu Province – the same province where General Zhai Yung had a spacious Buddhist temple build in 193 – and a miniature shrine of gilded bronze with both a sitting and a standing buddha in the centre and scenes from his life on both sidepieces, a vessel of celadon with four buddhas sitting on a lotus throne, a bronze mirror with sitting and standing buddhas, and seated buddha figures carved from rock within two cave gravesites at Leshan and Pengshan, Sichuan.[16] The last two examples show how Buddhist elements found entry into traditional Chinese burial art. The decoration of tombs with representations of Buddha was,

however, foreign to orthodox Buddhism, since buddha figures were never placed in graves but rather were designated as objects of veneration in temples, monasteries or private homes. But here in Sichuan Buddha no longer represented escape from the cycle of lives into nirvana but rather the opposite ideal: immortality or eternal life.

The oldest extant representation of Buddha in China is probably a 32 cm-tall gilded bronze statue of Buddha Shakyamuni seated on a lion throne with flames blazing from his shoulders. It is dated to around the year 300 CE. All examples, aside from the badly weathered stone carvings of Kongwang, show very clear influences from Gandhara; yet they are undoubtedly Chinese works. The earliest precisely dated figure comes from the year 338 and was created in the province of Hebei, east of Wutai Shan.[17] The marvellous 140 cm-tall gilded bronze statue of a standing Buddha Maitreya, which dates between 420 and 443 and is now in the Metropolitan Museum of Art in New York, was probably crafted in a monastery on Wutai Shan.[18]

The Buddhas of the Three Times, from left to right: the past buddha Randengfo (Dipankara), the present buddha Shijiafo (Shakyamuni), and the future buddha Milefo (Maitreya). Beside Shijiafo stand his chief disciples Anan (Ananda) and Dajiaye (Mahakashyapa). Great Hall, Gong Zhu Si, statues in the style of the eleventh/twelfth century from the Ming Dynasty (1368–1644).

In light of the non-personified forms of religion in pre-Buddhist China, it is not surprising that at this time religious sculpture portraying deities was hardly known. The terracotta or wooden figures placed in the burial chambers of deceased rulers or the mighty stone lions that guarded the gravesites do not represent deities to be worshipped. The only exceptions might be the mysterious bronze human figures from Sanxingdui, Sichuan; their symbolism, however, eludes our understanding. Also conspicuous in pre-Buddhist sculpture is the fact that people and particularly lions are portrayed in an expressive way, emphasising their vitality.

Buddhist art in China pursued entirely different goals, especially in its earliest centuries. It sought by means of simple forms and lines to express the noble and sublime. The Buddha and bodhisattva figures wanted neither to display their inner vitality nor to reveal the conflict between contradictory human impulses, as medieval portrayals of the suffering crucified Christ or the statues of Michelangelo so admirably do; they sought instead to suggest a sophisticated spiritual development, beyond those all-too-human contradictory tendencies. The Buddhas and bodhisattvas are the antipodes of tragic art, as they are freed from all earthly constraints. In them is displayed no struggle of one striving for purity, of a spirit dependent on divine help against a body inclined toward sin, but rather they signify a presence that has reached peace. In European sculpture we find a comparable radiance in the late Romanesque portrayals of the risen Christ in the tympana of Autun or Vézelay. In Buddhist sculpture, however, the figures were intended not only to be venerated in themselves but also to serve the faithful as guideposts to their own inner spiritual powers. The inwardly focused figures of Sino-Buddhist sculpture point to the latent Buddha-nature that slumbers in every living being, to the hidden spiritual abilities of each individual. From an art historical standpoint,

the introduction of divine figures of stone or metal was the decisive novelty that Buddhism brought to China from India and Central Asia.

The only exceptions to the early, tranquil Buddhist art of China were the muscular Tian Wang (Sanskrit Lokapala), the 'heavenly guardians', who watched over the four cardinal directions, and the gigantic Erjiang (Sanskrit Dvarapala), who stood sentinel at the entrances to monasteries. The Tian Wang, who appeared as armoured warriors, are, as guardians of the

An armoured celestial king from the time of the Northern Song (960–1127). Wenshu Hall, Huiji Si.

of Gandhara and especially the Mathura styles were dominant. In the cave temples of the Northern Wei in Yungang and Longmen, the shift from an artistic form adopted from Central Asia to a Chinese sculpture can be clearly seen. The first five grottoes of Tanyao, from the years 460–70, can be understood as a continuation of the caves of Dunhuang, which is not surprising in light of the fact that Tanyao had thousands of artists and craftsmen from Dunhuang sent to the Yungang caves.[19] Astonishingly, we find in caves 7, 8, and 10 again statues of almost purely Indian origin; for instance, the five-headed god of war Karttikeya, who entered the pantheon of Vajrayana Buddhism and who in the seventh and eighth centuries became very popular throughout China as a guardian deity in the form of a young General Weituo. Along with the four Tian Wang, he is absent from no Han Chinese monastery entrance on Wutai Shan. Further examples are the three-headed, four- or eight-armed deities that represent Shiva or the Buddhist guardian deity Mahesvara.[20]

The view found in the literature that the colossal Buddha figures of Yungang were inspired by those of Bamiyan, Afghanistan, is debated, however, since the latest radiocarbon analyses date these statues to the early sixth century. On the other hand, influence from the slightly older cave shrines of Wenshu Shan, Tianti Shan, Bingling Si (all in Gansu Province) and Maijishan (Shaanxi) is conceivable. Work in these four places was undertaken by the Northern Wei.[21] In the two succeeding periods of construction, which lasted until 494, more and more elements of Chinese style entered the canon of Buddhist sculpture. Thus the faces took on softer expressions, the eyes became slightly more almond-shaped, and the heads that had previously appeared squared-off became longer and more oval. This adoption of Chinese standards was taken further in the subsequent temples at Longmen.

The Indian god Shiva on his bull Nandi, whom Buddhism adopted as the patron deity Mahesvara; carved 470–94. Entrance to Cave 8, Yungang.

universe, the opposite of the Buddhas, whose representations did without anatomical details and proportions. In the case of the Tian Wang their anatomy was portrayed in an exaggerated style: with their ferocious gaze, their grimaces, their bulging muscles, and their dislocated bodies, they express a barely constrained violence, suggesting a savage Hercules. The same was true of the Erjiang, who resembled wrestlers.

In the first phase, until the start of the fifth century, the Indian and Central Asian influences

Under the brief dynasty of the Northern Qi (550–77) another important change occurred. Thanks to the artistic impulses of the Indian dynasty of the Gupta (330–550), whose artworks were known to Chinese pilgrims such as Faxian (in India *c.* 401–11), as well as Song Yun and Huiseng (both *c.* 519–21), who likely brought small bronze statues and scrolls back to Middle Kingdom, Chinese artists began to pay more attention to the portrayal of bodies under clothing. In this way the elongated body was idealised, adorned with overlapping necklaces and long chains of pearls, and the head again took on a somewhat rounded form. Especially clear Indian influence of the Gupta style of the school of Mathura was found in the cave temples of Tian Lung Shan, Shanxi, from the time of the Northern Qi, Sui, and Tang. This temple complex is found about 280 km south of Yungang and 190 km southwest of Wutai Shan. Unfortunately, most of the Buddhist stone statues of Tian Lung Shan dating from before the tenth century were either looted or wantonly destroyed during the first decades of the twentieth century.[22]

In the four decades of the Eastern Wei (534–50) and the Northern Qi (550–77) the faces of the buddhas took on a warm and benevolent expression, sympathetic to humans, which gave way under the Sui (581–618) and the early Tang (618–907) to an again distant, inward-looking, and meditative countenance. The faces then adopted a solemn, almost imperial look. The fact that in the sixth century buddha statues featured an especially benevolent – in the case of Buddha Maitreya also contemplative – facial expression is connected with particular eschatological anxieties. Buddhist philosophy has a cyclical understanding of time, according to which periods of sluggish decadence would follow every era of pure teaching of the Buddha, until a 'new' Buddha ushered in a renewed era of True Dharma (Chinese: Fa), the true teaching. According to a theory widespread

in China at the time, it was believed that Buddha Shakyamuni entered into nirvana in 1052 BCE and the two first epochs of the 'true dharma' and the 'form of the dharma' would together last 1,500 years. Thus the Buddhist community was convinced that a terrible age of 'disappearance of the dharma' would begin in 552. This would be characterised by anarchy, wars, catastrophes of all sorts, and the loss of religiosity.

These fears were reinforced by actual events: in the 550s political turmoil and civil

Karttikeya, the Indian god of war, sitting on a dragon, rather than on the usual peacock. He was accepted into Vajrayana Buddhism and appears in the Tian Wang halls of Chinese temples as General Weituo; carved 470–94. Entrance to Cave 8, Yungang.

wars afflicted all of China. And only 20 years earlier, in 535, a violent volcanic eruption in what is now Indonesia set off a worldwide climate catastrophe. The Byzantine historian Procopius reported that in the years 535–36 the sun lost much of its light for ten months, slowing the growth of plants.[23] Since China is much closer to Indonesia than Byzantium, it may be assumed that the climatic catastrophe had a more dramatic effect there and further stoked existing fears of the end times. In northern China these fears were increased by the simultaneous collapse of the Northern Wei Dynasty in the years 534/35 and the breaking up of the nation once again.

In this atmosphere of apocalyptic fears and visions of the end times, desire grew for the swift reincarnation of a Buddha on earth or at least for the possibility of escape into his paradise. The rapidly increasing spread of statues of the future Buddha Maitreya (Chinese: Milefo), whose Sanskrit name means 'universal love', shows the sense of urgency with which people eagerly anticipated the appearance of Maitreya, so that he could introduce a new age of Buddhist light and peaceful bliss as soon as possible. The popularity of Maitreya – the only bodhisattva also recognised by Hinayana – which had been growing rapidly already even the time of the Northern Wei, can be attributed to the influential monk and translator Dao An (312–85). In 370 he gathered his students before a statue of Maitreya and together they took an oath to do everything possible to be reborn in the paradise of Maitreya, Tushita (Chinese: Doushaitian or Zhizutian). Dao An's motivation was not, however, the hope of a comfortable rebirth in Tushita but rather the intention of receiving teaching there from Maitreya himself.[24] From this solemn vow of Dao An a popular Maitreya cult soon developed throughout China.

Three decades later, in 402, Dao An's student Huiyuan (334–416), along with 123 students, took a similar vow before a figure of Buddha Amitabha.

Amitabha (Chinese: Amituofo), whose name means 'infinite light', rules over the paradise of Sukhavati (Chinese: Xifang jile shijie), the 'blissful place'. A variant of the Buddha of light Amitabha is Amitayus (Chinese: Wuliang Shufo), the Buddha of 'immeasurable life'. Amitabha is said to have originally been a king, who upon his consecration as a monk swore to attain enlightenment only when he succeeded in creating a 'Pure Land', where still impure human beings could be reincarnated and he could teach them the perfect Dharma without suffering in his paradise. Those who were reborn after a stay of greater or lesser length in Sukhavati would then certainly enter nirvana. Like Dao An, Huiyuan, who in 370 founded the monastery of Bairenyan in his homeland at the far-northeastern foot of Wutai Shan, did not want to create a mass movement, but rather to commit himself and his following to extreme discipline and intensive meditation. Huiyuan and his students hoped for rebirth in Sukhavati not as personal reward for a virtuous life but instead to receive there deep insights into the doctrine from Buddha Amitabha.[25]

More than a century after Huiyuan's vow, Tanluan (476–542), born near Wutai Shan, popularised Huiyuan's intention to achieve great wisdom with the help of Amitabha. As the apocalyptic visions of the end times spread, he called on the faithful in 530 in the monastery of Xuanzhong, south of Wutai Shan, to seek refuge in the transcendental Buddha Amitabha. He preached that at the beginning of a wicked, Dharma-less time it was impossible, even arrogant, to believe one could achieve salvation in nirvana through one's own powers. Only the ceaseless repetition of Amitabha's name, 'Amituofo', would make possible a rebirth in his Pure Land. Such a rebirth in Sukhavati would guarantee in the next and last rebirth entrance into the desired nirvana; for after this 'in-between-paradise', no relapse back into an earthly incarnation is possible. Here

The future buddha Milefo (Maitreya) and bodhisattvas; created 855–57. Great Buddha Hall, Foguang Si.

Tanluan relied on the *Pratyup. Sutra*. Amitabha says, 'Anyone who wishes to be reborn in My land must constantly recollect Me. ... This bodhisattva, by recourse to this Buddha-recollection, shall be able to be reborn in the Amitabuddha's land.'[26]

From Tanluan's teaching there developed the school of Jingtu, whose name means 'pure (jing) land (tu)'. The 'easy path' of Jingtu to enlightenment requires neither the accumulation of merit through a righteous life (as in the other schools of Chinese Buddhism), nor radical meditation as in Chan, but only the internally repeated invocation of Amitabha. Thus a substantial part of Chinese Buddhism changed from a religion

of personal responsibility accessible in the end only to the literate to a religion of salvation open to all.[27] Tanluan's message built a bridge from an elitist monastic religion to a general religion of the people in the form of a lay Buddhism. This easily accessible school of Jingtu initiated a further revival of Buddhist sculpture, since it is natural to invoke Amitabha before a statue, whether at home in front of a private altar or in a temple. A precursor to this vocal and rhythmic invocation of Amitabha was the custom that arose in the fourth century of reciting sutras in unison.

In Jingtu temples Amitabha is often flanked by Avalokiteshvara (Chinese: Guanyin), the

bodhisattva symbolising the power of all Buddhas, replaced Mahasthamaprapta. As can be seen in the hundreds of dated stone statues at Longmen, at the start of the seventh century Amitabha and Avalokiteshvara overtook the previously dominant Shakyamuni and Maitreya in popularity; the compassionate Amitabha and Avalokiteshvara won the hearts of the people and pushed Shakyamuni and Maitreya, who projected more severity, into the background.[28] Finally, it has been noted that Buddhist sculpture contributed decisively to the expansion and establishment of Buddhism among common, illiterate people.

Kumarajiva and Buddhabhadra debate the Buddha-nature

At the beginning of the fifth century two scholars from Central Asia shaped the intellectual development of Chinese Buddhism. These were Kumarajiva (Chinese: Jiumoluoshi; 344 or 350–413), born in Kucha, and Buddhabhadra (Chinese: Fotuo Batuluo; 359–429), from southeastern Afghanistan, who met in Chang'an in 409/10 and engaged in a heated debate about the question of a universal Buddha-nature. Kumajariva was very learned, having studied first Sarvastivada Hinayana and then the Madhayamika doctrine of Mahayana, important in India.[29] In 384 the renowned scholar fell into the hands of General Lü Guang, who took him from Kucha to Gansu Province and detained him there, where in 386 he founded the short-lived empire of the Later Liang (386–403). Only the attack on Gansu by Emperor Yao Xing (ruled 394–416) from the eastern Tibetan dynasty of the Later Qin (384–417) freed Kumarajiva from his 17-year house arrest, and in 401 he reached Chang'an, where, with the generous support of the Buddhist emperor Yao Xing, he translated

bodhisattva of mercy and of the effective power of Amitabha, and by Mahasthamaprapta (Chinese: Dashizi), the guardian of Amitabha's wisdom. This triad of Jingtu shows that the two foundational virtues of Buddhism, compassion and wisdom, are united in Amitabha. With the spread of the cult of Amitabha, veneration of Guanyin also increased rapidly. Sometimes Manjushri (Wenshu), the bodhisattva of wisdom, or Vajrapani (Chinese: Jingang Shou Pusa), the

Buddhist sutras until his death. Since Kumarajiva knew Sanskrit, Prakrit and Chinese and carefully collated each sutra before the translation, his translations serve as definitive works.

Kumarajiva's rival was the Hinayana monk Buddhabhadra, a student of the famous Indian meditation master Buddhasena. In 409 Buddhabhadra entered Chang'an, where he advanced Buddhasena's teaching of meditation (Sanskrit Dhyana, Chinese: Chan). For personal and doctrinal reasons a debate soon flared up, which Kumarajiva manipulated to his own ends. For the celebrated Kumarajiva, the presence of the disciplined meditation master Buddhabhadra was the equivalent of a living reproach, as he had long since broken the vow of chastity and lived in decadent relationships with several women. A plot initiated by one of Kumarajiva's students forced Buddhabhadra to leave Chang'an in 410. First he visited the scholar Huiyuan on Mount Lushan in Jiangxi Province, after which, from 412 until his death, he translated important Mahayana texts in the southern Chinese city of Jiankang (now Nanking). Among these were

the sutras *Mahaparinirvana* and *Avatamsaka*, which were highly significant for the further development of Buddhism in China and which the pilgrim monk Faxian had recently brought back from India. Kumarajiva stands as the great translator of the north, and Buddhabhadra holds the same position for the south.

Viewed objectively, the two translators held different views in three general areas. First, Kumarajiva taught the Madhayamika doctrine of Mahayana, while Buddhabhadra advanced the meditation teaching of his master Buddhasena; the latter two both belonged to the school of Sarvastivada, which lies between Hinayana and Mahayana. Secondly, Buddhabhadra maintained the belief that every person, regardless of his position or lineage – even, for instance, a slave – is permeated by the Buddha-nature and therefore everyone has the potential to experience enlightenment. In this regard, Buddhabhadra had support from Dao Sheng (c. 360–434), although the latter was a colleague of Kumarajiva. Dao Sheng stated precisely that even an ichchantika (Chinese: yichanti), one who has lapsed into uncontrollable hedonism, who has consciously rejected the teaching of the Buddha, can achieve Buddhahood. This thesis affirming an indestructible kernel of Buddha-nature in every human being was a provocation for the Chinese class-based society of the time, in which there was enormous social differentiation according to lineage and social rank. It was inconceivable that a slave woman or a repentant criminal was, from an ontological or religious viewpoint, equal to a prince or a sage.

Dao Sheng went still further and claimed that 'goodness reaps no reward, and that one may have a sudden experience of enlightened intuition and achieve Buddhahood forthwith'.[30] This thesis overturned traditional doctrine, according to which enlightenment could be realised only after a long development extending over several

The merciful Guanyin Pusa (Bodhisattva Avalokiteshvara) saves all who call on her and believe in her, even sinners and those condemned to death. Southern side chapel of the Hall of a Thousand Buddhas, Xuanzhong Si.

rebirths. It also invalidated the principle, prized by every political authority, that the path to nirvana also followed along morally correct behaviour. The reaction of the public authorities was quick in coming: Buddhabhadra was banished from Chang'an also for this reason, and Dao

Sheng suffered the ignominy of being not only exiled from Jiankang but also expelled from the monastic community.[31] A new translation of the *Mahaparinirvana Sutra*, produced by Dharmaksema (385–433) in 421 and based on a Central Asian text, proves, however, that Dao Sheng's interpretation of the sutra was correct.[32] This view, recognising a Buddha-nature in all people, prevailed in China; it was shared by the most important Chinese schools of thought: Chan, Jingtu, Huayan and Tiantai. Individual schools such as Huayan and Tiantai flatly denied the existence of ichchantika. Buddhabhadra and Dao Sheng stand rightfully as the most important 'prophets' of the school of Chan.

The thesis of a Buddha-nature living within each person also contradicts a fundamental axiom of Indian Buddhism, whose representative Kumarajiva was, according to which there are absolutely no constant substances and thus also no eternal self. The idea of a an individual soul in the form of an individual Buddha-nature, identical to the cosmic Buddha-nature, the absolute, came very close to the belief, rejected by Buddha, of the pre-Buddhist Upanishads, according to which salvation from the circle of rebirth resulted from the union of the individual soul, atman, with the cosmic consciousness Brahman, the universal soul. For orthodox Buddhists it was a serious heresy to seek a self where there was no self and to presume a constant in the fundamentally inconstant.

With the theory of a general Buddha-nature, Buddhabhadra and Dao Sheng definitively set the course for the further development of Chinese Buddhism. In contrast to Indian Buddhism, which hardly concerned itself with the nature of the human being and concentrated on the cognitive processes of the mind; that is, on epistemological questions, the schools of Chinese Buddhism were intensively engaged with the nature of human beings.

Stone statue of Guanyin Pusa (Avalokiteshvara) from Foguang Si. Shanxi Provincial Museum, Taiyuan, Tang Dynasty (618–907).

Procession in honour of General Weituo, who often guards monasteries in China and is often venerated as a bodhisattva. Xuanzhong Si.

As is typical of Chinese thought, they were more interested in concrete changes than in metaphysical speculation. In this way the orientations of thought in Chinese Buddhism stand in the pre-Han traditions of the ancient philosophers Confucius, Mengzi, Mozi and Xun Kuang.[33] Thus, for instance, the Huayan and Chan schools taught that the human Buddha-nature was fundamentally good and without defects, in which they followed the beliefs of Mengzi. In this regard the sixth patriarch of Chan, Huineng (638–713), said, 'our original nature is Buddha and, apart from this nature, there is no other Buddha'. A millennium earlier Mengzi taught something similar in different words: 'All [natural] things in us are perfect and there is no greater joy than to find ourselves in harmony with our true nature.'[34] On the other hand, the Tiantai school emphasised that the human Buddha-nature still entailed a certain degree of ignorance and iniquity, which was

why not all people were enlightened, and there remained room for spiritual development. In this way Tiantai resembled Xun Kuang.

With this particular orientation of Chinese Buddhism it departed sharply from the original teaching of Buddha. In the Four Noble Truths Shakyamuni expressed the insight that, as a consequence of the transience of all beings, all of life was necessarily suffering or led to suffering, so the goal of his teaching was to escape suffering forever. With the exception of the Jingtu School, the problem of human suffering did not play a large role in the writings of Chinese Buddhism; in its place came ignorance of one's own Buddha-nature. Consequently enlightenment was understood as the experience and realisation of one's own Buddha-nature and no longer as a rescue from suffering, and thus the Chinese version of Buddhism transformed the original world-renouncing teaching of Buddha into a world-affirming worldview.

The Ten Schools of Chinese Buddhism

What can we gain by sailing to the moon if we are not able to cross the abyss that separates us from ourselves?

—Linji Yixuan (died 866), Master of Chan[1]

The further development and new direction of Buddhism

The significance of Chinese Buddhism lies not least in the creative advancement of Indian and Central Asian Buddhism at a time when it was coming under increasing pressure in its homeland of India in the fifth/sixth centuries. First came the invasion of the White Huns, the Hephthalites, who occupied the western region of northern India from about 480 to 528, and then from a powerful renaissance of Hindu movements, the absence of royal support, and the brutal and destructive invasions of Muslim warlords, of which the Turko-Afghan Mahmud Ghaznavi (970–1030) and Mohammed Ghuri (1162–1206) were the worst. In India Buddhism almost disappeared; today about 0.7% of the population is Buddhist, and there are three times as many Christians as Buddhists in the country. Buddhism was driven out of broad parts of Central Asia and Afghanistan even earlier. In China, however, learned and visionary monks gave new impetus to Buddhism, and from there it spread to Korea and Japan.

Ten schools crystallised out of the innumerable strands of Han Chinese Buddhism.[2] The following brief overview does not consider the four smaller schools of Pali Buddhism, Baliyu Fojiao, which spread only to the minority Dai peoples in the southwestern Chinese province of Yunnan. They belong to the early Buddhist tradition of Theravada; their principles and rituals are nearly identical to those of the neighbouring states of Myanmar (Burma), Thailand, and Laos. Tibetan Tantric Buddhism will be addressed in the section on esoteric Buddhism.

1. Sanlun Zong

This school (Chinese: zong) is called Sanlun, 'three treatises', because it is based on three scriptures of the Indian school of Madhyamika of Mahayana Buddhism, translated by Kumarajiva.[3] The spiritual fathers of the Sanlun School, which was organised by the monk Jizang (549–623),

Shijiafo (Buddha Shakyamuni) in parinirvana. Behind him Shijiafo makes the earth into a witness to his enlightenment. Statues of white Burmese jade. Ordination Hall in Bishan Si Monastery.

were Kumarajiva's student Sengzhao (378–413) and Dao Sheng, who also inspired the Niepan Shi School. The founder of the Indian Madhyamika, whose name means 'middle way', was the Indian philosopher Nagarjuna, from the second/third centuries CE. Regarding the fundamental question of the nature of being and non-being, Nagarjuna sought a mediating position between the extremes of the nihilistic and realistic approaches. The starting point of the argument is the axiom, formulated by Shakyamuni, that all life means suffering because everything is transitory. This universal transience stems from the fact that nothing has control over the cause of its own being but rather all beings depend on causes outside of themselves. If these causes were to change in themselves or cease to function, every being would, logically, likewise change or cease to exist. That which results only from causes is 'empty of its own self-nature' (Sanskrit sunya). It exists not from itself and possesses neither the sources of its own existence nor an unchanging self. If one thinks through this axiom consistently, one comes to the conclusion, with regard to ontology, that nothing really exists, including Buddha, and, with regard to epistemology, that therefore no statement, including Buddhist teaching, can have reference to reality. This is the position of nihilism and moral indifference with regard to suffering; its opposite extreme is realistic eternalism, which claims that being can arise out of itself, independent of causes and conditions.

Nagarjuna rejected this antithesis between being and non-being, between eternalism and nihilism, as an illusory contradiction. He introduced the concept of the 'two levels of truth' and taught that only the apprehension of the perceivable, apparent world would lead to the perfect wisdom beyond dualism. On the lower, ordinary level of perception, perceptible things have a relative reality; seen from the second level of truth, however, perception remains an illusion,

in the sense of a misperception, although it is not a hallucination. That which is perceived is not purely a product of our consciousness; rather there is also something really, if also conditionally, existing. To use an analogy popular in Buddhism, when at night we are frightened by a snake that reveals itself on closer inspection to be a rope, the rope really is lying on the floor. Since seen from the second, intuitive level of truth, everything perceptible is in fact an illusion without its own basis of existence, Sengzhao taught that things both exist and do not exist.[4]

This worldview enables Madhyamika Buddhists, such as the layman Vimalakirti, to lead a normal life in society, to accept the moral values of Buddha, and to keep others from suffering, as well as simultaneously to realise that the perceptible world and human activity are illusions and offer only a relative value. Thus the Sanlun School avoided the pitfalls of indifferent amorality, since, if all perceptions are illusions and ideas are empty, then human suffering is also an unremarkable illusion and values such as good and bad, helpful and criminal become mere verbiage devoid of content. The doctrine of the 'two truths', formulated by Sengzhao and Dao Sheng in China, formed the foundation for almost all other Chinese schools. After Jizang's death in 623 the School of the Three Treatises came under pressure from the school of Weishi (Faxiang), and its content was also absorbed by the schools of Tientai and Huayan. In 625 Jizang's Korean student Huiguan (Japanese: Ekwan) introduced the ideas of Sanlun into Japan, where it likewise served as the basis for many intellectual currents.

2. Niepan Shi

Niepan Shi, the Nirvana School, was less a religious group than a very influential school of thought. It emerged in the fifth century with the teaching of the monk Dao Sheng (c. 360–434), who has already been mentioned several times. Dao Sheng was especially concerned with the sutra *Mahaparinirvana*, which understood nirvana as eternal, pure, personal bliss, in contrast to the *Prajnaparamita* sutra, favoured by Kumarajiva, which interpreted nirvana as the realisation of absolute nothingness. Starting from this sutra, Dao Sheng revolutionised Chinese Buddhism with three theses:

- the Buddha-nature slumbers in everyone;
- criminals can also realise Buddha-nature;
- Buddhahood can be abruptly experienced in a sudden enlightenment.

With the participation of each person in the universal Buddha-nature, he granted to every individual a value unknown in China before that time. Dao Sheng was also the first to begin classifying the numerous, partially contradictory sutras according to the periods of Buddha's teaching and these according to the spiritual capacity of the audience of the time. Towards the end of the sixth century the Niepan School was absorbed into the Tientai School.

3. Jushe Zong

This school of the sixth and seventh centuries belonged to the realistic outlook of Hinayana. It held the basic Buddhist axiom of the non-existence of a constant self but believed in the essential reality of the dharma. This Sanskrit term has a special significance in Hinayana; Buddhism recognises a total of six meanings of the word 'dharma':

- the cosmic law governing rebirths
- the eternal teaching
- ethical norms
- observable phenomena
- mental content, an idea
- in Hinayana, an element of existence.

For the realistic Jushe School observable phenomena remain illusions, but the elements of existence underlying them really exist in the past, present, and future. This worldview is comparable to the atomism of the Greek philosophers Leucippos (fifth century BCE) and Democritos (c. 460–360 BCE). In the seventh century the Jushe School spread to Japan under the name Kusha, while in China toward the end of the eighth century it was considered a branch of the Weishi School.

4. Tiantai Zong

The school of Tiantai, whose name means 'heaven's (Tian) platform (Tai)' and which was founded by the monk Zhiyi (538–97), further developed the classification of the various sutras begun by Dao Sheng into a system of five teaching periods and eight types of teaching.[5] As the *Lotus Sutra* describes it, 'slightly differentiated' truths that appeal to simple people are resolved by 'higher' truths as soon as each has fulfilled its purpose. The numerous sutras may be compared to a staircase, whose highest step is the *Lotus Sutra*, which is why Tiantai is also called the School of the Lotus.

Starting from the concept of the two levels of truth, Zhiyi introduced the 'third truth', according to which there is no contradiction between the relative, illusory reality of phenomena and the insight into their emptiness because the absolute does not exist outside of phenomena. Zhiyi emphasised that all is interwoven with all and therefore included within all: 'In every particle of dust, in every moment of thought, the whole universe [and all Buddhas] is contained.'[6] Thus he followed the thought of Dao Sheng. Another key sentence of Tiantai states, 'For we ourselves and all living beings are already Buddha in a latent

Shijiafo (Buddha Shakyamuni) and four bodhisattvas, *c.* 1056. Second storey of the pagoda of Mu Ta.

China. To the traditionalists of the time, for whom Buddhahood was achievable only for select monks, the idea put forth by Saicho that all living things possessed the potential Buddhahood appeared as a scandal. Yet the doctrine prevailed, and its adherents grew into one of the strongest monastic communities in Japan, which, in a radical misrepresentation and perversion of Buddha's teaching, came in time not only to possess large landholdings but also to maintain armies of soldier monks. One of the most significant early masters of Tendai was the third patriarch, Ennin (793–864). Like his teacher Saicho before him, Ennin travelled to China to study and made a pilgrimage in 840 to Wutai Shan.[8] In China he was witness to the terrible anti-Buddhist persecutions of 843–45, which destroyed all the writings of Tiantai and nearly obliterated the intellectual school, which depended on the study of texts. A modest revival of the school succeeded only thanks to Japanese and Korean translations.

state; we could never become Buddha in fact if Buddhahood was not already within us'.[7] Later the ninth patriarch of Tiantai, Zhanran (711–82), stated more precisely that Buddha-nature is also contained in inanimate objects.

An important pillar of the identity of the absolute with illusory phenomena, postulated by Tiantai, is the idea of an absolute, universal mind, on which all things and phenomena depend. This cosmic mind has two aspects: a perfect and an impure. The perfect aspect produces the qualities of Buddha-nature, and the impure, all things and phenomena. Thus Tiantai recognises that the Buddha-nature that appears in phenomena can be imperfect, which leaves the necessary space to distinguish good from less good and to perfect the imperfect.

When in 805 the Japanese monk Saicho (767–822) introduced the Tiantai School to Japan, where it is called Tendai, he encountered in the established Buddhist schools of Japan the same opposition Dao Sheng had met with

5. Huayan Zong

The same fate as Tiantai was suffered by the likewise philosophically inclined Huayan School, which was destroyed by the persecutions of Emperor Wuzong (ruled 840–46). This school was based on the sutra *Avalamsaka* (Chinese: *Huayan*), whose name means 'garland of flowers'. It was founded and organised by the three masters Dushun (557–640), Zhiyan (602–68), and Fazang (643–712). It reordered the sutras into a five-part schema and supplemented the Tiantai School, whose basic principles it shared. As in Tiantai, Fazang taught that all things and phenomena were linked with one another and thus each individual phenomenon carried within itself the entire universe. In adding to the teaching of Tiantai he underlined the individual character of each phenomenon and maintained

that phenomena were not only identical with the absolute but were also interwoven with each other. For Fazang the cosmos resembled a net. In contrast to Tiantai, the school of Huayan assumed that the Buddha-nature in things and phenomena was generally pure, which blurred the boundaries between good and evil, right and wrong. The ideas of Huayan were taken to Japan by the Chinese monk Daoxuan in 736 and the Korean monk Shenxiang in 740, after which the Japanese Roben (689–773) became the first patriarch of the Kegon School. He had built in Nara the wooden temple of Todai-ji, which still stands today and which has been declared a world cultural heritage site by UNESCO. The triad of Shakyamuni, Wenshu, and Puxian Pusa, often encountered in the shrines of Wutai Shan, is also called the 'Three Saints of Huayan'.[9]

6. Weishi Zong

While the schools of Tiantai and Huayan were largely devoted to questions of logic, the school of Weishi explored the process of perception. Its approach is comparable to a kind of phenomenology of perception of modern psychology or phenomenological philosophy. The school called itself Weishi, which means 'consciousness only'; its opponents, however, such as the master of Huayan, Fazang, disparagingly called it Faxiang, meaning 'qualities of the dharma, of existence'. In this way Fazang insinuated that the Weishi School stayed only on the surface of perceptible appearances, while Huayan and Tiantai fathomed the nature of the existence underlying the appearances.

Weishi was founded by the most famous of all the pilgrim monks, Xuanzang (c. 602–64), and his student Kuiji (632–82), who undertook a pilgrimage to Wutai Shan with 500 monks in 673.[10] In 633 Xuanzang studied the Mahayana

Pious donors can place a slip with their name on it behind a clay tablet bearing the figure of Buddha Shakyamuni. Wenshu Pusa Hall, Shuxiang Si.

school of Yogacara at the Buddhist University of Nalanda in northern India and brought related texts with him back to China, where he translated them into Chinese. The Weishi School represented a consistent idealism, as for it all perceptible things and phenomena lack a substance of their own, since they arise only by means of the creative power of the mind. There exist no real things outside of subjective perceptions, and these are nothing but mental projections. But for Weishi not just the perceptible world is a mental idea, but the perceiving subject is as well. The entire world is only an idea; only consciousness.[11] Thus consciousness not only represents the condition of any awareness but also constitutes the perceived object.

Xuanzang hypothesised 100 factors of existence (dharmas) and eight types of consciousness. The first five types of consciousness correspond to the five senses, and the sixth is that of the thinking consciousness, which organises and coordinates the perceptions of the five senses. The seventh consciousness is the self-consciousness that thinks and wills; it is the basis of subjectivity. The eighth consciousness is the so-called 'storehouse consciousness', in which all impressions on the consciousness are preserved. It is a kind of complete memory of all elements of consciousness that affect karma, which have arisen from thoughts, feelings, and perceptions. This container of all the content of consciousness is purely passive; it becomes active only through contact with the seventh consciousness, the self-consciousness. Since this seventh consciousness forms the gateway between the first six types of consciousness and the storehouse consciousness, salvation emerges from the enlightenment of the self-consciousness, in which it finally recognises the illusory character of the world.

Despite the great renown of its founder Xuanzang, the decline of the Weishi School began only a few decades after his death, for two reasons. First, Weishi reproduced in their pure form ideas of Indian Yogacara, whose hair-splitting analyses and difficult terminology deterred the more practically oriented Chinese spirit. Secondly, Xuanzang denied that all people possessed the Buddha-nature and could realise Buddhahood. For him it was impossible that an unregenerate ichchantika, a faithless criminal, could achieve Buddhahood. However, Xuanzang did not define the ichchantika in the sense of an ontological preordination extending over multiple rebirths. For him someone was an ichchantika if he pursued a criminal lifestyle and refused over the course of several rebirths to pay heed to Buddha's message. One who chose the path of Buddha, however, could not be an ichchantika. Despite this differentiated view, the Weishi School was sharply attacked by Tiantai and Huayan on these grounds and rapidly lost prestige. In Japan, though, where the school was called Yui-shiki-shu or Hosso-shu, it remained a popular institution until the fourteenth century.

7. Lü Zong

While the first six approaches to doctrine fall into the category of philosophical Buddhism, the next four belong to praxis-oriented Buddhism. Lü Zong is the school of discipline, which is less concerned with religious and philosophical content and more with clarification and implementation of rules of conduct for Buddhist laypeople, novices, monks, and nuns. The school, founded by the famous Buddhist historian Daoxuan (596–667), proceeds from the Vinaya-Pitaka, the monastic rules, and is based on the rules of the Dharmaguptakas from the third century BCE.[12] Monastic discipline encompassed the five laws for the laity, the additional five requirements for novices, 250 rules for monks, and 348 for nuns.

Daoxuan wrote the authoritative commentary on the Dharmaguptakas and founded the Lü School as a reaction against the increasing disciplinary neglect in the large monasteries. He emphasised that there was no path to enlightenment outside strict monastic rules.

Although this school achieved no great popularity, Daoxuan's work gained wide acceptance. It is thanks to him that the large monasteries of other schools in China and Japan very often have a master of discipline, who is also responsible for the ordination ceremonies. In today's China the Lü School is enjoying a certain revival, as can be seen, for instance, on Wutai Shan at the new, very large convent of Pushou. In Japan the doctrine, spread by the blind monk Jianzhen (688–763) after 753, played a similar role as it had in China, where other schools began to erect special ordination platforms and establish consecration rites.[13]

8. Mi Zong

The name Mi Zong, commonly used today, means 'school' (Zong) of 'secrets' (Mi) and is the collective term for all the schools of esoteric Buddhism found in China, including Tibetan Buddhism. This type of Buddhism is called esoteric because it teaches that texts and formulas have a second meaning, accessible only to initiates. Specifically Han Chinese esoteric Buddhism calls itself Zhenyan Zong, 'school of the true word', which can also be translated as 'school of the mantras'. The school of Zhenyang emerged from Vajrayana, a further development of Mahayana. Vajrayana arose in India at the start of the seventh century as a populist reaction against the increasing intellectualism within Mahayana, which oriented itself strongly toward the teachings of the great monastic universities. Charismatic meditation masters, who were independent from the universities,

Entrance Hall and Tian Wang Hall in Pushou Si.

The titular god Zhuanlun Wangfo (Kalachakra) in sexual union with the female Zhuxiang Foma (Vishvamata). The Kalachakra Tantra is one of the most important tantras of Tibetan Buddhism. Great Hall, Wenshu Si.

recognised that the accumulation of knowledge was useless if it was not converted into action and experience. For them enlightenment was the result not of insights but rather of experiences.

To activate or hasten these experiences, the masters used psychological methods, which are common in Hindu religions, such as:

- mudra, certain gestures
- mantras, mystical syllables
- mandala, mystical cosmic designs
- abhisheka, special initiation rites.

These techniques assume a macro-microcosmic analogy in the universe, and, as external actions, are thought to precipitate inner psychic processes. Sexual symbolism also plays an important role, as a representation of the union of opposites. The esoteric teachings concerning these techniques and the many deities of Vajrayana Buddhism are called Tantra, which is why esoteric Buddhism is also called Tantrayana. Tantra is not accessible to all but is rather handed down successively from master to pupil. As the experience in India, China, and Tibet shows, the boundary between Tantra and magic, Tantrist and sorcerer, was often blurred. In fact, the conviction that believers could, by means of reciting a holy mantra or wearing a dharani text amulet, evade certain consequences of karma represented a faith in miracles. Since the Tantric masters appeared to have magical powers, such as the art of soothsaying or healing or the ability to cause rain, they were both valued and feared by rulers and the people. Insofar as the masters of Vajrayana believed in the possibility of a sudden and complete enlightenment in this body in the here and now, they resembled Chan.[14]

Tantrayana was distinguished by a complex pantheon. Starting with the principle of emanation or incarnation, esoteric Buddhism postulated five transcendental Tathagata-Buddhas (Chinese: rulai), who emerged from the original Buddha. Five female consorts correspond to these

five Tathagatas. From each Tathagata-Buddha there then emerged a bodhisattva; these five bodhisattvas likewise had their female counterparts. Finally, these deities had both a peaceful and an angry aspect, which they embodied according to the situation. Thus the pantheon of Vajrayana was separated into male and female, irenic and fearsome deities. Since in esoteric Buddhism statues and mandalas also served to communicate complex theological content, their

portrayal in statues and paintings was subject to strict rules. Only the correct rendering of bodily gestures, colour, mudras and attributes could ensure the effectiveness of a figure.

In China the charismatic monk Fotudeng (c. 232–348) was a forerunner of esoteric Buddhism insofar as he used his parapsychological abilities for predicting the future and influencing the weather. In 655 the Indian monk Punyodaya was the first to try to teach esoteric Buddhism in the capital Chang'an, but he failed because of the opposition of Xuanzang, who was very influential at the time. In the following century Vajrayana gained a foothold in China's capital city. First the Indian monk Subhakarasimha (Chinese: Shanwuwei, 637–735), who was renowned as a rainmaker and who settled in Chang'an in 716, translated the important sutra *Mahavairocana*, Chinese: *Darijing*. In it the highest Tathagata-Buddha, Vairocana, explains the essence of Tantrayana and describes various mandala and initiation rites. Next came the Indian Vajrabodhi (Chinese: Jingangshi, 663/71–741), who reached China in 720 and was active in both the capitals, Chang'an and Luoyang, and translated the most significant sutras of Vajrayana.

The decisive breakthrough occurred with the Indo–Sogdian monk Amoghavajra (Chinese: Bukong Jingang, 705–74), the most important student of Vajrabodhi. When Emperor Xuanzong (ruled 712–56) tried in 741 to reform the Buddhist institutions by reducing the number of monasteries and their landholdings, expelling foreign monks from the country, and returning 30,000 monks and nuns to the tax-paying lay state, Bukong undertook a pilgrimage to Southeast Asia, Sri Lanka and India.[15] He returned to China in 746. At this time Emperor Xuanzong was strictly regulating the ordination of monks and nuns, as only government-approved monks and nuns held the necessary warrant. Private consecrations were forbidden, and itinerant monks and

nuns not associated with any monastery were banned. But thanks to his power as a weather maker and magical healer, Amoghavajra won the trust of aging Emperor Xuanzong, as well as his successors Suzong (ruled 756–62) and Daizong (ruled 762–79). Daizong generously supported the monasteries on Wutai Shan, so that they would pray for the welfare of the empire.[16] In 759 Amoghavajra also declared Emperor Suzong a chakravartin, the image of Buddha on earth, and wrote out on slips of paper for him and later for Daizong magical formulas to lengthen life, which both emperors always wore on various parts of their bodies. Amoghavajra also developed special rituals with particular patron deities for the well-being of the state and the imperial ancestors. Amoghavajra was likewise of great significance for Wutai Shan, since he encouraged the cult of Wenshu Pusa (Manjushri), the protector of Wutai Shan, and in 766 had the monastery of Jinge, founded in 736, lavishly restored.[17]

The spread of Zhenyan Zong demonstrates that esoteric Buddhism established itself in China completely independently from Tibetan Buddhism. There are even clear indications that the veneration of the emperor as Buddhist world ruler, which arose at that time from Chinese Mi Zong, was adopted by the Tibetan royalty. So one finds, for instance, in the eastern Tibetan shrine of Bida near Yüshü, in today's Sichuan Province, a large stone relief sculpture from 804, in whose centre a Tathagata Vairocana, approximately three metres high, sits enthroned.[18] The figure of the cosmic world ruler Vairocana is not wearing the usual monk's clothing, however, but rather the typical robe of a Tibetan king. This portrayal of Vairocana shows that Tibetan kings – in the case of Bida, King Trisong Detsen (ruled 756–97), Mune Tsenpo (ruled 797–800), or Tride Songtsen (Sanalek, ruled 804–15) – took from China the custom of legitimating their authority through religion, by

The 1,000-armed and 11-headed Wenshu Pusa (Manjushri) in the 'Wenshu Pusa Hall of the Thousand Begging Bowls' in the monastery of Xiantong Si. The Indo-Sogdian scholar-monk Bukong Jingang (Amoghavajra) established esoteric Buddhism in China and promoted the cult of Wenshu Pusa.

Portrayal of the parental love of
Shijiafo (Buddha Shakyamuni),
Cave Temple 17 of Baoding Shan,
Dazu, Sichuan Province. Many
of the cave temples of Baoding
Shan from the Southern Song
Dynasty (1127–79) are masterpieces
of esoteric Buddhism.

having themselves presented visually as the earthly likeness of a powerful Buddhist deity.

Bukong was witness to a dramatic time. In his old age Emperor Xuanzong neglected the business of the state in favour of his concubine Yang Guifei, who abused her influence over the besotted emperor. She 'adopted' her lover, General Lushan, thus introducing him into the innermost circle of power. The upstart seized the moment, rebelled, and in 755 declared himself the new emperor of China. With his battle-tested veteran army, he conquered both capitals and forced Xuanzong to flee. Then his bodyguard rebelled and forced him to have his concubine Yang executed. Although An Lushan died in 757, the civil war did not end until seven years later, after the Tibetans conquered and plundered Chang'an in 763. The civil war instigated by An Lushan could only have been quelled with the help of the Turkic Uighurs, who, as the new protector power of the drastically weakened Middle Kingdom, ruthlessly exploited it. The Tang Dynasty never recovered from this blow, and according to official censuses, the population dropped from 53 million in 754 to just 17 million in 764.[19] Even if the numerous refugees were not included in the census of 764, this decline is shocking.

The decline of the Zhenyan School began after the death of Bukong in 774, not least because, apart from a few exceptions in the tenth century, no more Indian monks came to China to develop the tradition further. Although Bukong designated the Chinese monk Huiguo (746–805) as his successor, the already weakened school practically disappeared with the Buddhist persecutions of 843–45. The exception was the southwestern province of Sichuan, which was sporadically semi-autonomous, where esoteric Buddhism continued to flourish, since many Buddhists fled there in 845. In the immense, partially painted stone sculptures of Dazu (late ninth to mid-thirteenth

century), esoteric Buddhism left behind unique works of art. In Japan, by contrast, the school, known by the name Shingon, still flourishes today. It was Huiguo's Japanese student Kukai (775–835) and the founder of the school of Tendai, Saicho, who spread it to the island kingdom.

Under the Mongol dynasty of the Yuan (1271–1368) the esoteric Buddhism of China experienced a certain renaissance. In the process it drew much closer to Tibetan Vajrayana, not least because the Tibetan monks who lived at the imperial court enjoyed the trust of the Yuan

Stone relief sculpture of the highest Tatagatha Buddha and cosmic world ruler Vairocana in the garments of a Tibetan king, 804 CE. Bida Temple at Yüshü, Sichuan.

The standing bodhisattvas Dashizi
Pusa (Mahasthamaprapta, left)
and Jingang Pusa (Vajrapani,
right) flank the seated
Piluzhenafo (Buddha Vairocana).
Piluzhenafo Hall, Bishan Si.

emperors. This development was hastened under the first emperors of the Qing Dynasty, who out of political and personal motivations strongly encouraged Tibetan Buddhism, until Chinese esoteric Buddhism was largely absorbed into Tibetan Buddhism. In the nineteenth century Chinese esoteric Buddhism was reintroduced into China from Japan. Today on Wutai Shan the beliefs, scriptures and rituals of the so-called Mi Zong monasteries and the Lama monasteries are practically identical. The only difference is that Han Chinese or a combination of Han Chinese and Tibetan monks live in the former, while only Tibetans live in the latter.

9. Jingtu Zong

The apocalyptic fears of the civil war begun by An Lushan gave the salvation religion of Jingtu, which even before 755 had gained wide popularity among the lower classes, a decisive impetus among the upper classes as well. The movement of taking refuge in Buddha Amitabha,[20] born of the spirit of a pessimistic worldview of Huiyuan and Tanluan, was further refined by Tanluan's student Daochu (562–645). Like his master, he distinguished between the 'difficult path' to nirvana, open to only a few people, which led as a result of a monastic life to perfect enlightenment of the mind, and an 'easy path', open to all people, which depended on the help and grace of Amitabha. Daochu was the first to begin reciting aloud the supplication formula 'Namo Amituofo', 'respect is [rendered unto] Amitabha', created by Tanluan.[21]

Daochu's student Shandao (613–81), who studied with his master in the monastery of Xuanzhong, south of Wutai Shan, is the true founder of Jingtu. He popularised the doctrine and explained that only unreserved trust in the compassionate grace of Buddha Amitabha would

The monastery of Xuanzhong Si, founded in the fifth century, lies 76 km south of the provincial capital of Taiyuan and is one of the cradles of the school of Jingtu Zong. The name basically means 'the monastery that hangs in midair'.

lead to salvation. It sufficed to call upon Amitabha unceasingly, silently or aloud, and to think of him always. Later Fazhao (died *c.* 820), who founded the monastery of Zhulin on Wutai Shan between 777 and 796, defined the exact tune of the five-part invocation of Amitabha, as it is still heard today as a kind of perpetual background music in all the monasteries of Jingtu. Like Fazhao, his teacher Zimin (*c.* 680–748) concerned himself with uniting the veneration of Amitabha of Jingtu with the meditation practice of Chan. In fact, it is common to both schools that they pay little mind to textual study and emphasise praxis, in the fully complementary forms of humble devotion in Jingtu and mental concentration in Chan. It was these practical aspects of both schools, anchored in the general public, that allowed them to survive the severe persecutions of 843–45. The more intellectual schools, which primarily addressed educated monks and nuns rather than the illiterate

people, disappeared at that time. The movement of Jingtu, which had never organised itself as an institution in China, is today the most popular school in China, with a striking share of nuns and of laypeople of both sexes. In the temples of Jingtu, representations of Amitabha, Guanyin, and Dashizi (Mahastamaprapta) are especially popular; they serve as the Three Saints of the West.[22]

With Jingtu there emerged a Buddhist movement which distinguished itself sharply from the original Buddhism of Hinayana with regard to both its religious methods and its goal. While in Hinayana the overcoming of karma can result only through knowledge and the accumulation of merit from good deeds and intentions, in Jingtu above all prayer and faith are salvific. Apart from Jingtu and Mi Zong, faith plays only a subordinate role in Buddhism. For Jingtu the old behavioural ideals of personal responsibility and autonomous effort were just

To the left Wenshu Pusa (Manjushri Bodhisattva) rides his lion; to the right Buddha Amitabha sits enthroned. Between them stand bodhisattvas and in front of Wenshu Pusa are small statues of Shancai to the left and a black servant in a red robe to the right. The latter was replaced in the 10th century by the king of Udayana; 855–57. Great Buddha Hall, Foguang Si.

The mythical kingdom of Shambala, in the heart of the Himalayas, where justice and virtue reign. According to the prophecy of the Kalachakra Tantra, Rudra, the 25th king of Shambala, will defeat the attacking enemy with the help of the gods and found a perfect age lasting 1,800 years. This eschatological vision emerged at a time when the Muslim commander Mahmud Ghaznavi was systematically persecuting Buddhists and destroying their temples during his forays into northwestern India. Tian Wang Hall of Guangren Si.

A monk of Wanghai Si Monastery centres himself before beginning a sung recitation of the name of Amituofo (Buddha Amitabha).

signs of ignorant arrogance, which did not recognise that in times of complete decadence only trust in the saving power of Amitabha would lead to the goal. But this goal was also understood differently in Jingtu than in other schools. It is neither the final end of the karma-governed cycle of rebirths as in Hinayana nor the sudden enlightenment in the here and now as in Chan, but rather the penultimate rebirth in Sukhavati (Chinese: Jile), the paradise of Amitabha. Rebirth in the western paradise of Jile is a secure intermediary stage, since from here no relapse is possible, and the next and last rebirth will lead 'imperatively' to enlightenment.

That behind the goal of a rebirth in the Pure Land of Amitabha there glimmers the hope of eternal life is evident in the popularity of Amitabha's incarnation as Amitayus (Chinese:

Wuliang), whose name means 'immeasurable life'. For Jingtu a saving enlightenment is scarcely achievable in this present life; at most one might receive a vision of Buddha Amitabha as evidence that the believer or a monastic community is on the right path. In this regard, during my explorations of Wutai Shan I was several times shown photographs in which the figure of Amitabha was visible in a five-coloured cloud. In the eighth century the critique of Chan Buddhism assessed these points: there is no this-worldly paradisiacal Pure Land, but rather it is within us, it is the hidden Buddha-nature. 'The deluded person concentrates on the Buddha and wishes to be reborn in the other land; the awakened person makes pure his own mind ... If the mind is pure, wherever one is, there is the Pure Land.'[23] For Chan the message of Jingtu fosters adherence to

Man at prayer in the temple honouring Wenshu Pusa; Northern Song (960–1127). Huiji Si.

the transient and the inessential and is nothing but an illusory crutch for lazy people. In this sense, the Japanese Zen master Dogen (1200–53) derisively compared the continuous invocation of Amitabha to the croaking of frogs.[24]

Much more conciliatory was the Chan master Yungming (904–75), who recommended the

Man at prayer in the temple honouring Wenshu Pusa; Northern Song (960–1127). Huiji Si.

practice of meditation and humble prayer as complementary activities. For him the union of Chan and Jingtu was doubly effective, like 'a tiger with horns'.[25] Because Jingtu and Chan intermingled further beginning in the eleventh century, the differences in the monasteries today are not always immediately recognisable. They concern the daily routine of the monks and nuns, the texts studied, the content of the teaching, the ceremonies, the monastic festivals, and the figurative representations in individual temples. For the laity these differences hardly play any role anyway, so adherents of Jingtu on a pilgrimage would as a matter of course also visit the monasteries of Chan, and vice-versa. As can be observed on Wutai Shan, the Buddhism lived out by the people also adopted Daoist ideas.

The pious veneration of Amitabha is also widespread in Japan. It goes back to Ennin (793–864), the third patriarch of Tendai, who, after studying in China, was the first to teach the custom of invoking Amitabha in Japan. The two leading Japanese institutions are the 'School of the Pure Land', Jodo-Shu, which emerged in the twelfth century, and the 'True School of the Pure Land', Jodo-Shinshu, which split from the mother school as a reform movement in the fifteenth century.

10. Chan Zong

The name Chan'na (Japanese: Zen) is derived from the Sanskrit word Dhyana and denotes a mental or physical discipline that so calms the mind that it recognises the true nature of being, beyond dualistic opposites. Chan, which developed in China, is an outstanding example of the regenerating power of Buddhism. It arose as a reaction to both the hair-splitting and dogmatism of the philosophical schools of Tiantai, Huayan and Weishi, and the dependence on opulent ceremonies, which all represent obstacles on the path to enlightenment. Chan does not want to be a doctrine about enlightenment, Wu (Japanese: Satori), but rather an aid to the experience of it.

The spiritual fathers of Chan argued that philosophy, ceremonies and costly artworks represented only external appendages of Buddhism. The essence of Buddhism lies in the internal experiences that arise from meditation and concentration. They objected emphatically to the fundamental contradiction that the monastic institutions of Buddhism, which preached freedom from greed for material possessions, accumulated enormous wealth. The monasteries exploited the naïve hopes of the faithful that generous contributions would help them, their ancestors, and their families with regard to fortunate rebirths. An imperial edict from 707 calculated that approximately 70% of the total national wealth was held in tax-exempt Buddhist institutions.[26]

In Chan the goal was not to understand and interpret the world correctly from an intellectual point of view but rather to consistently live in it correctly. Thus it required neither an extended study of texts nor wealthy monasteries nor helpful bodhisattvas. On account of the universal Buddha-nature, every person, irrespective of his life circumstances, had the potential to live 'correctly' according to the principles of Chan. Chan combats our normal inclination to put off correct action until we feel strong enough or sufficiently prepared. For Chan every moment offers each of us the possibility to act and live correctly. A four-line strophe from the eighth or ninth century defines Chan as follows:

> Special transmission outside the Scriptures.
> No setting up of words and letters.
> Point directly at man's mind.
> See self-nature and attain Buddhahood.[27]

The intent of Chan consisted in recognising and experiencing the nature of Buddha in one's own nature and in the present life, not only in a distant rebirth. For outside of the universal Buddha-nature, there are no other Buddhas. This demythologising view comes forth in a famous statement of the Chan master Linji Yixuan (died 866):

There's a type of student who goes to Mt. Wutai to seek out Manjushri. [Wutai Shan serves as the residence of Manjushri, the patron of China.] That

Abbess of the Jingtu monastery of Baiyun Si, Shi Chang Long. She wears the ceremonial red garment 'jiasa' with the embroidered character 'fo' for Buddha.

*student has already made a mistake! There's no
Manjushri on Mt. Wutai. Do you want to know
Manjushri? It's just what is in front of your eyes!
From first to last it's not anything else. Don't doubt
it anywhere you go! It's the living Manjushri!*[28]

In these words are brought out the ascetic and
demythologising character of Chan, which
required students to give up all supporting illusions
such as ceremonies, figurative representations,
helpful buddhas and bodhisattvas, and visions.

The first two lines of the above strophe signal
the independence from established schools of
thought and metaphysical discussions, but not
the neglect of important sutras of Mahayana,
which form the foundation of Chan. Among them
are the sutras *Lankavatara*, *Mahaparinirvana*,
Vimalakirti, *Avamtamsaka*, and above all the
Diamond Sutra, which was widespread in China
and is part of the *Prajnaparamita Sutras*. Its full
name means 'the diamond that cuts through
illusions'. It is no coincidence that the earliest
printed book in the world is the *Diamond*

Sutra; it is a woodblock print dated to 11 May
868.[29] Meditative study can be a necessary but
not sufficient element in the establishment of a
correct life. Linji cautioned against the danger
that textual study becomes an end in itself with
provocative words: 'Sutras resemble hitching
posts for donkeys.'[30] Linji did not deny the value of
well-directed study of the sutras, because 'no one
is born wise and understanding. Everybody must
go through serious study and personal experience,
must be subjected to severe drills and trials, before
he can hope to come to an actual awakening in
his own heart some day'.[31] In Chan, however, the
study of the sutras was directed towards a deeper,
spiritual sense and not towards the literal meaning.

According to tradition, the semi-legendary
Indian Bodhidharma (Chinese: Putidamo,
c. 440–528 or c. 470–543) was the founder and first
patriarch of the school. His encounter in 520 with
the pious Emperor Wudi (ruled 502–49) of the
southern Chinese dynasty of Liang, who fostered
Buddhism through the building and support of
monasteries, is instructive for the mindset of
Chan. When the emperor asked him what merit he
had earned through his founding of monasteries
and copying of countless sutras, Bodhidharma
answered laconically, 'None whatsoever'.[32]

Bodhidharma did not want to somehow snub
the emperor but rather to indicate that the acquisi-
tion of positive merit could lead only to a more
positive rebirth or to a time-limited sojourn in a
paradise determined by karma. This striving for
merit would keep the cycle of rebirths going but
never lead to Buddhahood. The relative benefit of
the striving for merit follows deeds like a shadow
does the body but is as illusory as the shadow
itself. Bodhidharma consistently maintained that
'our mortal nature is our Buddha-nature. Beyond
this nature there's no Buddha'. Bodhidharma's
conversation partner asked, 'But suppose I don't
see my nature, can't I still attain enlightenment
by invoking Buddhas, reciting sutras, making

**Chan monk with ordination scars
on his shaved head, Bishan Si.**

offerings, observing precepts, practising devotions, or doing good works?' The master answered,

No, you can't. If you attain anything at all, it's conditional, it's karmic. It results in retribution. It turns the Wheel. ... They create karma in this life and receive their reward in the next. They never escape. Only someone who's perfect creates no karma in this life and receives no reward. The sutras say, 'Who creates no karma obtains the Dharma'.

The uselessness, indeed the obstructive character of all external fuss, was brought to the point by Bodhidharma: 'Those who worship don't know, and those who know don't worship'. Foyen expressed himself still more directly in the eleventh century: 'The one who seeks the ass on which he rides is foolish'. One who looks outside of one's own Buddha-nature finds nothing. Bodhidharma also pointed out, 'It's true, you have the Buddha-nature. But without the help of a teacher, you'll never know it.'[33] As in esoteric Buddhism, in Chan personal mentoring of the student by an experienced master is absolutely necessary.

Since Bodhidharma met with incomprehension on the part of Emperor Wudi, he took himself north to the monastery of Shaolin, which had been founded at the time of the Northern Wei in 495 southeast of the then capital, Luoyang. There he is said to have meditated before a rock wall in a cave for nine years. As he explained to his student and successor Huike (487–593), he sought in this manner the complete freeing of the mind, in order to recognise his own Buddha-nature:

When you start to meditate, you need to be unattached to everything and to observe your own mind with enormous concentration. You have to train your mind to be void or to be like a wall that nothing can hang onto. Not even your own anxieties, worries, and thoughts can cling to it.[34]

Earlier Bodhidharma had accepted Huike, whom he left standing unnoticed outside his cave for days in heavy snowfall, as a student only after a dramatic demonstration of his determination. When Bodhidharma pointed out that Buddha Shakyamuni attained enlightenment only after many, sometimes painful rebirths, Huike seized an axe and chopped off his left hand, which he presented to the stunned Bodhidharma. After Huike there followed three historically elusive patriarchs, Sengcan (died 606), Daoxin (580–651), and Hongren, the last patriarch recognised by all lines of the tradition.

Hongren's successor was the highly educated Shenxiu (died 706), who was recognised as the sixth patriarch until just under 30 years after his death. He spent the final six years of his life in the capital Chang'an, having been invited there by Empress Wu Zetian (ruled 690–705). The empress considered herself an incarnation of the future buddha Maitreya and was the first ruler to recognise Chan as an official school.[35] After Shenxiu's death, there was no agreement about his successor. In this context Abbot Shenhui (684–758 or 762), who had meditated under Shenxiu's guidance, publicly attacked Shenxiu in 732 or 734. He accused him on two grounds: first, Shenxiu taught the traditional, gradual enlightenment instead of the sudden and complete enlightenment propagated by Chan. Secondly, Shenxiu had been a usurper, since Hongren had not designated him as his successor but rather a monk named Huineng (638–713), little known before that time, who came from southern China. Thus Huineng represented the so-called Southern, only orthodox school of Chan, while Shenxiu belonged to the heretical Northern School (a term coined by Shenhui). Shenhui's attack was not selfless, as he considered himself Huineng's favourite student and demanded to be recognised as the seventh patriarch.

Like the semi-legendary first patriarch of Chan, Putidamo (Bodhidharma), who meditated for nine years in a cave, this hermit lives and meditates in a cave on Wutai Shan, in which are interred the bones of victims of the war of liberation against the Japanese occupiers of 1937–45. The custom of meditating on death and the cycle of rebirth in the presence of bones has been followed in northwestern China since the fifth century. One of the first depictions is in a mural in Cave 212 of Kizil, Xinjiang [Yaldiz et al.: Magische Götterwelten, pp. 202f].

Chan monks pray during the second morning devotion in the Great Hall of Xiantong Si. To the left in the front row stand two Tibetan pilgrim nuns and to the right two laywomen with shaved heads, who wear nun's clothing and live in the monastery for a month. They are called jushi, which means lay Buddhist. A statue of Shijiafo (Buddha Shakyamuni) can be seen in the background.

The official history of Chan, written only in the eleventh century, 'describes' the dramatic handover of office from Hongren to Huineng. When Hongren decided to designate his spiritual successor, both Shenxiu and Huineng lived in his monastery. Shenxiu was the respected master of all monks; Huineng chopped wood in the rice mill. Hongren announced to all the monks:

You strive every day to build up a field of merit and future happiness, rather than to overcome the ocean of rebirths. Your merit is worthless, since it will only cause further rebirths. You have lost your way at the gate of happiness and good deeds. Turn around, seek within your mind the truth of your true nature and write a verse about it for me. He who best understands the nature of the mind, I will name my successor.

The monks feared the test and asked Shenxiu to write the verse. At night he wrote on the wall of the meditation chamber:

The body is the bodhi tree
The mind is like a bright mirror's stand.
At all times we must strive to polish
it and must not let dust collect.

Hongren publicly praised Shenxiu. In private conversation he noted, however, that Shenxiu had only reached the door of wisdom but had not stepped through it, and encouraged him to go within himself again. On the next day another verse was there on the wall to read:

Bodhi originally has no tree.
The bright mirror also has no stand.
Fundamentally there is not a single thing.
Where could dust arise?

This second verse, which revealed a deeper, non-dualistic understanding of the

Buddha-nature, came, however, from the kitchen servant Huineng. Hongren at once recognised Huineng's wisdom and that night secretly gave him the insignia of the patriarchate. Out of fear that the monks who respected Shenxiu would rebel, he ordered Huineng to return to the south for the time being and assume the role of new patriarch only after a few years. After Hongren's death, however, Shenxui took advantage of the vacuum to declare himself the sixth patriarch.[36]

Shenhui's first criticism is unjustified, since Shenxui taught, according to the intended audience, both the slow and gradual and the sudden, complete enlightenment. In this case Shenxui could rely on the *Lankavatra Sutra*, recognised by Chan, which described both types of enlightenment. Huineng himself suggested that he considered this distinction unimportant: 'It is not the instructions leading to enlightenment that are sudden or gradual but rather the mind of the people is either sharp or dull.'[37] Shenhui's attack resembled a coup attempt that succeeded after 20 years. Lower and mid-level function-aries and scholars gathered around Shenhui, seeking to oust Shenxui's followers, who were influential at court. In 753, however, Shenhui was sent into exile, accused of inciting public unrest. But after the outbreak of the rebellion of An Lushan, Emperor Suzong called him back to Luoyang so that he could sell monastic certifi-cations on a grand scale, in order to replenish the empty state treasury – a violation Suzong's predecessor Xuanzong had forbidden. As a reward, Shenhui was recognised as the seventh patriarch, and Huineng posthumously as the sixth, while Shenxui, who was the uncontested sixth patriarch during his lifetime, was likewise posthumously condemned as a usurper from the heretical Northern School. This school vanished, however, at the end of the eighth century.

Huineng[38] and his successors emphasised that the concentration of the mind that led to enlightenment was not limited to the classical, time-limited sitting meditation, but rather at all times every concentrated and consciously pursued activity could itself become a liberating meditation. In this sense meditation became active, dynamic wisdom. Chan is not a specific type of meditation but rather a fundamental style of conscious living. Huineng warned, 'Sitting for a long time only weakens the body without strengthening the mind'. Huineng's student Nanyue Huairang (677–744) said the following to his pupil Mazu, who persisted in sitting meditation:

In learning sitting-in-meditation, do you aspire to learn the sitting Ch'an, or do you aspire to imitate the sitting Buddha? If the former, Ch'an does not consist in sitting or in lying down. If the latter, the Buddha has no fixed postures. The Dharma goes on forever, and never abides in anything. You must not therefore be attached to nor abandon, any particular phase of it. To sit yourself into Buddha is to kill the Buddha. To be attached to the sitting posture is to fail to comprehend the essential principle.[39]

Huineng warned against two additional dangers: complacency and social neglect. He underlined that a sudden and perfect enlightenment was not a free pass for vanity. 'When your mind is free from all clinging and thinks of neither good nor evil, you should be careful not to sink into a sheer emptiness and stick to a deathlike stillness; you should rather try to broaden your learning and increase your knowledge.'[40] Guishan Lingyou (771–853), the founder of the Chan school of Guiyang, echoed this sentiment: 'If a man is truly enlightened … yet there still remains the inertia of habit, formed since the beginning of time, which cannot be totally eliminated at a stroke. He must be taught to cut off completely the stream

of his habitual ideas and views caused by the still operative karmas.'[41] To guard against potential neglect on the part of Chan monks and nuns who overvalued themselves, Baizung Huaihai (720–814) developed strict monastic rules, which were the first to require daily productive work, under the motto, 'One day without work, one day without eating'.[42] The experience of enlightenment thus did not absolve people of the need to strive constantly for a 'right life'. To live according to the principles of Chan is a lifelong effort.

The second danger concerns neglect of the sufferings of others. Concentration on the present does not mean the adherent of Chan no longer wants to judge or change anything; that he is as unfeeling as a stone. Since everything is connected to everything, the suffering of others is also relevant to the adherent of Chan. Huineng noted, 'When you ignore the innumerable other phenomena and always interrupt your thoughts, you remain trapped in the cycle of rebirths'.[43] Huineng's models are the selfless bodhisattvas, who help out of compassion, without being trapped by emotions.

Like Jingtu, Chan survived Emperor Wuzong's persecutions relatively well, since it was not particularly dependent on texts or on imperial support. In the subsequent decades it reorganised itself into the Five Houses of Chan: Guiyang, Linji, Caodong, Yunmen and Fayan, of which only the traditions of Linji and Caodong still exist today. While Guiyang emphasised the need for an ongoing process of clarification even after enlightenment, Caodong developed a complex dialectical metaphysics in five levels and attached special significance to the sitting meditation. The tradition of Yunmen (864–949) was iconoclastic like its founder, who rejected all sutras and the popular traditions about Shakyamuni's life as restrictive. Fayan (885–958), by contrast, taught his students to recognise the Buddha-nature in the outside world as well. One of the most prominent followers of Fayan was

the above-mentioned Yungming, who not only
tried to bring together Chan and Jingtu but also
wrote a 100-volume compendium of Chan. It was
of course a paradox that Chan, which originally
questioned the authority of the sutras and spoke
of a 'direct communication of knowledge from
mind to mind', produced such a lengthy work.

The most influential of all the founders of
Chan schools, however, was Linji Yixuan (died
866). He further developed the method of
mental and physical 'shock therapy' introduced
by Mazu (709–88). In order to get students to
break out of their familiar patterns of thought and
experience, both masters confronted them with
a gong'an (Japanese: koan) and did not hesitate
to yell at them, pinch them, or hit them with
a stick of bamboo. A gong'an is a paradoxical
question, proposition, vignette, or dialogue,
which cannot be understood rationally but can
convey to the intuition a deep insight beyond
logical contradictions and dualistic thought. A
master presents a student with gong'an in order
first to question his mental and emotional
consciousness and to force him to open himself
to a higher level of consciousness. The intense
psychic pressure on the concentrating student
to give the master an answer eases the leap to
a higher level of consciousness. Secondly, a
master tests the consciousness level reached
by the student with a gong'an question, which
the student must answer. A famous gong'an
states, 'When you students encounter a Buddha,
kill the Buddha!'[44] On the level of logic, such a
saying seems to be the blasphemous raving of a
lunatic. Linji wants to show, however, that one
should not seek the Buddha in a temple, a sutra,
a Pure Land, or a vision, but rather in his own
Buddha-nature. One should realise the buddha,
not meet him as an other. Linji's shocking words
are to be understood as a warning that even
Buddhism itself can become a shackle. In this
sense Vimalakirti said about meditation, 'To

become infatuated with the taste of meditation
is the bondage of the bodhisattva'.[45] A gong'an is
never a puzzle that can be solved with intellectual
ingenuity. One who tries this remains hopelessly
stuck to the gong'an, like a fly on flypaper.

Even if the concept of the gong'an and
individual ideas of Chan show similarities to the
Daoism of a Zhuangzi and his aphorisms, there
are fundamental differences with regard to the
living out of one's life. Chan and especially Mazu
and Linji did not teach 'non-action' that peacefully
followed the course of natural development.
Instead they required from themselves and their
students that they set themselves against the

**Monk at the birthday celebration
for Wenshu Pusa, Tayuan Si.**

A larger-than-life statue of a bodhisattva, made in the year 782. Buddha Hall, Nanchan Si.

grain of the karma-dependent course of things. Expressed visually, the Daoist allows himself to be carried by the current, while the adherent of Chan swims upstream to the source in the mountains, in order there to break through the wall of rock – the customary patterns of thought and emotion. In this moment there opens up a non-dualistic experience of reality; the oppositions of subject and object, external nature and Buddha-nature, are nullified. While many Daoists take literally the term 'non-action' and abandon themselves to negligence and even sensual licence, adherents of Chan are neither daydreamers nor romantic nature-worshipers but rather highly disciplined, intrinsically hard-working people.

Insofar as Chan encompasses all aspects of life, it is not surprising that it influenced the arts, such as painting, especially brush painting, calligraphy, and poetry – three art forms that perfectly complemented one another in China. The landscape painter Guo Zhi of the eleventh century wrote, 'A poem, calligraphy, is a painting without images, and a painting is a poem in images'.[46] Such a painting is unacademic, unadorned, and almost minimalist. The objects are reduced to a minimum of complexity and often shrunken in size in relation to 'empty' space. The reduction of the world of objects to a single element, through which an individual flower evokes a forest; a pebble, a mountain; and a few lines, a seascape, adopts the key idea of Tiantai, shared by Chan, that every speck of dust contains the whole universe. Like a gong'an, a painting reduced to minimum forms can convey to spiritually open-minded viewers a second message, deeper than that of the immediately visible motif. The ascetic and self-restrained spirit of Chan is expressed most purely in brush painting, since here, as in calligraphy, every quickly made stroke must be perfect. Since the paper absorbs the ink, corrections are impossible. Every brushstroke arises from a

pure mind, which enables the practised hand to execute each spontaneous movement correctly. The Japanese D.T. Suzuki (1870–1966) compared life to a brush painting in the Chan sense:

Life delineates itself on the canvas called time; and time never repeats, once gone forever gone; and so is an act, once done, it is never undone. Life is a sumiye *(ink) painting, which must be executed once and for all time and without hesitation, without intellection, and no corrections are permissible or possible. Life is not like an oil painting, which can be rubbed out and done over time and again until the artist is satisfied. With the sumiye painting any brush-strokes painted over a second time results in a smudge; the life has left it. All corrections show when the ink dries. So is life.*[47]

In Japan Chan began to expand in the eighth century. As in China the two leading subgroups are Soto (Caodong) and Rinzai (Linji). In contrast with China, where Chan suffered a decline under the Song Dynasty (960–1279) and became intermingled with Jingtu, in Japan it experienced a strong upsurge during this time. The Japanese Dogen (1200–53), who lived in China from 1223 to 1237, founded the Japanese school of Soto. The sitting meditation of zazen plays a prominent role in Soto, while the use of koans is insignificant. During the period of the Meiji Restoration (1868–1912), Soto monks, like all monks, were secularised. This measure, applied for anti-Buddhist reasons, did not produce the desired effect. Instead of weakening Japanese Buddhism, as intended, the lay monks, often married and socially connected, began to take

Incense sticks up to 160 cm long in front of the Wenshu Temple, Zunsheng Si. The fragrance of burning incense is said to purify the spirit and encourage meditation.

**Incense holder in front of the
Prayer Hall of Wanghai Si.**

political action and bring to life influential,
militant-nationalist movements. Buddhism,
especially the two schools of Zen, increased
in influence over both domestic and foreign
politics. The school of Rinzai, for its part,
was introduced into Japan by Eisai Zenji
(1141–1215). The early death of his successor
Myozen Ryonen in 1225 plunged the school into

a severe crisis, but it soon blossomed again
in the second half of the thirteenth century
thanks to other masters. In Rinzai much less
importance is placed on the sitting meditation
than on the practice of koans, called Kanna
Zen, and on physical labour. Today Rinzai has
about 39 monasteries and 5,700 temples, and
Soto, 31 monasteries and 15,000 temples.

The nine sacred mountains of China and Mount Wutai Shan

Then the Great Enlightening Being Mind King said to the enlightening beings, 'In the northeast there is a place called Clear, Cool Mountain, where enlightening beings have lived since ancient times; now there is an enlightening being there name Manjushri, with a following of ten thousand enlightening beings, always expounding the Teaching'.

—Avatamsaka Sutra[1]

The Chan master Shi Yanwen practises Wushu martial arts on a boulder in front of the monastery of Shaolin Si on the sacred mountain Song Shan. The monastery, founded in 495, serves as the cradle of Chan Buddhism.

In China it is not buildings or graves that are pilgrimage sites, but rather mountains. In the traditional Chinese worldview the sacred is present in nature, especially in mountains. Mountains represent the fifth visible direction, which points upwards to heaven. On mountain peaks the ontological mist that conceals the spiritual spheres from our earth is thinner; for the awakened mind it is even permeable. The mountains, often shrouded in clouds, whose peaks break through those clouds and display themselves uncovered to the sun's rays, are cloaked in an aura of the numinous. Depending on the perspective, mountains bring heaven down to earth or raise the earth up to heaven. Mountains form the hinge between heaven and earth; here the worlds of the profane and the sacred merge into each another. A pilgrimage to a sacred mountain amounts to a journey to the centre of the universe.

Deities, bodhisattvas and Daoist immortals live in many mountains, so people seek to be close to them. Emperors pay respect to such mountains by making sacrifices on their peaks as if on enormous altars. Hermits seek refuge in caves in their flanks, monks and nuns build their monasteries, and laypeople hope to gain from a pilgrimage a spiritual awakening, forgiveness for their sins, or the fulfilment of wishes. Mountain landscapes, with their unspoiled and intact nature, symbolically approximate the object of many believers' desires: the paradisiacal Pure Land. Spiritually oriented pilgrims, however, try to advance during their pilgrimages from the formulaic and the forms to the formless.

Pilgrimages, of course, require freedom of movement of laypeople, monks, and nuns, which in medieval China was by no means always guaranteed. Ordinary people like farmers or serfs could leave their plot of earth for a pilgrimage only on very particular conditions, and the freedom of monks and nuns to travel was constrained by the central government. For Confucianism pilgrimages were a nuisance, since they called into question the established social order. Pilgrims in fact become nomads for a limited time. They separate themselves from their families and their social settings and form new communities with

their fellow pilgrims. Pilgrims live in worlds of meaning different from those of everyday life; their normal daily routine and their social obligations become insignificant and disappear from their mental horizon. Other dimensions come to the foreground instead. At the pilgrimage site pilgrims undergo extraordinary and meaningful experiences or at least believe that they are doing so. Then they must prepare for the return journey. In the end they must be able to return to their social environment, and that environment must be willing to accept them again. Such a reintegration does not happen smoothly; the seams remain. Every successful pilgrimage should represent a dying off of what is past and has become irrelevant, as well as herald the appearance of new horizons. The meaning of a pilgrimage lies in the will to rebirth.

Wutai Shan was promoted by many emperors, above all those of the Qing Dynasty (1644–1911). For political reasons the latter supported Tibetan esoteric Buddhism in Tibet and Mongolia and on Wutai Shan. By having themselves celebrated as the incarnation of Manjushri, protecting Buddhism, they hoped to be recognised by the Tibetans and Mongolians as patrons of religion. Esoteric Buddhism and the cult of Manjushri were means of cohesion that bound Tibetans and Mongolians to the emperor of China, although they rejected a connection with the Chinese state.[2]

Mountains enjoy high regard in other cultures as well. For instance, among the ancient Greeks Mount Olympus was considered the home of the gods, Moses received the Ten Commandments from Yahweh on Mount Sinai, and transfiguration of Jesus took place on a high mountain. While these mountains were made sacred by a deity or a person, in Japan Mount Miwa and Mount Fuji are sacred in themselves. Mount Kailash in western Tibet is likewise venerated by four religious groups; for Buddhists and Hindus it stands as the axis

One of the three rebuilt, gilded bronze pagodas at Xiantong Si.

of the world and the geographic counterpart to Sumeru, the centre of the world (Chinese: Xumi Shan). In Buddhist cosmology the mythical mountain of Meru, which came forth from the primeval ocean, is surrounded by seven rings of mountains and seven rings of oceans. The entire complex is encircled by the indomitable 'Iron Mountain', and between it and the seven rings of mountains, the four greater and eight lesser continents – of which the centre, larger of the southern group of three is said to represent our world, Jampudvida – lie in the salt ocean.

In China dozens of mountains are venerated, of which five Daoist and four Buddhist mountains come to the fore.[3] They are the nine sacred mountains of China. The five mountains of Daoism are:

- Tai Shan in the east, which is 1,545 m above sea level. The two most famous pre-Christian emperors, Qin Shihuangdi in 219 BCE and Han Wudi in 110 BCE, made pilgrimages and offered sacrifices here.
- In the south the Heng Shan Nan mountain chain, stretching 150 km and rising 1,290 m high.
- In the west the 1,997 m-high Hua Shan, which in parts is dangerous to climb.
- In the north the 2,017 m Heng Shan Bei, with its famous Hanging Monastery, Xuankong Si. This monastery, which stands 60 km north of Wutai Shan and dates from the period of the Northern Wei (386–534), clings to the face of a cliff. The small shrines and pavilions hang like balconies on the rock wall and are supported by thin wooden pillars. The renowned poet Jia Dao (779–843) said, 'It looks so dangerous that not even spirits can escape from it'. The monastery contains a unique shrine, in which Confucius, Laozi and Buddha Shakyamuni sit peacefully together and embody the coexistence of the traditional religions of China.

- The fifth Daoist mountain stands in the centre of the other four; it is the 1,494 m Song Shan, which is also claimed by Buddhists. Here stands the famous Shaolin Monastery, whose unarmed style of martial arts is traced back to the first patriarch of Zen, Bodhidharma, who meditated here for nine years.

The four sacred mountains of Buddhism are each consecrated to one of the four most important bodhisattvas:

These pilgrims carry Buddha statues purchased in Taihuai on their multi-day pilgrimages on Wutai Shan. In each temple they visit, they place their statues on the altar and ask the corresponding deity to bless their statues and give them strength. First inner courtyard of Xiantong Si Monastery.

- In the north, in Shanxi Province, is Wutai Shan, standing 3,058 m above sea level, the residence of Wenshu Pusa (Manjushri), the bodhisattva of wisdom and patron of writing.
- In the east, in Zhejiang Province, the female bodhisattva of compassion, Guanyin Pusa (Avalokiteshvara), is venerated on the small island mountain of Putuo Shan, which stands only 284 m high. Tradition says that in 847 an Indian monk had a vision of the then-Daoist mountain and noticed similarities to the island of Potalaka in the Indian Ocean. Potalaka

was the home of the bodhisattva Avalokiteshvara; this island gave its name not only to the 12.5 km² Putuo Shan, but also in Tibet to the palace of the Dalai Lama in the capital Lhasa because the Dalai Lamas are incarnations of Avalokiteshvara. Another tradition reports that in 916 the Japanese monk Huie suffered a shipwreck on the island of Putuo while taking a statue of Guanyin from Wutai Shan to Japan.[4] He prayed to Guanyin, who protected him and allowed him to reach land safely. But when he wanted to depart again, the statue refused to

Tibetan pilgrim monks in front of the pailou, the entrance gate to Longquan Si.

The 'hanging monastery' of Xuankong Si, founded in the sixth century, on Heng Shan Bei mountain.

The 71 m-tall Milefo (Buddha Maitreya) of Leshan, Sichuan, is the tallest stone buddha in the world and was carved out of the rock between 713 and 803. He looks toward the sacred mountain of Emei Shan, about 70 km away.

travel, whereupon Huie built for her on the coast the temple Bukenqu, whose name means 'reluctant to leave'. On the small island there stand about 20 monasteries and temples.

- The 1,341 m-high Jiuhua Shan is the third holy mountain of Buddhism and rises in the south, in the province of Anhui. The name of the mountain means 'nine flower mountain' and refers to its nine highest peaks. Jiuhua is dedicated to Dizang Pusa (Ksitigarbha), the bodhisattva who rescues people condemned to the ten different hells, or at least relieves their torments. This bodhisattva, very popular in Central Asia, China, and Japan, lives in the underworld but serves as patron of travellers. Because of Dizang's role in the underworld, Jiuhua Shan is visited in particular by pilgrims who want to beg for his saving help for recently deceased relatives. Dizang is also the patron of meditation. On the flanks of the mountain there arose in the third century a few of the first Daoist monasteries, but during the Tang period (618–907) Buddhist institutions claimed them. As in other parts of southern China, almost all buildings were destroyed during the Taiping Rebellion (1850–64) and the Cultural Revolution; today only about 80 have been reconstructed.

- The fourth sacred mountain of Buddhism stands in the west, in Sichuan Province; it is the 3,099 m high Emei Shan, consecrated to Puxian Pusa (Samantabhadra). This bodhisattva is seldom portrayed alone outside Emei Shan but rather flanks, together with Wenshu Pusa, either Buddha Shakyamuni or Tathagata Vairocana. In Chinese art he often rides a white elephant with six tusks. Emei Shan, frequently shrouded in clouds and fog, is known today primarily for its spectacular scenery. Its ascent is like a march through various climatic zones, as it begins in an evergreen tropical forest and travels over narrow stone steps into a wild mountain landscape with craggy rock overhangs. Like Jiuhua Shan, Emei Shan attracted Daoist monks beginning in the third century, and these were soon joined by Buddhist monks. During the time of the Ming Dynasty (1368–1644) at the latest, these four mountains represented four stations of a single pilgrimage journey.

On Emei Shan, of more than 150 Buddhist and Daoist monasteries that once stood, about 20 remain. Although this mountain and Tai Shan belong to the UNESCO World Cultural Heritage List, both sacred mountains are developing in the direction of Disneyland, where the priorities of mass tourism overwhelm the needs of the monasteries. In contrast, the monasteries and natural beauty on Wutai Shan are much better protected.

The sacred landscape of Wutai Shan and its numerical symbolism

Various sources provide information about the history, traditions and legends of Wutai Shan. These include state chronicles, monastic archives, commentaries on sutras, numerous autobiographies of monks and pilgrims, as well as four particular chronicles. These are the *Ancient Record of Clear and Cold* of the monk Huixiang, who in 667 made a pilgrimage to Wutai Shan, which was usually called Qingliang at that time. The latter name means 'clear, fresh, and cool'. It applies to Wutai Shan in two regards. In the concrete sense, it refers to the fresh, humid, and cool climate, caused by the elevated position of Wutai Shan relative to the northern Chinese plain. The sacred region lies at an altitude of 1,200 to 3,000 m above sea level and between 113° 15' and 113° 45' eastern longitude and 38° 45' and 39° 45' northern latitude.

Here neither winter temperatures of -40 °C nor a brief snowfall in June are rarities. The other three annals are the *Expanded Record of Clear and Cold* of the monk Yanyi, who lived on Wutai Shan, dating from 1060; the *Further Record of Clear and Cold* of the statesman and scholar Zhang Shangying (1043–1122), who made pilgrimages to Wutai Shan in 1088, 1089 and 1090; and the *Record of Clear Cold Mountain* of Zhencheng (1546–1617) from the year 1596.[5] To these is added the long report from Emperor Jiaqing's (ruled 1796–1820) inspection tour of Wutai Shan.

Wutai Shan, like the other sacred mountains of Buddhism, was first sacred to Daoists. It was then called Zifu Shan, meaning 'Purple Palace Mount', and served as the residence of the immortals.[6] Chinese documents linked the mountain directly with Manjushri early on. While the bodhisattva had been known in China since the second half of the second century CE, the *Manjushri Parinirvana Sutra*, translated into Chinese by the layman Nie Daozhen in the third century, was the first text to suggest that the bodhisattva lived in the snowy mountains. Although by snowy mountains the Indian text certainly meant the Himalayas, Chinese translators began to shift Manjushri's residence to China, more specifically to Wutai Shan. The interpretation resulted from the strong need to impart more prestige to Chinese Buddhism and to establish it as an authentically Chinese and seminal religion. This goal was reached by Chinese translators and commentators using the important *Avamtasaka Sutra*, whose Indian original is lost, to demonstrate that the coming revelation of Buddhist teaching, adapted to the new times, would take place on Wutai Shan or had in fact already begun there. Thus the source of Buddhism's message was no longer India but China.

Both the above-cited first translation of the sutra by Buddhabhadra (Chinese: Fotuo Batuluo) from 418 to 420 and the 695–99

version of Siksananda (652–710), who came from Khotan, provide indications that Bodhisattva Manjushri would someday preach Buddhist doctrine on the 'clear and cold' mountain Qingliang Shan. Qingliang Shan is, however, another name for Wutai Shan. The South Indian monk Bodhiruci (672–727) expressed himself still more clearly when he translated a scripture on the mantra of Manjushri in 710. In this work Shakyamuni prophesies,

After my final passing, in this Rose Apple Continent in the northeast sector, there is a country named Mahā Cīna. In its centre there is a mountain named Five Peaks. The youth Mañjuśrī shall roam about and dwell there, preaching the Dharma in its centre for the sake of all sentient beings. And at that time countless nāgas [snakelike lower deities], devas, yaksas, rāksasas [demons], kinnaras [heavenly musicians, half-bird and half-human], mahorāgas [chimeras in the shape of serpents or dragons], and other creatures human and non-human shall encircle him, making worship offerings and revering him.[7]

These texts elevate Wutai Shan to both the geographical origin and centre of Chinese Buddhism and the source of additional Buddhist revelations, which also encouraged streams of pilgrims from India, Central Asia, Japan, Korea and Southeast Asia. Later pilgrims came from Tibet and Mongolia, so that Wutai Shan connected China to many foreign people and cultures. At the same time Manjushri developed in the eyes of Chinese Buddhists into the patron of China.

Another close connection between the Five Terrace Mountain Wutai Shan and Chinese Buddhism resulted from the symbolism of the number five, which plays an important role in both Chinese thought and Buddhism. In ancient China they knew of five elements, corresponding to the five colours and the five directions:

View from Wanghai Si Monastery,
which stands on the peak of the
eastern terrace Dongtai, toward
the Wutai Shan mountain range,
which extends to the northeast.

An allegory of Wutai Shan as the residence of the gods, refuge of hermits and destination of pilgrims. Longquan Si.

- wood/east/blue
- fire/south/red
- metal/west/white
- water/north/black
- earth/centre/yellow.

Then there were five planets, five types of grain, five poisons, five classics, etc. There were believed to be 1,148 such groups of five.[8] In Mahayana Buddhism the five Tathagata Buddhas assume a prominent role, with the five directions and five colours assigned to them. These are:

- in the centre, the chief white Tathagata Vairocana
- in the east, the blue Tathagata Akshobhya
- in the south, the yellow Tathagata Ratnasambhava
- in the west, the red Tathagata Amitabha
- in the north, the green Tathagata Amoghasiddhi.[9]

The five terraces of Wutai Shan have a geographic parallel with one of the most important Buddhist pilgrimage sites of India, namely with the five peaks of Rajagriha, which lies in the southwest of the state of Bihar, east of Bodhgaya. Rajagriha, whose ruins can still be seen today, was one of Shakyamuni's favourite places and was presumably the first royal city of Buddhism. Five mountains encircle the city like a fortress with towers; the first Buddhist council after Buddha's nirvana is said to have taken place on the western peak, Vaibhagiri. The Rajagriha Mountains must not be mistaken for the five sacred mountains of Indian Buddhism, however, since only two of these are found in the Rajagriha range.[10] Additionally, Wutai Shan took on a cosmic dimension, insofar as its five peaks corresponded to the four continents and the central world-mountain Sumeru of Buddhist cosmology.

For the Tibetan monk Phagpa (1235–80), whom Kublai Khan appointed imperial preceptor and vice-king of Tibet and who made a pilgrimage to Wutai Shan in 1257, the five peaks corresponded to the five transcendental Tathagata Buddhas: the central peak symbolised Mahavairocana; the eastern, Aksobhya; the southern, Ratnasambhava; the western, Amitabha; and the northern, Amoghasiddhi.[11] By means of this correlation, the Five Terrace Mountain became a gigantic mandala, which made the five transcendental Buddhas symbolically visible. One who meditates moves spiritually from the edges to the central primordial Buddha Vairocana; the pilgrim does the same in physical steps from the outer terraces to the central peak with the centrally located monasteries. The five peaks were also connected with the five manifestations of Wenshu Pusa, elevating Wenshu to a status similar to that of the five Tathagata. The young Rutong Wenshu lived on the central peak Zhongtai; the keen-witted Conming Wenshu on the eastern peak Dongtai; the wise Zhihui Wenshu on the southern peak Nantai; Shihou Wenshu, who preaches while sitting on a lion, on the western peak Xitai; and the immaculate Wugou Wenshu on the northern peak Beitei.[12]

Finally, Wutai Shan has another point of reference with Manjushri, whose earlier Indian name was Panacasikha and means 'fivefold helmet' or 'fivefold ornament'. For this reason Manjushri, whose mantra consists of five syllables, is sometimes portrayed with a crown with five acute triangles, so that the five peaks of Wutai Shan may be interpreted as his crown.[13] Finally, Manjushri is believed to reveal himself to pilgrims sitting on a five-coloured cloud.

Wenshushili Pusa

Wenshushili Pusa (abbreviated to Wenshu; Sanskrit: Manjushri) is one of the most important figures in Mahayana Buddhism and has been known in China since Lokaksema's translation of the *Sukhavativyuha Sutra* between 168 and 186 CE. The youthful-appearing male Manjushri is the bodhisattva of wisdom and patron of scholarship, especially writing. In his right hand he often holds a double-edged sword of flames that destroys illusions, drives out the demons of ignorance, and helps the light of knowledge to break through. In his left hand he holds the *Prajnaparamita Sutra* in the form of a scroll or a book, which sometimes rests on an open lotus blossom. In many sutras he appears as a favoured conversation partner of the Buddha.

On Wutai Shan Wenshu Pusa is almost always portrayed in a semi-closed sitting position on an open lotus, which a powerful blue lion carries on its back. The lion's feet do not touch the ground but rather stand on lotus blossoms set upon clouds. The bodhisattva riding the lion and proclaiming doctrine is called Shihou Wenshu (Sanskrit: Simhanada Manjughosa). In the temples of Wutai Shan he typically flanks Buddha Shakyamuni, along with Puxian, but can sometimes also assume the dominant central position. The lion, which in India is a symbol of the powerful proclamation of Buddha's teaching, represents Wenshu's mission to lead people to spiritual awakening, to enlightenment, by destroying ignorance. The roar of the lion awakens lethargic, spiritually calcified human beings to a new life in the footsteps of the Buddha. In his angry form the bodhisattva appears as Yanmandejia (Sanskrit: Yamantaka), who has the face of a buffalo with the third eye and overcomes death or, in a deeper sense, puts an end to the cycle of rebirths.[14]

As to the 'biography' of Manjushri, there are several traditions. For Indian Hinayana sources he was the king of the Gandharva, a group of semi-divine musicians. For Mahayana traditions Manjushri was originally either a student of Shakyamuni, who developed spiritually into a bodhisattva, or the teacher of past buddhas as well as of the future Buddha Maitreya. In his Chinese context Wenshu is said to have come to China personally, whereupon he chose Wutai Shan as his residence. Particularly charming are the traditions in the Wutai Shan chronicles. In the *Ancient Record* of 667 and the *Expanded Record* of 1060 it says that at his first enlightenment Wenshu was the 'Tathagata King of all Dragons'. These records allude to the *Surangama Samadhi Sutra*, which Kumarajima translated. In this sutra Buddha Shakyamuni explains that from time immemorial, before his existence as a bodhisattva, Manjushri was a Buddha Tathagata of all dragons, who had rescued countless living beings.[15]

Even after Manjushri developed into a bodhisattva, he maintained his affinity for dragons; these correspond to the 'nagas' in Indian sutras. They are semi-divine water creatures that adopt the form of serpents or, in the Chinese understanding, dragons, and protect the Buddhas and the scriptures. The *Avatamsaka Sutra* says that at one of his teaching sessions innumerable dragons emerged from the ocean and, impelled by the wish to achieve Buddhahood themselves, 10,000 of them incarnated themselves as human or celestial beings and set out irreversibly on the path to enlightenment.[16] As we will see in the next chapter on the monasteries of Wutai Shan, several places, temples, and rituals are connected with dragons. For its part, the *Lotus Sutra* reports that Manjushri taught the sutra so successfully in the palace of the dragon king Sagara (Chinese: Suoqieluo) on the seafloor that the king's eight-year-old daughter Lungnü suddenly realised Buddhahood.[17]

Wenshu Pusa rides through the
mountain landscape of Wutai
Shan in the centre of the image; to
the right stands the patron deity
Jingang (Vajrapani). Mural from
Bezeklik, nineth/tenth century.
Hermitage Museum, St Petersburg.

The five manifestations of Wenshu Pusa (Manjushri) live on the five terraces of Wutai Shan, from left to right: Zhihui Wenshu lives on the southern terrace, Shihou Wenshu on the western terrace, Rutong Wenshu on the central terrace, Wugou Wenshu on the northern terrace, and Conming Wenshu on the eastern terrace. Lingfeng Si.

The history of Wutai Shan

If we apply scholarly standards, it is clear that the tradition that the two Indian missionaries Kasyapamatanga (Chinese: Jiaye Moteng) and Dharmaratna (Zhufalan) founded the first monastery on Wutai Shan, Xiantong, in 68 CE, is a legend. On the other hand, archaeological discoveries of stone axes, potsherds with cord ornaments, and pieces from three-footed cooking vessels demonstrate that Wutai Shan was settled as early as the Neolithic period, *c.* 5000–2000 BCE.[18] Concerning the establishment of the first three monasteries, various sources from the Tang Dynasty appear reliable, and these attribute the founding of these monasteries to Emperor Xiaowendi (ruled 471–99) of the Northern Wei Dynasty. At that time Xiaowendi supported the construction of the cave temples of Yungang, located 120 km north of Wutai Shan. These three earliest monasteries are Foguang Si in the western outer region; Qingliang Si on the border between the inner and outer regions; and Xiantong Si at the centre of Wutai Shan.[19] During the era of the Tang (618–907) Wutai Shan flourished with over 300 temples and monasteries.

One can assume that the cult of Wenshu Pusa took shape together with the construction of the first three monasteries at the end of the fifth century. The transformation of Wenshu Pusa from a mountain god who played an important role in the spread of Buddhism into the national patron deity of China and the powerful Tang Dynasty was the work of Amoghavajra (Chinese: Bukong Jingang). After Amoghavajra rebuilt from the ground up the Jinge Temple, dedicated to Manjushri and located on Wutai Shan, in 766–67, he succeeded five years later in persuading Emperor Daizong (ruled 762–79) to elevate Wenshu Pusa to patron of China. In 772 the emperor ordered that a shrine dedicated to Wenshu Pusa be put up in every Buddhist monastery in China, where monks would daily recite sutras for the welfare of the

Snow-covered pagodas on the central terrace.

Four of the five gilded bronze stupas in front of the Bronze Hall, Xiantong Si. The five stupas symbolize the five manifestations of Wenshu Pusa and the five terraces of Wutai Shan.

Wenshu Pusa (Bodhisattva Manjushri) is the patron deity of Wutai Shan. His mount, a blue lion with a green mane, shakes lazy people with his roars, so they set out on the path of enlightenment. Wenshu Pusa Hall, Shuxiang Si.

empire. From then on the veneration of Wenshu Pusa was a national cult.[20] The anti-Buddhist persecutions of Emperor Wuzong in the years 843–45 brought this to an abrupt end.

The significance of Wutai Shan may also be seen in the fact that the mountain is portrayed in a few Mogao caves of Dunhuang. The Buddhist cave temples of Mogao are found in the western part of Gansu Province, on the ancient Silk Road, not far from the imperial border at the time of the Sui and Tang dynasties. On an east-facing, 1.6 km-long cliff, about 1,000 cave temples were carved out between 344 or 366 CE and the Yuan Dynasty (1271–1368); of these, 735 remain, and 492 contain murals. For instance, there are murals portraying Wutai Shan in caves number 159 and 361 from the 830s, the period of the Tibetan occupation. The most famous is the large rendition in the 'Manjushri cave', number 61, from c. 980–95. Over an area of 54 m² all five terraces are portrayed with many monasteries, hermitages, pilgrims and allegorical scenes of

everyday life; it is a half-realistic, half-mythological pilgrimage map. The upper third shows heaven with three bodhisattvas and Lokapala Vaishravana, protector of the north and god of wealth, with 1,250 enlightened beings from the great following of Manjushri, which included a total of 10,000 bodhisattvas, and 300 arhats, as well as, somewhat lower in the picture, the 500 dragons he defeated. In the middle section one can recognise the five terraces and many monasteries, some of which are identifiable, while the lower third presents pilgrims travelling on foot, by horse, or by camel, as well as a delegation from the Korean kingdom of Goryeo.[21] We see just how important and internationally known the pilgrimage to Wutai Shan was at the time of the Tang in the fact that in 824 the Buddhist king of Tibet, Ralpachen (ruled 815–38), asked the Chinese emperor Muzong (ruled 820–24) for a map of Wutai Shan. The oldest extant map of Wutai Shan dates from even earlier; it is inscribed on a stone stele from the years 756–63,

Wenshu Pusa is said to have taught and meditated on this granite boulder. The Great Hall of Qingliang Si is in the background.

which stands by the entrance gate of Kaiyuan Monastery, near Zhengding in Hebei Province.[22]

Under the Yuan Dynasty (1271–1368) and the Qing Dynasty (1644–1911) Wutai Shan enjoyed imperial support. The twentieth century, however, brought to Wutai Shan, as to all of China, a turbulent and painful history. Although the warlord of Shanxi, Marshal Yan Xishan (1883–1960), who had been born in the Wutai region, was able to protect his province from the chaos of war until 1937, in the autumn of 1937 the Japanese invaders attacked and occupied the industrial cities of Datong and Taiyuan, despite fierce resistance. Until then there were still about 100 monasteries on Wutai Shan. At the same time, strong bands of the Red Army infiltrated the rural regions and used the Wutai Shan range, which stretched dozens of kilometres from east to west, as the headquarters of the Eighth Route Army. After the Japanese retreat and capitulation in 1945 there followed the civil war, in which Shanxi became the site of bloody battles. The civil war ended with the victory of the Communists, led by Mao Zedong, in October 1949, after which access to Wutai Shan remained forbidden to foreigners until 1985. After several unsettled periods of forced collectivisation, compulsory industrialisation, and subsequent famines came the Cultural Revolution, which was like a civil war. While the monasteries in the town of Taihuai more or less survived this turmoil, those outside this area largely fell victim to it. In 2007 a total of 64 monasteries and shrines were either restored, rebuilt from the ground up, or in the process of reconstruction; in each of these there lived at least one nun or monk year-round.

A dragon rising up from the water holds a jewel, a symbol of Buddhist teaching. Tian Wang Hall, Jixiang Si.

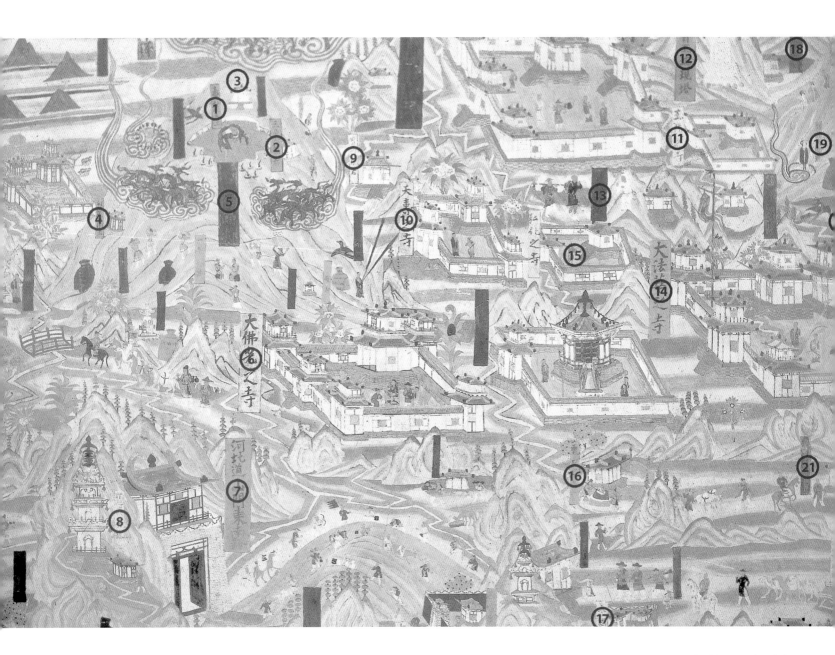

(Previous double-spread and above).
Section of the mural of Wutai Shan
on the western wall of Cave 61
of Mogao, Dunhuang, *c.* 980–95.
The section shows the region
between the northern and eastern
terraces as well as the Hebei gate.

Red number on picture	Name/identification
1	Du long tang: 'Hall of the poisonous dragon'
2	San quan lanruo: 'Meditation place beside the three fountains'
3	Northern Terrace
4	Bai long lanruo: 'Meditation place of/by the white dragon'
5	?? zhi ding: 'Peak of ...'
6	Da fo guang zhi si: 'Temple of the great Buddha light'
7	He bei dao shan meng dong nan lu: 'river—north—path—mountain—door—east—south—path,' that is, mountain pass to the Hebei gate
8	Shijia zhen shen ta: 'Pagoda of the true body of Shakyamuni'
9	?? lanruo: 'Meditation place of ...'
10	Tian shou zhi si: 'Temple of long life'
11	Yuhua zhi si: 'Jade blossom temple'
12	Ayu wang rui xian ta: 'Temple of the presence of King Ashoka, which brings good fortune'
13	The Indian monk and translator from Kashmir, Buddhapala (Chin. Fotuoboli), meets Wenshu Pusa, in the form of an elderly man, in 676
14	Da fa hua zhi si: 'Temple of the great dharma'
15	Honghua zhi si: 'Temple where Buddhist doctrine is taught'
16	Ling kou zhi ??: '... of the opening of the soul'
17	Yong chang ??: '... of the eternal magnificence'
18	Eastern Terrace
19	? de tian nü ?: '... of the heavenly daughter of ... virtue'
20	?? zhi ta: 'Four (?) pagoda'
21	Hunan song gong shi: 'The ambassador from [the region] south of the seas brings a gift.' (Hunan cannot refer to the present-day province of the same name, south of the Yangtze, since it was first separated from the province of Huguang under the Qing Dynasty (1644–1911).)

VII

Pilgrimage routes to the Five Terrace Mountain: The outer regions

There are records that provide accounts of the numinous vestiges of this mountain. When I was young, I investigated these texts, and each time I came to the relevant passages, I closed the scrolls with a drawn-out sigh. Thus, I did not consider ten thousand li as distant, and I yielded to an inner command, settling in refuge within the sacred precincts. I have been led to spend ten years here. The splendid display of its resonant qualities fills the eyes and ears, and even so there are still more such excellent matters. Dragon palaces each in turn open up at night to a thousand moons. ... Sometimes there are ten thousand sages arrayed in space. Sometimes five [-coloured] clouds are set firmly among the hill-gaps. ... One merely hears the name of the Great Sage [Mañjuśrī] and is no longer beset by the cares of human existence.

—Chengguan, Fourth Patriarch of Huayan (737–838)[1]

Chengguan was one of the most outstanding scholars of his era, who lived out the famous Chinese saying, 'to read ten thousand books and cover ten thousand Li'. He made pilgrimages to all the important monasteries and pilgrimage shrines of China in order to study there and experience the sacred aura of the pilgrimage sites. Although as fourth patriarch of the Huayan School he was particularly committed to this tradition, he also closely studied the scriptures of the schools of Tiantai, Sanlun, Zhenyan, Lü, and, above all, Chan. He produced new translations of many sutras and wrote over 30 books. Thanks to his writings on Chan, several elements of Huayan philosophy entered Chan.

Chengguan was closely linked with Wutai Shan, where he lived for ten years. He wrote a few of his most important commentaries

in the Xiantong Monastery, which was called at the time Da Huayan Si, meaning 'Great Huayan Monastery'. The monastery was then one of the most important centres of the school of the same name. After his death he was granted the honorary title 'National Master Qingliang'. Moreover, Chengguan was soon considered an incarnation of the bodhisattva Wenshu Pusa, who lived on Wutai Shan. In the following pages, I would like to present Wutai Shan, following in Chengguan's footsteps.

The outer region of the Wutai Shan pilgrimage route encompasses those places Wutai Shan pilgrims have traditionally visited. A few still enjoy high regard today; others have been closed for decades and are difficult to reach. I visited all the monasteries, temples, cave shrines and pagodas of the inner region, while

Bodhisattva from the twelfth century in the main hall of Hongfu Si.

in the outer region I limited myself to sites of art historical value or historical significance.

Three routes up Wutai Shan are available to pilgrims. The one from the southwest leads from the provincial capital of Taiyuan, by both the remaining Tang Dynasty temples, Foguang Si and Nanchan Si, to Wutai Shan. The northern route connects the onetime capital of the Northern Wei Dynasty, Datong, with the Five Terrace Mountain. A few dozen kilometres west of this route one can admire a few well-preserved, seldom visited monasteries dating from the eleventh to the sixteenth centuries. The third route, from the southeast, is less appealing, as it passes by hardly any historically important or artistically notable monasteries.

The southwestern outer region

My explorations began in the southwestern outer region, following the traces of many important missionaries from India and Central Asia, who approached Wutai Shan on the southwestern route.

Nanchan Si 南禅寺

About 180 km northeast of the provincial capital Taiyuan, I reached the sleepy village of Lijiazhuang on a bumpy dirt road in thick fog. Nothing suggested that the oldest shrine of the Tang Dynasty (618–907), made entirely of wood and wonderfully preserved, was found here. The entrance gate and the inner courtyard also made a modest impression. The jewel of Nanchan is the rear Hall of the Great Buddha, which follows the classical temple structure. At the end of a courtyard there rises a stone terrace on which the wooden temple stands; 12 strong wooden pillars support the hipped roof. No nails were used in the construction

of the hall. Some scholars speculate that the temple of Nanchan served as a model for the significantly larger Todaiji Temple, built in 752, in Nara, Japan.[2]

The name Nanchan means 'southern (nan) meditation (chan)'. This accords with the tradition that the shrine was founded by the Chan monk Zhuxi at the start of the eighth century. The name Nan indicates that Zhuxi belonged to the southern school of Chan. The earliest histori-cally certain date is provided by an inscription on a wooden beam; it states that the Huayan monk Faxian had the monastery rebuilt and the terracotta statues repainted or remounted in 782.[3] Thanks to its remote location, the Buddha Hall survived Emperor Wuzong's depredations of 843–45, which gives them a particular cultural historical value; the great terracotta statues are the oldest in the entire Wutai Shan region. The monastery, which later belonged to Jingtu, suffered some damage during the violent turmoil of the Five Dynasties (907–79) and was restored under the Song, Jin, Ming and Qing. Buddhist monks lived here until the Communist seizure of power in 1949, when

From left to right: Wenshu Pusa (Manjushri), Shancai (Sudhana, partially hidden behind the tablet), a bodhisattva, Anan (Ananda), Shijiafo (Shakyamuni), from 782. Buddha Hall, Nanchan Si.

The Buddha Hall of Nanchan Si, built toward the end of the eighth century, is the oldest wooden building in China, from the Tang Dynasty (618–907).

it was turned into a museum. It was declared an important cultural treasure on the provincial level in 1961 and on the national level in 2000. Like a few other temples of Shanxi, the Buddha Hall was spared the destruction of the Cultural Revolution. That a wooden structure has survived for more than 1,200 years in northern China, which has been plagued by countless wars, disorder, and bloody revolutions, seems to be a genuine miracle.

In the interior of the 11.6 x 10 m hall, I was surprised by 14 painted terracotta statues, ranging from about 80 cm to 3 m high, standing on a 70 cm-tall, 8.4 x 6.3 m platform. Until recently, 17 figures stood here, but in 1999 three small statues were forcibly removed from their pedestals and stolen. As at the monasteries of Foguang Si and Hongfu Si, which are also found in the southwestern outer region of Wutai Shan, a metal grate that reaches to the ceiling now guards the irreplaceable statues. In the centre sits an enthroned Buddha Shakyamuni in a teaching pose before an enormous mandorla made of wood; to his left stands his student Mahakashyapa (Chinese: Dajiaye) and to his right, Ananda (Chinese: Anan). The ascetically inclined Mahakashyapa presided over the First Buddhist Council, which took place soon after Buddha Shakyamuni's death in 483 BCE. The School of Chan claims him as its first mythic patriarch, since he was the only one to understand Shakyamuni's allegorical lotus teaching. Ananda, on the other hand, was the favourite pupil of Shakyamuni. Because he had accompanied the master for years on his missionary journeys, he was witness to all his preaching. Thus at the First Council he was the only one in a position to recite from memory all the preaching of the master, which provided the basis for the first

sutra collection, *Sutrapitaka*. Since Mahakashyapa and Ananda were the most important students of Shakyamuni, they are often portrayed beside him in temples and scrolls. To the left of Shakyamuni and Mahakashyapa, Bodhisattva Puxian rides his white elephant, with an open lotus blossom serving as a saddle, while to the right of Ananda, Shihou Wenshu Pusa, likewise sitting on a lotus blossom, rides his blue-green lion.

On each side of the dais stands a powerful heavenly guardian, Tian Wang, about 3 m tall, wearing typical armour from the period of the Tang Dynasty. On each side, between the heavenly guardian and the mounted bodhisattva, stands an almost 3 m-tall female bodhisattva figure, dressed in the traditional clothing of noblewomen at court at the time of the Tang. In the background, between the students of Shakyamuni and the mounted bodhisattvas, are two more female bodhisattvas. To the right, in front of Puxian Pusa, stand two small figures, each about 80 cm tall, the smaller of which looks up reverently at the bodhisattva. It represents Sudhana (Chinese: Shancai), to whose quest for perfect understanding of Buddhist teaching the final and longest chapter of the *Avatamsaka Sutra* is devoted.

In this way the legendary boy Sudhana, whose name means 'wealthy' (in wisdom), appealed for the first time to Wenshu Pusa, who offered him a first instruction. After that Sudhana sought out 52 teachers and sages, corresponding to 52 steps on the path of the bodhisattvas. Finally he met, as the 53rd teacher, Puxian Pusa, who helped him reach enlightenment. For this reason the Buddha Hall of Nanchan has a second, identical statue of Sudhana before Wenshu Pusa. Shancai represents the perfect pilgrim, whose pilgrimage signifies continuous spiritual development. Since 1999 the figure of the functionary Fulin to the left and two bodhisattva figures kneeling in a lotus blossom in the centre-front have been missing; they were victims of a brazen break-in. As I have unfortunately seen in China since about 1995, cases of art theft have grown more common in remote temples. Security provisions there are often minimal, and the guards in charge corrupt. Professionally organised art theft has become a plague and threatens the integrity of the cultural heritage.

Hongfu Si 洪福寺

About 35 km southwest of Nanchan in the county of Dingxian there is a poor farming village, whose city walls made of clay are well preserved. On the way there I crossed paths with carts pulled by oxen, mules and donkeys. Here stands another small jewel of ancient Chinese temple architecture. It is the former monastery of Hongfu. The earlier monastery structure stands on a small hill with the citadel and is bordered on the southeastern side by the village wall. As is the case in China with many small, remote cultural treasures, the

entrance gate was closed and probably had not been opened for some time. After a long search through the village and with the help of a RMB 100 bill (about US$14) my translator Yin was able to persuade the custodian of the key to open the temple. Then Yin magically produced from his bag a small flask of cheap liquor, which kept the sullen guard happy for an hour.

A stone stele standing before the main hall reports that in 1132 Hongfu-Si, whose name means 'temple of flowing good fortune', developed close relations with the monasteries Tayuan and Zhenrong (Pusading) in Taihuai, the main city of Wutai Shan. This inscription also shows that Hongfu has existed since the time of the Jin Dynasty (1115–1234). The treasure of Hongfu is the wonderfully preserved painted figures in the Great Hall from the twelfth century. In the centre are seated statues of, from left to right, the Buddhas Amitabha, Shakyamuni and Akshobhya, whose backs are surrounded by a large and richly decorated mandorla made of

From left to right: a heavenly guardian, a bodhisattva, and Amituofo (Buddha Amitabha) from the twelfth century in the main hall of Hongfu Si.

wood. As at Nanchan, the Buddha is flanked by his students Mahakashyapa and Ananda, and on each side stand both a magnificently painted, noble-looking female bodhisattva figure and a fierce heavenly guardian. On each side wall there are niches for the 500 luohans, but except for a handful, all the statuettes have disappeared. While the eastern wing of the temple serves as a storage shed, in the western wing there is a seated buddha statue surrounded twice by nine luohans, from the period of the Qing (1644–1911).

Foguang Si 佛光寺

My next destination on the way to Wutai Shan was the museum of the former monastery Foguang Si, which lies less than 50 km southwest of Taihuai, not far from the city of Ducun. If one believes the *Ancient Record of Clear and Cold*, the founding of the monastery goes back to Emperor Xiaowendi (ruled 471–99). The emperor is said to have

seen here a vision of the Buddha, whose body was surrounded by a luminous aureole. For this reason he had built the temple of Foguang, whose name means 'brilliance of the Buddha'. The same chronicle goes on to report that Foguang Si was linked with the southern terrace of Wutai Shan as early as the second quarter of the seventh century and that the famous master of Chan, Jietuo, left his hermitage on Wutai Shan at that time in order to take up residence at Foguang Si, where he died between 642 and 656. He had Foguang Si greatly expanded in 633 in order to accommodate the many pilgrims who wanted to hear his teachings on their pilgrimage to Wutai Shan.[4]

Since under the Tang Foguang Si was an important way station on the pilgrimage to Wutai Shan, it did not have the good fortune of the monastery of Nanchan, located not far away. It fell victim to the wave of destruction of Buddhist monasteries in 845. An octagonal stone stele from 857 tells of the reconstruction of Foguang Si. It states that the wealthy female

Shijiafo (Shakyamuni) surrounded by his students Anan (Ananda) and Dajiaye (Mahakashyapa, hidden), as well as bodhisattvas; created 855–57. Great Buddha Hall, Foguang Si.

大佛光之寺

河北

The monastery of Foguang Si, probably founded at the end of the fifth century. This depiction dates from the end of the tenth century. Northern section of the western wall of Cave 61, Mogao.

Buddhist Ning Gongyu financed the rebuilding, which was led by the monk Yuancheng. The restoration took place between 855 and 857.[5] Because Foguang Si was declared to be a cultural treasure of the first order in 1961, it escaped the destruction of the Cultural Revolution.

The monastery nestles against a flank of the mountain, where small forests border fields. The great Buddha Hall is found on the eastern side of the third and final inner courtyard on the highest point of the entire complex; it stands on the site where a shrine dedicated to Maitreya stood before 845. After the last and very steep flight of steps, I was greeted by the stele of Ning Gongyu, and I stood before the hall, built exclusively of wood, which is 35 m long and 18 m wide. Thirty-six wooden pillars

support the slightly flared roof. Upon entering the darkened hall I was overwhelmed by the sight of 35 colourfully painted terracotta statues, which stand on a 75 cm-high brick platform. Soon my eyes were able to discern the splendid figures from the ninth century, which underwent an unfortunately rather drastic repainting between 1922 and 1925 and again in 1975. This collection is unique in China and is unparalleled from an art-historic point of view. It can be compared only to the Buddhist cave shrines of Mogao near Dunhuang. Here, as there, the artistic magnificence and perfection is so overwhelming that the spirit becomes drunk on them.

As in the case of Nanchan, the great Buddha Hall of Fuguang has similarities to temple structures of Japan, namely to the great Buddha Hall in the monastery of Toshodaiji in Nara.[6] Since the latter was built in 759; that is, a century before the reconstruction of Foguang Si, there are two possibilities. Either the earlier building at Foguang from the sixth century influenced the hall of Toshodaiji, or, conversely, the Japanese structure was the model for the reconstruction of Foguang Si.

The hall is ruled by the Buddhas of the Three Times. In the centre in the lotus position sits the present Buddha, Shakyamuni (Shijiafo), to his right would sit the past Buddha, Dipankara (Chinese: Randengfo), whose position here is taken by Amitabha, and to Shakyamuni's left sits the future Buddha, Maitreya (Milefo), with his legs tucked under in the European style. The portrayal of the Buddhas of the Three Times shows that since time immemorial there had been an incarnation of the eternal Buddhahood and that there would also be such in the future. The faces of the three buddhas are painted gold; they wear the typical imperial clothing of the Tang, with green, yellow, and blue dragons embroidered on red cloth. The portrayal of the most important buddhas in imperial dress accorded with the political strategy of caesaropapism[7] then current in China. Through such portrayals the emperors sought to appear as legitimate representatives of Buddha. Before each of the three buddhas two small bodhisattvas kneel in an open lotus blossom, presenting the Buddha with a bowl of fruit or other offering.

As in Nanchan and Hongfu, Shakyamuni's favourite students Mahakashyapa and Ananda flank the present Buddha, who holds his begging bowl in his left hand and with his right calls on the earth as witness to his enlightenment. Before each of the two students stands a bodhisattva with feminine facial features. Buddha Amitabha makes with his hands the dharma chakra mudra, which symbolises the setting in motion of the Wheel of Dharma; that is, teaching. He is surrounded by four female bodhisattvas. To the

right of Amitabha; that is, to the left from the viewer's perspective, Wenshu Pusa rides his blue lion, which is led by a red-clothed man. Beside the lion, Sudhana stands in a reverential pose, and on each side of the Buddha stands a female bodhisattva. On the outer edge stands a fierce-looking heavenly guardian, with sword held high.

Four female bodhisattvas also surround the future Buddha, Maitreya, who makes with his right hand the gesture of encouragement, abhyamudra. To the left of Maitreya; that is, to the right from the viewer's perspective, Puxian Pusa rides his white elephant, which has not just two but six tusks. Beside the elephant stands again the boy Sudhana and a second small figure, presumably representing the monk Yuancheng. Before Puxian sits General Weituo, who wears a heavy suit of armour. The armoured general Weituo, sometimes venerated as a bodhisattva, is identical to the Indian deity Skanda, whom Buddhism adopted as one of the eight guardians of the south. Eight generals are under the control of each of the four celestial kings, and Weituo is

The Great Buddha Hall of Foguang Si dating from the year 855.

their leader. It was the founder of the Lü School of discipline, Daoxuan, who spread the belief in Weituo, since the latter exemplified for him the deep sense of discipline.[8] Presumably on the left side there was once a corresponding figure of General Qielan, the protector of monks and nuns, which has disappeared. As beside Wenshu, there stand by Puxian two female bodhisattvas and on the outer right edge a combat-ready Tian Wang. Between this heavenly guardian and the next standing bodhisattva there sits on a pedestal a statue, about 80 cm tall, of a woman dressed in blue and red; she represents the donor Ning Gongyu, who financed the reconstruction of the monastery in the mid-ninth century.

With the exception of the statues of Sudhana, the benefactor Ning Gongyu, the monk Yuancheng, Weituo, the red-clothed man beside Wenshu Pusa, and the demon-like beings supporting the Buddha's throne, all the figures, including the lion and the elephant, stand, kneel or sit on open lotus blossoms. Contrary to the widely held belief that the lotus

motif, omnipresent in Buddhism and symbolising the development of the pure mind out of the earthly swamp of sin and desire, came out of India to China with Buddhism, this motif was widespread in the Middle Kingdom about 1,000 years before the introduction of Buddha's teaching. The bronze vessels from the Spring and Autumn Period (770–475 BCE), with lids in the form of open lotus blossoms, can be cited as examples and are found in the Historical Provincial Museum of Taiyuan, Shanxi.

The Manjushri Hall in Foguang Si, dating from the Liao Dynasty (907–1125) and located on the north side of the first inner courtyard, is also well worth seeing. In the centre stands a group of six large, painted terracotta statues from the time of the Jin (1115–1234). In the centre a majestic figure of Wenshu Pusa rides a lion; rider and mount are together about 7 m high. The bodhisattva of wisdom is surrounded by two other enlightened beings, Sudhana, Weituo, and two more helpers. The 500 arhats from the Ming Dynasty are painted on the

In the centre Puxian Pusa (Samantabhadra) rides his white elephant; to the far right stands a heavenly guardian, Tian Wang, and to his right sits, partially hidden, the sponsor of the monastery, Ning Gongyu. In the foreground stand small statues of Shancai and the monk Yuancheng, who oversaw the reconstruction of 855–57, in front of the seated, armoured General Weituo; from 855–57. Great Buddha Hall, Foguang Si.

The buddhas of the three times;
from left to right, Buddha Amitabha
(in place of the usual past buddha
Randengfo (Dipankara)), the present
buddha Shijiafo (Shakyamuni),
and the future buddha Milefo
(Maitreya), as well as bodhisattvas
and attendants; dating from 855–57.
Great Buddha Hall, Foguang Si.

walls. A visit to Foguang Si allows pilgrims who are interested in art history to get a sense of how marvellous monasteries of a similar age in the heart of Wutai Shan, such as Qingliang Si or Xiantong Si, may once have been.

Zunsheng Si 尊胜寺

On the way to Wutai Shan, 14 km southeast of Fuguang Si, pilgrims come upon the active monastery of Zunsheng, 'monastery of the honoured and victorious', in the village of Rucun. The monastery, oriented precisely to the north, consists of a series of seven inner courtyards with five shrines and a 39 m-high, nine-storey octagonal stupa. The monastery was founded during the time of the Tang and rebuilt under the Song. In the first shrine stand the four heavenly guardians Tian Wang, also called Hushize, who all wear armour. They are former Hindu guardian deities who protected the world-centre, the mountain of Sumeru.[9]

Following the entrance hall with the Four Tian Wang is the Great Hall with more recent paintings of the life of Buddha Shakyamuni and then the shrine of the Buddhas of the Three Times, who sit in tall lotus blossoms. On the chest of each buddha is carved the wheel of life, the swastika, and on the front edge of each lotus throne stands a red and gold lotus blossom made of paper with writing on the petals. Two bodhisattvas stand before the three buddhas, and six additional bodhisattvas sit on each side wall.

In the next shrine, of the 24 deities, a religious potpourri prevails. Beside the four Buddhist Tian Wang stand Daoist gods and other deified beings. It is an 'ecumenical' collection of Chinese deities, corresponding to the lived religion of the people. Two dozen huge sticks of incense burn in front of the fifth shrine, honouring the five manifestations of Wenshu Pusa on Wutai Shan. At the temple

entrance there stand 'monks' who do not belong to the monastery – I assumed they were clever merchants dressed as monks who had bribed the monastery – and who sell the incense sticks, which are as long as 160 cm, for RMB 99 and 180 (about US$14 and $26). One of these pseudo-monks led a group of pious pilgrims through the monastery and loudly and at length encouraged them to buy. He succeeded, as this group lit about US$380 worth of incense before the shrine of

The 39m tall pagoda with an octagonal plan crowns the monastery of Zunsheng Si.

Wenshu Pusa alone! That this commerce did not involve real monks I determined from the fact that as soon as the group of pilgrims left the monastery, they closed their stand, put civilian clothes on over their monks' habits, and rode off on bicycles.

Within the temple a remarkable brass statue of Bodhisattva Wenshu caught my eye, because it had two heads. The seated, four-armed Wenshu holds in his upper right hand a sword, and the second head of the bodhisattva looks at it. This newer statue is puzzling, since Wenshu Pusa is usually portrayed with one, three or four heads, but never with two. The monks in the monastery were also unable to give me a satisfactory explanation. In a small niche at the foot of the octagonal stupa is a rare bronze or brass statue of the single-headed and 18-armed bodhisattva Guanyin. In this masculine form he is called Astadasabhuja-Padmanarteshvara (Chinese: Shipapei Lienhuamiao Wuzuzai).

On the next floor are found 24 groups of three statues, in the same number of niches. Each triad, made of painted terracotta, consists of a deity from the pantheon of Buddhist folk religion, with two servants standing by its side. The red-clothed, life-size General Weituo leads these 72 figures. Another storey higher is found the larger-than-life-size brass statue of a seated, three-headed, and eight-armed deity. It holds in its hands a small buddha statue, an arrow, a bow, a small jewelled vase, a noose, and a double

vajra. The vajra, also called the thunderbolt, is shaped like a small sceptre and symbolises the masculine principle of the methods and indivisibility of enlightenment. The opposite of the vajra is the bell, which symbolises the feminine principle of wisdom. The two remaining hands make the gestures of encouragement (adhayamudra) and the granting of wishes (varadamudra). The centre and right faces are peaceful; the left is angry. The figure represents the female Ushnishavijaya (Chinese: Foding Zunsheng); her name means 'the one who is victorious through enlightenment'. She is the keeper of wisdom of the Buddhas and is thus characterised as the 'mother of all Buddhas'. While in temples of Han Chinese Buddhism statues of Foding are rarely encountered today, the goddess, who is associated with longevity, was very popular until the fourteenth century. For instance, in 762 Amoghavajra presented Emperor Daizong (ruled 762–79) on his birthday with a copy of his translation of the *Dharani* text, dedicated to Ushnishavijaya, as an amulet and advised him to wear it always.[10]

(Left) The rare statue of a two-headed Wenshu Pusa (Manjushri), Wenshu Temple, Zunsheng Si.

(Below) The three-headed and eight-armed deity Foding Zunsheng (Ushnishavijaya), chapel of the pagoda of Zunsheng Si.

The luohans

On both side walls of the Great Buddha Hall of Foguang Si there sit in closely packed rows small stereotypical figures of the 500 luohans from the Ming Dynasty; in fact there are only 296 of them. The luohans (Sanskrit: arhat) enjoy great esteem in Chinese Mahayana Buddhism. This is in contrast with Indian Mahayana, where they are barely valued as they are considered to be lower, even misguided stages in the process of enlightenment. In early Chinese Buddhism, however, they were interpreted first as a kind of Daoist immortal, and they increased greatly in significance under the influence of Chan beginning in the ninth century. Since Chan emphasises the human element in the path to enlightenment, and thus shies away from an all-embracing worship of deities, it saw in the luohans, who achieved enlightenment and the realisation of Buddhahood through their own power, admirable models. First in Chan and then in Jingtu the luohans personified complete liberation.

In Chinese temples a group of 16 favoured students of Buddha Shakyamuni are often portrayed as luohans or, since the famous painter-monk Guanxiu (832–912), a group expanded to 18 luohans.[11] The two additional luohans vary according to school and temple; Emperor Liang Wudi (ruled 502–49), Kumarajiva, the layman Dhamatala, and Budai Heshang are often encountered. Budai Heshang, whose name means 'hemp bag (Budai) monk (Heshang)', is portrayed as a laughing, big-bellied monk. A popular legend says that, as an envoy for Emperor Taizong, he invited the 16 arhats who lived in India to China, whereupon they flew together over the Himalayas to China. Beginning in the tenth century, Budai Heshang was venerated as an incarnation of the future Buddha Maitreya who brought good fortune; his statue most often greets pilgrims in the first temple hall of the Four Tian Wang.[12] In pictorial representations six small children sometimes surround Budai; they not only commemorate his kindness toward children but also symbolise the six senses, consisting of the five perceptive senses and reason. The third group contains 500 luohans; it refers to the First Buddhist Council, in which the 500 enlightened students of Shakyamuni participated. They are believed to have settled later in the Kun Lun Mountains, which separate northern Tibet from the Taklamakan Desert in northwestern China.

The 500 luohans (arhats) on the interior wall of the Hall of Wenshu Pusa, Foguang Si, Ming Dynasty (1368–1644).

The northwestern outer region

Approaching Wutai Shan from the northwest is likewise lovely and very worthwhile. The starting point for this pilgrimage route is Datong, the capital of the Northern Wei until 494.

Huayan Si, Datong 华严寺

Modern Datong is a centre of industry, mining and coal processing and is thus plagued by smog. Nevertheless, a visit to the city is always well worth the effort. The nearby cave temples of Yungang from the fifth–sixth century CE are a cultural treasure of the first rank, as are the two Huayan temples in the city centre from the period of the Liao (907–1125). Their name refers to their affiliation with the School of Huayan. In 1038 construction of the Three Buddha Hall, now known as the Lower Huayan Temple, was completed. In contrast to the Han Chinese temples, whose entrance gates are oriented towards the south, temples of the Liao, who originated in eastern Mongolia, are oriented eastward, towards the rising sun. In 1122 the Jurchen, also of eastern Mongolian origin, conquered the western capital of the Liao, Datong. Except for the Three Buddha Hall, the monastery complex was lost in a fire. The Great Hall of the Five Buddhas, which had been destroyed in the fire, was rebuilt in 1140; today it is called the Upper Huayan Temple. In the early fifteenth century the temple was renovated and the statues there today were added.

The Lower Huayan Temple, which had been built for the safekeeping of Buddhist scriptures, houses 29 Buddhist terracotta statues from 1038, a unique piece of cultural history. On the rear wall sit enthroned the Buddhas of the Three Times, Dipankara, Shakyamuni and Maitreya. The pilgrim recognises the bodhisattvas Dizang, Wenshu, Puxian, and Guanyin, in front of and looking at them. In between stand the bodhisattvas of the ten directions, as well as two more bodhisattvas, Shakyamuni's students Ananda and Mahakashyapa, four kneeling helpers, left and right two small bodhisattvas sitting on lotus blossoms, and on each edge two heavenly guardians. Despite a millimetre-thick layer of dust, the statues are wonderfully preserved and project a singular harmony.

The Great Hall of the Upper Huayan Temple, located 300 m away, is the largest ancient Buddhist hall in all of China. In it the five seated transcendent buddhas dominate, with the three in the middle made of wood and the two on the sides made of clay. Before them stand six bodhisattvas and on each short side are arrayed ten additional standing deities, who respectfully bend far forward with their whole bodies toward the buddhas, as though the laws of gravity did not apply to them. Also unique in this hall are the paintings, which fill the rear and side walls to an area of 875 m². Six buddhas are painted on the back wall and five buddhas on each side wall; in between and on the front wall episodes from Shakyamuni's life and scenes from everyday religious life are there to admire. Dragons, phoenixes, flowers, and Sanskrit inscriptions are painted on the 1,012 shingles of the wooden roof.

In Datong on the eve of my second pilgrimage to Wutai Shan I read in the *China Daily* newspaper a terrible story documenting the continuation of a tradition that was thought to have disappeared from China more than 2,000 years ago. It concerned the practice of providing the body of a woman as a grave gift at the burial of a man. In May 2007 in the neighbouring province of Hebei a 53-year-old man had been arrested on the charge of murdering six mentally ill women in order to sell their corpses as grave gifts. The dead men were bachelors. The brief story ended with

The 67 m-tall, octagonal, wooden pagoda of Mu Ta, built 1056.

the following words: 'The custom of marrying the dead is ancient and is still followed in a few remote villages in rural areas.' This raises the alarming question of whether, on the death of a husband, the wife might sometimes be killed in order to be laid in the grave with him.

Mu Ta 木塔

Eighty-five km south of Datong the pilgrimage route runs beside the district capital Ying Xian to the 67 m-high, five-storey wooden pagoda Mu Ta – 'wooden (mu) pagoda (ta)'. It belonged earlier to the Fogong Monastery, the 'Temple of Sacrifices to Buddha'; today it is a museum. It was built in 1056 during the Liao Dynasty (907–1125) exclusively of cedar, weighs 7,000 tons, and has an octagonal floorplan. The wood, which came from Shanxi, is said to be so hard that it would not be infested by woodworms or insects. The pagoda withstood two strong earthquakes, after which the ground floor was reinforced with a brick wall under the Ming and the Qing. The design of the pagoda shows that traditional Chinese pagodas were strongly influenced by the ancient towers of the Eastern Han Dynasty (25–220 CE).[13] Such multi-storeyed, pavilion-shaped towers did not serve much of a military purpose, with the exception of those towers standing near borders and used to send fire and smoke signals, but rather symbolised an entrance to heaven and to the world of the immortals. This is why miniature multi-storeyed towers were popular as grave goods.

The four upper levels have both an inner and an outer gallery; in the middle of the five storeys stand a total of 26 Buddhist statues. On the ground floor there is an 11 m-tall seated Buddha Shakyamuni; on the second level Buddha Shakyamuni and four bodhisattvas; on the third floor the Buddhas of the four directions; on the fourth floor Buddha Shakyamuni, Puxian Pusa

and Wenshu Pusa, Mahakashyapa and Ananda, as well as two smaller figures; and on the fifth floor Buddha Vairocana and the eight most important bodhisattvas. Between each level with statues there is a mezzanine level, so pilgrims experience the pagoda's interior as a nine-storey building. In 1974 160 artifacts from the Liao period, such as printed sutras, scrolls, coins, gemstones, and a purported 'tooth' of Shakyamuni – which in a photo on display looks more like the molar of a dog – were discovered in the body of Buddha Shakyamuni on the fourth floor.

Bairenyan Si 白仁岩寺

About 65 km southwest of the Mu Ta pagoda I arrived at the monastery of Bairenyan, important for the school of Jingtu. The name means 'rocks (yan) of the white (bai) people (ren)' and alludes to the nearby bizarre rock formation; the name is

The Janus-faced sculpture in the Guanyin Temple of Bairenyan Si symbolises the fact that whether one has a healthy or sickly baby is a matter of fate.

The monastery of Bairenyan, originally founded in the fourth century, is venerated as one of the founding monasteries of Jingtu and has been rebuilt since the year 2000.

also interpreted as 'merit'. The monastery stands at the top of a narrow chasm and is reached by means of an almost endless flight of stairs. The mountain landscape with its densely forested slopes and craggy rock formations corresponds perfectly to the classical Chinese ideas of an unspoiled landscape; it seems to lack only a waterfall or stream. For this reason Bairenyan was originally a refuge for Daoist hermits.

The Buddhist monastery was founded by the monk Huiyuan (334–416) during the period of the Eastern Jin (316–420). Huiyuan was a student of Dao'an (312–85) and founded the monastery of Bairenyan in 370, first as a simple hermitage. Since in 402, along with 123 students, he swore an oath before a statue of Buddha Amitabha to be reborn in his paradise Sukhavati, he stands as the spiritual founder of Jingtu. The ashes of Huiyuan, who died in southern China, were solemnly transferred to Bairenyan in 2005, which is why the site now serves as one of the oldest monasteries of Jingtu. Its significance for Jingtu is increased by the fact that Tanluan (476–542),

another spiritual father of Jingtu, from the Dai region, belonged to Bairenyan. The monastery was restored under the dynasties of the Tang and the Song, but completely destroyed by the Cultural Revolution. Reconstruction began again in 2000. Today five Jingtu monks live here.

When I visited the monastery in May 2007, the terracotta statues in most of the halls awaited painting or were only in the early stages of creation. The statues were made using the same methods as in the Tang period. First the 'skeleton' was built, consisting of a wooden model covered with straw. Artists shape the statues around this framework using clay that is mixed with cotton fibres, straw or paper pulp to increase its stability. The figures must then rest and dry for a few weeks. Cracks form. The largest are filled with fragments of dried clay, and uneven spots are smoothed over with slightly damp clay. Once dried, such places, as well as hairline cracks, are sanded down. The figures are left for a few weeks then the artists apply three different coats of colour from natural pigments. As I observed in other temples on Wutai Shan, the makers of such terracotta statues come from the eastern Tibetan province of Qinghai. In contrast to central China, in eastern Tibet the art of creating large Buddhist terracotta statues lives on and represents a respected profession.

Right beside the entrance to the monasteries a small shrine dedicated to Bodhisattva Guanyin stands on a small rock spur. Behind the main figure of Guanyin, who holds a child in her lap, stand a pair of parents and, to the right of Guanyin, a red-haired demon, which carries on its shoulders a small child, whose eyes are covered with a green ribbon. On the left side stands a remarkable Janus-faced statue: the right-side face, turned toward the visitor, is pleasant, and on this side the figure carries two happy children in a pouch. The left-side face, on the back, however, looks fierce and mean, and this side carries a single baby. The figure symbolises how fate and karma determine what kind of

child a woman will bear – healthy or sick, intelligent or stupid, etc. This small shrine was eagerly visited by pregnant women, even though the renovation of the monastery is not yet complete. They undertake the arduous climb in order in the small shrine to implore the female bodhisattva of compassion Guanyin for a good and healthy child.

Huiji Si 慧济寺

Before reaching the city of Dai Xian I made a short detour of 60 km to the southwest to Huiji Temple in the village of Lianjiagang. Huiji, meaning in effect 'granted (ji) wisdom (hui)', was presumably the name of a monk who had an important connection to the monastery, which was founded toward the end of the Tang Dynasty. No monks have lived here since the Communist seizure of power. Three shrines are all that remain of the complex. I was able to visit them only after

Four bodhisattvas and a scholar. The statues come from the Northern Song Dynasty (960–1127), the mural from the time of the Ming (1368–1644). Guanyin Hall, Huiji Si.

hours of searching for the custodian of the keys.
The largest shrine is the Wenshu Hall from the
time of the Northern Song (960–1127), where
nine statues are still preserved: Shihou Wenshu
Pusa on his lion, the young pilgrim Shancai
and the young dragon maiden led to enlightenment by Wenshu Pusa, two bodhisattvas,
two helpers and two huge heavenly guardians.
Unfortunately, the head of Wenshu Pusa is a
more recent, crude copy; since 2003 the temple
has been the victim of three break-ins, during
which Wenshu's head, as well as at least one
other head from the Guanyin Hall, was stolen.

In the Guanyin Hall across from the Wenshu
shrine, Bodhisattva Guanyin sits enthroned in the
centre; to her right and left sit eight bodhisattvas
on each side, their painted surface well preserved.
The statues also originate from the period of the
Northern Song (960–1127), but the murals on
both side walls date to the time of the early Ming
(1368–1644). The shrine, which is nominally
under the protection of the Cultural Relics Bureau,
serves today as a storage shed where cement sacks
are piled up. Between the two larger shrines
stands a smaller one honouring Puxian, who
is encircled by the 18 arhats. The statues date
from the period of the late Qing (1644–1911).

Ayuwang Ta 阿育王塔

East of Huiji stand the 40 m-high Ayuwang
Pagoda in the centre of the small city of Dai Xian,
a coal mining centre. The air reeks terribly of
burning coal, and the tap water leaves a distinct
aftertaste of sulphur. I found the Ayuwang
Pagoda in the large compound of the district
police, where military music blared from clanging
loudspeakers. The pagoda belonged earlier to the
Yuan Guo Temple, which has now disappeared
and whose name means 'completed (yuan) fruit
(guo)', i.e., 'nirvana'. The monastery was founded

The pagoda of Ayuwang Ta
in Dai Xian, dating from the
thirteenth or fourteenth century.

during the time of the Sui Dynasty (581–618).
The pagoda's name is the Chinese transliteration of Ashoka (ruled *c.* 268–32 BCE), who is
said to have given China the gift of 19 stupa-
shaped reliquary shrines. The wooden pagoda,
which had been built after 845, was destroyed
by a lightning strike in 1079, after which it was
rebuilt in 1102. In 1218 it was destroyed when
the attacking Mongols left the city in rubble and
ashes. Only afterwards was it built of brick.

Zhao Gao Si 赵呆寺

Twenty-three km south of Dai Xian the Buddhist
temple complex of Zhao Gao is found on the
northern slope of Mount Tiantai, the 'Mountain
of the Heavenly Terrace'. The spacious compound
was built during the time of the Northern Wei
(386–534) in honour of Minister Zhao Gao; the

temples spread along the mountain slope are also called Tiantai Si. This name recalls the fact that until the persecutions of 843–45 the monastery maintained close relations with the main monastery of the Tiantai School, called Guoqing, found in Zhejiang Province in the Tiantai Mountains, west of today's Shanghai. Today four monks and a nun of the Lingji Chan School live at the main temple of the Great Buddha Hall, which was rebuilt in 1993 after the destruction of the Cultural Revolution.

The path to the entrance gate of Chaoyuang Temple travels along a mountain stream through a sparse forest of deciduous and conifer trees. Along the path I saw several places where 10 to 30 cm-long wooden rods had been placed vertically between stones and rocks. Each rod symbolised a wish for recovery for oneself or another ill person. I had observed this practice before at the pilgrimage site of Kongpo Bönri in Tibet. There, however, the rods, which are

somewhat thicker and marked with notches, symbolise a ladder to heaven, so that errant souls of deceased people can find their way into the afterlife and stop frightening or troubling the living. The Chaoyuang Temple, lying next to the Great Buddha Hall, looks spectacular; its seven storeys abut a natural cave, which tapers at the top, so it looks like a slightly curved pagoda. Near the Chaoyuang Temple two small shrines hang from the rock wall; they can be reached only with the help of iron chains, the longest of which is 35 m long. A narrow, dark tunnel carved into the mountain leads to a third stone shrine hanging in the air. Earlier these rugged cliffs also offered shelter to Daoist hermits.

After another quarter-hour's walk through the woods I reached one of the temples, rare in China, honouring the medicine buddha Bhaisajyaguru (Chinese: Yaoshi Liuliguang Rulai, shortened to Yaoshifo). Yaoshifo heals not only bodily ailments but also spiritual ones, including the three basic

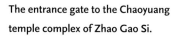

The entrance gate to the Chaoyuang temple complex of Zhao Gao Si.

The seven-storey Chaoyuang
cave temple, Zhao Gao Si.

evils of lust, hatred and delusion. The medicine buddha embodies one of the essential elements of Buddha Shakyamuni, who often characterised himself as a healer. Many sutras also interpret Shakyamuni as a physician, the faithful as sick people, the Dharma as medicine, and nirvana as cure. The medicine buddha holds in his left hand an eight-storey miniature stupa and makes with his right hand the gesture of instruction, vitarkamudra. At the sides of Yaoshifo stand two slender female bodhisattvas, who hold the sun- or moon-disc in their raised hands and are only rarely portrayed figuratively. To the right of Yaoshifo stands Suryaprabha (Chinese: Riguang Pusa), bodhisattva of sunlight, and to the left Chandraprabha (Yueguang Pusa), bodhisattva of moonlight.[14] Five additional Buddhist medicine deities sit on each side of Yaoshifo, and six Daoist medicine deities stand on each side wall.

Yan Shan Si 岩山寺

My next destination on the way to Wutai Shan was the former monastery of Yan Shan, whose name means 'stone (yan) mountain (shan)'. On the journey along very dusty dirt roads it became apparent how poor the north of Shanxi Province is. It is dominated by scraggly soil, where ploughing is done almost exclusively by horses, donkeys and cows. After 20 animals in harness came a motorised plough or an antiquated tractor. Even on the main road I saw clear signs of widespread poverty. Ragged figures gathered up the small pieces of coal that had fallen off the overloaded wagons onto the road. In fact, Shanxi is among the poorer provinces of China; here the immense economic difference between the wealthy coastal provinces in the east and the poor rural provinces of northern and central China reveals itself.

The medicine buddha Yaoshi Liuliguang Rulai (Bhaisajyaguru) between Riguang Pusa (Suryaprabha, right) and Yueguang Pusa (Chandraprabha, left), Yaoshifo Temple, Zhao Gao Si.

The monastery of Yan Shan Si,
founded in the twelfth century.

As so often in monasteries of the outer region, neither monks nor nuns live in Yan Shan, just a guard, who could only be persuaded to open the Wenshu Hall by means of a large tip. It was the only hall here not completely plundered of its contents during the Cultural Revolution. In the front, northern part of the 15 x 11 m hall from the time of the Jin (1115–1234) there once stood a south-facing statue of Shihou Wenshu Pusa. Unfortunately the figure of the bodhisattva has disappeared, and the lion is missing its head. Behind the lion a north-facing terracotta statue of Bodhisattva Guanyin sits in a relaxed pose on a wooden plank, which earlier was part of a throne. Viewed from the front there stand to the left two more figures, which look toward Wenshu, and to the right a powerful celestial king. Wooden stubs in the floor indicate that at least two more statues once stood on the small dais. Both side walls are decorated with murals from the year 1167, which show episodes from the life of Shakyamuni on the west side and, on the east, meritorious highlights from his earlier

incarnations, in which the future buddha sacrificed himself selflessly for the sake of living beings – whether humans or animals – in need of help. The murals convey valuable information about both the architecture of the time and everyday life, since they show in a realistic style palaces, temples, administrative buildings and ordinary houses, residential streets and bridges. People are also realistically portrayed in concrete situations. For instance, scenes include two carts crossing in a narrow street and causing a traffic jam, a ship anchored near a bridge being loaded with barrels, and wealthy merchants are having a garden party.

Gong Zhu Si 公主寺

Before I tackled the mountain pass to Wutai Shan, I toured the 'Princess Temple' Gong Zhu Si in Fanzhi County. It was built in honour of a princess of the Yuan Dynasty (1271–1368). In the small monastery lived a lone nun of the Huayan School,

Shijiafo (Buddha Shakyamuni) makes the gesture of dispensing favour, varadamudra, with his left hand, mural from 1167, Wenshu Hall, Yan Shan Si.

The Great Wall on the outer northern flank of Wutai Shan in the period 1906–9. Photo by Ernst Boerschmann.

Side temple at Gong Zhu Si.

from the time of the Ming. The Buddhas of the Three Times sit enthroned in the 20 x 12 m room; Ananda and Kashpaya stand in front of Shakyamuni. All the walls are decorated with well-preserved paintings from the Ming Dynasty; stylistically, however, they borrow heavily from the murals of the Northern Song (960–1127).

On returning to the main road in the afternoon, I encountered dozens of stopped trucks. Their destination was Beijing. The trucks had to wait at a barrier every day until 5:00 p.m. because in the centre of the capital city trucks are only allowed on the road at night, between 10:00 p.m. and 5:00 a.m. It is a pilgrimage not of pilgrims but of trucks.

About 30 km from the summit of the pass between the eastern and central peaks I caught sight of three watchtowers on the Great Wall, which was originally built under the Han Dynasty and restored from the ground up under the Ming, when the clay walls were replaced by stone. The wall shows that here we had reached the boundary between the settled, agricultural culture of China and the nomadic world of the Mongols. Even in the twentieth century these walls witnessed bitter conflict. First at the start of 1901, when Graf von Waldersee, who led the alliance of eight foreign powers in 1900 in order to break the siege of the Legation Quarter by the Boxers, ordered German and French troops to Shaanxi to pressure Empress Cixi, who had fled to Xian, to return to Beijing. After a few skirmishes with Chinese gangs, these foreign troops passed the inner Great Wall not far from Wutai Shan.[15] Almost 40 years later, in September 1937, at the nearby Pingxing Pass, the 115th Division of the Red Army won China's first victory in the war of resistance against the Japanese occupiers. Thus Wutai Shan is a pilgrimage destination not only for believing Buddhists but also for war veterans and nostalgic patriots.

rare in China today. She had, however, no key to the two locked, culturally significant temples. It was kept at the local Cultural Relics Bureau. There an employee roused himself to open the shrine only after lengthy negotiations and thanks to the prospect of generous baksheesh. Just past the entrance gate of the monastery grounds I entered the Hall of the Eighteen Luohans. In the 10 x 9 m inner chamber there sits enthroned in the front a Buddha Shakyamuni, whose hands make the 'gesture of the highest enlightenment', uttarabodhimudra. In the back sits Bodhisattva Guanyin and on the side walls the 18 luohans. Unfortunately, in 1996 all 20 heads of these valuable statues from the Ming Dynasty (1368–1644) were cut off and stolen. They have been replaced with copies. Behind this first shrine stands the much more significant Mahavira Hall, likewise

Mural in the Great Hall, Gong Zhu Si, in the style of the eleventh/twelfth century from the Ming Dynasty (1368–1644). In the upper left are the seven astral deities of the north star, which correspond to the constellation of the Little Dipper, with the north star marking the end of the shaft bending toward the north. In the upper right are Bodhisattva Baolan Hua and Milefo (Maitreya); in the lower left are deities of the 12 signs of the zodiac and in the lower right, Jingang Pusa (Vajrapani).

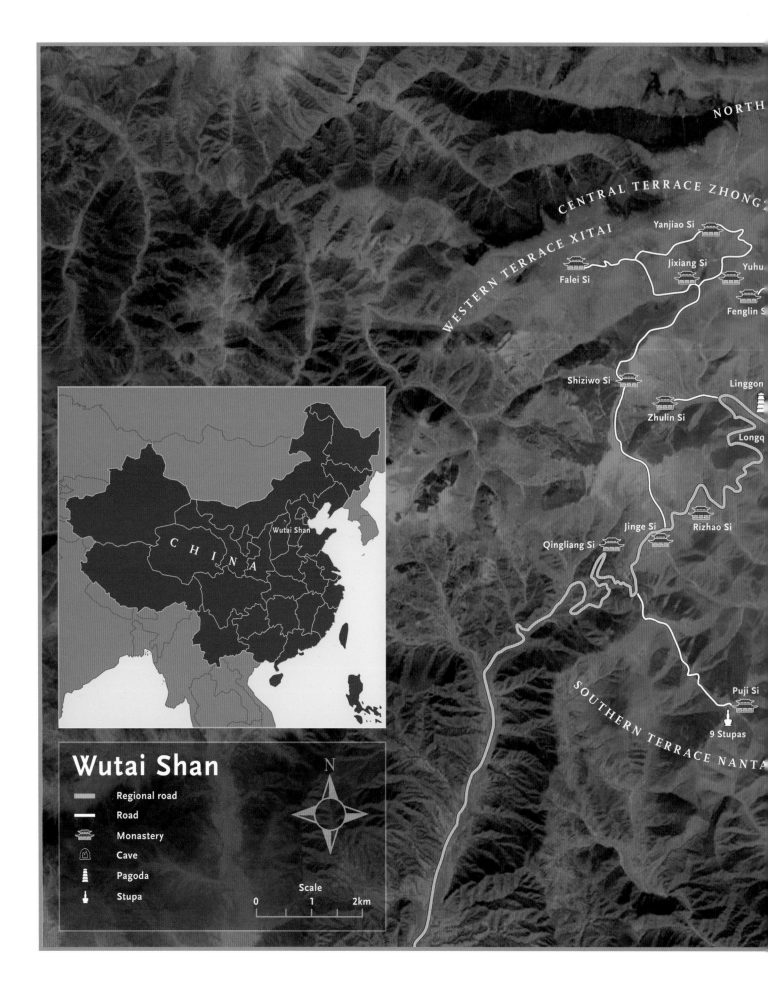

NORTH

CENTRAL TERRACE ZHONG

WESTERN TERRACE XITAI

Yanjiao Si

Jixiang Si

Yuhu

Falei Si

Fenglin S

Shiziwo Si

Linggon

Zhulin Si

Longq

Jinge Si

Rizhao Si

Qingliang Si

Puji Si

9 Stupas

SOUTHERN TERRACE NANTA

Wutai Shan

CHINA

Wutai Shan

N

Regional road

Road

Monastery

Cave

Pagoda

Stupa

Scale

0   1   2km

RACE BEITAI

Zhaoyuanwai Tang

ling An

Baohua Si

EASTERN TERRACE DONGTAI

Wanghai Si

Jingang Ku

Guangming Si

Bishan Si

Cifu Si   Jifu Si

Sanquan Si   Qifo Si

Shouning Si   Shangshi Tayuan Si

Si   Dailuoding Si

Shuxiang Si   **Taihuai**

gying Si   Wenshu Si   Wenshu Dong

g Si   Huayan Dong

Dong   Puhua Si

Guanyin Dong

Nanshan Si

Youguo Si

Wanyuan An

Zhenhai Si

Mingyue Chi

Jingang Bao Ta

Puan Si

Guandi Si

aiyun Si   Baitou An

nu Dong

Haihui An

Jingang An

Gufo Si

VIII

The five terraces and their monasteries

The Buddha says, 'Countless ages ago there was a buddha called the model and tathagata of all dragons. For four million four hundred thousand years he saved people and gods and then entered nirvana. After his complete enlightenment [he manifested himself] as Manjushri, prince of the Dharma'.

—Surangama Samadhi Sutra[1]

The northern terrace Beitai 北台 and Lingying Si 灵应寺

Coming from the northern outer region, I reached the northern pass that lies between the northern and eastern terraces. A few metres from the summit the street is crossed by a stone ceremonial gate called a 'pailou'. Traditional pailous consist of several arches, sometimes feature swooping roofs, and always bear inscriptions. Here the pailou marks the entrance to the sacred zone of the inner Wutai Shan, the home of Wenshu Pusa. The region, almost 300 km² in size, is strictly protected as a nature preserve. An entrance fee is payable, and only vehicles licensed specially for Wutai Shan may remain there for an extended time. In fact, although it hosts thousands of pilgrims from China, Taiwan, Korea and Japan, Wutai Shan gives a very clean and well-tended impression.

Only a few kilometres from the northern pailou rises the northern peak Beitai, which is dedicated to the Tathagata Buddha Amoghasiddhi. (Bei means 'north' and tai 'terrace'.) It is also

called Yedou Feng. The word 'feng' means 'peak'; 'ye' refers to the Daoist Black Emperor, a deity symbolising the north and winter, and 'dou' means 'plough'. The name is connected to the belief that the northern peak looks similar to the shaft in the constellation the Big Dipper.[2] At a height of 3,058 m above sea level, the flat peak is the highest mountain not only of Wutai Shan but in all of northern China. During the ascent through a sparse landscape of stone and short grass, fierce and cold wind from Mongolia whipped at my face. Wutai Shan, especially the northern peak, is notorious for sudden drops in temperature. It is not uncommon that even at the end of May or the beginning of September hailstorms hit during the day and snow falls at night. In the winter temperatures of -40 °C or even lower are not unusual. I had to fight my way forward with my body bent down and reached an isolated pailou which heralded the nearby peak.

On the peak the winds reached near hurricane strength; from all directions they assaulted the small Daoist shrine of Lungwang Si, which is dedicated to the five dragon kings. The name means 'dragon (lung) king (wang)'. It originally belonged to the monastery complex of Lingying, 'Temple of the Divine Answer', which was likewise founded during the time of the Sui and was rebuilt in 1986. Today 13 Daoist monks of the Zhengyi School live here. It seems that anyone who willingly subjects himself to such furies of the heavens as endless windstorms, hail and blizzards surely earns double or triple merit. Tibetan prayer flags hang on long cords between the shrine and a white stupa about 20 m away, facing the raging winds with strength and flexibility. Only with effort was I able to defy the wind and stand upright. The dark gray clouds had long since swallowed up the sun; now the mountain peaks disappeared one after another into the mouths of the dragons, who had demonstrated their unbroken power.

In the interior of the shrine the five dragon kings and their wives sit enthroned. The Daoist priest explained that the central, largest dragon king represented Manjushri, who had turned himself into a dragon! When I think of the Chinese Buddhist monastery Wanfo Ge in the city of Taihuai, which celebrates the conversion of the black dragon king Wuye by Manjushri, the close connection between the Buddhist bodhisattva and the Daoist dragon king stands out. As early as the year 840, the Japanese pilgrim monk Ennin reported that in the centre of the Dragon Hall of the northern terrace 'the central portion was occupied by an image of the Dragon King of Wutai, but on either side of him stood images of Manjushri'.[3]

This surprising placement of Daoist deities in a Buddhist monastic complex relates to the mythological treatment of a historical process. Wutai Shan was originally a stronghold of Daoists, after which Buddhist monks, beginning in the fourth and fifth centuries, gradually took it over, without completely ousting the Daoists. Thus the story was handed down that the bodhisattva

overpowered and converted the dragon king and the 500 poisonous dragons of Wutai Shan. The Daoist temple of Lungwang Si re-established the original relationships, since the ostensible usurper Wenshu Pusa turned back into a dragon king of the autochthonous mountain deities of Wutai Shan, as the Daoist priest explained. According to the *Surangama Samadhi Sutra,* Manjushri, before he took on the form of a bodhisattva, was said to be the 'highest Tathagata of the dragon race'.

In the lived faith of the people the two religions, Buddhism and Daoism, have intermixed. This can be seen not only in the proximity of Buddhist and Daoist deities in other monasteries but also in the fact that pilgrims bring as offerings and ritually burn before the great stupa of Tayuan Monastery sticks of incense wrapped in a box bearing images of both Wenshu and the dragon king. Wenshu and the dragon king are like two sides of the same coin or two faces of the same Janus head.

Not far from the shrine of the dragon king stands the hall of the five manifestations of Wenshu, which represent the five terraces of Wutai Shan. Here five bronze statues of

Entrance gate, called the 'pailou', in front of the shrine of Lungwang Si and the monastery of Lingying Si on the northern terrace Beitai.

The northern terrace is the most popular home for dragons on Wutai Shan. In the centre of the picture a dragon king swims in the dragon pool. Middle section of the western wall of Cave 61 in Mogao, late tenth century.

Dragons, clouds and bodhisattvas

The topics of clouds, mountains, dragons and Wenshu Pusa are connected in a special way. In an agrarian society rain has great significance. In ancient Daoist thought dragons are the lords of the rain-giving clouds and bodies of water. Thus it is understandable that in the spectacular and storm-prone landscape of Wutai Shan, worship of the dragon king played an important role in pre-Buddhist times. That this mythical animal is still present in China today is shown in the popular pastime of flying dragon kites. In China this is not only child's play but a recreational or competitive activity for adults – whether on Tiananmen Square in Beijing or in a championship competition.

The cloud and the dragon are age-old motifs, which are found on bronze vessels from the Shang Period (sixteenth–eleventh centuries BCE). The dragon has also been the most important emblem of the Chinese emperor since the unifier of the empire Qin Shihuangdi (ruled 221–10 BCE). According to the Daoist worldview, the emperor, as the son of heaven, was responsible for harmony between heaven and earth, between the deities who determined the weather and the human beings who depended on it. The dragon released the life-giving rain, and the emperor was responsible for making this happen. If the dragon refused the desired rain, the people had the right to call the emperor to account for it or, in the end, to rebel.

In light of the great significance of Wutai Shan as a stronghold of rain-giving dragons, it was imperative that Buddhism place a symbol there. Thus Wenshu Pusa subdued all the dragons of Wutai Shan. He did not destroy them, however, but rather left them in their roles under his supervision. Buddhism employed exactly the same strategy in Tibet in the eighth century when the Buddhist Tantrist and sorcerer Padmasambhava subordinated the deities of the autochthonous Bön religion and repurposed them as guardians of Buddhism. The connection between Manjushri and other Buddhist deities such as Amitabha, Puxian or Guanyin and clouds is seen in the fact that these transcendental beings often manifest themselves in cloud formations. By forcing out the dragons, they took over the function of weather gods. That clouds are the ideal guise for beings that remain the same despite changing form was already known by the famous Daoist philosopher Zhuangzi (c. 369–286 BCE). He replied to the king of Wei when the latter offered him a permanent position as his personal adviser, 'My form is like the clouds in the heavens or smoke on the ground; how can you ask to tie me down? My body is like a wave in the river or like falling snow, how can it stay any longer?'

Four of the five manifestations of Wenshu Pusa in the main hall of Lingying Si, northern terrace Beitai.

Together with the four other dragon kings, the chief dragon king resides in the Daoist temple of Lungwang Si on the northern terrace Beitai.

Wenshu with slightly different attributes sit enthroned. Thus the erstwhile rivals Wenshu and the dragon king are peacefully united within the same complex of Lingying. They share not only the highest mountain of the range but also the pilgrims, who pay homage and present offerings first to the Daoist dragon king and then to the Buddhist bodhisattva.

The eastern terrace Dongtai 东台, Wanghai Si 望海寺 and Nayuolan Dong 那罗延洞

The 'eastern' (Chinese: dong) terrace of Dongtai, rising 2,732 m above sea level and also called Wanghai Feng, is dedicated to Tathagata Aksobhya. My pilgrimage began in Taihuai at 4.00 a.m. under a sky filled with twinkling stars, since I wanted to experience sunrise on the peak

of the eastern terrace. After travelling over a rugged field path in the crisp cold I reached the foot of the temple complex of Wanghai, whose name means 'view of the sea [of clouds]'. I was lucky, as the atmosphere was quite clear and offered good visibility. Simultaneously with the end of the morning devotions of the monks a red-orange streak appeared on the horizon and the sky began to display all the shades between dark blue and violet. Shortly before sunrise there gathered a group of about ten Chinese women, who bowed to the rising sun with folded hands. For them the sunrise meant more than an aesthetic natural phenomenon.

Also after sunrise strong winds swirled around Wanghai Monastery's Great Hall, built in 1998 in an octagonal shape and painted bright red. The monastery is said to have been founded at the time of the Sui (581–618), after which the structure was renovated under the Yuan (1271–1368) and the Qing (1644–1911/12). Today

Wenshu Pusa (Manjushri) in
the Prayer Hall of Wanghai Si,
eastern terrace Dongtai.

Puxian Pusa (Samantabhadra),
Shijiafo (Buddha Shakyamuni),
and Wenshu Pusa (Manjushri).
White Burmese jade. Prayer Hall of
Wanghai Si, eastern terrace Dongtai.

Shijiafo (Buddha Shakyamuni) entering nirvana, in front of the Prayer Hall of Wanghai Si, eastern terrace Dongtai.

28 Jingtu monks live here. Before the hall lies an approximately 7 m-long white marble statue of Buddha Shakyamuni in the state of nirvana. In the interior there sits enthroned a brass statue, dedicated in 2006, of the four-armed Wenshu Pusa Minjie (Sanskrit: Tikshna Manjushri). Behind it stand three beautiful white jade figures from Burma, representing Shakyamuni, Puxian, and Wenshu. A harmonious peace prevails in the light-filled room. A monk recites the name of Amitabha while lighting incense, while purifying the altar, and when pilgrims enter the room. At the same time, as in every monastery on Wutai Shan, he lightly strikes once a bronze vessel that stands on the altar. The tone is supposed to symbolically direct the attention of the deity being addressed to the desire of the donor. An endless loop of tape heralds the name Amitabha melodiously in five variations. The style of chanting the name of Amitabha in five tones goes back to the monk Fazhao in the eighth century. He claimed that Amitabha himself had taught him this type of mantra-chanting at the monastery of Zhulin.[4]

The older statue of Wenshu Pusa from the Great Hall is now found in the small Wenshu shrine, as it had to make room for the new one two months earlier. Much more interesting are two old but newly repainted stone statues, which could come from the period of the Yuan. The left portrays Wenshu as a simple monk, the right, as four-armed bodhisattva. Three hundred metres below the prayer hall is the

Nayuolan (Sanskrit: Narayana) Cave (Chinese: dong). Nayuolan Fo is one of the 35 buddhas of confession.[5] The cave is greatly revered by pilgrims, since Wenshu Pusa is said to have meditated in it in the form of a monk during the time of the Northern Song Dynasty (960–1126).

The southern terrace
Nantai 南台 and Puji Si 普济寺

The 'southern' (nan) terrace Nantai is dedicated to Buddha Ratnasambhava; at a height of 2,410 m above sea level it is the lowest peak of Wutai Shan. The former Puji Monastery, said to date back to the time of the Sui (581–618), was razed to the ground during the Cultural Revolution. In its place there is now a weather station. The new monastery, whose name means 'universal salvation', was built on a neighbouring peak and houses 18 Jingtu monks. The rare pilgrims entering the monastery find themselves first in the Hall of the Three Buddhas and the Wenshu Hall and then step up to a humble one-storey brick structure, which serves as a substitute for three caves that were part of the old monastery. To the west stands a new stupa built of concrete. The Puji Monastery lies apart from the streams of pilgrims and is little visited, but I imagine that there is another reason for the lack of visitors. The monks give a sullen and unwelcoming impression. They refused to open the pseudo-caves for a group of local pilgrims and offered monosyllabic answers to my questions, if they bothered to answer them at alll. Below the monastery a collection of new stupas, which had been erected over the urns of high-ranking monks, stood in a sea of nasturtiums and chrysanthemums, among which grew smooth, reddish mushrooms. Photographs of the deceased were placed on the southern side of the stupas. On account of these magnificent flowers, the terrace is also called Jinxiu Feng, 'brocade peak'.

The western terrace
Xitai 西台 and Falei Si 法雷寺

In contrast to the southern peak, which is protected from the wind, the 'western' (xi) terrace Xitai, which rises 2,781 m above sea level, is exposed to the rush of the wind. It is dedicated to the transcendental Buddha Amitabha. The terrace also bears the name Guayue Feng, which basically means the peak of the hanging moon. The terrace is of great significance for adherents of Jingtu, since the moon 'hanging' over them symbolises the Pure Land of Buddha Amitabha, to whom the peak is dedicated. The travelogue of Ennin underscores the importance of the western terrace. He writes that about 3 km west of Xitai two 10 m-high boulders with 'great stone chairs' faced each other. Wenshu Pusa and the enlightened layman Vimalakirti would have sat in them and debated Buddhist doctrine, so the place was called Duitanshi, 'stones of discussion'.[6] The monastery of Falei, founded during the time of the Sui, whose name means the 'rolling thunder (lei) of Buddhist doctrine (fa)', was destroyed several

The cave dedicated to Nayuolan (Narayana) on the eastern terrace Dongtai.

Memorial pagodas for distinguished nuns and monks, southern terrace Nantai.

times, most recently in 1923. The reconstruction of the Jingtu monastery, begun in 1986, is more modest. In the rear shrine honouring Wenshu Pusa three brass statues of Puxian, Wenshu, and Guanyin sit enthroned, and before them colourful prayer flags crackle in the wind.

The central terrace Zhongtai 中台 and Yanjiao Si 演教寺

The 'central' (zhong) terrace Zhongtai, rising 2,893 m above sea level, is consecrated to the highest transcendental Buddha Tathagata Vaicorana. Traditional pilgrims climb it on foot by choosing the direct path from Taihuai to the monasteries of Fenglin and Jixiang. Modern pilgrims, by contrast, can catch a taxi in town and ride first along the road to the west to the Jinge Monastery and there turn toward a slope heading north. This leads through a larch forest to Jixiang Si, where it forks toward the central and western peaks. The tree line is reached at 2,500 m above sea level. That this lay no higher more than a millennium ago we can gather from the travelogue of the famous historian and founder of the Lü School Daoxuan (596–667): 'There are five terraces. Grass and trees do not grow on the peaks. Thick pine forests grow in the valley bottoms.'[7]

Fierce winds seemed to want to blow me off the mountain, as the central terrace rivals the northern terrace in terms of the power of the wind and the wintery cold. The terrace is strewn with huge stone boulders, covered with moss, which is why it is also called Cuiyan Feng, 'green stone peak'. This terrace is also closely tied to Wenshu Pusa, as the bodhisattva is said to have taught here, sitting on such a stone. This legend provided the name of the present-day monastery of Yanjiao, the temple of the instruction. The monastery, exposed to the wind, likewise originated during the time of the Sui and was spectacularly rebuilt in the late 1980s. The monastery serves as an institution of Chan, but more than half of the approximately 20 monks belong to the esoteric Buddhism of Mi Zong. A monk said that the young Eleventh Panchen Lama, enthroned by China, had visited

Wenshu Pusa, wielding
the sword of wisdom, in
Falei Monastery on the
western terrace Xitai.

Monk praying at sunrise
at Wanghai Si Monastery
on the eastern terrace,
2,732 m above sea level.

the monastery a few years earlier. The strong influence of Tibetan Buddhism on Yanjiao Monastery goes back to Emperor Zhengde (ruled 1506–21), who was fascinated by Tibetan culture and had the monastery revived by a Tibetan monk in 1512. The initiative to rebuild after the Cultural Revolution came from Master Qinghai (1922–90). He was Han Chinese and studied Tibetan Buddhism first in Sichuan and then on Wutai Shan. In 1985 he began the reconstruction on both the southern and central peaks.

Before the Hall of Wenshu Pusa stands a reliquary stupa, which pilgrims circle either nine or 108 times. In the Manjushri Hall 1,000 small metal statues of Wenshu Pusa stand on a long, step-shaped altar. The 12 large, colourfully painted relief statues on both side walls and the rear wall surprised me, because they portrayed gods that play an important role above all in the Tibeto-Buddhist pantheon, for example the black,

buffalo-faced Yamantaka (Chinese: Yanmandejia), the 'conqueror of death', standing on a crouching blue bull, or the nine-headed, dark blue Vajrabhairava (Chinese: Weilowa Jingang), with the main head of a bull, in a sexual embrace with his yogini Vajravetali. Vajrabhairava is the patron of the Tibetan Gelugpa School, to which the Dalai Lamas belong. The highest head of Vajrabhairava is irenic, as it represents the bodhisattva Manjushri, whose wrathful incarnation he is.[8] Additional deities are Bodhisattva Vajrapani (Chinese: Jingang Shou Pusa), the four-headed Buddha Vairocana (Chinese: Piluzhena Fo), and, riding a donkey through a sea of blood, the female guardian goddess Palden Lhamo, patron of Lhasa and both the Dalai and the Panchen Lamas. The portrayal of these deities accords with Tibetan iconography. The floor is painted with mandalas. North of the Wenshu Hall stands the newly built Great Hall. Three

The Buddhas of the Three Times and four of the eight transcendental bodhisattvas. Great Hall of Yanjiao Si on the central terrace Zhongtai.

**Great Hall of Yanjiao Si,
central terrace Zhongtai.**

11 m-high copper statues of the Buddhas of the Three Times sit enthroned in it, and before them stand the eight transcendental Buddhas.

In 840 the central peak bore witness to a deed by the monk Wuran as surprising as it was spectacular. He came as a young man to Wutai Shan in 791 and over the course of the following decades made pilgrimages no fewer than 72 times to all its sacred sites, temples and shrines. At the same time he collected money in order to be able to invite all the monks and nuns living on Wutai Shan to a periodical vegetarian banquet – a custom that was revived in the late 1990s. Today it is not monks but rather wealthy bankers or industrialists who underwrite such large banquets, in which in the summer as many as 300 monks take part. Wuran celebrated the successful feeding of these countless monks by

ceremonially burning one of his fingers on the altar as an offering of thanksgiving at regular intervals, until none of his fingers remained.

When he was 74 years old, he announced he would 'burn a stick of incense on the highest point of the central terrace to honour the Five Terraces and their inhabitants'. The stick of incense he referred to was, however, his own body. After he had called on Buddha all night long and prostrated himself, he covered himself in an oil-soaked cloth, sat down on the ground in a meditation position, poured oil over his head, and set himself on fire. Sitting in this position he burned like a stick of incense, from top to bottom. His disciples gathered up his ashes and carried them to the mound of Fanxian, south of the present-day monastery town of Taihuai, where they erected a reliquary pagoda, which has since disappeared.[9]

The monastery city of Taihuai 台怀景区

When a son becomes a monk, nine generations enter heaven.
—Chinese saying

Xiantong Si 显通寺

From the northern pass the road descends almost 1,000 m down to the monastery town of Taihuai, the centre of Wutai Shan and the place with the highest concentration of Buddhist monasteries. No fewer than 14 monasteries stand here in a small area west of the Qingshui River. In total, in the summer 4,000 monks, over 1,000 nuns and 8,000 laypeople live in the whole of the inner region; in the winter this number falls to about 2,000 monks and nuns and 6,000 laypeople. The overwhelming majority of the seasonal monks and nuns come from China, Taiwan and eastern Tibet, then from Mongolia, Korea, and, depending on the political climate, Japan. After a quarter of an hour, deep in the valley of the Qingshui River, in the fading evening light, the landmark of Taihuai came into view. It is a 56.4 m-high white stupa from the early fourteenth century, which is said to contain a reliquary of Shakyamuni given by the Indian emperor Ashoka. I gazed over the valley and saw more than 20 monasteries and temples dotting the landscape – a view suggesting the

mythical paradise of Shangri-La. By the time I reached Taihuai, night had fallen and the small shops that line the main street had just closed.

The next day typical autumn weather prevailed, with sunny days of clear skies alternating with days of drizzle and fog. The monumental reliquary shrine of Tayuan Monastery seemed to want to pierce the sky, its peak no longer visible in the fog. I went to the oldest and second-largest monastery, Xiantong Si. The Chan monastery counts 60 monks in the winter and 150 in the summer. It prides itself on being, along with the monasteries of Baima Si in Luoyang and Qingliang Si on Wutai Shan, among the oldest Buddhist institutions in all of China, as it is said to have been founded in the year 68 CE by the Eastern Han emperor Mingdi.[1] While this tradition belongs to the realm of legend, it is quite possible that the founding of the monastery goes back to Emperor Xiaowendi (ruled 471–99).

Xiantong Monastery, whose name means 'clear (tong) understanding (xian)', was originally called Dafu Lingjiu Si, 'Vulture Mountain of the Great Buddha Monastery', analogous to the Indian

994 hands of the 1,000-armed Wenshu Pusa hold small Buddha statues in begging bowls, Qian Bo Wenshudian (Wenshu Pusa Hall of the Thousand Begging Bowls), Xiantong Si.

Tibetan prayer flags and the pagoda of Tayuan Si, view from Pusading Si to the south.

mountain Gridhrakuta, the vulture peak of the five-peak mountain Rajagriha. There Buddha instructed his early disciples and is believed to have preached the *Lotus Sutra* and other important sutras of Mahayana. At that time the present-day monastery of Pusading Si, lying on a ridge north of Xiantong, also belonged to the Lingjiu Si, as did the present-day Tayuan Monastery, south of Xiantong. This association of Lingjiu on Wutai Shan with Mount Gridhrakuta in India is said to go back to the Indian itinerant monks Kasyapamatanga and Dharmaratna, who in the year 68 allegedly reported to Emperor Mingdi that Wenshu Pusa had given instruction on Wutai Shan.[2] Later Empress Wu Zetian (ruled 690–705) gave the monastery the new name Da Huayan Si, 'Great Huayan Temple', to honour the *Avatamsaka (Huayan) Sutra*, which alluded to Wutai Shan as the residence of Wenshu Pusa. We can also see the significance of the then Huayan Monastery

in the fact that the fourth patriarch of Huayan, Chengguan (737–838) taught here from 771 until about 795.[3] The complex, which over time fell into disrepair, was completely renovated and split into three separate monasteries: Xiantong, Pusading and Tayuan, by the emperors Hongwu (ruled 1368–98) and Yongle (ruled 1403–25).[4] At that time two high-ranking Tibetan dignitaries were staying in the monastery, the fifth Karmapa in 1407 or 1408 and Tsongkhapa's student Shakya Yeshe (Chinese: Jiangquanquerji, 1354–1435) in 1415. Emperor Shunzhi (ruled 1644–61) gave the monastery its present name, Xiantong Si.

The present building plan goes back to the renovation of 1579–1606, ordered by Empress Dowager Li (1546–1613). The lead architect was the ingenious Chan master Miaofeng (1540–1613), whose friend the Chan master Deqing (1546–1623) lived on Wutai Shan and was among the four greatest Chan masters of the Ming Dynasty.

The potbellied future buddha
Milefo (Maitreya) greets
pilgrims in Taihuai on the way
to Tayuan Si and Xiantong Si.

Miaofeng was purely an architect, who never strove for the grandeur of an abbot but remained a builder of monasteries. Miaofeng designed here, among other things, the 'pillar-less hall', two of the five slender bronze pagodas south of the bronze shrine, and this shrine itself, which stands as the only structure preserved unchanged.

As everywhere on Wutai Shan, indeed in all of China, a high, blood-red wall surrounds the monastery. This not only marks the religious zone off from the profane surroundings but also goes back to China's ancient need to protect itself by building high walls. Cities and palaces are surrounded by walls, as are monasteries. Since two pavilions, each with a large stele, stand in front of the second of the seven shrines, the complex is compared by the local people to the shape of a dragon, with the two stele pavilions forming its eyes. Another interpretation sees in Xiantong Monastery the body of a dragon, whose neck is formed by the long stairway to the elevated monastery of Pusading and whose head is Pusading itself. Along with the bell and drum towers, the monastery consists of seven large temples, which lie along the north–south axis, and dozens of smaller side shrines and rooms.

Since Xiantong lacks the traditional entrance hall with the four heavenly guardians, this is replaced by a side entrance with two steles, on which the characters 'long' (dragon) and 'hu' (tiger) are written. Between the bell tower, where a 5,000 kg bell from the Ming period hangs, and the drum tower stands the Guanyin shrine with seated figures of, from left to right, the bodhisattvas Puxian, Guanyin, and Wenshu. During my second stay on Wutai Shan in May 2007 I was able to observe the celebration of dead souls, which takes place annually from the ninth to the sixteenth day of the fourth lunar month. It is called Shui Hu Fa Hui, meaning 'water and land prayers'. As a monk explained to me, although such rituals stand in the Confucian

tradition of ancestor worship, they are also grounded in Buddhist thought, according to which every person is reincarnated in one of the six possible existences – unless he enters nirvana. For this reason the ritual is directed to all spirits, in water, on earth and in the air. In the hall about 30 monks and just as many lay

Drum tower, Xiantong Si.

pilgrims, who return every year, chant sutras; the latter pray in particular for deceased relatives.

North of the Guanyin shrine stands the Manjushri Temple Wenshuyuan with an impressive statue of Bodhisattva Manjushri sitting on his blue lion. This figure, like that in Shuxian Monastery, is supposed to represent the archetype of Wenshu Pusa. The Japanese pilgrim monk Ennin, who stayed here for a month and a half in 840, reported in his travelogue that at the end of the seventh century the artist tried six times in vain to pour a metal statue of the bodhisattva, which shattered each time. Finally, in despair, he asked Wenshu Pusa for help and for forgiveness, in case the six earlier, unsuccessful statues had aroused his ire. The bodhisattva revealed himself, astride his lion, and the artist was able to complete the seventh, perfect statue. Since then these statues have served as models for all artists who work on Wutai Shan.[5] Three smaller statues, representing Buddha Shakyamuni and two bodhisattvas, sit in front of Wenshu Pusa.

Next comes the Great Hall with the statues of the seated Buddhas of the Three Times, with Bhaisajyaguru (Chinese: Yaoshifo) replacing Dikanpara, who is usually found here, as the past Buddha, and Amitabha replacing Maitreya as the future Buddha. Since Amitabha's paradise of the Pure Land is found in the west, Amitabha sits to the west of the south-facing Buddha Shakyamuni; that is, at his right hand. Yaoshifo's paradise, by contrast, is linked with the east, so he sits to the left, east of Shakyamuni.[6] It is understandable that on Wutai Shan Amitabha often takes the place of Maitreya, since the Jingtu School, which predominates on Wutai Shan, places Buddha Amitabha at the centre of its religious efforts. Furthermore, Wutai Shan serves as a kind of foretaste of his paradise; for especially pious pilgrims Wutai Shan is like the earthly Pure Land.

At this point a strict adherent of Chan would assert, however, that every person carries the Pure Land within himself. It is the Buddha-nature latent in every human being; we must

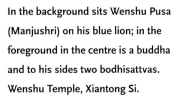

In the background sits Wenshu Pusa (Manjushri) on his blue lion; in the foreground in the centre is a buddha and to his sides two bodhisattvas. Wenshu Temple, Xiantong Si.

'just' realise it, and this realisation corresponds to enlightenment. Thus pilgrimages are really superfluous, since the Buddha-nature can also be realised in everyday life. For centuries, however, many Chinese Chan masters have granted that a pilgrimage can help to purge the spirit of unnecessary and troublesome baggage. Finally, Shakyamuni's two chief students, Mahakashyapa and Ananda, stand before him. Before the Cultural Revolution, official consecrations of monks and nuns took place in this hall; today on Wutai Shan only Bishan Monastery is authorised to do this.

Behind the Great Hall stands the 20 m-high, whitewashed 'pillar-less hall' with two aisles. Its Chinese name 'Wuliang Dian' evokes the boundless presence of the Buddha. Miaofeng actualised the idea of expressing this omnipresence of Buddha through the construction of a 'pillar-less, unbounded hall' in other places in China, too. Here a gigantic statue of the highest Tathagata Buddha Mahavairocana, the most important

buddha of the *Huayan Sutra*, sits enthroned in the centre of a white, pink, and blue lotus blossom.

The next hall is the second temple honouring Wenshu Pusa. It is called the 'One Thousand Begging Bowls Wenshu Pusa Temple' (Chinese: Qian Bo Wenshudian) because it contains an approximately 8 m-high, 11-headed and 1,000-armed metal statue of the bodhisattva from the Ming Dynasty. Of the thousand arms, 994 each hold a small buddha figure, sitting in a begging bowl; four more arms hold two vajras and two bells; and the last two arms lift over the head additional buddha figures in the unusual gesture of greeting. The model for this rarely encountered portrayal of Manjushri goes back to murals in Dunhuang, where it appears paired with the much more commonly portrayed thousand-armed bodhisattva Avalokiteshvara. It was the tireless Amoghavajra who in 740 translated into Chinese the *Sahsrapatra Sutra*, dedicated to this exceptional incarnation of Wenshu Pusa.[7]

(Below left) The words on both sides of the picture exhort readers not to disdain elderly people but to respect them. The text that forms the old man's garment is a popular folk song with a similar message. Side chapel in Xiantong Si.

(Below right) A pilgrim has placed his own Buddha statue on the altar before the 1,000-armed and 11-headed Wenshu Pusa and asks the bodhisattva to impart protective power to his statue. Qian Bo Wenshudian (Wenshu Pusa Hall of the Thousand Begging Bowls), Xiantong Si.

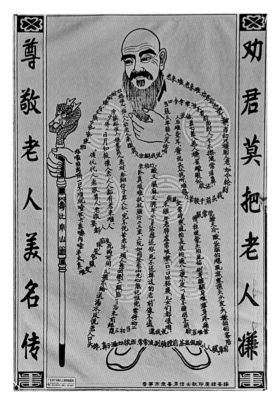

In the centre is the Bronze Hall,
built in 1606 and newly gilded in
the late 1990s; beyond it is the
monastery library of Xiantong Si.

The statue is regularly visited by groups of pilgrims, each of whom carries a new buddha or bodhisattva, which is up to 40 cm tall. At the thousand-armed Wenshu Pusa, they place their buddha on the altar, light three sticks of incense and recite prayers. They hope that some of the blessing power of the large statue is transmitted to their own statue, which they will then put up at home after their pilgrimage. Pilgrims almost always use exactly three incense sticks, since these symbolise the three basic elements of Buddhism: the Buddha, the Dharma and the community of believers.

North of this shrine a staircase leads the Bronze Hall, 6 m higher up the mountain side. The hall, built in 1606 from 50 tons of bronze, has a rectangular foundation of 4.8 x 4.2 m and is, without the roof, just under 5 m tall. In front of the shrine stand five slender bronze pagodas, three of which were rebuilt in the late 1990s and all of which, along with the hall, were newly gilded. The two needle-shaped, 13-storey pagodas to the southwest and southeast have the elegance of Ottoman minarets. Not only do the five stupas symbolise

the five terraces of Wutai Shan, their mandala-shaped arrangement refers to the five manifestations of Wenshu Pusa and the five Tathagata Buddhas. In the interior a brass statue of Wenshu Pusa is enthroned, and the walls are decorated with some 10,000 small gilded figures in high relief, which represent the meditating Buddha Shakyamuni. They commemorate the famous miracle of Sravasti, when Buddha Shakyamuni multiplied himself ceaselessly to demonstrate the omnipresence and universality of his teaching. The small statues could, however, also be related to the 10,000 disciples of Bodhisattva Wenshu Pusa, described in the *Avatamsaka Sutra*.

Another 4 m higher the stairs lead to the highest hall, the monastery library. It is hardly ever visited by pilgrims, however; neither the figure of Wenshu Pusa nor the statues of eight seated monks on the ground floor seem to enjoy their esteem. In the inaccessible upper storey sacred books, as well as a 5.7 m-long and 1.2 m-high paper scroll, are said to be protected. At the time of Emperor Kangxi (ruled 1661–1722), the layman Xu Dexin wrote the

(Above) The Bronze Hall of Xiantong with a statue of Wenshu Pusa.

(Left) Like the interior walls, the inside of the roof of the Bronze Hall at Xiantong Si is also decorated with countless Buddha figurines.

General Weituo (right) guards the monastery while Milefo or Budai Heshang (left) benevolently greets pilgrims. Tian Wang Hall, Guangming Si.

entire *Avatamsaka Sutra,* which has 630,043 Chinese characters, in tiny script in the shape of a seven-storey stupa on this scroll.[8]

The next morning I knocked on the closed entrance gate at 4:30, in order to take part in the morning meditation. As arranged with the porter the previous evening, he opened a wing of the heavy, red-painted entrance gate and led me to the Great Hall. First a monk struck the wooden simandron, in the shape of a hollow fish, to call all the monks to the mandatory early morning prayer. The Chinese word for fish is yü, which also means 'more'; that is, wealth or abundance. Thus fish are very popular throughout China. Since the fish, with its eyes always open, seems never to sleep, it also symbolises the ceaseless concentration on their spiritual mission desired by monks and nuns. Now the monks must quickly get up. After a few minutes the loud sound of a bronze gong followed and finally a young, strong monk beat a huge drum, about 250 cm in diameter, in a rapid tempo. Coughing and spitting shadows scurried through the night and entered the barely lit, unheated hall. As

soon as they stood before the high altar, they prostrated themselves three times and touched their foreheads to the floor. Older, frail monks were content to touch their foreheads to the lotus throne of Shakyamuni. Then they took their traditional place standing behind their meditation cushions. They formed two groups that faced each other, one on the eastern and the other on the western side of the hall.

Now the monks, three Tibetan pilgrim nuns and two female lay Buddhists called jishu and staying three months as guests, recited sutras for half an hour to the beat of a rhythmically struck wooden instrument shaped like a shell. Then they lined up to the side of the three high altars and walked quickly, one after another with eyes lowered, between the rows of cushions as through a labyrinth and clockwise around the three large buddha statues. They ceaselessly called on Wenshu Pusa. After several circum-ambulations of the three altars they returned to their places and continued the recitation of sutras. The striking of a bronze bowl signalled the end of the 40-minute devotion. They hurried to the centre of the room, bowed quickly before the statue of Shakyamuni, and streamed out into the gleaming dawn. All monasteries on Wutai Shan carry out such morning devotions; additional communal prayer follows, depending on the monastery, at 9:00 a.m. and 4:30 p.m.

A monk strikes the fish-shaped simandron, called Muyü, 'wooden fish', to call others to communal prayer, Xuanzhong Si.

The spatial arrangement of monasteries

Xiantong Si displays most of the features of traditional Chinese temple architecture. These developed out of the traditional palace architecture of China and took on influences from the cave temples of India and Central Asia. The main temples extend along a central axis, while the side chapels, living quarters and administrative buildings, and the refectory stand parallel on both sides across from them. When the topography allows, temple complexes are laid out along the north–south axis, with the entrance to the south. Since in Chinese thought every structure built by human hands threatens to damage the natural harmony between heaven and earth, it is necessary not only that buildings take into account the natural conditions but also that the complex itself be harmonious. Whenever possible Buddhist monasteries stand in a location with a harmonious landscape in a so-called dragon position, which means that the entrance looks out at a body of water and the rear buildings are placed up against a mountain.

The faithful normally enter a walled monastery complex through the main gate, on which is written the monastery's name. They then come into a wide, open courtyard, with a pond on each side, one filled with lotus plants and the other with fish. They next enter a small entrance hall, where the pot-bellied Milefo or Budai Heshang greets them. In the very human-appearing form of an incarnation of the future buddha, he suggests to all visitors that there is hope of a better rebirth even for them.

Back to back with Milefo stands a statue of General Weituo, who looks at the succession of temples. In the hall there also stand the four heavenly kings, Tian Wang, as well as sometimes Heng and Ha, the two Erjiang marshals. They are portrayed as giants with muscular, mostly naked upper bodies and armed with clubs or swords. For instance, two such figures stand in the convent of Guangming Si. They represent the double incarnation of the Yaksha guardian deity Vajrapani (Miji Jingang). Their appearance at the temple entrance is said to go back to Buddha Shakyamuni, when he asked the sponsor of a park for two guardian demons armed with clubs.[9]

Although the four Tian Wang had been known in China since Faxian's report of his travels in India from 401 to 411, Emperor Xuanzong (ruled 712–56) in 742 was the first to order the building of the first Tian Wang halls, after the king of the north Vaishravana assisted him in battle.[10] That all the deities seen in this entrance hall are neither buddhas nor high-ranking bodhisattvas eases access for pilgrims. They can proceed from a world of celestial kings and warriors, which stands relatively close to them, to the halls of the highest bodhisattvas and buddhas and finally to the library, which contains the holy scriptures, the Dharma. Seen from the perspective of an entering visitor, the bell tower stands to the right and the drum tower to the left of the Tian Wang Hall. The sound of the bells is thought to summon the bodhisattvas, especially Dizang Pusa, while striking the drum scares away evil spirits.[11]

After the Tian Wang shrine pilgrims reach the temple of the patron of the monastery, such as Wenshu or Guanyin Pusa. A second statue of Weituo often stands at the back of this temple. The next temple is the Great Hall Da Tian with the Buddhas of the Three Times, where monks and nuns hold their daily meditations. The description 'great' refers not only to the physical size of the hall but also primarily to Buddha Shakyamuni's title 'the great hero'.[12] At the rear of this hall are usually found either Guanyin Pusa, standing between the young model pilgrim Shancai and the converted dragon

Chan monks walk around the Buddha statues in the Great Hall of Xiantong Si during their second morning devotions. At the front of the photo to the left are three Tibetan pilgrim nuns and to the right two laywomen. In the background one can see a statue of Shijiafo (Buddha Shakyamuni).

maiden Lungnü, or the three saints of Jingtu, Amitabha, Guanyin, and Dashizi. Since monasteries change their school association frequently over the course of their history with the ascension of a new abbot, the statues of buddhas and bodhisattvas encountered in the halls do not necessarily allow for conclusions about the present school affiliation.

In large complexes a second shrine to honour the patron deity follows. The 16 or 18 luohans are found on the side walls of this shrine or the Great Hall. While the classroom with its benches and tables is a side building, the monastery library is located next along the main axis. Here Buddha is no longer present concretely but rather abstractly in the form of his recorded teaching. However, only educated monks and nuns with authorisation from the abbot have access to the books and scrolls. At some monasteries, such as Zunsheng, a high pagoda completes the complex. While monks may invite visitors during the day into their small, often spartanly appointed cells, the separate cloister, in which monks and nuns spend one to three years in deep meditation, is hermetically closed.

The monastery of Jinge Si shows the classical architectural arrangement of Buddhist monasteries on Wutai Shan. After the entrance gate, located to the south, there follow the Tian Wang Hall, the hall honouring the bodhisattvas, and the Great Hall. A red-painted wall surrounds the entire complex.

View from the Bronze Hall
southward to the pillar-
less hall of Xiantong Si.

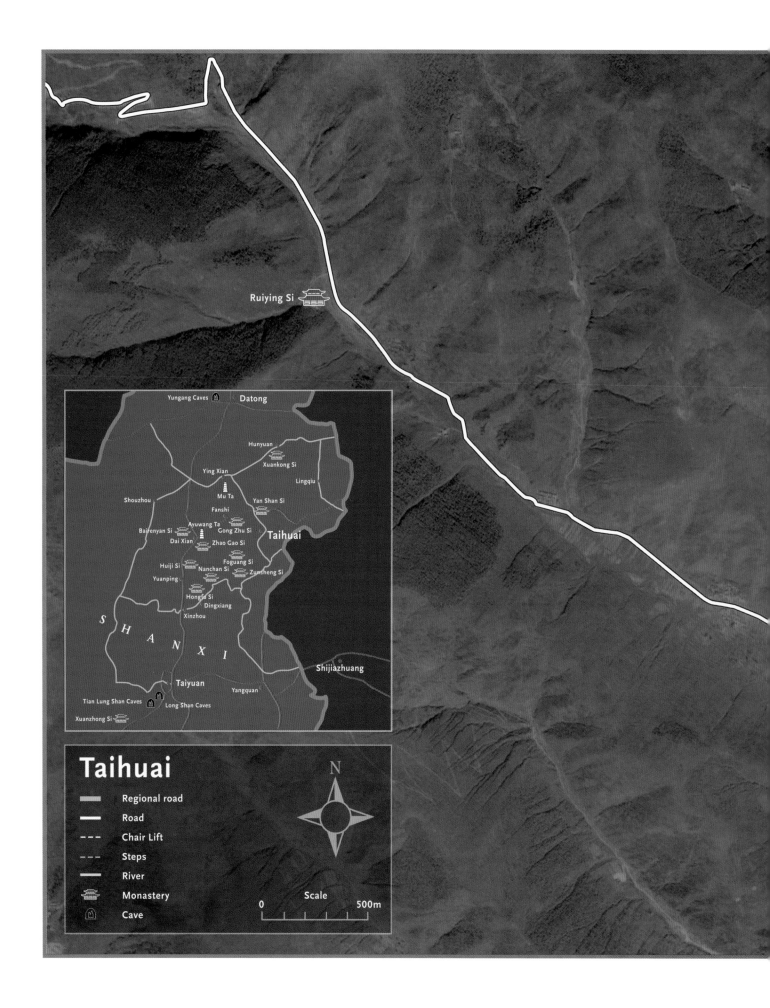

Ruiying Si

Yungang Caves   Datong

Hunyuan

Xuankong Si

Ying Xian   Lingqiu

Mu Ta

Shouzhou   Fanshi

Yan Shan Si

Ayuwang Ta

Bairenyan Si   Gong Zhu Si

Dai Xian   Zhao Gao Si   **Taihuai**

Foguang Si

Huiji Si   Nanchan Si   Zunsheng Si

Yuanping

Hongfu Si

Dingxiang

Xinzhou

S H A N X I

Shijiazhuang

Taiyuan   Yangquan

Tian Lung Shan Caves

Long Shan Caves

Xuanzhong Si

Taihuai

	Regional road
	Road
	Chair Lift
	Steps
	River
	Monastery
	Cave

N

Scale

0   500m

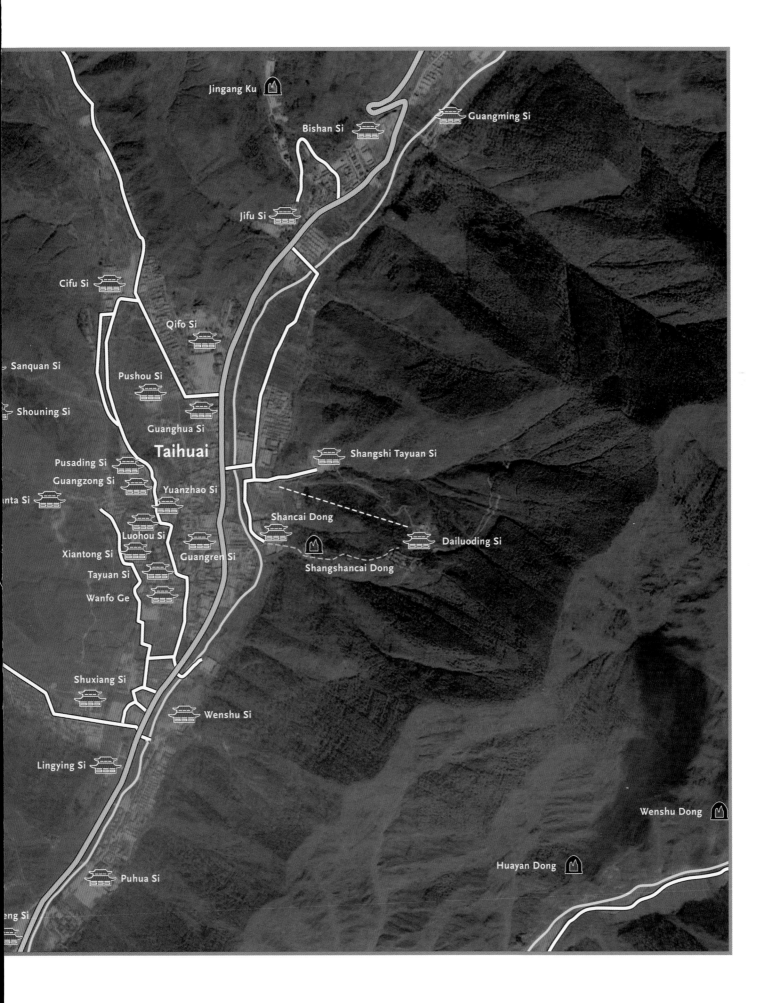

Jingang Ku

Bishan Si

Guangming Si

Jifu Si

Cifu Si

Qifo Si

Sanquan Si

Pushou Si

Shouning Si

Guanghua Si

Taihuai

Shangshi Tayuan Si

Pusading Si

Guangzong Si

Yuanzhao Si

...nta Si

Shancai Dong

Luohou Si

Dailuoding Si

Xiantong Si

Guangren Si

Shangshancai Dong

Tayuan Si

Wanfo Ge

Shuxiang Si

Wenshu Si

Lingying Si

Wenshu Dong

Huayan Dong

Puhua Si

...eng Si

Tayuan Si 塔院寺

South of Xiantong stands the monastery of Tayuan of the Chan Zong, which until the beginning of the fifteenth century belonged to Xiantong Si. At the end of the sixteenth century it was renovated and took the present name, which means the 'court (yuan) of the pagoda (ta)'. In fact the 56.4 m-high Great White Pagoda, which stands in the monastery's inner courtyard, dominates the monastery city; it is the emblem of Wutai Shan. The pagoda, which ostensibly contains a reliquary of Buddha Shakyamuni, was built in 1301 by the renowned Nepalese artist Anige (in Chinese Aniko, 1245–1306), who had already in 1279 built the White Pagoda in Beijing, which is

similar in appearance.[13] The bell-shaped pagoda, reminiscent of Tibetan stupas, clearly distinguishes itself from the surrounding Chinese temple architecture. It culminates in a 13-part cone, tapering at the top, and above that a ceremonial roof on which hang 252 wind chimes.

In 1407 the fifth Karmapa Deshin Shegpa (1384–1415) financed a restoration of the pagoda, which indicates early close contact between Wutai Shan and Tibetan institutions. Pilgrims take care to circle the pagoda once, 12, or 108 times clockwise and simultaneously to gently turn the prayer wheels found in the base of the pagoda. They also seek out in a niche of the pagoda's base a stele on which a 50 cm pair of feet is chiselled, representing Buddha Shakyamuni's footprint,

The large stupa to the left is said to hold a relic of Buddha Shakyamuni; the smaller stupa to the right, a hair of Wenshu Pusa. Pusading Si can be seen in the background.

Buddhapada. The footprint represents one of the earliest, non-figurative portrayals of the Buddha and symbolises the blessing of the earth by Buddha and his teaching. It also emblemises both Buddha's presence in the form of his message and his absence insofar as he has entered into nirvana and encourages us to forsake all attachments and desires that precipitate the mechanism of rebirth.

A significantly smaller pagoda that stands in an eastern side court of Tayuan is almost as important for pilgrims because it is said to contain a hair of Wenshu Pusa. The corresponding legend says that at the time of the Northern Wei (386–534) a rich man gave a banquet for all the monks of Wutai Shan. He was bothered, however, by the many laypeople who also came. Finally a ragged, pregnant woman appeared, carrying a baby, holding a boy by the hand, and accompanied by a dog. Since money was being collected in the temple but she was penniless, she snipped off a lock of her hair as a symbolic donation. Then she asked for food for herself and those with her. She received two portions, for herself and the boy. When she asked for two more helpings, for the baby and the dog, she was given them only grudgingly. Her third request, however, for another portion for the unborn child, was roundly denied. The woman then contemptuously rejected the four portions and walked to the exit of the hall. There she transformed herself into the luminous bodhisattva Wenshu Pusa, the two children into heavenly children, and the dog into Wenshu's lion. They rose up to heaven and disappeared. The insensitive benefactor then blinded himself, since his eyes had not recognised the presence of Bodhisattva Manjushri, and he vowed to all present to treat all supplicants and people equally and not to discriminate against anyone. The lock of hair from the pregnant beggar was from then on venerated as a relic in the small stupa.[14] When I heard this legend for the first time, the last parable in Chapter 25 of

the Gospel of Matthew came to mind, in which Jesus speaks of the Last Judgement: 'I tell you the truth, whatever you did for one of the least of these brothers of mine, you did for me ... whatever you did not do for one of the least of these, you did not do for me' (Matt. 25:40, 45; NIV).

On holidays and weekends the furnace in front of the southern entrance to the monastery does a brisk business. Pilgrims buy rectangular boxes, measuring about 70 x 50 cm, which are filled with sticks of incense. Wenshu Pusa sitting on his lion or the highest dragon king is pictured on the front. On the back, on the nine quivers filled with incense sticks, are lucky formulas: 'Good destiny'; 'Luck and wisdom'; 'Health and longevity'; 'Luck and safety'; 'Good wishes of the ancient Buddha'; 'Happy marriage'; 'Sons and daughters'; 'Luck and Wealth'; 'All your problems will disappear'. Pilgrims light the centre incense stick, bow slowly toward each of the cardinal directions, and toss the burning box into the blazing furnace.

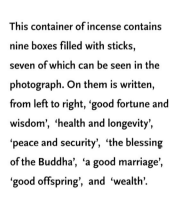

This container of incense contains nine boxes filled with sticks, seven of which can be seen in the photograph. On them is written, from left to right, 'good fortune and wisdom', 'health and longevity', 'peace and security', 'the blessing of the Buddha', 'a good marriage', 'good offspring', and 'wealth'.

Just past the main entrance Tibetan pilgrims prostrate themselves ceaselessly before the pagoda and the Great Hall with the statues of Shakyamuni, Puxian, and Wenshu Pusa, 108 or 1,080 times. Before each pilgrim lies a 3 m-long wooden board, a few of which are covered with cushions. First they press their palms together above their heads and then bring them down to their hearts. Then they bend down to the board, hold on to the sides, and push their entire bodies forward onto the board until they are lying flat on it with arms outstretched in front of them. Now, while lying on the board, they again lift their folded hands above their heads, after which they stand up again, like a striking cobra, and raise their hands above their heads, ready for the next prostration.

North of the pagoda stands the monastery library and in its centre a two-storey, 11 m-high, octagonal, rotatable bookcase. Today small Buddha figures fill the book niches; the valuable books in Chinese, Mongolian, and Tibetan are kept in the second storey. Such rotating,

octagonal bookcases – really forerunners of the prayer wheels – are very old and date back as far as 544 CE. Such a tower-shaped library in another shrine caught the attention of Ennin in 840.[15] Around 1,000 years later Mao Zedong – who during the Cultural Revolution unleashed anti-Buddhist fury – and Zhou Enlai gave the monastery a dubious honour by spending the night in one of the side buildings on 9 April 1948.

On 19 May 2007, the celebration in honour of Wenshu Pusa's birthday took place in the inner courtyard of Tayuan Si. In that year the festival was moved one day from the fourth to the third day of the fourth lunar month, probably because the third day promises greater luck than does the fourth.

When I arrived before 7:00 a.m., I stood, along with dozens of monks and nuns, as well as laypeople, before the closed entrance gate; access was limited for security reasons. Only after a few lay pilgrims had left the monastery was I able to squeeze in. Monks and nuns from many monasteries, along with numerous

(Above) A pilgrim throws a carton of burning incense sticks into the offering fire in front of Tayuan Si.

(Left) In front of the southern entrance to Tayuan Si a pilgrim prays while holding up a carton of incense sticks toward the four cardinal directions. The text on the carton states that the incense will cause the dragon king Wuye to grant good fortune.

The rotating, octagonal
bookshelf in the library of
Tayuan Si, which today is filled
with small Buddha figurines.

pilgrim monks, had gathered here for prayer, so the courtyard was full to overflowing. In the courtyard about 2,500 monks were reciting in unison sutras and the mantra of Wenshu Pusa. Another 300 or so pilgrims stood along the outer wall. During the prayer a solemn and at the same time joyful mood prevailed. The approximately 500 Tibetan and Mongolian monks sat in rows on the floor; the Chinese nuns and monks stood in somewhat more casual order. They really needed stamina, since the festival began at 5:30 in the morning and lasted four hours. But the monks were rewarded for their endurance; at the end of the festival they each received a 50-yuan note, about US$7. Later I found out that the sponsor, a merchant from Taiyuan, had spent a total of about US$40,000.

Pusading Si 菩萨顶寺

The monastery of Pusading, whose name means 'peak, crown of the bodhisattva' and which is also called Zhenrong Yuan 真容院, 'court of the true appearance', stands on the rock outcropping north of Xiantong Si, to which it belonged until the fifteenth century. The steps leading to it number 108; this corresponds to the 108 tests human beings must withstand during their lives. The rather steep ascent symbolises a spiritual refining. The steps begin and end with a 'blind' gate to protect against ghosts, on which a red, 3 m-high and 1 m-wide inscription of the name of Buddha is painted on a yellow background. Pilgrims making the ascent close their eyes on the lowest step and step confidently

A procession of Chinese monks walks between seated Tibetan and Mongolian monks. Birthday celebration of Wenshu Pusa at Tayuan Si.

or hesitantly toward the written name. Those who miss the calligraphy are laughed at by their fellow pilgrims and must repeat the exercise.

In front of the steps a bronze statue of the legendary monk and outlaw Lu Zhi Sheng stands guard over the entrance to the monastery complex. In the classic novel *Water Margin*, also called *Outlaws of the Marsh* (*Shuihu Zhuan*), Lu Zhi Sheng is a leader of the robbers of Liangshan and the 36 heavenly robbers. In his youth Lu had killed a butcher – other sources say it was a high-ranking functionary – who had molested a poor singer, after which he fled to Wutai Shan. But as monk he also still ate meat and drank wine. While drunk he once beat all the monks of Pusading and damaged the temple with his 31 kg metal staff and his 40.5 kg knife, after which the abbot expelled him from the monastery, and he became a robber baron.

Beside the bronze statue are many stands offering devotional objects such as small statues of buddhas and bodhisattvas, scrolls, amulets, prayer flags, and Buddhist rosaries with 108 beads. It is a fact that commerce is an unavoidable by-product of any pilgrimage. One who does not gain an inner experience on the pilgrimage must get an external sign of it. It should also be kept in mind that pilgrimage journeys to famous pilgrimage sites, which focus on a particular place and do not extend to the great outdoors, as in the case of the circumambulation of a sacred mountain, hardly inspire experiences of silence and individual self-discovery, but rather collective experiences with fellow pilgrims, who share similar expect-ations and desires. Until now there have been hardly any foreign tourists; visitors have consisted of many Chinese groups, as well as individual Tibetan and Mongolian monks. Are they tourists or pilgrims? Where does the boundary lie between pilgrims and tourists? Probably not only is it blurred but the two terms are not mutually exclusive; they can in part overlap. Modern

pilgrim tourists, as well as monks and nuns, take photographs and send text messages. By way of comparison, in the Middle Ages European pilgrims bought inexpensive paintings or statues, copies of relics, or letters of indulgence.

All in all, during a longer stay the strict discipline and quiet spirit in the large monasteries stand out, in contrast to Tibet. There it is not unusual to see monks strolling about in the streets or watching television or playing billiards in a restaurant. One encounters such activity on Wutai Shan only very rarely. This difference is certainly related to the fact that monks here enter monastic life largely voluntarily and out of their own

A pilgrim with eyes closed approaches the character representing the Buddha; inner spirit wall at Pusading Si.

Tibetan and Mongolian
monks in the inner courtyard
of Tayuan Si at the birthday
celebration for Wenshu Pusa.

motivation. In Tibet, by contrast, it is the custom that the second-eldest – clearly under the direction of the parents – enters a monastery. Economic distress can also force parents to place 'surplus' children in a monastery. I believe the fact that the overwhelming majority of monks and nuns on Wutai Shan chose this lifestyle of their own accord can also be seen in their spiritual concentration during communal prayer and sitting meditation. In Tibet, however, I sometimes had the impression that the sutras were rattled off mechanically and in spiritual lethargy. However, even in ancient imperial China the saying applied: 'When a son becomes a monk, nine generations enter heaven'.[16]

Pusading Si, which belonged to Xiantong Si for about 900 years and was at that time called Da Wenshu Huayan Si, meaning 'Great Wenshu Temple of the Huayan Monastery', was rebuilt in 1404 by Emperor Yongle. Four centuries earlier, in 980, Emperor Taizong of the Northern Song Dynasty gave the monastery a large, gilded statue of Wenshu Pusa.[17] In 1659 the first emperor of the Manchurian Qing Dynasty, Shunzhi (ruled 1644–61), made the seminal decision to convert the monastery to the Tibeto-Buddhist school of Gelugpa. Furthermore, the abbot of Pusading was given administrative authority over not only the other Tibetan monasteries but also over all the monasteries on Wutai Shan.[18] Today eighty monks live here in the summer, of which 20 Chinese monks belong to the esoteric school of Mi Zong; the remainder are Gelugpas from Tibet and Inner Mongolia. The current abbot is a 48-year-old Han Chinese from Hohhot, Inner Mongolia, whom the provincial authorities appointed 20 years ago.

After pilgrims have tackled the steep steps, they reach the pailou, the three-part wooden entrance gate, from which another dozen steps lead to the Tian Wang Hall, which stands between the bell tower and the drum tower. As everywhere,

(Right) Nuns and monks wait in the morning in front of the closed gate to Tayuan Si, until they are granted entrance. Birthday celebration for Wenshu Pusa.

(Far right) A wealthy merchant from the provincial capital Taiyuan sponsors the birthday celebration for Wenshu Pusa in Tayuan Monastery and gives each of the monks and nuns present a 50-yuan bill.

the pot-bellied, laughing Milefo receives the pilgrims, and at his back General Weituo guards the interior of the monastery. On the opposite side of the small courtyard stands the Great Hall, in which the Tibetan and Chinese monks gather for communal prayer at 4:00 a.m. and 3:00 p.m. Apart from signs written in Chinese the room is no different from a Tibetan shrine. Long temple flags hang from the ceiling. At the altar the buddhas Bhaisajyaguru, Vairocana, and Amitabha bless visitors. In front of the statue of Vairocana there is a brass figure of Tsongkhapa, founder of the Gelugpa School, and in front of him a photograph of the Tenth Panchen Lama (1938–1989). The liturgy is also

Tibetan, as the monks recite the sutras in the Tibetan language from Tibetan books. As in Tibet, four metre-long horns, reminiscent of alpenhorns, drone throughout the room, and the master of ceremonies recites the sutras in an incredibly deep, gravelly voice. The shrine honouring Wenshu Pusa, in front of which stand four stone steles, follows to the north of the Great Hall. One stele is blank; it was put up under Emperor Qianlong (ruled 1736–95). Another stele without inscription, from the time of Kangxi (ruled 1661–1722), stands in the Xiantong temple. According to popular lore, these rulers are said to have refused a text in praise of them, trusting that posterity would recognise their merits.

View of Pusading Si from the two pagodas of Santa Si.

Tibetan Gelugpa monks recite sutras in the Great Hall of Pusading Si.

The pailou entrance gate at the top of the 108-step stairway of Pusading Si.

The founder of the Tibetan
Gelugpa order, Tsongkhapa (right),
is venerated as a manifestation
of Wenshu Pusa (Manjushri).
Mural on linen in the Wenshu
Hall of Guanghua Si.

Wutai Shan – Bridgehead of Tibetan Buddhism in China

There were close ties early on between Tibet and Wutai Shan, called 'Riwo Tsenga (Ri-bo-rtse-lnga)' in Tibetan. Tibetan hierarchs, such as Phagpa (1235–80), verifiably visited Wutai Shan beginning in the thirteenth century at the latest. An early flourishing of Tibetan Buddhism occurred at the start of the dynasty of the Ming (1368–1644), when Emperor Xuande gave the abbot of the first Tibetan monastery Yuanzhao important administrative authority. The second upsurge of Tibetan Buddhism, specifically the Gelugpa School, on Wutai Shan began at the time of the Fifth Dalai Lama (1617–82) and the first Qing emperor Shunzhi (ruled 1644–61). In 1653 the Fifth Dalai Lama visited the capital of the Qing, Beijing, and 300 Chinese monks of Wutai Shan seized the opportunity to meet the him in Beijing.[19]

The visit of the Fifth Dalai Lama prompted Emperor Shunzhi to give the Dalai Lama the authority to name the most senior administrator for all monks of Wutai Shan; that is, not only for Tibetan monks but also for Mongolian and Chinese ones. The first to assume this office, called the 'Zongli Wutai Shan Fan Han Lama' (Mongolian: Dzasak), was Ngakwang Lozang (Chinese: Awang Laozang) in 1659.[20] His successor in 1668 was the Mongol Lozang Tenpel (Chinese: Laozang Danbei, 1632–84). After Emperor Kangxi (ruled 1661–1722) visited Wutai Shan in 1683, Lozang Tenpel was able to put a new roof on the monastery using tiles in the colour of yellow gold, which could otherwise only be used for imperial residences. Kangxi, who converted a total of ten monasteries on Wutai Shan to Gelugpa, certified his successor Lozang Tenpa (Chinese: Laozang Danba) as administrator of all the monks of Wutai Shan in 1698. Now the Dalai Lama indirectly held jurisdiction over all the monasteries of Wutai Shan. Tenzing Gyatso (Chinese: Dingzeng Jianzuo) followed Lozang in 1704. In this way Wutai Shan became the bridgehead of Tibetan Buddhism in China, and was joined in 1744 by the Yonghegong Monastery in Beijing. Until the Republic of China (1912–49) the administrators of Wutai Shan and Yonghegong, appointed from Lhasa, were the most important representatives of Tibet in China.[21]

This indirect power of the Dalai Lama and the administrators appointed by him on ancient Chinese territory must have unsettled even the Qing emperors who were so well-disposed toward Wutai Shan – Kangxi visited it five times and Qianlong six. They began to support other Tibetan and Mongolian dignitaries; that is, to develop them into counterweights to the Dalai Lama and the Dzasak. With regard to Wutai Shan, the Zhangjia (Tibetan: I cang skya; Mongolian: Jangjia) line of reincarnations, which the emperor supported as an alternative to the Dzasak, was the most important. The first Zhangjia Rinpoche confirmed by Emperor Kangxi was in fact the thirteenth of an already existing lineage of rebirths.[22] The Zhangjia lamas had residences in Beijing, Jehol, on Wutai Shan and in Labrang in present-day Gansu. Thus they could exercise their influence in terms of the emperor among Mongols as well as Tibetans.

The most significant Zhangjia lama was Zhangjia Hutuku Rölpai Dorje (1717–86), whose pagoda stands in Zhenhai Monastery on Wutai Shan. He studied with the future Emperor Qianlong (ruled 1736–95), who named him 'Lama of the Seal' in 1736. Qianlong's father and predecessor had appointed Rölpai national master in 1734. Rölpai thanked him for the great honour by praising Qianlong as an incarnation of Manjushri, just as the Tibetan Sakya hierarch Phagpa had recognised the Mongol emperor Kubilai Khan as an incarnation of Manjushri about 450 years earlier. As the

Dalai Lama is thought to be an incarnation of Avalokiteshvara, the Manchu emperor Qianlong was regarded as an emanation of Manjushri. It is sometimes claimed that the founder of the future Qing Dynasty, Nurhaci (1559–1626), took his new tribal name, 'Manchu' from Manjushri. This is simply a legend, however.

In 1744 Rölpai Dorje founded a monastic university for Mongols, Manchurians and Chinese in the former palace of Yonghegong in Beijing. Since he had already obtained good results from a delicate diplomatic mission to Lhasa in 1734–35, he had become the most influential Tibetan Buddhist monk in the capital city.[23] Rölpai Dorje went to Wutai Shan at least 18 times, twice together with Emperor Qianlong. He died on 2 April 1786, in a sitting meditation pose in Pusading Monastery.

Rölpai Dorje was not Tibetan but rather Monguor. The Monguor were descendants of the Mongol garrison troops stationed in Gansu and Qinghai at the time of the Yuan (1271–1368). The Monguor largely adopted Tibetan culture but maintained their Mongol dialect. They were nominally under the authority of the central government in Beijing. Thus the Monguor were destined to mediate among Chinese, Tibetans and Mongols.[24] In 1947 the penultimate Seventh Zhangjia Hutuku, Lozang Penden Tenpe Drönme (1890–1957), was appointed head of the Buddhist Association of China, which was based in Nanjing and stood under the authority of the Kuomintang government. When Chiang Kai-Shek lost the civil war against the Communists in 1949, the Zhangjia Hutuku followed him into exile in Taiwan. With his death in 1957 the lineage practically disappeared. His eighth reincarnation was recognised in India by the Dalai Lama only in the year 2000.[25]

The support given to Tibetan Buddhism by the Qing emperors was complex and followed not only from personal convictions. It also served to win over the Tibetan and Mongol vassals and tie them to the empire. By having themselves celebrated as incarnations of Manjushri and Buddhist dharma kings or chakravartins, the emperors were able to win from the Tibetans and Mongols, who were adherents of esoteric Buddhism, the recognition these peoples had denied the Chinese state. Tibetans and Mongols felt bound to the Manchu emperors but not to China. Thus esoteric Buddhism in the Tibetan-Mongol mould became the state religion of the northern and western border regions of the Qing Dynasty and was an essential contributor to the unification of the empire.

That Wutai Shan was of great significance in the eyes of Tibetans as well can also be seen in the fact that it is shown in murals of important monasteries in Tibet, such as in Potala Palace and in the summer residence Norbulinka in Lhasa, the monastery of Samye, as well as Donggu Monastery in Kandze.[26] Southwest of Lhasa there is also a sacred place called Riwo Tsenga, which also bears the Tibetan name of Wutai Shan. It consists of a mountain ridge with five peaks.[27]

The present revitalisation of Tibetan Buddhism on Wutai Shan is partly the work of the two Han Chinese Nenghai (1886–1967) and Fazun (1902–80), who studied and absorbed Tibetan Buddhism. Beginning in 1926, Nenghai taught Tibetan Buddhism in Bishan Si Monastery on Wutai Shan, where he encountered opposition from the monks. The Chinese monks objected to the integration of esoteric practices and rituals. When the Japanese advanced into the province of Shanxi in 1937, he returned to Sichuan, where he had acquired his knowledge of Tibetan Buddhism. In 1953 Nenghai went back to Wutai Shan and opened his own Vajra instruction hall in the remote monastery of Jixiang, which lies on the southern slope of the central terrace of Wutai Shan. When the Buddhist Association of China was founded in 1953, Nenghai was appointed its vice president. During the

Gilded silver statue of the
second Zhanggjia Hutuku Rölpai
Dorje (1717–86) in the Palace
Museum of Beijing. The 75 cm-tall
statue was made in the year of
Rölpai Dorje's death, 1786.

Pagoda honouring Rölpai Dorje (1717–86), the Second Zhangjia Hutuku and friend of Emperor Qianlong. Yongle courtyard, Zhenhai Si.

Preparations for the Tibetan Cham dances on the 14th and 15th days of the sixth lunar month.

Cultural Revolution, the Red Guard tortured him, forced him to eat meat and drink alcohol, and locked him with a nun in a cell of Jixiang Si. In order not to further break his monastic vows, Nenghai chose suicide. Since he was found dead in the sitting meditation pose, he had presumably intentionally held his breath to the point of death. Although Fazun survived the Cultural Revolution, he was unable to recover from the abuses suffered between 1966 and 1972. He died in 1980, shortly after he had been named head of the reopened Chinese Buddhist College.[28]

Today Nenghai's third- and fourth-generation students are active on Wutai Shan. At the same time, since the late 1990s well-educated young people have also chosen to be consecrated monks and nuns. I observed several times that wealthy individuals or Chinese corporations were generously financing the reconstruction of monasteries on Wutai Shan. Buddhism in China has come back to life and is again socially acceptable; the government has to come to terms with this phenomenon.

Nenghai and Fazun were convinced that with the help of Tibetan Buddhism they could revive the moribund Chinese Buddhism. This was extraordinarily optimistic, since under the Republic of China (1912–49) a deep mistrust prevailed between the leading personalities of Tibetan and Chinese Buddhism. We must not forget that before 1912 Tibetan Buddhism was present in China proper only thanks to the support of the Qing emperor, and this only selectively, in the imperial residences of Beijing and Jehol, as well as on Wutai Shan, the hinge between the two Buddhist schools. For the Chinese, esoteric practices of Tibetan Buddhism such as tantra and mantras seemed suspect, if not decadent and corrupt. The Tibetans, for their part, condemned the funeral practices of the Chinese Buddhists, such as the burning of joss paper, paper houses and paper ships, as superstition. Gelugpa especially condemned Chan Buddhism, since it had little regard for scripture and scholastic training in logic and analytical thought.

The approach of Nenghai and Faxun accorded with the ideas of the Chinese monk Taixu (1890–1947) and the Guomindang politician Dai Jitao (1891–1949), who had also studied with the Panchen Lama. Taixu believed that cooperation with the republic was the best strategy to protect Buddhism from governmental encroachments such as expropriations. Dai Jitao, by contrast, sought in the Buddhist religion a mechanism for holding together the empire, which was breaking apart. Since the fall of the Qing in the autumn of 1911, Tibet and Mongolia had declared themselves independent, and in Central Asia the Xinjiang governor Yang (ruled 1912–28) reigned as an independent despot. Since the proclamation of the republic, the empire had shrunk to those territories inhabited by Han Chinese.

The Republic of China tried to maintain the unity of the empire ideologically with the principle of Wuzu gonghe, 'five races harmoniously united'. These five races were the Han, Tibetans, Mongols, Manchurians and Hui Muslims. The first four races were more or less distinctly adherents of a Buddhist church. This discourse quickly proved not to be credible, however, since the Han Chinese were not prepared to share power with representatives of the other groups. As an alternative to the dubious principle of the five peacefully united races, Dai Jitao, with the support of Taixu, put forth the idea of a pan-Asiatic Buddhism in different ethnic forms. While this formula excluded the Muslims, it was able to provide a collective Buddhist basis for Han, Tibetans, Mongols and Manchurians. Now Tibetan Buddhism (Xizang Fojiao) appeared to be an ethnic variant of the global Buddhist religion,

Great Hall of Guanyin Dong, built in the Tibetan style.

equal to Chinese Buddhism (Zhongguo Fujiao). In this sense Nenghai and Fazun tried to build bridges between Han Chinese and Tibetan Buddhism.[29]

One of Nenghai's students was Zhidu, born in 1908, the former abbot of the monastery of Tayuan. When major flooding devastated southern China in 1998 and threatened to break through important dams, the affected provincial government asked the 90-year-old master to perform a seven-day prayer ritual to prevent a still greater catastrophe. The combined efforts of Zhidu, the People's Army, and 10,000 volunteers finally mastered the dangerous situation. Zhidu died in 2003 at the age of 95; his pagoda at Santa Monastery was completed in 2007.

Today there are three purely Tibetan monasteries of Gelugpa on Wutai Shan; these are Guangren, Guanghua and the Guanyin cave monastery. To these are added eight additional monasteries of the esoteric Buddhism Mi Zong, in which Tibetan monks live with their Han Chinese confreres, at least in the summer: Pusading, Luohou, Guangzong, Yuanzhao, Santa, Shangshi Tayuan, Wuye and its Wenshu Temple, as well as Zhenhai. At the time of Kangxi there were ten Tibetan monasteries on Wutai Shan; before 1956 there were 25 Tibetan and 99 Chinese monasteries, for a total of 124.[30] On Wutai Shan the denominational affiliation of a monastery is defined not only by the monastic institution but also by the monks living there at the time. Thus I encountered on Wutai Shan several monasteries where nuns and monks of different schools lived together.

Wanfo Ge 万佛阁

Next to the former monastery complex of
Huayan are five more monasteries. A few
metres southeast of Tayuan Si, to which it once
belonged, stands the monastery of Wanfo Ge.
Built in 1616, its name means 'pavilion of the
ten thousand buddhas'. Today Wanfo belongs to
the school of Mi Zong. Its other name is Wuye
Miao and refers to a legend that Manjushri
transformed the black dragon king Wuye
into a golden, healing dragon. Right beside
the entrance, on the southern side of the first
courtyard, stands a stage for classical Chinese
opera performances, the only one in Taihuai.
A legend recounts that the dragon king Wuye,
whose name means 'fifth man' and to whom the
shrine on the northern side is dedicated, loved
opera above all. For this reason opera performances take place on every holiday and on

**Novice of the Gelugpa
School at prayer in the
Great Hall of Pusading Si.**

weekends, attracting many spectators. The music,
shrill to Western ears, and the strident singing
blast so loudly from the loudspeakers that they
can be heard in the neighbouring Tayuan Si.

On the eastern side of the first courtyard
stands a small shrine with a seated brass figure
of Piluzhenafo (Sanskrit: Vairocana). The
buddha's hands are folded, and the forefingers
are parallel to each other and point upwards in
the gesture of highest enlightenment uttarabodhimudra; this suggests that all oppositions have
been nullified. Statues of Dipankara and Maitreya
stand at Vairocana's sides. Behind the shrine
of the five dragon kings stands the Wenshu
shrine, which was completely destroyed during
the Cultural Revolution. Metal statues of Puxian,
Wenshu and Guanyin Pusa, which came from the
convent of Miaoding, stand in the rebuilt temple.

Guangren Si 广仁寺

The Guangren Monastery stands to the north
of Wanfo Ge and originally belonged to the
neighbouring monastery of Luohou. In 1831
a master of the eastern Tibetan monastery of
Choni founded it as an independent institution, belonging to the Tibetan school of Gelugpa.
Since its founding it has cultivated close relations
with the northeastern Tibetan region of Amdo
and serves almost exclusively Tibetan and
Mongolian pilgrims as a residence; in the early
summer of 2007 27 Tibetan monks were staying
there. In 1983 the Tenth Panchen Lama stayed
in the monastery, and in 2004 the Eleventh
Panchen Lama, who is recognised by China,
did so. The name Guangren means 'universal
(guang) humanity (ren)', while the second name
Shifang 十方 means 'ten directions'; that is,
north, east, south, west, northeast, northwest,
southeast, southwest, over and under. This
implies that Buddhist teaching is universal.

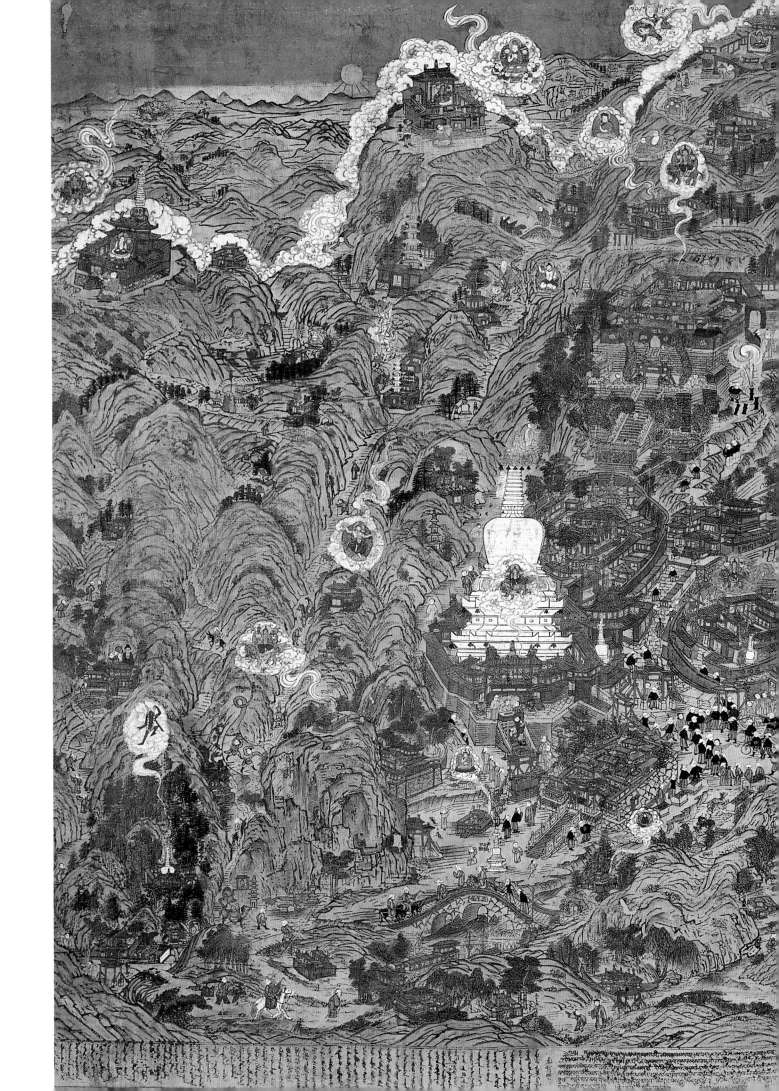

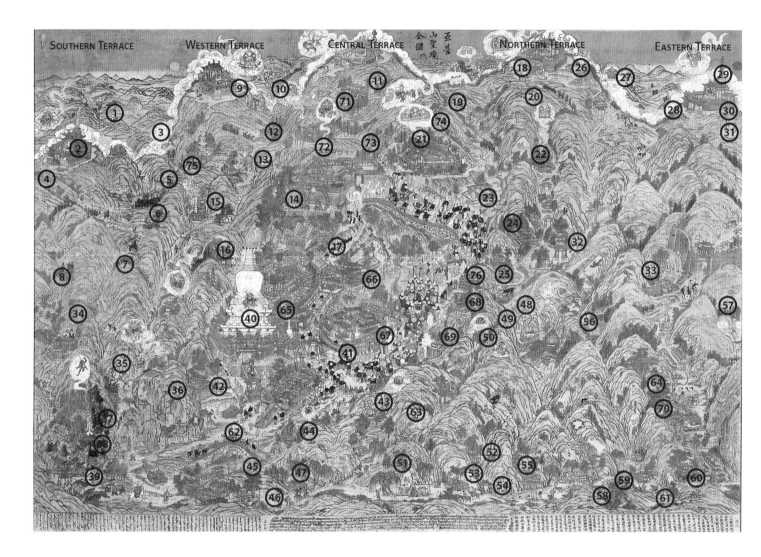

SOUTHERN TERRACE   WESTERN TERRACE   CENTRAL TERRACE   NORTHERN TERRACE   EASTERN TERRACE

Historical panoramic map of Wutai Shan

One hundred and twenty-seven Buddhist monasteries and temples, Daoist temples, pagodas and religious places, and historic sites, as well as monks, nuns, laypeople, and deities, are portrayed on this map from Cifu Si Monastery. As on the mural of Wutai Shan in Cave 61 of Mogao, Dunhuang, the southern terrace is shown to the far left and the eastern terrace to the far right, with the western, central and northern terraces in between. In the centre of the picture the procession on the 'imperially mandated prayer festival' on the 14th and 15th days of the sixth lunar month begins at Pusading Si Monastery and ends at the Great Stupa of Tayuan Si.

Previous double-spread and above: Hand-tinted wood-engraving on linen in sino-mongol style from *c.* 1846. Size 118 x 165 cm. Rubin Museum of Art, New York.

Red Nr. on picture	Name
1	古竹林; Guzhu Lin 佛光寺; Foguang Si
2	南台; Nantai 普賢塔; Puxian Ta
3	永安寺; Yongan Si
4	白龍池; Bailong Chi
5	羅漢洞; Luohan Dong 清涼石; Qingliang Shi
6	金閣寺; Jinge Si
7	日照寺; Rizhao Si
8	金灯寺; Jindeng Si
9	西台; Xitai
10	秘庵; Mi'an
11	中台; Zhongtai 演教寺; Yanjiao Si
12	清涼橋; Qingliang Qiao
13	西天洞; Xitian Dong
14	菩薩頂; Pusading Si
15	竹林寺; Zhulin Si 凤林寺; Fenglin Si
16	三塔寺; Santa Si
17	廣宗寺; Guangzong Si
18	北台; Beitai
19	萬年冰; Wannian Bing
20	黑龍池; Heilong Chi
21	慈福寺; Cifu Si
22	普樂院; Pule Yuan
23	兩房院; Liangfang Yuan
24	吉福寺; Jifu Si
25	七佛寺; Qifo Si
26	罗汗台; Luohan Tai
27	闃然寺; Lanran Si
28	東台; Dongtai
29	笠子塔; Lizi Ta
30	望海樓; Wanghai Lou
31	罗罗洞; Luoluo Dong
32	西天寺; Xitian Si
33	湧泉寺; Yongquan Si
34	千佛洞; Qianfo Dong
35	蛇溝寺; Shegou Si
36	梵仙山; Fanxian Shan

37	鎮海寺; Zhenhai Si
38	行宮; Xinggong
39	白雲寺; Baiyun Si
40	塔院寺; Tayuan Si
41	羅睺寺; Luohou Si
42	殊像寺; Shuxiang Si
43	觀音洞; Guanyin Dong
44	奶奶庙; Nainai Miao
45	慈福庙; Cifu Miao
46	玉皇庙; Yuhuang Miao
47	棲賢寺; Qixian Si
48	文殊洞; Wenshu Dong
49	公布山; Gongbu Shan
50	朝陽洞; Chaoyang Dong
51	南山寺; Nanshan Si
52	明月池; Mingyue Chi
53	萬綠庵; Wanyuan An
54	黑崖洞; Heiya Dong
55	普安寺; Puan Si
56	水連洞; Shuilian Dong
57	白雲洞; Baiyun Dong
58	金剛窟; Jingang Ku
59	海回庵; Haihui An
60	大寺; Da Si
61	黑馬石; Heima Shi
62	Taranatha Stupa
63	Cave of Sixth Dalai Lama
64	射虎川; Shehu Chuan
65	顯通寺; Xiantong Si
66	圓照寺; Yuanzhao Si
67	十方堂; Shifang Tang
68	大螺頂; Dailuo Ding
69	善財洞; Shancai Dong
70	台麓寺; Tailu Si
71	玉花池; Yuhua Chi
72	壽寧寺; Shouning Si
73	三泉寺(三全寺) ; Sanquan Si
74	鐵瓦寺; Tiewa Si
75	獅子窩; Shizi Wo
76	龍王庙; Longwang Miao

In the entrance hall the four heavenly guardians are not portrayed in statues but rather painted. I also found here pictures of the Wheel of Becoming and the mythical kingdom of Shambala. In front of the Great Hall a Tibetan monk prostrated himself unceasingly and touched the ground with his forehead and outstretched arms; on his knees and hands he wore wooden protective gear.

On the traditional day for the birthday celebration in honour of Wenshu Pusa, the fourth day of the fourth lunar month, a ritual in honour of Weilowa Jingang, a manifestation of Yanmandejia, is performed in the small courtyard in front of the prayer hall. The Buddhist deity Yanmandejia is identical to Yamantaka, the conqueror of death, and, in the form of Weilowa Jingang, is also identical with Vajrabhairava, the patron of Gelugpa. Ten Tibetan monks sit on the ground, with a small fire burning before them. The leader of the ritual wears a yellow monk's

hat and the two monks to his left and right wear five-petalled crowns with pictures of the five Tathagata Buddhas. All five monks in the front row swing thunderbolt-shaped instruments and ring bells. The monks perform such a ritual only upon request, when it is financed by a sponsor. This type of fundraising is legitimate because in China, unlike in some European countries, religious institutions receive no subsidies so that monks and nuns are dependent on private donations. After the ritual the monks recite sutras in the main hall, and the sponsor sits among them. For a few minutes a monk holds a tablet with about eight burning candles over the sponsor's head, to symbolically purify him. The ritual recalled for me the fire cult of the ancient Turkic and Mongol peoples, which I observed several times in Central Asia. The Byzantine envoy Zemarkos, who travelled in 568 to the khan of the Western Turks in the Talas valley in southern Kazakhstan,

Wenshu Pusa (Manjushri) sits European-style on his blue lion. Wenshu Temple, Wanfo Ge.

A monk holds a platter of burning candles over the head of the sponsor of the preceding ritual for Weilowa Jingang, in order to purify his karma.

also reported that the Turks 'purified themselves with fire'. John of Plano Carpini, whom Pope Innocent IV sent as ambassador to Mongolia in 1245, reported as well, 'The purification took place in the following manner: they light two fires, stick two lances in the earth close to the fires. Then they have people, animals, and dwellings [yurts placed on carts] pass between the two fires'.[31]

While lively commerce prevailed in the small shops between Guangren Monastery and the main street during the autumn of 2006, in the spring 2007 noisy bulldozers were at work. Because in 2006 China applied to UNESCO for acceptance of Wutai Shan into the World Cultural Heritage List, the centre of Taihuai was to be 'beautified'. Thus many buildings housing businesses, souvenir shops, snack bars and even the post office were torn down. This 'clean-up' aroused mixed feelings in me. Although these small shops were not particularly aesthetically pleasing, they were clean and they met the need of pilgrims to purchase religious

souvenirs. They belonged to the vital everyday life of a very popular pilgrimage site. Clearing them out raised the fear that a sterile environment would be created here, like that at the southern foot of the Potala Palace in Lhasa, where the traditionally built Shöl Quarter, with its artisans and their shops, had to give way to a gigantic concrete plaza. On Wutai Shan a living pilgrimage site threatens to ossify into a museum. Even worse, as an abbot who wishes to remain anonymous shared with me confidentially, about 1,000 residents of Taihuai were to be forcibly resettled.

After my second research trip I noticed that the prevailing politics of ruthless modernisation in China is finding further victims on Wutai Shan. In May 2007 I heard almost daily sporadic explosions coming from the northwest. In a monastery in the northwestern region I also noticed fresh-looking cracks in the murals. I was then told that this had something to do with rock blasting in connection with the

In Guangren Monastery Tibetan
and Mongolian monks perform a
ritual honouring the patron deity
and meditation god Weilowa
Jingang (Vajrabhairava) on the
birthday of Wenshu Pusa.

The most important monastic festivals

Just as in the Catholic Church the saints are celebrated on annually recurring feast days, the monasteries of Wutai Shan commemorate their Buddhas and bodhisattvas each year. The most important holidays pertain to events in the life of Buddha Shakyamuni or Wenshu Pusa; these are observed in all monasteries although at greatly varying expense. A few of the large monasteries, such as Xiantong Si, Tayuan Si, Shuxian Si or Baiyun Si each year hold a ceremony lasting several hours, others only when a sponsor underwrites the celebration, and smaller monasteries content themselves with the recitation of a few extra sutras or take part in the ceremonies of a large monastery. Other holidays concern only a certain school of thought and for that reason are observed only in the corresponding monasteries.

All holidays are arranged according to the Chinese lunar calendar, with Gelugpa monasteries also following the Tibetan lunar calendar. As I quickly noticed on Wutai Shan, both calendars acknowledge astrologically auspicious and inauspicious days, so monastic festivals that would fall on an inauspicious date in a given year are moved forward a day. In the Tibetan calendar days are also doubled or deleted in order to conform to the lunar calendar, numbering only 354 days, to the 365-day solar calendar. For pilgrims the situation is made more difficult by the fact that the same holiday may be celebrated at different times. For instance, the ceremony of the washing of the newborn Buddha Shakyamuni, which is an important part of his birthday celebration, takes place between 9:00 a.m. and 12:00 a.m. at Baiyun Si but from 2:00 to 3:00 a.m. at Bishan Si. For this reason it is advisable for pilgrims and visitors to ask shortly ahead of time about the day and exact time of a celebration.

The most important monastic festivals according to the Chinese calendar are the following:

Chinese and Tibetan New Year, which sometimes but not always fall at the same time	8th–15th day of the 1st lunar month
Birthday of Maitreya Pusa	1st day of the 1st month
Siddhartha, the future Buddha Shakyamuni, leaves his family	8th day of the 2nd month
Birthday of the sixth patriarch of Chan, Huineng (638–713) (only in Chan monasteries)	9th day of the 2nd month
Buddha Shakyamuni's entrance into nirvana	15th day of the 2nd month
Birthday of Guanyin Pusa	19th day of the 2nd month
Birthday of Puxian Pusa	21st day of the 2nd month
Kalachakra instruction (only in Gelugpa monasteries)	15th day of the 3rd month (Tibetan calendar)
Birthday of Zhunti Pusa, a female bodhisattva	16th day of the 3rd month
Birthday of Molizhi Tian, also called Jikuang Fomu Pusa (Marici), a female bodhisattva	23rd day of the 3rd month
Birthday of Wenshu Pusa	4th day of the 4th month
Birthday of Buddha Shakyamuni	8th day of the 4th month
Feast of the Dead Souls	9th–16th day of the 4th month
Birthday of Guanyin Pusa (Avalokiteshvara), according to the Tibetan calendar	13th–16th day of the 4th month

Birthday of the Medicine Bodhisattva Yiqie Zhongsheng Xijian (Sarvasattvapriyadarsana). Yiqie burned his arms and his body in honour of Buddha and incarnated himself later as the Medicine Bodhisattva Yaowang Pusa (Bhaisajyaraja)	28th day of the 4th month
Birthday of Weituo Pusa	3rd day of the 6th month
Prayer festival for universal peace and security, the former 'imperially mandated prayer festival'	8th and 15th day of the 6th month, in Pusading Si and other Tibetan monasteries. On the 14th and 15th days Cham dances take place.
Horse and livestock market in Taihuai	Middle of the 6th month
Guanyin Pusa achieves enlightenment	19th day of the 6th month
Birthday of Dashizi Pusa (Mahastamaprapta)	13th day of the 7th month
Yulanpen (Ullambana), the feast for the 'hungry souls', which is also called 'Buddha's happy day'. It is the end of the three-month meditation period that begins on the 15th day of the fourth month	15th–30th day of the 7th month
Birthday of Longsuzixi Pusa (Nagarjuna, a co-founder of Mahayana, second century CE)	24th day of the 7th month
Birthday of Dizang Pusa (Ksitigarbha)	30th day of the 7th month
Birthday of Buddha Dingguangfo, also called Jantengfo or Randengfo (Dipankara, first past Buddha)	22nd day of the 8th month
The future Guanyin Pusa leaves his family	19th day of the 9th month
Birthday of the Medicine Buddha Yaoshi Liuliguang Rulai (Bhaisajyaguru)	30th day of the 9th month
Birthday of Putidamo (Bodhidharma), the semi-legendary patriarch of Chan from the fifth/sixth centuries (only in Chan monasteries)	5th day of the 10th month
Birthday of Tsongkhapa (only in Gelugpa monasteries)	25th day of the 10th month
Birthday of Buddha Amitabha	17th day of the 11th month
Enlightenment of Shakyamuni	8th day of the 12th month
Birthday of Huayan Pusa (Avatamsaka)	29th day of the 12th month

In the upper centre image the sleeping Maya receives the future Buddha Shakyamuni in the form of a white elephant. Below, the newborn Prince Siddhartha takes seven steps in each of the four directions and announces the purpose of his appearance, while the rain gods, portrayed as dragons, pour waters of good fortune over him. Nirvana Hall, Puhua Si.

construction of a road. Since the explosions were very loud, despite the distance, I believed they came from artillery drills. After I returned from China, I learned on the internet that to the north of Wutai Shan prospecting was taking place to find ores such as iron, copper, gold and molybdenum. The powerful exploratory blasts carried out in this process had caused damage to murals and terracotta statues at the monastery of Jinge Si.[32] That UNESCO permitted such activities, and the destruction of an entire quarter in Taihuai, is incomprehensible but not unexpected.

Luohou Si 罗[目侯]寺

Luohou Si, which is separated by just a wall from Guangren Monastery, was founded at the time of the Tang (618–907) and completely renovated in 1492. Toward the end of the seventeenth century it came into the possession of the Tibetan Gelugpa Order and since then has been a popular destination for Tibetan and especially Mongolian pilgrims. The name Luohou is the Chinese transliteration of the Sanskrit name Rahula. This was the name of the son of Buddha Shakyamuni, who took monastic vows at age 15 and belonged to the inner circle of Shakyamuni's first ten disciples; he is one of the 18 luohans. The most important shrines of the monastery, which has 40 monks, are: first the Wenshu Hall with the central brass statue of the bodhisattva seated in a lotus blossom, carried by his blue-green lion. The bird of prey Garuda sits on the upper end of the mandorla standing behind Wenshu and guards the bodhisattva. Then follows the Great Hall with a mighty Buddha statue. A very particular arrangement of statues stands in the centre of the Hall of Buddha's Revelation. It includes a red-painted lotus blossom, about 4 m tall and made of wood (opposite p.1). By means of a hidden crank mechanism, the eight petals can bend outward. The flower opens and gives

(Left) Mongolian monk at Luohou Si.
(Below) Great Hall, Luohou Si.

Great Buddha Hall, Yuanzhao Si.

view to four symmetrically arranged Shakyamuni statues, facing the four cardinal directions. The lotus blossom stands on a square dais, on which sit 42 small figures; these are the 18 luohans and the 24 bodhisattvas. Such extraordinary and today rarely encountered three-dimensional lotus mandalas were popular at the time of the Ming as much smaller, gilded bronze or copper statues; there were dedicated to, for instance, the meditation deity Cakrasamvara or the eight medicine buddhas. They hark back to earlier Indian models from the Pala Dynasty (750–1174), which ruled in northeastern India.[33]

Here as in other monasteries on Wutai Shan one notices photographs of the Tenth Panchen Lama, who died in 1989. As a young reincarnation, the Panchen Lama was built up into a rival to the Fourteenth Dalai Lama by the Chinese invaders of Tibet, and he held the politically meaningless office of a vice president of the Chinese People's Congress. In light of the dramatic destruction in eastern Tibet in 1956, in 1962 he denounced Chinese policies in occupied Tibet in the famous '70,000-character Memorandum', after which he was deposed from all his offices, tortured, and arrested in 1964. After his release in 1977 he dedicated himself to the reconstruction of monasteries of all schools. The initially somewhat naïve collaborator had become an active patriot, who paid for his devotion with his life. On 27 January 1989, in a public speech at his Tibetan home monastery of Tashilümpo, he acknowledged the Dalai Lama as the spiritual and political head of all Tibetans. He 'fell ill' the following day under mysterious circumstances and died in the 'care' of Chinese military doctors; his own Tibetan doctors were denied access to the dying man. There is much evidence to suggest that he was poisoned because of his public commitment to a free Tibet.

Yuanzhao Si 圆照寺

North of Luohuo Si stands the monastery of Yuanzhao, founded in 1309, which was formerly called Puning 普宁. The current name means 'complete enlightenment', and the earlier one 'universal peace'. Tsongkhapa's important student Shakya Yeshe (1355–1435) stayed at the monastery several times, after which the pilgrimages of Tibetan pilgrims to Wutai Shan began. In 1426 Emperor Xuande of the Ming Dynasty (1368–1644) appointed the abbot of Yuanzhao, the first Gelugpa monastery on Wutai Shan, as overseer of all the monasteries of the region.[34] More than 200 years later Emperor Shunzhi transferred this honour to the abbot of Pusading Monastery. Despite such indications of favour from the early Ming emperors toward high-ranking Tibetan dignitaries, they emphasised the establishment of impermeable boundaries between Tibetan and Chinese Buddhism. This end was served by a law that forbade Han Chinese from becoming monks of Tibetan Buddhism.[35]

Especially worth seeing here is the Great Hall with its mighty statues of the Buddhas of the Three Times. In front of Shakyamuni Wenshu Pusa rides his lion, and on the side walls the 500 luohans dwell in their mountain niches. Song-style bodhisattva statues made of terracotta stand in the corners. To the rear of the main statue are three new statues to admire: Wenshu in the middle, Puxian to the left and Guanyin to the right – a classic bodhisattva triad on Wutai Shan. In a rear courtyard stands the 16.5 m tall, white Bao Lisha pagoda, built in 1434 for an 'Indian', probably Tibetan, master. In 1984 the Han Chinese master Qinghai (1922–90), who represented Tibetan Buddhism, moved from Guangzong Monastery to Yuanzhao Si and revived the centuries-old links between the monastery and the esoteric Buddhism of

Wenshu Pusa (Manjushri) sits on his lion in front of Shijiafo (Buddha Shakyamuni), Yuanzhao Si.

View from Pusading Si toward
the monasteries of Yuanzhao Si
(front), Shancai Dong (centre),
and Dailuoding Si (on the hill).

The monastery of Guangzong Si in the foreground and the stupa of Tayuan Si in the background, as seen from Pusading Si.

The stupa honouring the Han Chinese master of Tibetan Buddhism, Fazun, who died in 1980, Guangzong Si.

Octagonal stele at Guanghua Si, Northern Song Dynasty (960–1127). The motif of the lions' heads harks back to the famous columns of the Indian emperor Ashoka (ruled *c.* 268–232 BCE).

Mi Zong and the Gelugpa School. A year later Qinghai began the initially modest reconstruction of smaller temples and shrines on Wutai Shan, such as on the southern and central terraces.

Guangzong Si 广宗寺

A few metres north of Yuanzhao stands the monastery of Guangzong, whose name means 'universal (Guang) orthodox teaching, school (zong)'. The monastery, founded in 1507 by a Tibetan monk, is home to about ten Mi Zong monks. The upper roof of the Tongwa Dian Hall is made of bronze tiles. Unfortunately, the 18 luohans made of iron, which were still here in the 1990s, have been replaced by crude clay copies; the originals are allegedly on the second floor of the library, which is closed to all visitors. A statue of Wenshu Pusa with two of his students is found on the ground floor of the monastery. In the northeastern part of the monastery stands the stupa for the Buddhist master Fazun (1902–80), who as a Han Chinese had studied Tibetan Buddhism in Kham and central Tibet and taught it in China beginning in 1935. Behind the whitewashed stupa stands a newer, Tibetan-style temple, whose entrance is guarded by two bronze lions.

Guanghua Si 广化寺

The monastery of Guanghua is located northeast of Pusading Si in the northern part of Taihuai. Its name means 'universal transformation'. It dates to the time of the Northern Song (960–1126), as a 230 cm-tall stele from that period testifies. It ends in four lions' heads, which open out into a lotus bud. The four lions recall the columns of the Indian patron of Buddhism Emperor Ashoka (ruled *c.* 268–32 BCE), who was also crowned

by four lions. These indicate that Buddhist teaching should be spread in all four directions. Guanghua was originally a Huayan institution and is now largely a Gelugpa monastery.

After the gate and the entrance hall with the Four Tian Wang follows the Manjushri Hall with the three bodhisattvas Wenshu, Guanyin and Puxian Pusa. Unfortunately, the famous 100 cm-tall stone statues of the 16 luohans were smashed to pieces during the Cultural Revolution; at that time the remaining buildings served as a high school. The interior walls are decorated with murals painted in the eastern Tibetan style of Amdo, portraying scenes from the life of Buddha Shakyamuni. They were painted on canvas and attached to the walls in red-painted wooden frames. In autumn of 2006 money was collected for the reconstruction of the Great Gathering Hall, which had burned down. The interim building is found to its west; a Tibetan stupa stands in front of it.

Pushou Si 普寿寺

A few dozen metres from Guanghua Si stands the gigantic convent of Pushou, currently under construction, whose name means 'universal longevity'. It was founded under the Jin Dynasty in 1202 and rebuilt as a Gelugpa monastery in 1908 on the initiative of the Thirteenth Dalai Lama. Earlier it was called Guangming, which means 'shining light'. Then it fell victim to anti-Buddhist agitation, and the few surviving residential buildings served from 1962 as a home for the elderly. In 1981 local authorities granted permission for construction of a convent, which ten years later began offering instruction. Today it can house 600 nuns and

temporary female pilgrims in the summer. During this season it functions as a kind of Buddhist Summer University, admitting nuns not only from China, Hong Kong and Macao but also Taiwan, Malaysia and Singapore. The approximately 250 nuns who live here year-round must first complete a three-year novitiate before the monastic leadership under Abbess Miao Yin finally accepts them. Since the inception of the instructional programme about 2,500 nuns are believed to have completed the entire curriculum at this largest monastery on Wutai Shan.

Pushou belongs to the Lü School (Sanskrit Vinaya), rarely seen today, which emphasises exact observation of monastic rules and places great value on discipline. Right beside the

Various episodes from the life of Shijiafo (Buddha Shakyamuni). In the upper left he calls upon the earth to witness to his enlightenment; in the centre the Buddha descends from heaven to earth after he has given instruction to his deceased mother; and on the right he enters nirvana. Mural on linen in the Wenshu Hall of Guanghua Si.

entrance gate two female porters stand guard so that no unauthorised people, including ordinary lay pilgrims, enter the monastery. Nuns and novices rise at 3:00 a.m., and their long days are filled with the recitation of sutras, meditation, study and physical labour. The novices work in the kitchen, keep the monastery and all the statues in the temples clean and dust-free, unload building materials from trucks, or take active part in the construction of the monastery complex. From the monastery of Shangshi Tayuan, which lies slightly higher up, I saw three large, new residential buildings made of gray tiles and an enormous hall under construction. By way of comparison, the smaller, existing hall offers space for just under 1,000 nuns.

The monastery of Santa Si, destroyed during the Cultural Revolution and rebuilt in recent years.

Santa Si 三塔寺

West of Pusading stands the small monastery of Santa, surrounded by broadleaf and pine trees, whose name means 'three (san) pagodas (ta)'. The monastery, founded in the late sixteenth century, was destroyed by the Cultural Revolution except for the entrance gate, which dates to the time of the Qing; it was still being rebuilt in the fall of 2006. The new brass statues in the Great Hall indicate that the monastery belongs to esoteric Buddhism. The three pagodas that give the monastery its name rise in the large courtyard. In early summer 2007, two newly built pagodas, each about 4 m tall, stood south of the monastery. One pagoda was erected for Master Zhidu, an important

student of Nenghai who died in 2003. From here one gets a magnificent view of Pusading Si.

On Wutai Shan deceased nuns and monks, whether Chinese or Tibetan, are always cremated. Unlike in Tibet, sky burials are uncommon, as are burials in the earth. The ashes of ordinary monks are buried in a mountain forest, marked with a small stele or a small stupa standing about 20 cm tall. The ashes of exceptional monks are buried on certain geomantically advantageous sites on a mountainside, where other outstanding dead people already rest; such sites are comparable to cemeteries. One such cemetery is found a few dozen metres south of the pagoda honouring Zhidu near Santa in a small grove, where an old, well-preserved, five-storey pagoda made of yellow tiles stands; it could date from the time of the Yuan or the Ming. There the pagodas for the dead, made of gray tiles or concrete, are some 50 to 200 cm tall. Memorial pagodas are built within a monastery only for founders of monasteries and especially outstanding and holy monks; there are, however, very rare exceptions.

and even brought the ashes of their dead there, since it was considered especially auspicious to have one's final resting place in the earthly paradise of Manjushri. Monks from Wutai Shan also travelled to Mongolia to collect money and to sell products, such as scrolls, made on Wutai Shan. The monastery was destroyed during the Cultural Revolution. After it had been rebuilt, the seven Jingtu monks living here embarked on a complete renovation of the entire complex. At the entrance the rare visitors are welcomed by dozens of already cut wooden pillars, which await use; all building except the Great Buddha Hall have been emptied out and filled with scaffolding. The monks hope to be able to ceremonially dedicate the new construction by 2010.

It was in Cifu Si that the Mongolian monk Lhudrup in 1846 or somewhat earlier cut a set of printing blocks out of wood to print a panoramic map of Wutai Shan. The hand-tinted, 118 x 165 cm map, printed on linen, incorporates 127 Buddhist monasteries and shrines, Daoist temples, pagodas, places of religious significance, and historical

Great Hall of Cifu Si.

Cifu Si 慈福寺

In the autumn of 2006 the monastery of Cifu, lying northwest of Pushou, offered the surprising view of a large construction site. The compound was founded in 1822 by Lama Nabuhai, who belonged to the Gelugpa School of Tibetan Buddhism, in order to provide monks from Pusading with a secluded place for extended periods of meditation. Just seven years later Cifu, whose name means 'kindness and good fortune', became an independent monastery. It often served as a residence for Mongolian pilgrims, for whom a pilgrimage to Wutai Shan substituted for one to Tibet. At that time close relations prevailed between the Five Terrace Mountain and Mongolia. Mongolian pilgrims streamed to Wutai Shan

Monks' cemetery between Cifu Si and Sanquan Si.

sites, as well as monks, nuns, laypeople, and deities. The map, with text in Chinese, Tibetan and Mongolian, served not only as a concrete orientation aid for pilgrims but also as a substitute for a physical pilgrimage, as the visual basis for a mental-spiritual pilgrimage in meditation. Paths included in the map suggest certain pilgrimage routes. This map stands in the tradition of older maps, such as one from 1596 and the famous mural in Cave 61 of Mogao, Dunhuang. All offer a panoramic view with the identical orientation of the five terraces: from left to right, the southern terrace, then the western, central, northern and eastern terraces. This map was quite widespread in the nineteenth century; there are at least six extant exemplars, easily distinguished from one another by their coloration.[36]

The centre of the map shows the ceremonial procession that took place annually on the occasion of the 'imperially mandated prayer festival' on the fourteenth and fifteenth days of the sixth lunar month. After the Cham dances,

which hark back to pre-Buddhist fertility rites and symbolise the victory of good over evil, ended, the procession began. It started at Pusading Monastery and was made up of Tibetan and Chinese monks, high-ranking functionaries, musicians, masked dancers with conch shell trumpets, tubas, cymbals, drums, horsemen, two riderless white horses, over which monks held umbrella-like standards, and two litters. At the rear sat the Dzasak, the most senior overseer of all the monks of Wutai Shan; at the front monks carried a gilded bronze statue of the future Buddha Maitreya. The Briton John Blofeld (1913–87), who stayed on Wutai Shan in 1936, noted, 'As the sedan-chair approached [with the statue of Maitreya], individuals would spring from the ranks of spectators lining both sides of the route, hurl themselves under this screen and then roll hurriedly out of the way of the oncoming Lama.'[37] The procession moved slowly past the monasteries of Guanzong Si, Yuanzhao Si, Luohou Si and Guangren Si and ended at Tayuan Si.

Sanquan Si 三泉寺

From Cifu Monastery a path leads through a small forest to the monastery of Sanquan, which is about 2 km northwest of Taihuai. When I visited it, just before the path slopes upward I came upon another monks' cemetery with dozens of small pagodas and steles inscribed in Chinese or Tibetan. Soon I reached the small and impoverished-looking monastery, which is only rarely visited. Its name means 'three (san) springs (quan)', which allegedly can never run dry. Sanquan Si was founded at the time of the Yuan (1271–1368) and restored in the second quarter of the fifteenth century. Later, the Tibetan Lobsang Tashi renovated it again at the start of the eighteenth century.

The monastery, which was completely destroyed during the Cultural Revolution, is today inhabited by three Jingtu monks. During my visit, one of them sat writing in his cell, while a television broadcast a military parade. As in several other monasteries, I noticed that the monks spoke of the horrors of the Cultural Revolution only very hesitantly and anxiously. The conversation quickly turned to another topic. The question of the destructions of that time seemed to be an awkward taboo; I assumed that the authorities had instructed all monasteries not to speak of this topic with foreigners.

In the entrance hall of Sanquan Si the fat Budai sits alone; the Four Tian Wang are absent. After the modest Guanyin shrine follows the Hall of the Buddhas of the Three Times; in its interior one encounters in front of the three buddha figures, statues of Puxian and Wenshu Pusa made of white Burmese jade, as well as one of General Guandi. General Guandi, venerated by both Daoists and Buddhists, is here portrayed standing and carries a halberd. He serves as the personification of fundamental Confucian values, such as loyalty to the state, respect for parents, goodwill toward fellow human beings, and fidelity to friends.

The monastery of Sanquan Si.

Shouning Si 寿宁寺

A few hundred metres from Sanquan Si, on
a terrace in the middle of a hill rising to the
northwest of Taihuai, stands the monastery of
Shouning. The monastery, founded at the time
of the Northern Wei (386–534) or the Northern
Qi (550–77), was originally called Wangzi Fen
Shen, 'the prince who immolated himself'. The
name honours the third son of the founder of
the Northern Qi dynasty, Emperor Wenxuandi
(ruled 550–59). According to tradition the
prince, as military commander of a punitive
expedition against tribes of eastern Turks and
Khitan, killed many people. Out of remorse
for the massacre in 557 he took the monk's
tonsure on Wutai Shan. He later sacrificed
himself to honour Manjushri.[38] As the panel
explains, such excesses were not unusual.

In the years 1296–97 the future builder of
the Great Pagoda in the monastery of Tayuan Si,
the architect Aniko, designed the new building
of Shouning Si, whose name means 'longevity and
peace'.[39] In 1415 Shakya Yeshe had the monastery
renovated and converted it into a Gelugpa institution.
Today it is inhabited by eight Jingtu monks and is
regularly visited by Tibetan monks in the summer.

A 4 m-high wall surrounds the monastery,
which is built along the north–south axis. In the
south admittance is granted by the triple-arched
entrance gate, which is flanked by the drum
and bell towers. Then follows the Hall of the
Tian Wang, a small pavilion honouring Wenshu
Pusa, and the Great Hall, in front of which stand
three steles from the eighteenth century. Finally
comes the Guanyin Hall, in which are found
on the altar statues of, from left to right, the
Tibetan poet and mystic Milarepa (1040–1123 or
1052–1135), Guanyin, and the Indian Tantra master
Padmasambhava , who spread Buddhism to Tibet
in the second half of the eighth century. The right
side chapel is dedicated to the deified General
Guandi; in the left, which is misused to store
waste, stands a discarded statue of Confucius.

The monastery of Shouning Si,
founded in the sixth century,
commemorates the self-immolation
of a prince who became a monk.

Self-immolation and self-mutilation as the greatest sacrifice

Self-immolation committed out of religious conviction is a peculiarity of Chinese Mahayana Buddhism; in Indian Buddhism it was a very rare exception. It can be interpreted as an extreme consequence, absurd to rationally thinking people, of the Third Noble Truth of Shakyamuni, according to which the suffering that is inextricably linked to life can be ended only by the annihilation of desire for existence and sensual pleasure. Buddhist discipline forbids all killing, including suicide; nonetheless there is in Buddhist scriptures stimulus for such action. The first sources are the edifying stories of the pre-existences of Buddha, called jatakas. They praise the heroic self-sacrifice that the bodhisattva makes many times. In these he, for instance, sacrifices his body to feed hungry animals or, in the form of a giant tortoise, he saves from drowning 500 merchants in distress at sea, after which they kill and eat their rescuer.[40] Another jataka tale anticipates the sacrifice of the prince, telling of how the bodhisattva showed the way to lost merchants in the night with his burning hands.[41]

The second, much more important, source of inspiration are at least eight Mahayana sutras, of which the *Lotus Sutra* is the most famous. The 23rd chapter recounts how a bodhisattva 'gave his body to the Buddha as an offering' by covering his body with oil and setting himself on fire. In another form the same bodhisattva burned his arms as an offering. About this Buddha Shakyamuni said,

> *He is in fact none other than the present bodhisattva Medicine King! He cast aside his body as an offering in this fashion immeasurable hundreds, thousands, ten thousands, millions of nayutas of times. Constellation King Flower, if there are those who have made up their minds and wish to gain anuttara-samyak-sambodhi, they would do well to burn a finger or one toe of their foot as an offering to the Buddha towers. It is better than offering one's realm and cities, wife and children [etc.]. [This] brings the most numerous blessings of all.*[42]

Whether these words and the praise of self-immolation as the greatest form of sacrifice in the seven other sutras are meant purely allegorically seems to me doubtful.[43] In any case, in the first known instance of a publicly staged self-immolation, in 396 CE, the monk Fayu expressly invoked the model of the medicine king and his self-sacrifice for the Buddha. Also at other self-immolations, including those of a few nuns, the motivation consisted in both the imitation of the medicine king and the hope of achieving enlightenment through an act of radical surrender. Others hoped to be rewarded for such a suicide in honour of Amitabha with rebirth in his paradise. When around 550 fears arose about the end of the age, a few masters called on their students to mutilate themselves or burn themselves together to atone for the 'sins' of all living beings and to implore the future Buddha to come quickly.[44]

There are other forms of religiously motivated suicide, such as falling into the void from the peak of Emei Shan, jumping into a deep cave at Putuo Shan, or a conscious kind of self-mummification that is practised in both China and Japan. In this case monks choose a radical diet, lasting three years that culminates in the relinquishment of water and the taking of diuretics.[45] It also happens that people mutilate themselves by burning or cutting off individual fingers or ears. Thus an eyewitness reported in 873 that on the occasion of the procession of the relic of the Buddha's finger from the Famen temple to Chang'an a soldier cut off his left arm in front of the relic and other 'believers' bit off their fingers or singed their heads.[46] A milder form of self-sacrifice consisted of writing sutras in one's own blood.[47]

These self-immolations and self-mutilations evoke not only admiration but also harsh criticism. The biographer of the renowned monk Daoxuan (596–667) objected that suicide was concerned only with the effect of karma, with the body instead of with its cause, the greed for existence. In this case he could refer to Shakyamuni who commented on a monk's self-castration with the words that he would have better cut off his greed than his penis.[48] That such self-immolations and mutilations were not rare, isolated events can be seen in the fact that several imperial edicts tried to forbid them, such as an order from Emperor Huizong (ruled 1101–25): 'The following ordination rites are forbidden: singeing the head, burning the arm, bleeding oneself, and cutting off fingers.'[49] In fact self-mutilations and self-immolations reveal no superior, peaceful spirit but rather demonstrate how in Buddhism aggressive and violent tendencies are directed not outward but inward, similar to the extreme mortifications of early Christian monks or the reciprocal flagellation of the Shi'ites on the day honouring their Imam Hussein.[50]

Writing sutras in one's own blood or mixing one's blood with ochre-coloured ink was once considered highly meritorious. Watercolour-tinted drawing. Museum of Yunju Si.

The North

Destroy the Four Olds – ideas, customs, habits, and cultures – and establish the Four News.

—Propaganda slogan of the Cultural Revolution

Bishan Si 碧山寺

The northern inner region begins at the northern border of Taihuai and stretches over the southern side of the northern terrace. Here are found, among others, the great monastery of Bishan Si, the historically significant cave of Jingang Ku, and four convents.

A kilometre north of the city limits of Taihuai stands the important monastery of Bishan, whose name means 'emerald green mountain'. Earlier it was called Puji Si 普济寺, 'temple of universal salvation', and Guangji Maopeng, 'straw hut of universal salvation'. The monastery is said to go back to the time of the Northern Wei; it was greatly expanded in 1486 by Chan monks and in 1698 was restored from the ground up by Emperor Kangxi (ruled 1661–1722). It is famous throughout all of East Asia for two reasons. First, before the Communist takeover, renowned masters presented and interpreted doctrine on the ordination platform annually between the fifteenth day of the fourth lunar month and the fifteenth day of the seventh lunar month. Second,

Bishan Si is traditionally the most important pilgrim residence on all of Wutai Shan, as it accepts any monk, regardless of his affiliated order, and any layperson, as long as he or she follows the rules of the monastery. For this purpose a large complex was built north of the monastery proper, consisting of several meditation halls, shrines, and two- or three-storey residences. It serves monks and laypeople undertaking extended periods of meditation. In the summer more than 100 monks of the Linji tradition of Chan live in the monastery, as do additional guest monks and laypeople in the separate meditation complex; about 50 monks also spend the winter in the compound. After the wooden entrance pailou come four shrines. Pilgrims first encounter the traditionally designed entrance hall with the four heavenly guardians, the fat future Buddha Maitreya, and General Weituo.

Then they come to the hall dedicated to the Tathagata Vairocana. Over the entrance portal a calligraphic inscription of Emperor Qianlong (ruled 1736–95) proclaims, 'Hall of the thunderous sound'. The name refers to the tradition that

Recently ordained monk with 12 burn marks on his scalp from the Pusajie ordination ceremony.

The future buddha Milefo (Maitreya)
in the two-storey library of the
Chan monastery of Bishan Si.

Buddha Shakyamuni's teachings sounded as loud as thunder and shook the world. In imperial China it was a great honour when the emperor gave a temple a calligraphic inscription done by his own hand. This custom is being revived today, as I saw in Xiantong Si Monastery in the autumn of 2006. There, in a newly built entrance hall, large photographs of former president Jiang Zemin (in office 1993–2003) show how he wrote a calligraphy for the monastery. On the altar in the interior of the hall sits enthroned in the centre a statue of a seated Buddha Vairocana, and to his sides stand Dashizi Pusa (Mahastamaprapta) and Jingang Pusa (Vajrapani). All three figures are surrounded by a flame-shaped mandorla. Along the side walls stand statues of the 12 bodhisat-tvas of complete enlightenment, Yuanjue.

The third hall, the Jietan Ordination Hall, is not only the most significant of the monastery but also one of the most important on Wutai Shan. In the 24.5 m-long and 17 m-deep room lies a 3 m-long white jade statue from Burma of Buddha Shakyamuni in nirvana in a sea of colourful sculpted flowers. Behind this is a smaller, seated statue of Shakyamuni, as he appealed to the earth as witness to his enlightenment. The seated statue was donated in 1980; the figure in repose, in 1995. The 1 m-high, 5 x 5 m ordination platform rises behind the two statues. During official consecra-tion ceremonies about 30 candidates take their places here, in order to receive final ordination after the preceding preparations and rites. On the back end of the dais stands a huge, gold-painted wooden mandorla, which is missing the accom-panying Buddha statue. Along both sides sit seven luohans, with four more on the back wall. Above, at the roofline, 1,000 buddha and bodhisattva statues sit in two rows. These and the 18 luohans participate in the ordination ceremonies as witnesses and lend them an especially solemn note. Today in the region of Wutai Shan only Bishan Monastery has the authorisation to perform

official ordination ceremonies; earlier there were ordinations also in the monasteries of Xiantong and Zhulin. They take place every three years in the summer and must be approved in advance by the appropriate government authorities. The ordination ceremonies of Bishan Si are open to monks and nuns of all Han Chinese schools.

The most precious Buddhist treasure, the teaching of the Buddha in the form of the Tripitaka, is kept in the fourth hall, the Hall of Scripture. A two-storey-tall terracotta statue of Buddha Maitreya, made in 1986, sits European-style in its centre. His hands form the dharmacakra gesture, which symbolises the setting in motion of the Wheel of Dharma. During my visit a monk struck the fish-shaped simandron at 3:00 p.m. to call the monks to common prayer, which took place in the Vairocana Hall. The recitation of sutras in time with the deep, thudding rhythm emanating from the wooden instrument exuded peace and harmony; it was as if time had stopped centuries ago.

The consecration ceremony of monks and nuns

In the Jietan Hall of the monastery of Bishan Si a Chan monk explained to me the course of the ceremony of highest consecration to fully ordained monks, called in Chinese heshang or biqiu (Sanskrit bhikshu), and nuns, nigu (bhikshuni). Before the candidates are admitted to this final consecration they have already taken basic and monastic vows. The very first vows are the 'five vows' of Wu jie, taken by all novices and sometimes also by laypeople who want to dedicate their lives to Buddha. These are:

- Do not kill!
- Do not steal!
- Maintain chastity, no illicit sexual activity!
- Do not lie!
- Do not drink alcohol!

The second level of vows for monks, or shami (Sanskrit: sramanera), and nuns, or xiushi (sramaneri) includes five additional vows:

- No lipstick, no face powder, and no perfume!
- Do not sing or dance or listen to or watch such activities!
- No fancy or expensive bed!
- No private property!
- No eating between the permitted mealtimes!

The future heshang and nigu can, beginning at age 20, take a third step and make all the vows, 250 for monks and 348 for nuns. Monastic ordination is called shou biqiu jie and means literally 'to take on the renunciations of an ordained monk'; the ordination of a nun is called, correspondingly, shou nigu jie. Many monks and nuns, however, forgo full ordination and remain shami and xiushi.

The final, highest consecration is the ordination ceremony of pusajie (Sanskrit: pranidhana), in which monks and nuns vow to follow the path of a bodhisattva. Before they may take the four highest vows they must first provide a meal to all the monks and nuns taking part in the ordination and secondly go through the painful moxa ceremony. They mount the ordination platform and kneel down. Then, on the freshly shaved head of each monk and nun are placed three, six, nine or 12 small balls of incense and dried grass, which are affixed with wax and lit. These little balls burn down and leave behind such scars that no hair will grow there anymore. The candidates must withstand this painful test in motionless prayer. Then they may take the Four Vows of the Bodhisattva. They vow:

- to lead all living beings to enlightenment
- to relieve the suffering of all living beings
- to study the teachings of the great masters
- to perfect themselves tirelessly until they have achieved Buddhahood.

In conclusion the ordained monks and nuns receive their certificates.

A monk of Bishan Si gave me three reasons for carrying out the moxa test: first, perseverance through the pain is thought to show that

Piluzhenafo (Vairocana) Hall in Bishan Si.

In the year 676 the white-clothed Wenshu Pusa, in the form of an elderly man, meets the Indian monk Buddhapala (Fotuoboli) and asks him to bring the original text of a certain sutra from India to China. Southern section of the western wall of Cave 61, Mogao, late tenth century.

the monks and nuns have dispensed with all personal needs and that they are capable of the utmost self-denial, in order to help fellow human beings in need. Secondly, in Chinese Buddhism there arose very early a tradition of honouring the Buddha by singeing a piece of one's own skin. The theoretical background is provided by the *Lotus Sutra* and two apocryphal Chinese sutras: the sutra *Fanwang Jing (Brahmajala Sutra)*, which appeared in China between 420 and 480, and the sutra *Shouleng'yan Jing (Suramgama Sutra)*, which was 'translated' into Chinese around 705. Thirdly, this test leaves behind an easily recognisable sign testifying to the authenticity of a monk's ordination and distinguishes true from false monks. Early on, beginning in the time of the Northern Wei (386–534), Buddhist monasteries attracted dubious and shady figures who eluded the grasp of justice as pseudo-monks. Thus this painful test, which could be undertaken only at the end of a process lasting many years, really attested to the authenticity of a monastic claim.

Jingang Ku 金刚窟 and the Wulang 五郎寺 ancestor shrine

Northwest of Bishan Si, behind the tiny village of Huafang, is the cave of Jingang Ku, 'diamond cave', which is shrouded in legend. The Japanese pilgrim monk Ennin visited the cave in 840 and reported on the stories associated with it. In 676 the Indian monk and translator Buddhapala (Chinese. Fotuoboli), who came from Kashmir, made a pilgrimage to Wutai Shan in the hope of meeting Wenshu Pusa in a vision. As he neared the inner region of Wutai Shan along the southwestern pilgrimage route, Wenshu Pusa met him in the form of an old man. He informed the pilgrim that he would only be able to see the bodhisattva if he brought the original text of the sutra *Sarvadurgati-Parisodhana-Ushnishavijaya-Dharani* (Chinese: *Zunsheng Foding Tuoluoni Jing*) from India. Before Ennin visited the cave, he had seen in the monastery of Zhulin Si a mural illustrating this encounter. It is also shown in the famous mural of Wutai Shan in Cave 61 of Mogao. The monk obeyed, returned to India, and gave the sutra in the capital Chang'an to Emperor Gaozong, who commissioned him to translate it into Chinese. When in 683 he took the original sutra to Wutai Shan, he again met the old man, who revealed himself as Wenshu Pusa and led him to the Diamond Cave. 'Just as Buddhapala entered the cave, it shut itself up and has not been opened again to this day.'[1] Legend holds that a secret tunnel connects the cave to the peak of the northern terrace. A century after Buddhapala's mysterious disappearance a Chan monk had the temple of Banruo, whose name means 'wisdom', built next to the cave. Ennin described it as a high tower, in which he saw a rotating, octagonal bookshelf. During the time of Emperor Daoguang (ruled 1821–50) the temple was expanded into the Tibetan monastery of Pule, whose name means 'universal peace'.[2]

Also near the cave stood the Buddhist ancestor temple of the Wulang family, which likewise features a peculiar history. Yang Wulang was the fifth son of the military commander Yang Ye, who served Emperor Taizong (ruled 976–97) of the Northern Song Dynasty (960–1127). During a battle against the Liao south of Datong in 986, which was lost on account of a betrayal, Yang Ye fell into the hands of his enemies, who starved him to death because he refused to swear loyalty to them. Four of his eight sons, who were nicknamed the 'eight tigers', fell in the battle, and two more were taken prisoner; the fifth son, Yang Wulang, succeeded in breaking out of the encircling troops. He fled to Wutai Shan and was ordained a monk in the monastery of Tai Ping Xin Guo ('the Chinese nation prospers in peace'), which had been founded in 982. After his death the monastery was renamed for him; the name 'Wulang' means simply 'fifth son'. His statue stands in a side shrine of the nearby convent of Jifu Si. In 1968 Marshall Lin Biao, the commander of the Chinese People's Army and one of the most radical compatriots of Mao Zedong, stayed here. Both monasteries were later razed to the ground.

Today in the former monastery district there is a military museum honouring the People's Army. Since it lies in a military area, admittance is forbidden to foreigners. Nevertheless, by pulling the hood of my coat far over my head and joining a group of pilgrims, I made it past the inattentive guard. Of the two once-great monasteries I found only isolated piles of stones, overgrown fragments of walls, and paved pathways. Vegetation has taken over the monastery area, and colourful prayer flags flutter between the many trees. Until 2007 nothing had been rebuilt, aside from the white stupa, which stand just under 4 m high. Hundreds of photographs of officers of the People's Army hang in the pavilions of the military museum. They seem to interest hardly anyone, however; the few pilgrims pay no attention to the museum but instead visit the many ruins and the ostensible entrance to the cave.

Yang Wulang was a son of General Yang Ye, in whose honour he built the Linggong Pagoda on Wutai Shan and who subsequently became a monk. Side chapel at the convent of Jifu Si.

Entrance to the cave of Jingang Ku, in which Wenshu Pusa reportedly sealed up the Indian monk Buddhapala forever in the year 683. The surrounding monastery complex around the Wulang ancestor temple was completely destroyed during the Cultural Revolution. Today a military museum stands on the site.

Jifu Si 集福寺

A few hundred metres south of Bishan Si stands the convent of Jifu Si. The complex, founded in 1875, whose name means 'accumulated good fortune', was until the Cultural Revolution a monastery of esoteric Buddhism. After its complete destruction it has been painstakingly rebuilt as a convent beginning in the 1990s. After the entrance hall with the Four Tian Wang follows the Great Hall with statues of Buddha Shakyamuni and his two favourite students Mahakashyapa and Ananda; behind them are statues of the bodhisattvas Guanyin and Dashizi. In the third, rear hall, the Manjushri Hall, visitors encounter three superbly painted clay figures. To the left sits Puxian Pusa on his white elephant, in the middle Wenshu Pusa on his lion, and to the right Guanyin Pusa on a hou, a mythological combination of a dragon and a lion.

Qifo Si 七佛寺

Just a few hundred metres further south stands the convent of Qifo. It was founded during the time of the Northern Song (960–1127), restored under the Ming in 1466, and converted into a Tibeto-Mongolian monastery under Emperor Kangxi (ruled 1661–1722). After vandalisation by the Red Guards, which left only a few walls standing, in 1994 it began to return to operation as a convent of the Chan School. The name Qifo means 'seven Buddhas', and refers to the seven Buddhas of the past: Vipasyin, Sikhin, Visvabuj, Krakucchandra, Kanakamuni, Kasyapa and Shakyamuni. They are portrayed in the Great Prayer Hall in the form of white jade statues. South of the monastery buildings stands a seven-storey, 22 m-tall pagoda made of white marble, which is circled by pilgrims 12, 108 or 1,080 times. In early 2007 a gold-painted

Guanyin Pusa on his mythological chimera called a hou made up of a dragon and a lion (left) and Puxian Pusa on his elephant (right), Wenshu Hall, Jifu Si.

statue of the standing bodhisattva Wenshu Pusa was erected between the pagoda and the monastery buildings. Like Pushou Si, the convent runs a small summer university for advanced female students from China, Hong Kong, Taiwan, Europe and the United States.

Guangming Si 光明寺

Northeast of the monastery of Bishan Si, on the eastern bank of the Qingshui River, stands the convent of Guangming, whose name means 'shining light'. It was ostensibly founded during the time of the Northern Qi (550–77) and completely renovated under the Ming (1368–1644). The stately monastery was then called Xi Tian Si, which means 'monastery of the western heaven' and indicated its connection to the Jingtu School, which proclaimed a rebirth in the Western Paradise of Amitabha. It was completely destroyed before the Cultural Revolution and its reconstruction as a Jingtu convent began after the start of the new millennium. When I visited

it in early summer of 2007, there stood only two empty residences and the Heavenly Guardian Hall with the two Erjiang generals Heng and Ha, which had been built in 2002. General Ha holds a club in his right hand and a diamond bell in his left; his mouth is open. General Heng, by contrast, has his mouth closed and holds a sword and a ring.[3] The four Tian Wang, for their part, are identifiable by their attributes, as follows:[4]

- Vaishravana (Chinese: Duowen) holds a pearl-spitting mongoose (or, as in this monastery, a white bird) in his hand, symbolising wealth, as well as a standard representing the victory of Buddhism; he commands the other three Tian Wang and is lord of the north and the winter. In China his body is coloured either green or black.
- Dhritarashtra (Chinese: Chiguo) plays a pipa, a kind of lute; sometimes he holds a sword instead of a lute. He is lord of the east and the spring; his body is red or blue-green.
- Virudhaka (Chinese: Zengzhang) holds a double-edged sword and is yellow, red or white; he is lord of the south and the summer.

The 22 m-tall marble pagoda of Qifo Si and the statue of Wenshu Pusa erected in 2007, as seen from Shangshi Tayuan Si.

The convent of Qifo Si.

The Tian Wang Duowen
(Vaishravana) and Guangmu
(Virupaksha) as well as the Erjiang
general Ha (left to right), in the
Tian Wang Hall, Guangming Si.

From left to right: the Erjiang
Heng and the Tian Wang
Zengshang (Virudhaka) and
Chiguo (Dhritarashtra) in the
Tian Wang Hall, Guangming Si.

It is said of the white pagoda in the centre of Baohua Si that it was miraculously flown to its present location in three parts 'independently' from central and eastern Tibet as well as from Nepal.

- Virupaksha (Chinese: Guangmu) holds a snake or a dragon and is white or red; he is lord of the west and the autumn.

In the large courtyard countless logs lay on the ground; there were great piles of gray and red tiles, and dozens of bags of cement were stacked along the walls of the Tian Wang Hall. I got the impression that construction had stalled because of a lack of money. This was confirmed by the two nuns living in a poor stone hut. They said that the abbess was in the process of raising money. It was unknown when construction would begin again.

Baohua Si 宝华寺

Baohua Si, whose name means 'temple of the precious [lotus] blossom', stands just under 4 km north of Taihuai in the Taergou valley at the southern foot of the northern terrace. It was founded under the Ming as a convent of the Huayan School and was originally known as Zahua Si. In 1711 it was completely renovated and converted into a Tibetan Gelugpa monastery. It received the name Baohua Si only in 1903. The changing of monastery names is not unusual in China, because monasteries can receive new names on the occasion of an imperial donation or visit, when a new abbot assumes office, or if the monks or nuns feel drawn to another school. After the destructions of the Cultural Revolution Abbot Yanlin has led reconstruction since 1990. The main buildings of the monastery are the Hall of the Heavenly Guardians, the shrine in honour of Wenshu Pusa, and the Great Prayer Hall. In the centre of the first courtyard stands a 4 m-high, bell-shaped pagoda in the Tibetan style. It bears the Tibetan kalachakra symbol and is dedicated to the mother of the first Buddha of the past Dipankara. It is said that the square foundation of the pagoda flew to the monastery from central Tibet, the bell-shaped body of the stupa from the eastern Tibetan monastery of Kumbum, and the steeple from Nepal.

During my visit in autumn of 2006 Baohua Si and its 15 Jingtu monks made an unfavourable

A temple at Qifo Si, destroyed during the Cultural Revolution (1966–76). Photograph from *c.* 1991.

The 'Great Proletarian Cultural Revolution'

The Cultural Revolution, which lasted from 1966 to 1976, was a campaign of Mao Zedong (1893–1976) that created civil-war-like circumstances in China and led the country to the brink of the abyss. With it Mao tried to eliminate his political opponents and regain his former position of political power. The political background was formed by the 'Great Leap Forward', the industrial policy initiated by Mao that failed spectacularly. This had as its goal both to raise the Communist consciousness and to overtake the Soviet Union industrially. To this end, beginning in 1958 Mao enforced the collectivisation of all areas of life and wealth and in all of China forced the production of steel to the detriment of agriculture. This led not only to the production of inferior steel but also to agricultural collapse, which resulted in a catastrophic famine, to which 20 to 30 million people had fallen victim by 1961. President Liu Shaoqi (1898–1969) condemned the Great Leap – and, indirectly, Mao as well – for the human tragedy. The centrist pragmatists Liu Shaoqi and Deng Xiaoping (1904–97) then brought both agriculture and industrial production back to strong growth and increased standard of living of the people. Mao, however, lost power in the party and was relegated to a symbolic figure.

Since Mao was in an inferior position in internal party power struggles in 1962, he decided to seize the party from the outside. He mobilised the easily manipulated youth, many of whom were unemployed, to lead the class struggle against the internal enemies of the people; that is, the party leadership and the government. Increasing tensions with the Soviet Union gave him an additional pretence for criticising the party leadership. First he mounted the so-called Great Proletarian Cultural Revolution against the traditional ideas of culture, cultural goods and all intellectuals. In the summer of 1966, under the motto 'War against the Four Olds' – old ideas, old customs, old habits, and old culture – youths organised into the Red Guards attacked first artists, writers and professors as reactionary enemies and traitors. Throughout China a hunt for 'anti-proletarian elements' began, during which university professors were openly beaten, humiliated, and forced to run the gauntlet in the streets. Universities and high schools ceased all instruction and closed.

The lust for senseless destruction having been stimulated, throughout China the Red Guards began to raze cultural sites such as temples, monasteries, mosques, cemeteries and palaces. They burned paintings, shattered terracotta statues and melted down metal figures. The Red Guards also violently invaded private homes, where they forced people to hand over everything 'old', such as artworks, religious pictures and statues, and non-Marxist books. Anyone who resisted was beaten, arrested, and sent to a labour camp. In Tibet, Xinjiang, and Inner Mongolia, hatred toward ethnic minorities reinforced the destructive wrath. This orgy of violence was escaped only by cultural goods of national significance, whose military protection had been ordered by Premier Zhou Enlai (1898–1976), or when army units stood up to the Red Guards in the provinces. Finally, local administrators and party associations protected their cultural sites by seizing monasteries and temples, white-washing the murals, and using the buildings as party meeting rooms, workhouses or granaries. While Westerners are more or less familiar with the destruction of Tibetan cultural goods that took place at that time, they have turned a blind eye to the devastation of cultural goods carried out by Mao in China proper.

The persecution of intellectuals was simply a prologue to a more comprehensive hunt for human beings. Soon officially pardoned former officers and functionaries of the Kuomintang Party, which had been suppressed in 1949, were arrested by the tens of thousands, sentenced to forced labour, or shot. The Cultural Revolution gathered momentum, so that Mao was able to attack and destroy his alleged personal enemies. Among the most prominent victims, all highly decorated veterans, were the former defence minister and marshal Peng Dehuai (1898–1974), who was badly tortured by members of the Red Guards in 1966; President Liu Shaoqi, who died in 1969 as a result of the torture he suffered two years earlier; Deng Xiaoping; and his son Deng Pufang, whom the Guards so abused that he became paraplegic.

The most driving and radical forces were the head of the internal security apparatus, despised by the people, Kang Sheng (1898–1975); Marshal and Defence Minister Lin Biao (1917–71); and Mao's fourth wife Jiang Qing (1914–91), who spearheaded the Cultural Revolution and was the most prominent member of the so-called Gang of Four. But when China threatened to collapse into complete chaos, Defence Minister Lin Biao mobilised the army, which brutally crushed the rebellion of the Red Guards. Now the army, instead of the weakened party, ruled China, and its leader, Lin Biao, was officially named successor to Mao. Since Mao saw that his return to power was threatened, and Lin Biao demanded an end to the Cultural Revolution and the return to social and political normalcy, Mao and his wife Jiang Qing began to plot against the defence minister. He died in September 1971 in a still-unexplained plane crash; presumably the cause was sabotage. The Cultural Revolution came to an end only with Mao Zedong's death on 9 September 1976, and the fall of the Gang of Four a month later. In those years priceless cultural treasures were destroyed and about five million people lost their lives. As I heard often in China, 'the true liberation of China came only with Mao's death'.

impression. As soon as I arrived a monk begged me for dollars and another monk explained that he had left his home monastery Wanfo Ge in Taihuai because there was too little to eat and too much work there. The monastery, whose restoration was finally completed in 1998, was grubby and dilapidated. The closed Great Hall, dedicated in 1998, seemed to stand on the brink of collapse. In the second courtyard a giant pile of coal was heaped up in front of the Prayer Hall, and a large iron bell languished, silent and rusting. Rubbish lay all over the ground. The Manjushri Hall, erected in 1990, had obviously been out of use for a fairly long time, as I saw through the windows that the statues in it had never been unpacked and countless cardboard boxes were piled up. The two closed up halls suggested that no communal ceremonies had taken place here for quite some time.

Miaoding An 庙顶庵

The nunnery of Miaoding An lies 1.5 km northwest of Baohua Si in the neighbouring Zixia Valley, near the western branch of the Qingshui River. The Chan master Hanshan founded the monastery in 1575 and called it Mituo Si 弥托寺, which means 'temple of Amitabha'. The present name means essentially 'temple on the highest point of the monastery'. Like most monasteries outside Taihuai, it was destroyed during the Cultural Revolution. In 1996 Abbess Shenglian began the reconstruction of Miaoding An as a convent of the Jingtu School. The current 43-year-old abbess welcomed me very cordially in autumn of 2006. She took over the office from her predecessor Shenglian in 2005 and now leads 20 nuns and four novices, who may be accepted as nuns after a two-year novitiate.

In front of the Tian Wang shrine bubbles the well of the convent, which has no access to running water. In the inner courtyard a white, 4 m-tall statue of Guanyin greets visitors, who

then proceed to the Great Hall. In the modern, very clean room sit enthroned the Buddhas of the Three Times, as well as gold-painted statues of Amitabha, Puxian, and Wenshu Pusa; on the side walls stand figures of the 18 arhats. On the floor, white cushions in the form of an open, white-and-pink lotus blossom await the nuns – similar to the cushions held by the buddha and bodhisattva statues in the ancient monasteries of Foguang and Nanchan.

Upon leaving I asked the abbess whether there was a shortage of novice nuns and monks on Wutai Shan. She laughed and said that more and more young, educated urban people are seeking entrance into monasteries. Most will leave the monastery at the end of the novitiate, whether to study at a university or to return to secular life, while a minority choose to stay after taking final vows. When I expressed my astonishment that well-off young people with career prospects entered the monastery, she replied with a parable:

A poor woodcutter sought from Buddha the ability to take on other, desirable forms. The Buddha granted him this gift but warned him of eventual disadvantages that could result from such changes in existence. But the woodcutter was dazzled by the potential for social advancement and transformed himself into a rich merchant. He enjoyed his new wealth, until two robbers attacked him on a trip and threatened to kill him. To save his life he had no choice but to transform himself into an eagle and fly away from the daggers into the sky. In the air, however, such bad weather assaulted him that he adopted the form of his presumed aggressor and became heavy clouds. But soon he discovered that great forests growing on the steep mountain slopes would force the clouds to rain. So he transformed himself into a strong oak tree, which gazed haughtily over the smaller trees and the valley lying deep below. Suddenly a great pain, which he felt way down at ground level, disturbed

The convent of Miaoding An.

his sublime and self-important feeling. Then he heard the clear tone of an axe striking wood. At each sound his pain increased. He looked down and saw to his horror that a woodcutter had begun to chop him down. In a panic, he again saw no other option than again to take on the form of his aggressor – he was again a woodcutter.

'You see', concluded the abbess, 'every form of existence entails its own dangers. Thus it is better not to be driven by greed for material things but rather to overcome this by following the Eightfold Path. A monastic life offers the best conditions for this.'

Zhaoyuanwai Tang 赵员外塘

About 2 km northwest of the nunnery and around 350 to 400 m higher in elevation lies the small shrine of Zhaoyuanwai Tang, the 'lake of the magistrate Zhao'. Two monks of the Jingtu School, who regularly descend to the hamlet near Miaoding An Monastery, live there.[5]

The East

You should not assume that this sort of sitting [in quiet meditation under a tree in the forest] is true quiet sitting! ... Not abandoning the principles of the Way and yet showing yourself in the activities of a common mortal – this is quiet sitting.

—Vimalakirti Sutra[1]

Shangshi Tayuan Si 上士塔院寺

The eastern inner region extends from the newly built monastery of Shangshi Tayuan Si in the north to the Guanyin and Huayan caves in the south. All the monasteries and caves are found east of the Qingshui River.

On the eastern bank of the Qingshui River, at the same height as the Pushou Monastery that lies opposite it, is the monastery of Shangshi Tayuan Si. It was destroyed during the Cultural Revolution but reconstruction started in 2004. Of the old monastery, whose name means 'courtyard (yuan) of the pagodas (ta) of the master (shangshi)', only a stele from Emperor Kangxi (ruled 1661–1722) still stands. As of early summer of 2007, the eight monks and their few labourers had erected only the skeleton of the three-storey main hall. In front of this hall stand three white, Tibetan-looking pagodas with the Tibetan kalachakra symbol, the middle one of which is dedicated to Master Nenghai (1886–1967). South of the monastery a narrow iron bridge crosses a small

The 'flying' luohan Jigong looks down from the ceiling at pilgrims in the Buddha Hall of Puhua Si.

ravine, on the other side of which a mountain path leads to the monastery of Dailuoding. Because the monastery of Shangshi Tayuan Si stands on a slightly elevated site, it offers a good view of the northern part of Taihuai

Shancai Dong 善财洞

The monastery of Shancai Dong – 'cave of Shancai' (Sudhana) – constitutes, together with Shanshancai Dong, the 'upper Shancai cave monastery', a double monastery of the Jingtu School. The lower monastery was founded during the time of Emperor Qianlong (ruled 1736–95) and stands near the market, close to the start of the 1,080 stairs leading up to Dailuoding Monastery. It is dedicated to the ideal of the perfect pilgrim Shancai, who configured his life as a pilgrimage to his own Buddha-nature. After visitors have passed through one of the three portals of the massive entrance gate, they reach the Great Hall. In it a statue of Buddha Shakyamuni sits enthroned, flanked by Puxian

Shangshancai Dong 上善财洞

Bridge leading to the monastery of Shangshi Tayuan Si, which is under reconstruction.

Just under 100 m above the Shangcai Monastery is Suddhana's meditation cave, Shangshancai. Tradition says that during the construction of the two cave shrines during the Ming Dynasty (1368–1644) three ancient bronze statues of Maitreya, Wenshu Pusa and Shancai were found in the ground, which would suggest there had been an earlier temple. Unfortunately here, too, the statues fell victim to the Cultural Revolution; they have been replaced with modern figures. In the front, larger cave a bronze statue of Guanyin welcomes pilgrims; in the rear cave, one of Shancai does. This smaller cave is also connected to Wenshu Pusa, who is said to have debated with Vimalakirti here.[2] The layman Vimalakirti is the main character of the *Vimalakirti Sutra* of Mahayana from the end of the first century CE. He used his wealth and wisdom to help all living beings. Once he pretended to be sick so that the people of the city would come to his sickbed, and he could teach them. When Buddha Shakyamuni heard of this, he instructed first his 500 students and then all bodhisattvas to visit Vimalakirti and ascertain the state of his health. But they feared his phenomenal wisdom and keen intellect, since earlier he had rebuked them all. Only Wenshu Pusa dared to visit him. Vimalakirti immediately took over the discussion and taught those present that a married layman, a woman, a dragon maiden and even a repentant criminal could experience enlightenment. In this way he stood the old school of Theravada on its head, since for this school only monks, not even nuns, could gain enlightenment; nuns and laypeople could only hope to be reborn as monks as a result of a well-lived life. The *Vimalakirti Sutra* was a radical reaction to the elitist requirements of Theravada and was very popular among the laity. This famous discussion is portrayed several times in the murals of Dunhuang, for instance in caves 103, 159 and 237.

and Wenshu Pusa. In front of Shakyamuni stand two brass figures, which look very similar, of Shancai and the dragon maiden Lungnü, whom Wenshu Pusa converted to Buddhism. While Shancai by his example spurs pilgrims to unfailing efforts in pursuit of Buddhahood, Lungnü's fate teaches that on the path to enlightenment even the most disadvantageous karma can be overcome.

The Great Hall leads to the Maitreya Hall, with its metal statues of Guanyin, Maitreya, and Wenshu Pusa, as well as Shancai once again. Immediately in front of Maitreya, on the altar, is a seated figure of Tsongkhapa (1357–1419), founder of the Tibetan Gelugpa Order. The statue recalls the fact that Shancai Dong was originally founded as a Tibetan monastery. In the rear of the hall pilgrims again find statues of Lungnü and Shancai, which stand at the sides of Guanyin Pusa. Behind the Maitreya shrine, ten new, multi-storey red-painted pagodas rise into the sky.

Guanyin Pusa (Avalokiteshvara) stands between the enlightened dragon maiden Lungnü (left) and the model pilgrim Shancai (right). Rear of the Milefo Hall, Shancai Dong.

Shancai Dong lies at the foot of the 1,080-step stairway that leads to Dailuoding Monastery.

Founder of the Tibetan Gelugpa
order, Tsongkhapa (1357–1419),
in front of Milefo (Maitreya).
Milefo Hall, Shancai Dong.

The young pilgrim Shancai, rear cave of Shangshancai Dong.

Dailuoding Si 黛螺顶寺

After the Shangshancai shrine I accompanied a group of pilgrims on the way to the monastery of Dailuoding – 'temple of the peak of the dark shells' – which stands 300 m above the valley floor. Lazy pilgrims and tourists take the chairlift, motivated pilgrims climb the 1,080 steps on foot, and those who either want to earn a lot of merit or rid themselves of many sins measure off the entire length with their bodies, which entails 1,080 kowtows and a four- or five-hour effort. After about 200 steps pilgrims are offered another opportunity to earn merit. A man has in a cage five pigeons, which he sells for RMB 20 (US$3). By buying a bird and setting it free, they earn moral merit, because they have liberated a living being from a miserable imprisonment. I seized the opportunity and 'freed' two pigeons, which surely flew back to their master's dovecote straight away to be offered for sale again the next day. This custom is widespread in the Buddhist part of Asia.

In ancient Tibet, for instance, virtuous Buddhists ransomed caught fish or yaks on their way to the slaughterhouse. This custom benefits all parties: the merchant gets money, the believer earns merit, and the animal is not eaten for the moment. In the spring of 2007 I observed the same practice even in predominantly Muslim Pakistan. In the city of Lahore a merchant in front of the Golden Mosque held over 20 pigeons captive in a cage, selling them to benefactors for 25 rupees (US$0.50) so that they could set the birds free.

Near a small terrace halfway up the ascent hundreds of metal locks are fastened onto chains that are decorated with prayer flags. The locks symbolise the personal desires that enslave human beings and prolong the suffering earthly existence over many rebirths. Pilgrims promise to leave these desires here. They throw the key into the abyss so that the desires stay imprisoned here forever and can no longer torment them. The hanging keys have another meaning as well, however, as they are said to symbolically maintain

It is considered meritorious to buy a pigeon from a vendor in order to set it free, although the pigeon is trained to fly back to the vendor's cage.

Pious pilgrims measure out the 1,080-step staircase to Dailuoding Si Monastery with their bodies.

a young love for eternity. Young couples have a phrase like 'eternal love' or 'eternal happiness' engraved on the lock and then together hang it on the chain. They also throw the key away as a sign that their vow of love will never be broken. On the way I passed innumerable pilgrims who prostrated themselves at each step. There were young and old, athletes and overweight people, lone pilgrims and married couples who asked for the blessing of children, as well as a monk who sent a text message between kowtows.

The monastery of Dailuoding offers a wide view of the village of Taihuai, of a labyrinth of more than a dozen walled monasteries, and of the northern, central and southern terraces. Seen from here, the entire Wutai Shan region appears as a single, gigantic temple complex.

The monastery was founded by the Ming emperor Chenghua (ruled 1465–87) as the Foding Convent, after which it was renovated by Emperor Wanli (ruled 1573–1620). The present name, Dailuoding, was given by

Emperor Qianlong in 1786. On previous pilgrimages bad weather had always prevented the emperor from showing his respect to the statues of Wenshu Pusa on all five terraces. For this reason the monk Qingyuan had copies of statues of the five manifestations of Wenshu Pusa erected in the Manjushri Hall, as they stood in the temples of the five terraces at that time. Now the aging emperor could symbolically complete the strenuous pilgrimage to the five terraces at the monastery of Dailuoding.[3]

Today more than 20 Jingtu monks live at Dailuoding. As at all monasteries, right beside the entrance a table with sticks of incense invites pilgrims to light a few of them from the nearby stove. The faithful usually take exactly three sticks, since they symbolise the Buddha, the Dharma, and the community of believers. In the Manjushri Hall pilgrims bow before the five brass statues of Manjushri sitting behind glass, and in the following Great Hall, before the Buddhas of the Three Times.

Padlocks hanging on chains
symbolise either the locking up
of morally reprehensible desires
or eternal fidelity between lovers.
In the background one can see
the monastery of Pusading Si.

The monastery of Dailuoding Si sits enthroned above the cave-monastery of Shangshancai and, below that, Shancai Dong.

Shijiafo with his two chief disciples Anan and Dajiaye in the Great Hall of the Buddhas of the Three Times in Dailuoding Si.

Wenshu Si 文殊寺

Southwest of Taihuai, on the eastern bank of the river, stands the monastery of Wenshu Si, founded in the eighteenth century, which belongs to the monastery of Wanfo Ge. Only three monks of esoteric Buddhism, Mi Zong, live in the rather stately monastery. The monastery, which was destroyed in the Cultural Revolution, was rebuilt in 1994. The Great Hall is dominated by a new brass statue that stands more than 3 m high, of the Tantric meditation god (Yidam) Kalachakra (Chinese: Zhuanlun Wangfo) from the Kalachakra Tantra, in the sexual union called Yab Yum with his partner (Shakti), called Vishvamata (Zhuxiang Foma).[4] Kalachakra has four heads, 24 arms, and two legs; Vishvamata, four heads, eight arms, and two legs. The tantra was introduced in Tibet in 1027 and is the final significant tantra; its name means 'wheel of time', or 'wheel of becoming'. Kalachakra is one of the most important deities of the Tibetan Gelugpa

School, and the Dalai Lama regularly provides private and public initiations and introductions into the teaching of Kalachakra. The paintings on the two side walls show the 500 luohans. In the lower frieze, 25 future, peaceful rulers and the victorious king of Shambala are portrayed on the left, and on the right 12 sequences from the life of Buddha Shakyamuni. The mythical kingdom of Shambala, said to lie northwest of India, serves as the homeland of the Kalachakra teaching.

On the walls of the inner courtyard stand 200 stone steles with poems about Wutai Shan from various authors. One of these is the eight-line poem of the monk Zheng Cheng from the monastery of Jinge Si:

Such marvellous temples stand on the sunny peak,

Look at them and the fascination of them never ends,

The pleasure of looking and everything changes,

Monks, nuns, and laypeople studying Buddhist books. Mural in the Great Hall of Wenshu Si.

I bow reverentially before the merciful face of the Buddha,

Let a cord fall from the window and rain falls over 1,000 mountains,

The wind from the mountain blows close by the window,

Standing by the rail, what do I think?

From the moon falls icy fog and it conceals itself in the cold heavens.

Puhua Si 普化寺

Likewise on the left bank of the Qingshui stands the large monastery of Puhua Si, which today belongs to the Jingtu School. In the winter it houses 30 monks and in summer 50. As I soon noticed, Puhua is unusual in more than one respect. In front of the monastery entrance, a long stone wall prevents evil spirits from entering. Not Buddhist but Daoist figures are portrayed

in the three medallions, however. In the centre medallion stand three older men with long, thin beards: Fu embodies happiness, Lu, good health and Shou, longevity.[5] On the interior of the spirit wall, however, I encountered a medallion with the Buddhist figures Lungnü, Guanyin, and Shancai. The puzzle was solved when I learned the history of the monastery. It was built in the last years of the Ming Dynasty, between 1628 and 1644, as a Daoist monastery to honour the celestial king Yü Huangdi. Later the Daoist shrine was reinterpreted as Indra's palace, since the Hindu god-king Indra (Chinese: Dishi) entered the Buddhist pantheon as a powerful patron god. In 1922 the institution of the 'Nine Daoist Palaces' was converted into the Buddhist monastery of Puhua, whose name means 'universal transformation'. The remodelling of the buildings lasted until 1935, making Puhua the last monastery built on Wutai Shan before the Communists seized power.

The spirit wall is followed by the Tian Wang Hall with statues of the celestial kings and two mounted luohans: Fuhu, whose name

Wenshu Pusa as an old man, the way he appeared to the Indian monk Buddhapala (Fotuoboli) in 676. Great Hall, Puhua Si.

means 'tamer of the tiger', rides a tiger, and
Shang Lung rides a dragon. The fact that both
luohans ride wild animals symbolises not only
their magical powers but also that they have
mastered their fantasies and passions. While
in the Great Hall seated figures of Wenshu
Pusa, Shakyamuni, and Puxian Pusa receive
pilgrims, there is here an unusual portrayal
of Wenshu Pusa as an elderly man with a
white beard. The statue refers to the tradition
that the bodhisattva met the itinerant monk
Buddhapala in 676 in the form of an old man.

The Three Buddha Hall also offers visitors
a surprising sight. The Buddhas of the Three
Times sit enthroned on the high altar, but it is
the figures of the 18 luohans that catch the eye.
Sixteen arhats sit along the side walls, and two –
among them the famous Chinese monk Jigong
– hover in space. Jigong was a legendary monk
from the twelfth century who had clairvoyant
powers and could fly. One day he saw a mighty
mountain, coming from India, fly to China
and threaten a village where a great wedding

celebration was taking place. At first Jigong was
puzzled as to how he could persuasively warn
the wedding celebrants of the impending but
not yet visible danger. He flew quickly to the
village and kidnapped the bride in front of all
the guests, who angrily chased after both of
them. No sooner had the guests left the village
than the flying mountain buried it. Thanks to
this ploy, the villagers escaped certain death.

In the shrine all the luohans have odd if not
grotesque facial features, which is a characteristic of Chinese portrayals of arhats. This is
to symbolise that as enlightened beings they
stand outside everyday norms, similar to the
great masters of Chan. Their appearance is
just as surprising as the behaviour of a Chan
master can be unpredictable. Finally, the last
hall was rebuilt in 2000, after it had been
destroyed in 1967 by a landslide caused by
heavy rains. In it lies a gold-painted buddha
in the pose of entrance into nirvana, and the
most important scenes from his earthly life
are painted on the walls in a modern style.

A heavenly guardian and the past
buddha, Randengfo (Dipankara),
Buddha Hall, Puhua Si.

Luohans along the southern wall of the Buddha Hall, Puhua Si.

Guanyin Dong 观音洞

In a side valley, 3 km east of Taihuai, the cave monastery of Guanyin Dong clings to the mountain like an eagle's nest. It is venerated by Mongolians and Tibetans in particular, because not only Bodhisattva Guanyin but also two of his human incarnations are said to have meditated here. The first such incarnation was the Sixth Dalai Lama (1683–1706 or 1746), who reportedly did not die in Tibet in 1706 but rather found refuge on Wutai Shan. The Sixth Dalai Lama, Tsangyang Gyatso, enthroned at age 14, was an enigmatic personality. After breaking into tears during his tonsuring as a novice, four years later he refused to receive consecration as a monk and threatened suicide if his wishes were not respected. He preferred to occupy himself as a

gifted archer and poet and to court pretty women. He rejected the role of religious leader of Gelugpa, plunging the order and Tibet into a crisis. In 1706 Emperor Kangxi ordered the deportation of the Dalai Lama to China. He was arrested and died, supposedly of poisoning, at the end of 1706 in the present-day province of Qinghai. After half a century, however, a Mongolian monk published a document claiming that the Dalai Lama had fled and found refuge in a cave on Wutai Shan for six years.[6]

By contrast, the other incarnation of Guanyin connected to the cave monastery did in fact stay here. This was the thirteenth Dalai Lama (1876–1933), who fled here in exile in 1904 ahead of the British invasion and lived on Wutai Shan in the summer of 1908. The Dalai Lama remained politically active here and

Brass statue of the Sixth Dalai Lama, who reportedly lived incognito in a cave at the Guanyin Monastery after his escape from Tibet in 1706. Guanyin Chapel, Guanyin Dong.

The Tibetan Sakyapa master Gyanak Tulku extends a ray of light over the Yangtze as a bridge for his students. Guanyin Chapel, Guanyin Dong.

established contacts with Western dignitaries. Thus he had talks with the then-Russian officer and later Finnish president C.G. Mannerheim, as well as with the American diplomat and explorer of Tibet, Minister William Rockhill; he asked him for advice on whether he should return to Lhasa.[7] As a Tibetan monk from Labrang informed me, the Eleventh Panchen Lama, Gyaltsen Norbu, appointed by China, made a pilgrimage to Guanyin Dong, as did the Seventeenth Karmapa Urgyen Trinley Dorje. However, heavy snowfall prevented the Fourteenth Dalai Lama from visiting Wutai Shan on his return from Beijing in 1955.

Today ten Tibetan monks from the East Tibetan monastery of Labrang live year-round at Guanyin Dong, which in the summer is one of the most popular pilgrimage destinations for Tibetans. As I neared the monastery, a few monks standing around the entrance gate were engaging in athletic activities. Three monks turned pirouettes in a wild dance, as they do at the annual Cham celebrations in which masked dancers embody stags and skeletons. The young, strong abbot, for his part, used the upper part of the iron gate as a high bar and demonstrated bold moves that would have done a gymnast proud. As I had observed on my previous travels in Tibet, it is not uncommon for novices and younger monks to play sports, not least as a counterweight to the long sitting during the communal recitation of sutras. In the early summer of 2007 Tibetan monks even played soccer every afternoon on an empty stretch of ground north of Pushou Monastery.

Another striking thing about this monastery was the loud barking of dogs that greeted me. Half a dozen Tibetan mastiffs romped around the monastery courtyard; accustomed to the visits of pilgrims, however, they took no notice of me. In contrast with Chinese monasteries, where dogs are unwanted, it is normal to encounter dogs in Tibetan monasteries. In Tibet no nomadic family

could protect their herds from wolves without the fearsome mastiffs, and at monasteries as well they loudly announce every visitor.

Above the Great Hall, rebuilt on the floor of the valley, is the erstwhile sanctum of the Thirteenth Dalai Lama, in which new scrolls hang on the walls and an 11-headed brass statue of Guanyin stands. If pilgrims follow the steep steps further upwards, they go by reliefs of stupas, buddhas, and masters carved into the rocks, on which they place a small coin as an offering. Halfway to the Guanyin chapel is another cave, where the Tibetan Sakyapa monk Phagpa (1235–80) reportedly stayed in 1257. Finally they reach the highest shrine dedicated to Guanyin, where a rare brass statue of the Sixth Dalai Lama stands. A mural portrays how the Sakyapa master Gyanak Tulku from the thirteenth century laid a beam of light across the Yangtze, so his students could cross the river.

The Gelugpa cave monastery Guanyin Dong is one of the most popular destinations on Wutai Shan for Tibetan and Mongolian pilgrims.

Huayan Dong 华严洞

A few kilometres east of Guanyin Dong a second cave monastery, Huayan Dong, is nestled high above the Xi Xian valley like a swallow's nest. The monastery's name, 'wonderful (hua) rigour (yan)', fits the location, as the small monastery is accessible only by a steep and narrow path, which is impassable for days after snowfalls in the winter. Three Jingtu monks live here, two of whom hold out during the very cold winters as well. As I knocked on the entrance gate, wheezing heavily, a mastiff began to bark loudly and all three monks hurried out, astonished that a 'long-nose' wanted to visit their modest cave monastery. Hardly any pilgrims stray to their remote shrine. The earlier main shrine in the Huayan cave was reached through a tunnel carved out of the rock, with the mouth of the cave offering a spectacular view of the valley. In a rather long building nestled up against the rock, there is a little prayer shrine; next to it is the small Puxian cave.

Wenshu Dong 文殊洞

Almost an hour's walk further east of the Huayan cave, the infrequent pilgrims reach a third cave monastery. It is called Wenshu Dong, because the bodhisattva of that name is said to have once meditated in this natural cave. The tiger-taming luohan Fuhu, whose statue stands in the entrance hall of the monastery of Puhua, is also said to have lived here with his tiger. Like the other two cave monasteries of the Xi Xian valley, this one was also destroyed during the Cultural Revolution. When I visited the shrine in 2007, three nuns had been leading the rebuilding for a few years. Two belonged to the school of Jingtu and one to Mi Zong. After the completion of construction of their small shrine, the energetic nuns had a meditation hall built. They were now taking on the construction of a larger temple on the valley floor, where I saw a dozen stonemasons at work. In the narrow cave there are three statues of Manjushri, two new ones of bronze in the Tibetan style, in which the

Monks from the eastern Tibetan
monastery of Labrang using the
entrance gate of Guanyin Dong
as a gymnastics apparatus.

The main shrine of Huayan Dong is accessible only through a tunnel.

bodhisattva wields a flaming sword, and a third of stone and in the Chinese style. These statues, completely blackened by soot from the butter lamps, could be old and might have been chiselled out of the rock before the Cultural Revolution.

Tiewa Si 铁瓦寺

My quest for the monastery of Tiewa Si, whose name means 'iron tile', remained fruitless. On a Chinese map from 1993, which was based on a significantly older sketch from before the Cultural Revolution, the monastery was some 6 or 7 km east of the Wenshu cave monastery. In another Chinese brochure I had read that the monastery

had been destroyed during the Japanese occupation in the late 1930s. Despite hours of searching I found no trace of the monastery until I came to a hamlet of fewer than ten poor houses. Goats and sheep searched for sparse grass between stone blocks. When I asked an elderly farmer about the ruins of a monastery, he said hesitantly, after long thought, that a very long time ago a monastery may have stood north of the last house. He led me to a place where there was nothing to see except for a low stone terrace and a three-part arch. While it cannot be ruled out that the arch belonged to a temple and that the stone houses, plastered with clay, had been built with materials from the monastery ruins, I found no positive proof that Tiewa had in fact stood here.

The luohan Fuhu is said once to have lived with his tiger in the cave of Wenshu Dong. Tian Wang Hall, Puhua Si.

The South

Buddha Amitabha will soon send an incarnation of Manjushri to the West to teach there a form of Buddhism appropriate for today's Western zeitgeist.

—Abbess Shi Chang Long, 2007

Shuxiang Si 殊像寺

The southern inner region encompasses those monasteries that stand south of the city limits in the valley of the Qingshui River and on the neighbouring mountainsides. This region begins in the north at Shuxiang Si and ends about 25 km further south at Gufo Si.

One of the most distinguished monasteries of Wutai Shan is Shuxiang Si, which stands 1.5 km south of Taihuai. The monastery's name means 'image of [Wen]shu'. It refers to a legend, according to which the bodhisattva revealed the great Manjushri statue to its creator in a vision, similar to what happened at Xiantong Si. In the Wenshu Pusa Hall of the monastery, which was founded at the time of the Tang Dynasty (618–907), stands a truly majestic 9.87 m-tall statue of the bodhisattva. He sits on a lotus throne, which is carried by a lion with a green mane and a blue body. Eight bodhisattvas flank the main figure, and on both side walls, dwelling in their mountain caves, are the 500 luohans, whom I imagined coming to life on Wutai Shan. The

monastery, which was completely rebuilt in 1487, is surrounded by a red wall marking off an area more than twice the size of the present complex. Comparison with photograph taken by Ernst Boerschmann in 1906 or 1909, however, shows that the monastery was no bigger then than now.[1]

Shuxiang Si is famous not only for its Manjushri statue but also for its abbot, Sheng Zong, who received me for a conversation in the long sitting room in autumn 2007. Despite his advanced age of 77 and the privations he suffered during the Cultural Revolution, the abbot remains full of life. While we talked, he was also tuning into conversations his two secretaries were having with other guests, and he joined in now and then. He handled calls on his mobile telephone speedily with a sharp voice. The fact he enjoyed great respect in China was evident from the large photographs in the sitting room showing him with the former Chinese president Jiang Zemin (in office 1993–2003) and with the present officeholder Hu Jintao (since 2003).

The abbot's civilian name is Er Nü, and he comes from the neighbouring province of Hebei.

A young nun carries an altar bearing three bowls and walks through a symbolic sea of fabric lotus blossoms. Birthday celebration for Shijiafo, Baiyun Si.

View from Fanxian hill of Shuxiang Si (foreground), the town of Taihuai, the pagoda of Tayuan Si, and Pusading Si (centre), and the monasteries of Shancai Dong, Shangshancai Dong, and Dailuoding Si (background right). Photograph by Ernst Boerschmann, taken between 1906 and 1909. (Opposite) Photograph from 2006 taken from the same place.

His parents gave him, at the age of three, to a monastery, where just a year later he was consecrated as a monk. At the age of only 19 he was appointed abbot on Wutai Shan. Like all his fellow inhabitants of the region he was confronted with the horrors of the Second World War. The Japanese invaders occupied his monastery for three years. At first the Japanese soldiers behaved decently and took part in the prayers, but later they murdered civilians and monks and plundered monasteries. Then he left his monastery to serve as a soldier for three years in the anti-Japanese guerrilla war. After the war he returned to monastic life and was elected abbot of Shuxiang Si in 1948. Even then such an election had to be ratified by the local government.

Regarding the later developments the abbot said,

Up until a few years before the start of the Cultural Revolution life on Wutai Shan went on quite as normal. We were little harassed and could accept novices. At the beginning of the Sixties the situation deteriorated dramatically. The monks were banished from their monasteries and forced to work as farmers or factory workers in their home villages.

I assume that many monks were also deported to labour camps. The abbot continued,

I was expelled in 1964, two years before the outbreak of the Cultural Revolution, and worked as a farmer in my home village until 1984, when I finally received permission to return to Shuxiang Si. In the 20 years in Hebei I remained a monk, as far as that went. During the Cultural Revolution, when there were no monks on Wutai Shan and the Red Guards destroyed all the monasteries outside Taihuai, pious laypeople and sympathetic functionaries occupied Shuxiang Si and the other monasteries, with the approval of the local military leadership, in order to protect them. Fortunately, only a little was destroyed. When I returned, only one monk lived in the monastery. Today we are over 30 monks of Jingtu.

The attraction of Wutai Shan, which has lasted for almost two millennia, was explained by the abbot as follows:

Wenshu Pusa blessed Wutai Shan through his presence and his spiritual teachings. His presence can still be felt today, and this holy aura draws believers, monks, and nuns. Today in the summer as many as 5,000 nuns and monks live on Wutai Shan; in the winter there are still almost 2,000. It is easy to find novices; many young people, including the well educated and well-to-do, want to enter the monastery. I decide on their acceptance. Unlike earlier, we no longer ordain children, although we accept children from difficult circumstances, such as orphans. Our youngest novice is 15 years old.

To my question about what he hopes for the future, the abbot answered, 'That the Buddhist family of Jingtu, Chan, and Tibetan Gelugpa monks on Wutai Shan develops further and that Buddhism throughout China continues to gain strength'.

Abbot Sheng Zhong of Shuxiang Si Monastery.

Jingtu monks during afternoon prayer in the Wenshu Pusa Hall of Shuxiang Si.

Lingying Si 灵应寺

A few hundred metres south rises the Fanxian 梵仙山 hill, which is also called the 'small southern terrace'. The name of this small mountain refers to the ritual, widespread in Daoism and Buddhism, of 'rice for the wise', a banquet given for monks. Here it can be understood as 'food leading to immortality'. In a little forest on the mountain stands the small monastery of Lingying Si, whose name means 'temple of the divine answer'. The visit is surprising, since, although the four monks present there characterise themselves as adherents of Chan, three of the four shrines are dedicated to Daoist deities; namely, the god of wealth Cai Shen, the medicine king Yao Wang, and a fox spirit that once lived on the mountain.

Cai Shen is one of the most popular deities in the Daoist-influenced Chinese folk religion, and his statue is also encountered in temples of Buddhist Jingtu and in many private shrines.

Likewise in many businesses, stores and banks there are altars dedicated to Cai Shen or at least his statue. He is invoked in particular at the start of the Chinese lunar year, because at this moment he is thought to come down from heaven to earth to inspect the living conditions of his followers. He also protects against lightning strikes and hail. He is said to have originally been a general in the service of the Jade Emperor, one of the highest deities of Daoism. Later he served the Qin Dynasty (221–206 BCE), named Zhao Xuantan or Zhao Gongming.[2]

The medicine king Yao Wang is also very popular among believers and, like Cai Shen, is said to have originally been a mortal who gained entrance into the Daoist pantheon after his death. Sun Simiao (581–682) was a renowned doctor who several times refused an appointment as imperial physician in the capital because he preferred healing simple folk as an anonymous itinerant doctor. Thanks to his great powers of observation he discovered new treatments for then incurable

Like the hermits who once lived in caves on Wutai Shan, the 500 luohans are depicted in the Wenshu Hall of Shuxiang Si.

diseases. For example, Sun Simiao noticed that night blindness affected in particular poor farmers who could not afford meat. He suspected that liver was connected to sight and travelled to Wutai Shan to purchase the livers of boars, wild sheep, and birds. After he had treated farmers suffering from night blindness for a certain time with liver, their vision improved. In fact, a deficiency of retinol, whose natural sources include liver products, leads to impaired night vision. Sun Simiao regularly sought healing herbs on Wutai Shan, of which more than 300 are still known today.[3]

The belief in fox spirits was widespread in the rural regions of northern China. It was believed that foxes, who sometimes build their dens near gravesites, could be the spirits of dead people who died under unjust circumstances or had not received an adequate funeral. Fox spirits lived for a long time, and they could transform at age 50 into an elderly woman, at age 100 into a young woman and at age 1,000 into a heavenly fox. Fox spirits were greatly feared, since they could, in the

form of a seductive maiden, entice men, especially scholars, and enslave them. Because the fox spirit sucked the vitality out of its beloved in order to gain immortality – like a vampire – the man quickly lost strength and could be saved only by the magical powers of a Daoist master. When people dedicated a shrine to a fox spirit, however, it redounded to their prosperity and health.[4]

Only the fourth deity venerated in Lingying, Guanyin, is Buddhist. Despite this heterogeneous religious affiliation, the monastery is very popular among Tibetan pilgrims, as in the inner courtyard the trees are swathed in Tibetan prayer flags and the ground is covered with Tibetan printed lung ta papers. These are square, very thin, printed papers. In the centre is the wind horse, facing left, which gives the Lung Ta paper its name, since the Tibetan word 'lung' means wind and 'ta', horse. The horse carries on its back the flaming jewel that brings good fortune and fulfils wishes; the wind carries the prayers to the bodhisattva being appealed to. Four other animals occupy the corners of the paper: in the east, a dragon; in the south, a raptor; in the north, a snow lion; and in the west, a tiger. The corresponding character often replaces the animal, however. The lung-ta symbol, whose name can be understood as breath-horse, also means the internal energy of the human being, which holds the four elements in balance. In this context, the dragon symbolises water; the raptor, fire; the snow lion, earth; and the tiger, air. A strong lung-ta ensures health, vitality, and stamina; a weak one leads to sickness, accidents, and generally to misfortune.

Lingfeng Si 灵峰寺

Likewise on the southern edge of Taihuai stands the monastery of Lingfeng Si from the time of the Tang. The monastery, made up of three halls, was razed during the Cultural Revolution,

The god of wealth Cai Shen was originally a general who served the mythical Jade Emperor. Lingying Si.

General Weituo stands in front of the rebuilt monastery of Lingfeng Si, whose five temples are dedicated to the five manifestations of Wenshu Pusa and symbolise the five terraces of Wutai Shan.

and was rebuilt by Abbot Miosheng of the Chan School according to a new plan beginning in 1998. Although the temple is oriented toward the west, the five new shrines lie, unusually, in a line along the north–south axis. Normally the main halls lie behind and not beside one another. The uncommon arrangement of the temples stems from the fact that the monastery is dedicated to the five terraces, which is why a statue of one of the manifestations of Wenshu Pusa is found in each of the five chapels. If pilgrims stand in front of the monastery by the statue of General Weituo, these are, from left to right: Zhihui Wenshu of the southern terrace, Shihou Wenshu of the western terrace, Rutong Wenshu of the central terrace, Wugou Wenshu of the northern terrace, and Conming Wenshu of the eastern terrace. In this sense the monastery represents a three-dimensional interpretation of the ancient map of Wutai Shan, in which the five terraces are in the same order. The monastery offers hurried pilgrims the possibility to symbolically

demonstrate respect to all five incarnations of Manjushri who reside on the five terraces. The monastery's name means 'temple of the spiritual peak'. Lingfeng Si lies somewhat apart from the streams of pilgrims, however, and, located behind administrative buildings, is hard to find.

Wanfo Dong　万佛洞

The once-great cave monastery of Wanfo Dong is found at the intersection where the approach from the west enters the main road that crosses Taihuai on the north–south axis. Today at this intersection two huge placards stand side-by-side, showing President Hu Jintao and former president Jiang Zemin in front of the white stupa of Tayuan Si. On the other side of the road are the sparse remains of Wanfo Dong. On the southern end of the earlier complex a brick building nestles against the rocks, where a Jingtu monk lives alone and tends to a tiny shrine. Before the Cultural Revolution the

the rocks and from which the plaster had fallen away. Either a temple had stood here earlier, with its rear wall against the rocks, or additional caves had been walled off. When I asked the monk about this, he became nervous, shrugged his shoulders, and led me back down to show me a stele commemorating the advance of the German troops of Graf von Waldersee in 1901.

Brick pagoda from the Yuan Dynasty (1271–1368) at Wanfo Dong. The pagoda's monastery was razed during the Cultural Revolution.

Nanshan Si 南山寺

The double monastery of Nanshan Si and Youguo Si is located above the eastern bank of the Qingshui River across from Wanfo Dong. The double monastery, which clings to the mountain side 3 km south of Taihuai, consists of seven terraces, of which the three lower belong to Nanshan Si and the three upper to Youguo Si with residences and guest quarters on the middle terrace. Today in the summer nearly 40 Chan monks live at Nanshan Si, whose name means 'southern mountain'. It was the Yuan emperor Temür Oljeitu (ruled 1294–1307) who in 1295 commissioned the Tibeto-Nepalese architect Aniko with the construction, in order to accumulate religious merit for his mother Hongjilie. Aniko completed the project in just two years; however, he triggered severe social unrest on account of the forced labour it required and the attendant rise in taxes. This provoked sharp criticism

monastery, which had been founded at the time of the Yuan Dynasty (1271–1368), extended more than 100 m to the north, where only a hexagonal, five-storey pagoda now stands. Today between the cave shrine and the pagoda there are apartment buildings and a factory area. During the building of the monastery cave tens of thousands of small buddha statues were reportedly found in the cave. Made of pressed clay, these statues are called 'tsa tsa' in Tibetan and were produced in great numbers by means of wooden or metal moulds. They are the reason why the monastery was given the name Wanfo, which means 'ten thousand buddhas'.

After receiving me with some suspicion, the lone monk led me up the rock face where there was a single new buddha statue in a small cave. Next to the cave I noticed stone walls built into

Billboards depicting President Hu Jintao (left) and former president Jiang Zemin in front of the silhouette of Taihuai.

The second pailou of
Nanshan Si, built in 1937.

from high-ranking functionaries at the imperial
court.[5] Temür Oljeitu's generally uncontrolled
spending led over time to an unsustainable
national deficit, and eventually the amount of
money in circulation had to be increased to such
an extent that paper money became worthless and
was no longer accepted as a means of payment.

Later, under the Ming and the later Qing,
the temple was almost entirely rebuilt.

The entrance to the monastery begins with
an 18 m-wide and 8 m-high pailou made of brick
covered with marble slabs. From here a steep
staircase of 108 deep steps leads to a second
gate, built in 1937, which looks like a Roman
triumphal arch topped by a Chinese roof. After
a few more steps the panting pilgrims reach
the three-part entrance portal and, behind it, a
jumbled array of mostly closed temples and
shrines. In neglected and run-down Nanshan
Si I was impressed only by the statue of a seated
Buddha Shakyamuni against the background
of a great aureole of flames in the Great Hall.

Youguo Si 佑国寺

Youguo Si, whose name means 'temple of the
defence of the empire' and where only six monks
still live, also appeared neglected. On the fifth
terrace stands the Hall of the Heavenly Guardians;
on the sixth, a Great Hall, opened only rarely;
and on the seventh, the Hall of the Thundering
Storm, with murals from the late nineteenth
century. Well worth seeing at Youguo Si are
the sandstone reliefs in front of the entrance
to the Tian Wang Hall, from the end of the
nineteenth century, which portray Daoist figures.

The surprising encounter with the Daoist
immortals in a Buddhist monastery goes back to
an important religious personality from the turn
of the late nineteenth and early twentieth century.
The Buddhist monk Puji (died 1917), who was
renowned on Wutai Shan and throughout Shanxi
Province for his charitable work, enjoyed the
confidence of the ruling Empress Dowager Cixi
(ruled *de facto* 1861–1908), who considered herself

The double monastery of Nanshan Si (below) and Youguo Si (above).

The Eight Immortals of Daoism

Although the idea of immortals is very old, the legend of the Eight Immortals emerged in the twelfth or thirteenth century. Since immortals symbolise wealth and longevity, they are popular among people of different beliefs. They are recognisable by particular attributes:

- Zhang Guo Lao rides a donkey, often backwards. He has the ability at the end of a journey to fold up his donkey like a piece of paper and tuck it in his bag.
- Zongli Quan is a pleasure-seeking, well-loved man with a big belly, similar to Milefo.
- He Xiangu is the only female immortal and carries a magic lotus blossom.
- Cao Guojiu is said to be the uncle of an emperor and always wears official royal clothes.
- Lan Caihe is a strange figure and presumably a hermaphrodite, who wears winter clothes in summer and summer clothes in winter.
- Han Xiang is always happy and content; with his flute he tames the wildest animals and always makes flowers blossom.
- Li Tieguai is portrayed as a lame and ragged beggar. Earlier, when he had a well-formed body, his spirit is said to have left its own body regularly in order to be able to travel more quickly on earth and in heaven as pure spirit. One day one of his students found the lifeless body of the master, believed him to be dead, and cremated him. When Li Tieguai's spirit later returned and did not find his body, he entered the first body he found, that of a lame beggar.
- Lü Dongbing carries a magical sword, with which he freed the earth from most dragons over the course of 400 years; he serves as leader of the immortals.

Taibai Jinxing riding his ox (upper right). He is the messenger of the Jade Emperor and one of the most popular Daoist deities. Sandstone relief sculpture on the Hall of the Four Heavenly Guardians at the Buddhist monastery of Youguo Si.

an incarnation of the bodhisattva Guanyin. At the time of the restoration of the double monastery in 1883, Puji was abbot of Youguo Si. He harboured sympathies for Daoist ideas and had Daoist scenes put on the entrance of the monastery. In the last period of his life he professed Daoism and became the local representative of the institution of 'Daoism of the Nine Palaces'.[6]

Zhenhai Si 镇海寺

The monastery of esoteric Buddhism, Zhenhai Si, which is home to 23 Chinese and a few Tibetan monks, lies in a picturesque forest clearing 5 km south of Taihuai. According to legend, a dragon that was in love with a maiden was spurned by the object of his desire. In his anger he flooded the nearby mountain streams by bringing forth a new spring, threatening the houses of the neighbouring farmers. Wenshu Pusa then intervened. He restrained the angry

dragon and stopped the threatening spring with a copper pan. Thus the monastery bears the name Zhenhai Si, 'temple of the restraining of the flood'. As in other contexts, Wenshu Pusa appears as a dragon-tamer, like the Christian St George or St Sergius. The monastery was founded at the beginning of the fifteenth century and in 1430 served Tsongkhapa's student Shakya Yeshe (1355–1435) as a temporary residence. Emperor Kangxi (ruled 1661–1722) later had the monastery restored, and its main halls were mostly spared in the Cultural Revolution. The shrines higher on the slope, which were destroyed, are being rebuilt.

Pilgrims enter the monastery, which stands right up against the mountain, through the Tian Wang Hall, which is flanked by the drum and bell towers, and then reach the Great Hall. On its exterior walls are images of Wenshu Pusa, Shakyamuni, and the Buddhas of the Three Times, painted in the Tibetan style with acrylic paints on canvas, which have defied bad weather since 1986. Three wooden statues of

Great Hall of Zhenhai Si with recent murals on canvas panels.

From left to right: the bodhisattvas Wenshu Pusa (Manjushri), Guanyin Pusa (Avalokiteshvara) and Puxian Pusa (Samantabhdra) in the Guanying Hall of Zhenhai Si.

the Buddhas Bhaisajyaguru, Shakyamuni and Amitabha sit enthroned in the interior of the hall. The next hall, which honours Guanyin, contains a surprise: the statues of the bodhisattvas Wenshu, Puxian, and Guanyin Pusa are done in the Indian style. All three have Indo-European facial features and have blue-black beards and moustaches. They are among the oldest temple statues inside Wutai Shan. South of the main courtyard with the two shrines is the smaller Yongle courtyard, in the centre of which stands a white, 9 m-tall stupa in honour of the famous second Zhangjia Hutuku Rölpai Dorje (1717–86), who was a friend of Emperor Qianlong. On the tambour of the stupa are figures of the eight most important bodhisattvas as well as the Buddhas of the Three Times, while in the lower frieze the most important events in the life of Buddha Shakyamuni are portrayed.

Wanyuan An   万缘庵

Across from Zhenhai Si, on the left bank of the Qingshui, stands the convent of Wanyuan An, whose name means 'temple of the ten thousand predestined relationships' and refers to the doctrine of karma. The monastery, which was built under the late Ming and destroyed during the Cultural Revolution, was rebuilt starting in 1998 as a combination convent and guesthouse for pilgrims. Two long, two-storey buildings on both sides of the complex serve as guest quarters; of monastic buildings at the end of 2006 there stood only the still incomplete Tian Wang Hall and the main hall with the three bodhisattvas Wenshu, Guanyin, and Puxian Pusa. The reconstruction and operation of Wanyuan An, where three Jingtu nuns live, is led by a married lay couple.

When I visited the monastery it was very interesting to observe in the Tian Wang Hall the production of four heavenly guardian and two Erjiang statues. Three artists from the village of Wutun in the eastern Tibetan province of Qinghai, which is known throughout the Tibetan cultural realm for its outstanding scrolls, murals, and terracotta statues, had begun work on the 4 m-tall statues four months earlier. Their technique was the same as I had encountered in the monastery of Bairenyan Si.[7] At Wanyuan An they were busy filling the cracks of the statues, which were in an unfinished state, with small bridges of dried clay, and smoothing out the uneven places with moist clay. After a two-week drying period they planned to apply the three required coats of paint made from natural mineral pigments.

Mingyue Chi 明月池 and Jingang Bao Ta 金刚宝塔

About 2 km south of Wanyuan An stands, also on the left bank of the river, the small monastery of Mingyue Chi. It lies hidden in a forest and is accessible from the road on foot in less than a quarter of an hour. The monastery's real name is Guanhai 观海, which means 'view of the sea [of fog]', but it is known by the name Mingyue, 'shining moon spring'. This second name refers to a spring that never runs dry, in which the moon is especially clearly reflected at night. Today a small shrine stands over the spring, to which female pilgrims in particular flock. Inside the shrine an altar with a kitsch-looking statue of the seated, female Guanyin,

holding a naked little boy on her right knee – similar to a Catholic statue of Mary with the baby Jesus – stands immediately above the spring. In this manifestation the bodhisattva is called Songzi Guanyin, the 'child-granting Guanyin'. In folk belief she is venerated not only for her all-encompassing compassion but also as the protector of children and as a child-granting deity, which positions her as a kind of fertility goddess.

The monastery, ostensibly founded at the time of the Northern Wei and renovated under Emperor Kangxi, served as a meditation space for Emperor Qianlong during his sixth visit to Wutai Shan. Until 1949 Mingyue Chi belonged to esoteric Buddhism; today ten Jingtu monks live here. In the Vajra Hall stands a unique wooden statue, more than 5 m tall and lacquered pitch

Eastern Tibetan artists from Qinghai working on new statues of the heavenly kings and the two Erjiang in the Tian Wang Hall of the convent of Wanyuan An.

Wooden statue of the patron deity Miji Jingang Pusa (Bodhisattva Vajrapani) in the Vajra Hall of Mingyue Chi.

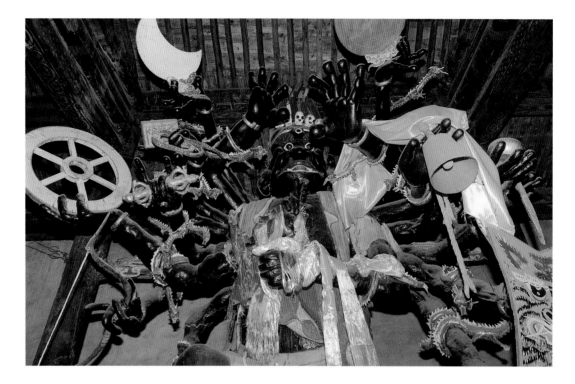

black, of a fierce-looking Bodhisattva Vajrapani (Chinese: Miji Jingang Pusa).[8] The wrathful guardian of Buddha and his teaching has 18 arms and seven heads. The foremost face is terrifying, featuring protruding eyes and a slightly open mouth with two pointed, jutting eyeteeth; behind it to the left a monkey or marten face gazes at pilgrims, and behind and to the right, the face of a demon. Above the tongues of flame adorning the five white crowns of the first face, four white, peaceful Buddha faces look out into the distance. Vajrapani's hands hold objects characteristic of him, such as the Wheel of Dharma, a bow, a sword, a lance, a bell, a thunderbolt, and, in the uppermost hand, the sun and moon. Dragons twine around some of his arms. Within sight of Mingyue Chi, in a higher location 1 km south, the pagoda of Jingang Bao Ta, the 'precious pagoda of diamonds', presumably from the time of the Yuan, stands in a forest clearing.

Puan Si 菩提庵寺

Two kilometres south of Mingyue Chi, on the left riverbank, stands the monastery of Puan, which once housed 100 monks and was razed to the ground during the Cultural Revolution. As the abbot assured me, the monastery's name 菩提庵寺 means in effect 'temple (an) of liberation (puti)'. The name on maps 普庵寺 which in this spelling would mean 'temple of all monasteries', is thus incorrect. In autumn of 2006 I met six Jingtu monks, who were working on new construction, under the leadership of the young Abbot Jende from Beijing. At that time the shrine consisted of only three tiny rooms, in front of which two statues of Guanyin and one of Buddha Shakyamuni stood under a small veranda. In the main shrine were seated statues of the Buddhas of the Three Times.

The monastery of Mingyue Chi, which stands in a forest.

Baiyun Si 白云寺

Three kilometres south of Puan Si, on the right riverbank, stands the large monastery of Baiyun Si, the 'monastery of the white cloud', from the time of the Tang (618–907). The famous traveller and geographer Xu Xiake (1587–1641), who undertook 22 exploratory journeys on foot throughout China from 1607 to 1640, in order to empirically study the geography of his homeland, visited Baiyun Si in 1633. During the Qing Dynasty (1644–1911), the emperors Kangxi (ruled 1661–1722), Yongzheng (ruled 1723–1735), Qianlong (ruled 1736–95), and Jiaqing (ruled 1796–1820) stayed at the monastery. Like many monasteries outside of Taihuai, this Jingtu monastery was completely destroyed by the Red Guards.

Today Baiyun Si numbers 54 Jingtu nuns. It is opulently built and carefully planned, down to the floor of the great meditation and soul hall. An open lotus blossom is portrayed in the centre of each white floor tile, so that each meditating

person sits on a lotus blossom like a buddha or bodhisattva. This symbolism also applies to Wutai Shan, which is likewise understood as an open lotus blossom. One could almost speak of a designer monastery. At the entrance to the monastery stands a stone wall with three engraved and gold-painted inscriptions on a black background. In front of it stand two fearsome guardian figures of white marble and between them the female bodhisattva Guanyin. After pilgrims have crossed the large Tian Wang Hall, they reach the first inner courtyard, where the Hall of the Buddhas of the Three Times stands. Along the side walls stand statues of the sixteen luohans; on the rear wall, the triad of Jingtu: Shakyamuni, Wenshu and Puxian Pusa. Statues of this triad also stand on the main altar of the Bodhisattva Hall. East of the Hall of the Buddhas of the Three Times stands the instruction hall, the 'Hall of Dharma'. Along the stairs leading to it and on the rear of the hall hang small marble plaques on which the names of deceased people are written.

Start of the birthday celebration for Shijiafo (Buddha Shakyamuni) in Baiyun Si. Buddhist maxims are written on the banners.

Nuns and lay pilgrims living temporarily in the monastery walk around the standing statues of Wenshu Pusa, Shijiafo (Buddha Shakyamuni) and Guanyin (from left to right) in the Bodhisattva Hall of the Jingtu Monastery of Baiyun Si.

Abbess Shi Chang Long carrying a statue of the newborn Shakyamuni during the birthday celebration for Shijiafo in the Great Hall of Baiyun Si.

Abbess Shi Chang Long

In Baiyun Si I had the good fortune to engage in two conversations with Abbess Shi Chang Long. The abbess, born in 1945 in Liaoning Province, was given by her parents at the age of seven to a monastery in her home province, where she took the vows of a nun. During the Cultural Revolution she had to leave her monastery and work in a food factory. She conformed herself externally to her new circumstances but remained a nun on the inside. In 1989 she came to Wutai Shan and entered the Jifu Convent. In 1995 she received permission from the State Administration for Religious Affairs to build a new convent on the site of Baiyun Si, which had been destroyed during the Cultural Revolution. She took on the project with only two nuns. The Hall of the Great Buddha was opened in 1997 and the Hall of the Three Bodhisattvas in 2005. At the dedications of both shrines Buddhist deities are said to have appeared in the clouds: Buddha Amitabha in 1997 and Bodhisattva Guanyin in 2005. Shi Chan Long's assistant proudly showed me the photographs of cloud images and apparitional forms. These ostensible manifestations, observed by all faithful participants in the dedications, are entirely within the tradition of earlier pilgrim stories. Thus, for instance, the Japanese monk Ennin (793–864) and the high-ranking Chinese magistrate Zhang Shangying (1043–1122) reported several visions they experienced on the Five Terrace Mountain. In these many buddhas and bodhisattvas appeared to them in clouds and light phenomena.

Abbess Shi Chang Lung is filled with missionary fervour for the things of Buddhism. The motto printed on her calling card reads, 'Filled through suffering and care with true Buddhist spirit, I no longer wander about but have decided to teach Buddhism'. She fulfils this self-imposed charge by building monasteries, which she herself plans down to the smallest detail and whose construction she oversees. Baiyun is not her only monastery; she has had additional monasteries built in the provinces of Liaoning, Shandong, Shaanxi and Henan, over all of which she presides. She explains, 'It is my purpose to build Buddhist monasteries'. In order to finance the construction of the monasteries she keeps up an active schedule of international travel to collect donations. All her institutions belong to the Jingtu School. Her monasteries have neither a minimum age for entry nor a minimum educational level; the youngest novice is nine years old.

Shi Chang Long believes that in each epoch a particular type of religiosity leads to the goal of enlightenment. Until the second or third century CE the study of sutras was of utmost importance. Thereafter Wenshu Pusa taught the esoteric Buddhism of Mi Zong and later the school of Jingtu. Thus she interprets Wenshu Pusa as a type of prophet from Buddha Amitabha, who periodically incarnates himself in order to adapt the message of Buddhism to the new historical circumstances. At this time, Shi Chang believes, no salvation is possible without humble devotion to Amitabha; he will accept all people who sincerely appeal to him into his Western Paradise. With regard to the West, Amitabha will soon send a new incarnation of Manjushri there with a special message adapted to Western civilisation.

Lay pilgrims taking part in communal prayer. Birthday celebration for Shijiafo at Baiyun Si.

Buddha Shakyamuni's birthday celebration in Baiyun Si

May 24, 2007, was a big day for the convent of Baiyun Si, since the birthday of Buddha Shakyamuni fell on this date. The date corresponds to the eighth day of the fourth lunar month. At 7:00 a.m. the final preparations were taking place. More than 250 laypeople registered with a donation at the registration booth set up in front of the main hall. They then dressed in monks' and nuns' garments and arranged themselves into rows according to the instructions of the abbess and her two assistants. The abbess oversaw the proceedings and used a microphone to direct nuns and pilgrims to their appointed places and explained the course of the ceremony. No detail escaped her; if someone broke ranks, that person was whistled mercilessly back into place.

After a short address in front of the main hall, the abbess proceeded to the reception hall to change clothes. She soon returned in the ceremonial garb of Chinese abbesses and abbots. Under a bright yellow robe she wore the red cloak called jiasa, on which the character 'fo' for Buddha was embroidered dozens of times in gold thread. During the whole celebration red and gold served as colourful accents, since in China red symbolises happiness, wealth and honour, and yellow, nobility. Thus the cushions that connected the two halls were yellow and red. During the procession, Shi Chang was accompanied by four nuns who carried red and yellow lotus blossoms made of fabric.

After such a procession three times through the courtyard the abbess proceeded to the main temple, where she delivered another short speech. Judging by the reaction of those present, the speech was not only earnest but also funny, because a few times the pilgrims broke into loud laughter. Then some 80 pilgrims arranged themselves in two rows, across from each other, between the two halls. They knelt down and the abbess walked through the space between them and blessed the kneeling women with a red lotus blossom made of cloth. Immediately after that another procession left the main temple. A young nun led it; she carried a small altar with three bowls. She proceeded to the reception hall to receive a small figure of the newborn Buddha Shakyamuni, as the ceremony was to culminate in the washing of the just-born Buddha. It recalls the story that nine nagas, snake- or dragon-shaped spirits, washed the newborn Siddhartha, after which he immediately began to speak and made seven steps in each direction to indicate that he would show the entire cosmos a path to salvation. The Buddha received the name Siddhartha, which means in essence 'one who has attained a goal', from his parents; Shakyamuni is an honorary title and means 'sage from the lineage of the Shakya'.

After a few minutes the procession returned from the reception hall to the main hall. The young nun again held her portable altar, and behind her followed the abbess with a small statue of the baby Buddha. As is traditional, he raises his right hand to heaven and points toward the earth with his left. In the meantime two nuns had distributed to the lined-up pilgrims a dozen large, red, yellow and pink fabric lotus blossoms, which they then tossed to the front like Frisbees. It seemed as if the procession was wending through a sea of moving lotus blossoms. This detail commemorates the tradition that lotus blossoms sprouted up under the feet of the newborn Buddha, as he made his first steps in the four directions. Shi Chang then entered the main temple, where on the altar, in front of the statue of Shakyamuni, she washed the small figure with a tiny pine bough.

In the interim the courtyard had filled with many more pilgrims, who also wanted to participate in the highpoint of the ceremony. Nuns then placed the small Buddha statue in front of the main hall on a small altar, and all present pressed forward in order to kneel and symbolically briefly wash the Buddha themselves. On both sides of the statue stood a pail, in which pilgrims put their offerings. Depending on income level, offerings varied from US$50 to 50 cents. For the people present, participation was an emotional experience, and a few could no longer stand up unassisted. Four pilgrims fainted and had to be carried away by helpful nuns.

In retrospect I noticed, despite all the external differences, structural similarities to Christian festivals: the celebrant leads the ceremony and gives speeches. Important themes are peace, mercy, helpfulness, and confidence. The people recite and sing prayers together. The second half of the ceremony leads purposefully to the solemn climax – whether it be the Lord's Supper or the washing of the Buddha – which is completed first by the celebrant and then by all present. Immediately after follows the offering. And, as in early Christianity or today in Eastern churches, where the shared meal, the agape, concludes the worship service, at Baiyun Si all participants are invited to lunch.

Procession during the birthday
celebration for Shijiafo in front
of the Great Hall of Baiyun Si.

Abbess Shi Chang Long blesses lay pilgrims (called jushi in Chinese) during the birthday celebration for Shijiafo at Baiyun Si.

Fomu Dong 佛母洞

From Baiyun Si a mountain road leads west in
the direction of the cave temple of Fomu Dong.
The name means 'mother (mu) of the Buddha
(fo) cave (dong)'. It is dedicated to Siddhartha's
mother Mahamaya, who died a few days after
Siddhartha's birth. A few hundred metres beyond
Baiyun Si the road passes a group of newly built
white pagodas. The main pagoda is dedicated to
the mother of the abbess of Baiyun Si, who died
in 1998. Her Buddhist name was Guofoxing,
which means in effect 'perfection of the Buddha'.
As befits a pilgrimage, pilgrims must suffer
somewhat before they reach their goal. The
street soon ends, and pilgrims must surmount
the 260 m difference in elevation on a staircase
of 1,680 steps. On the way I passed people of
various ages, from small children who used their
hands to help clamber over the steps, to very old
pilgrims who walked with crutches. Nevertheless
they refused to accept the services of the litter-
bearers who stood at the ready, since this would
greatly decrease the merit of the pilgrimage.

Arriving at the shrine, I joined about 300
pilgrims who were waiting patiently to be
admitted to the two caves. A narrow passage led
from the larger, outer cave to the smaller, interior,
stalactite cave, which had room for at most five
or six people. Since the inner cave was compared
to the womb of Siddhartha's mother, passage
from the outer to the inner cave symbolises
liberation from prior cares and sins, and the
return to daylight represents rebirth into a new
life. At the entrance to the first cave plaques and
drawings provide exact instructions as to how
pilgrims should force themselves through the
truly narrow passageway. This represents a test,
since it is said that only good people can push
through the narrow passage; evil ones get stuck.
When I asked a monk standing at the entrance if
it might not be possible that a slender miscreant

Rapid, constant rubbing of the
handles of this bronze bowl creates
vibrations that cause the water in
it to spray. Busker on the stairway
to the caves of Fomu Dong.

would get through, but a chubby virtuous person
would get stuck, he replied indignantly that the
shape of a body could not influence the outcome
of the test; it simply reflected the moral worth
of the pilgrim. I encountered a similar test in
1991 during the pilgrimage around the sacred
Mount Kailash in western Tibet, where at a
particular place some 5,300 m above sea level
pilgrims had to crawl through a narrow gap
between two rocks. Those who came through
were purified; those who got stuck still had not
stripped away their sins and their poor morals.

Lingjing Si 灵境寺

This monastery, the 'temple of the spiritual region',
is found at the southern foot of the southern
terrace, about 25 km from Taihuai.[9] Ostensibly
founded during the time of the Tang, it has been
renovated and rebuilt several times, most recently

after the Cultural Revolution. Two steles from 1612 and 1804 remain from the old monastery. Despite its isolation, Lingjing Si is an important pilgrimage destination for Japanese pilgrims, for in this monastery the Japanese pilgrim monk Ryosen, who lived on Wutai Shan from 820 on, was poisoned between 825 and 828.[10]

Baitou An 白头庵

The convent of Baitou An, located on the eastern side of the Qingshui River, is the exact opposite of Baiyun An. When I visited it, I found only two nuns, presumably self-designated, who lived in a dilapidated private house. They neither knew the history of Baitou An, which had been destroyed by the Red Guards, nor were they able to say which religious school they belonged to. They refused to show me their shrine and after a few minutes brought the conversation to an end and fled back

into their house. The meaning of the monastery's name, 'monastery of the white head', was also unknown to them. Perhaps it referred earlier to Buddha Vairocana, whose body was white. I assumed that these were pseudo-nuns, who were rejected by or expelled from another monastery. They wore typical monastic clothing, however, and their heads were shaved bare, as befits nuns.

Guandi Si 关帝寺

The Daoist monastery of Guandi Si lies 4.5 km northeast of the main road in a hidden side valley. Guandi, who was originally called Guan Yü, served as a general during the last two decades of the Eastern Han Dynasty (25–220 CE) and was renowned for his courage and loyalty. His deification took place under the dynasty of the Sui (581–618). In the sixteenth century Emperor Wanli (ruled 1573–1620) elevated him to national

Temporary shelter for the Daoist monks of Guandi Si.

Autumn fog at Gufo Si.

they spoke to me. Then a man in civilian clothes appeared, who harshly forbade me from taking any more photographs. Later I learned that the village authorities had ordered that the monastery be razed in 2005, although the cultural authorities wanted to protect it under all circumstances. As for the reasons, one can only speculate.

Gufo Si 古佛寺

Twenty-five kilometres south of Taihuai stands Gufo Si, the monastery of the 'old Buddha', rebuilt by Abbot Puji. When he came to the badly neglected monastery at the beginning of the twentieth century, there was only a single terracotta statue of a buddha in an open hall lacking a roof. Since the statue had been exposed to the elements, no one could identify it, not even

Puji, so they called it 'the old buddha'. Seized with compassion, the monk promised to build the old buddha a new, gilded statue and a new temple.

Today the monastery houses 20 monks of the Jingtu School, who tend their complex well. First pilgrims walk through a stone pailou and reach the hall with the heavenly kings as well as the two flanking towers. Then they move to the Guanyin Hall with its statues of the bodhisattva triad of Jingtu and colourfully painted figures of the 500 luohans, sitting in their niches. Finally, in the Great Hall there are gold-painted statues of the Buddhas of the Three Times as well as the 18 luohans. On both side walls and on the rear wall the 500 luohans are portrayed figuratively, residing in their hermitages in a colourful, blue-green mountain landscape. North of this shrine stands a seven-storey pagoda, completed only in 1998.

after the Cultural Revolution. Two steles from
1612 and 1804 remain from the old monastery.
Despite its isolation, Lingjing Si is an important
pilgrimage destination for Japanese pilgrims,
for in this monastery the Japanese pilgrim
monk Ryosen, who lived on Wutai Shan from
820 on, was poisoned between 825 and 828.[10]

Baitou An 白头庵

The convent of Baitou An, located on the eastern
side of the Qingshui River, is the exact opposite
of Baiyun An. When I visited it, I found only two
nuns, presumably self-designated, who lived in a
dilapidated private house. They neither knew the
history of Baitou An, which had been destroyed by
the Red Guards, nor were they able to say which
religious school they belonged to. They refused
to show me their shrine and after a few minutes
brought the conversation to an end and fled back

into their house. The meaning of the monastery's
name, 'monastery of the white head', was also
unknown to them. Perhaps it referred earlier
to Buddha Vairocana, whose body was white. I
assumed that these were pseudo-nuns, who were
rejected by or expelled from another monastery.
They wore typical monastic clothing, however,
and their heads were shaved bare, as befits nuns.

Guandi Si 关帝寺

The Daoist monastery of Guandi Si lies 4.5 km
northeast of the main road in a hidden side valley.
Guandi, who was originally called Guan Yü,
served as a general during the last two decades
of the Eastern Han Dynasty (25–220 CE) and
was renowned for his courage and loyalty. His
deification took place under the dynasty of the
Sui (581–618). In the sixteenth century Emperor
Wanli (ruled 1573–1620) elevated him to national

Temporary shelter for the Daoist monks of Guandi Si.

Autumn fog at Gufo Si.

they spoke to me. Then a man in civilian clothes appeared, who harshly forbade me from taking any more photographs. Later I learned that the village authorities had ordered that the monastery be razed in 2005, although the cultural authorities wanted to protect it under all circumstances. As for the reasons, one can only speculate.

Gufo Si 古佛寺

Twenty-five kilometres south of Taihuai stands Gufo Si, the monastery of the 'old Buddha', rebuilt by Abbot Puji. When he came to the badly neglected monastery at the beginning of the twentieth century, there was only a single terracotta statue of a buddha in an open hall lacking a roof. Since the statue had been exposed to the elements, no one could identify it, not even

Puji, so they called it 'the old buddha'. Seized with compassion, the monk promised to build the old buddha a new, gilded statue and a new temple.

Today the monastery houses 20 monks of the Jingtu School, who tend their complex well. First pilgrims walk through a stone pailou and reach the hall with the heavenly kings as well as the two flanking towers. Then they move to the Guanyin Hall with its statues of the bodhisattva triad of Jingtu and colourfully painted figures of the 500 luohans, sitting in their niches. Finally, in the Great Hall there are gold-painted statues of the Buddhas of the Three Times as well as the 18 luohans. On both side walls and on the rear wall the 500 luohans are portrayed figuratively, residing in their hermitages in a colourful, blue-green mountain landscape. North of this shrine stands a seven-storey pagoda, completed only in 1998.

after the Cultural Revolution. Two steles from 1612 and 1804 remain from the old monastery. Despite its isolation, Lingjing Si is an important pilgrimage destination for Japanese pilgrims, for in this monastery the Japanese pilgrim monk Ryosen, who lived on Wutai Shan from 820 on, was poisoned between 825 and 828.[10]

Baitou An 白头庵

The convent of Baitou An, located on the eastern side of the Qingshui River, is the exact opposite of Baiyun An. When I visited it, I found only two nuns, presumably self-designated, who lived in a dilapidated private house. They neither knew the history of Baitou An, which had been destroyed by the Red Guards, nor were they able to say which religious school they belonged to. They refused to show me their shrine and after a few minutes brought the conversation to an end and fled back into their house. The meaning of the monastery's name, 'monastery of the white head', was also unknown to them. Perhaps it referred earlier to Buddha Vairocana, whose body was white. I assumed that these were pseudo-nuns, who were rejected by or expelled from another monastery. They wore typical monastic clothing, however, and their heads were shaved bare, as befits nuns.

Guandi Si 关帝寺

The Daoist monastery of Guandi Si lies 4.5 km northeast of the main road in a hidden side valley. Guandi, who was originally called Guan Yü, served as a general during the last two decades of the Eastern Han Dynasty (25–220 CE) and was renowned for his courage and loyalty. His deification took place under the dynasty of the Sui (581–618). In the sixteenth century Emperor Wanli (ruled 1573–1620) elevated him to national

Temporary shelter for the
Daoist monks of Guandi Si.

god of war and gave him the title Guan Sheng Di Jun, which means in effect 'holy Emperor Guan'. In the nineteenth century he was further elevated to 'military emperor'. Guandi provides a clear example of how in China deities were supported or demoted by emperors – not vice versa. But the common people could also punish Guandi, if he did not fulfil his duties. Since in popular belief he was not only god of war but was also responsible for local security, he was held to account in the case of natural disasters, such as a drought. Then the people in charge of the temple removed wooden statues of him from the shrines and carried them out into the blazing sun, so that the god could feel the heat on his own body.[11]

Over time Guandi developed into one of the most popular gods of China, who not only enjoyed high regard in Confucianism but was also venerated as an outstanding patron deity in Daoism and was admitted into the Buddhist pantheon under the name Qielan Pusa. Qielan Pusa is the counterpart to Weituo Pusa, as in monasteries he protects monks and nuns, while Weituo watches over the monastery complex. In large monasteries, such as Xiantong Si, his side shrine is found to the left of the most important temple, and Weituo's side shrine, by contrast, to the right. Before the revolution of 1911 Guandi also served as god of justice, so civil court cases were often held in his temple. He is portrayed as an armoured, muscular man with a red face and black beard, who carries a cut and thrust weapon, similar to a halberd.[12]

The monastery, which was completely destroyed during the Cultural Revolution, was rebuilt in a new, more auspicious location under the leadership of eight Daoist monks, who lived in humble tents. In autumn 2006 two stone lions and the popular Milefo watched over the still empty Great Hall. A small hut formed the provisional shrine, next to which stood next to a white statue of the eight-armed

General Guandi (left) guards the Jade Emperor (centre). Guandi Si.

goddess Daumu, the 'mother of the Dao'. In the interior of the shrine sits a statue of the Jade Emperor; Guandi stand to his right.

Haihui An 海会庵

About 20 km south of Taihuai, on the eastern bank of the river, stands the convent of Haihui An. The name means in essence 'temple of the meeting point of the whole world'. The 15 nuns belong to the Chan subgroup Lingji. The monastery, founded under the Qing (1644–1912), was restored at the turn of the twentieth century by the famous abbot of Youguo, Puji. The complex was a convent from the start, and it features a classical plan: after the Tian Wang Hall with the bell and drum towers follows the temple honouring Guanyin and after that the Great Hall, in which Shakyamuni, the Medicine Buddha, and Amitabha are venerated. As in the kiosk over the spring at Mingyue Chi there is also a statue of a Catholic-looking Songzi Guanyin, who holds

Ritual in front of the Great Hall of Haihui An in honour of the abbess who died a year earlier.

(Right) Daoist statues from the monastery of Jingang An, which was destroyed in 2005 and is being rebuilt as a convent.

a naked baby on her left arm. During my visit a small yellow tent was also set up in front of this hall, in honour of the abbess who had died a year earlier. On the altar, between blooming branches, stood a photograph of the late abbess, in front of which were piled offerings of apples. In front of the tent a few nuns and laypeople sat in communal prayer. After the two-day observance the urn with her ashes would be placed in a forest clearing near the monastery and a pagoda would be built over it. As the abbess-designate explained to me, Haihui An has strict criteria for admittance. The candidate must be a proven Buddhist believer and have successfully completed high school. Provided her parents give permission for entry into the monastery, she must undergo a one-year novitiate.

Jingang An 金刚庵

A few kilometres south of Haihui An, on the western side of the river, stands the convent of Jingang An, the 'monastery of diamonds',

whose visit was a bitter disappointment to me. I had read in a Chinese brochure that the monastery, founded in 1838 in honour of the deified general Guandi, still possessed rare Daoist murals portraying Guandi, his son Guanping, and another general and companion called Zhoucang.[13] As soon as I arrived I noticed that something was not right, for in front of the monastery stood three old-looking painted statues of Daoist deities under a transparent plastic tarpaulin, and a pile of debris lay in the grass. The murals, for their part, were nowhere to be found, and the monastery consisted of one empty and two unfinished shrines as well as an ordinary house. When in the monastery I asked two of the seven nuns, who belong to the school of Mi Zong, about the reason for the destruction of the old monastery, they became nervous. At the same time, a few suspicious-looking construction workers drew near, after which the two nuns quickly disappeared. My translator explained that they feared being expelled from the monastery if

Autumn fog at Gufo Si.

they spoke to me. Then a man in civilian clothes appeared, who harshly forbade me from taking any more photographs. Later I learned that the village authorities had ordered that the monastery be razed in 2005, although the cultural authorities wanted to protect it under all circumstances. As for the reasons, one can only speculate.

Gufo Si 古佛寺

Twenty-five kilometres south of Taihuai stands Gufo Si, the monastery of the 'old Buddha', rebuilt by Abbot Puji. When he came to the badly neglected monastery at the beginning of the twentieth century, there was only a single terracotta statue of a buddha in an open hall lacking a roof. Since the statue had been exposed to the elements, no one could identify it, not even

Puji, so they called it 'the old buddha'. Seized with compassion, the monk promised to build the old buddha a new, gilded statue and a new temple.

Today the monastery houses 20 monks of the Jingtu School, who tend their complex well. First pilgrims walk through a stone pailou and reach the hall with the heavenly kings as well as the two flanking towers. Then they move to the Guanyin Hall with its statues of the bodhisattva triad of Jingtu and colourfully painted figures of the 500 luohans, sitting in their niches. Finally, in the Great Hall there are gold-painted statues of the Buddhas of the Three Times as well as the 18 luohans. On both side walls and on the rear wall the 500 luohans are portrayed figuratively, residing in their hermitages in a colourful, blue-green mountain landscape. North of this shrine stands a seven-storey pagoda, completed only in 1998.

A few of the 500 luohans,
Guanyin Hall, Gufo Si.

The West

*Everything before one's eyes raises thoughts of the manifestations
of Monju [Manjurshri].*

—Ennin, Japanese pilgrim monk[1]

Ruiying Si 瑞应寺

The western inner region begins on the western
edge of Taihuai at Ruiying Si and extends to
Qingliang Si, which lies on the outermost
western flank of Wutai Shan.

The monastery of Ruiying Si, founded under
Emperor Kangxi (ruled 1661–1722) and quite
large at that time, was razed to the ground
during the Cultural Revolution. It lies 4 km from
Taihuai, northwest of Shuxian Si. Today eight
monks from Inner Mongolia and Manchuria,
who belong to the school of Mi Zong, live there
in a simple house. In 2003 they rebuilt the
pagoda honouring the Buddhist prince of the
Qoshot Mongols, Tsagaan Danjin (died 1735),
who was associated with Emperor Kangxi.[2] In
1642 the Qoshot Mongols established a protec-
torate over Tibet, after Gushri Khan (ruled
1642–55) responded to the appeal of the Fifth
Dalai Lama (1617–82) and destroyed his political
opponents in a war lasting from 1636 to 1642.

The monks of Ruiying Si have been working
on the reconstruction of the monastery since

2006. The abbot also planned to install a
17 m-tall copper statue of the Buddha from
India. On both sides of the monastery burble two
springs, interpreted as the eyes of a dragon. The
silhouette of the mountain ridge across from
the stupa is compared to the shadow of Buddha
Shakyamuni lying in nirvana. The abbot was
clearly proud of living in a sacred landscape, as
well as of the name of his monastery, which
means 'temple of the fortunate answer'.

Fenglin Si 凤林寺

About 3 km along the way from Ruiying Si
to Fenglin Si, I passed a cemetery with eight
pagodas and a few memorial steles, which stood
in honour of important monks of the monasteries
of Pusading Si and Fenglin Si. Since the urn of
an abbot from Pusading Si is buried here, monks
from this monastery come here to pray annually
on the first day of the fourth and the tenth lunar
months. Founded at the time of the Yuan Dynasty
(1271–1368), Fenglin Si, the 'forest of the phoenix',

**The monastery of Jixiang
Si at the foot of the central
terrace Zhongtai.**

The monks of Fenglin Si Monastery belong to the Chan subgroup Linji. A path leads from Fenglin Si to the monasteries of Yuhua and Jixiang Si.

stands at the end of a valley of the same name, 8 km from Taihuai. This monastery also fell victim to the destructive frenzy of the Red Guards; it was rebuilt starting in 1994. Today 15 monks live there, members of the Linji subgroup of Chan. Northeast of the very well tended monastery stands the rebuilt pagoda honouring a monk from the Ming Dynasty. A long, steep stairway leads to the two entrance gates. Behind them stand the Tian Wang Hall, the Great Hall with seated statues of Bhaisajyaguru, Shakyamuni and Amitabha, and the Pilufo Hall. In this shrine the transcendent Buddha Piluzhenafo (Sanskrit: Vairocana) sits enthroned; next to him Puxian Pusa rides his elephant and Wenshu Pusa his lion. Beside the two bodhisattvas stand four 3 m-tall cone-shaped objects, each of which is decorated with 1,000 clay figures of Shakyamuni. In the interior of these tsa tsas there are small red cards bearing the names of donors.

Yuhua Si 玉花寺

Less than 2 km northwest of Fenglin, about half the distance to the monastery of Jixiang Si, stands Yuhua Si, the 'monastery of the jade flower'. It is said that the lotus flowers that grow in a nearby pond were white as jade. For this reason hundreds of luohans once spent the summer by this pond. Thus the main hall of the monastery was called the 'Hall of the Luohans'. In it and in the neighbouring Great Hall there were more than 350 bronze statues of luohans from the Ming Dynasty (1368–1644). Each statue was about a metre tall and weighed about 60 kg; the facial expression and body position of each statue was different.[3] Unfortunately, this monastery with its art historical treasures also fell victim to the Cultural Revolution; reconstruction has only just begun.

Jixiang Si 吉祥寺

Below the central terrace, in a very remote location, stands the monastery of Jixiang Si, whose name means 'promise of happiness'. It is said to have been founded during the time of the Tang as a convent called Gufo and over the course of centuries was destroyed several times, most recently during the Cultural Revolution. The monastery, which was called at the time Qingliang Qiao, 'fresh and cool bridge', became a centre of esoteric Buddhism in 1953, when Master Nenghai began to teach Tibetan Buddhism there.[4] While the monastery lies to the west of a stream that becomes a torrent during the snowmelt, a newly erected white pagoda stands to the east of it. A dramatically arched bridge, likewise new, spans the stream; it symbolises the crossing over to the 'other bank', to the start of the path to salvation. When I visited the monastery in autumn 2006

it seemed deserted, since the few monks of the school of Mi Zong had, with one exception, gone to Taihuai to participate in a vegetarian banquet given by a wealthy merchant. Besides the Great Hall and the shrine honouring Wenshu Pusa, the entrance shrine, in which each of the heavenly kings is portrayed in both sculpture and painting, is also noteworthy. The painstakingly rendered paintings are in the eastern Tibetan style of Amdo and were painted on canvas that was directly attached to the wall, instead of first putting them in wooden frames for their protection.

Longquan Si 龙泉寺

This monastery of Chan has ten monks and lies 5 km west of Taihuai on the road leading to the provincial capital of Taiyuan. The name means 'dragon spring', since the nine hills surrounding

From left to right: the Buddhas Yaoshifo (Bhaisajyaguru), Shijiafo (Shakyamuni), and Amituofo (Amitabha) sit enthroned in the Great Hall of Fenglin Si.

In the Tian Wang Hall of Jixiang Si the heavenly guardian Chiguo (Dhritarashtra) is portrayed in both a statue and a painting.

Figures of Buddhist folk
iconography holding
or giving out jewels
in the Tian Wang
Hall of Jixiang Si.

the monastery are interpreted as dragons who refresh themselves at the nearby spring. As at Pusading Si, Nanshan Si and Jinge Si, at Longquan Si a steep, 108-step stairway leads from the lower walls, which guard against spirits, to the white marble portal, the pailou. In the centre of the gate, completed in 1924, an inscription proclaims, 'The light of Buddhism enlightens the world'. Buddhist and Daoist scenes are engraved on medallions on both the wall protecting against spirits and the lintels of the gate; there are also 108 large and small figures of dragons on the pailou. Between the portal and the Tian Wang Hall, two stone lions guard the complex. As in Puhua Si there stand here not only statues of the guardians of heaven but also the luohans Fuhu on his tiger and Shang Lung on a dragon.

The shrine of Guanyin lies at the end of the large interior courtyard that follows. Here on the side walls the 12 bodhisattvas of perfect enlightenment Yuanjue sit on lotus blossoms and flank the statues of Guanyin,

Wenshu, and Puxian Pusa. The calligraphy on the temple entrance reads, 'The merciful Guanyin helps all those who call on her'. In the following Great Hall sit the Buddhas of the Three Times; beside them stand Shakyamuni's students Ananda and Mahakashyapa, as well as Indra and Mahasthamaprapta. To the west of this row of halls stands a marble pagoda honouring the monk Puji, who died in 1917 and who built or completely renovated a total of 18 monasteries. In the onion-shaped tambour of the pagoda the future Buddha Maitreya is depicted in four niches, bearing the face of Puji in four different stages of life: as a youth, a young man, a mature man and an old man.

Linggong Ta 令公塔

The 13 m-tall, three-storey pagoda of Linggong Ta, from the late tenth or eleventh century, stands 1 km northwest of Longquan Si. It is almost a miracle that it was spared by the Red Guards. The ashes of the loyal general of the Northern Song Dynasty (960–1127), Yang Ye, rest here. In 986 he lost an important battle against the hostile emperor Liao-Shengzong (ruled 982–1031) from the dynasty of the Liao (907–1125), because his ministerial colleague Pan Renmei betrayed him.[5] Four of his eight sons fell and two were taken prisoner, as was Yang Ye. Because he refused to swear an oath of loyalty to the victorious Liao, water and food were denied him, and he died a slow death. His fifth son, Wulang, who escaped and became a monk on Wutai Shan, placed his father's ashes here. General Yang Ye serves as an example of unconditional loyalty, so the pagoda is called 'esteemed man'. In front of the pagoda stands a stele, where I found recently presented offerings in the form of plastic flowers, cookies and liquor flasks, a sign that pilgrims still find their way to the pagoda.

108 steps lead from the spirit wall to the pailou, the entrance gate to Longquan Si.

The pagoda commemorating the Daoist-Buddhist abbot Puji, who restored Longquan Si, among other sites, and who died in 1917. The four statues of Milefo in the tambour bear the features of Puji in four stages of life. Longquan Si.

Zhulin Si 竹林寺

The Chan monastery Zhulin Si lies just 7 km west of Taihuai, not far from the main road. The name means 'bamboo grove', as bamboo symbolises purity and silence. It refers to one of the very first Buddhist monasteries, the Veluvanara-maya Monastery, whose name in Pali also means 'bamboo grove'. King Bimbisara of Magadha had it built for the Buddha in Rajagriha. Prior to that the Buddha and his disciples lived in forests and caves, like Hindu ascetics.[6] The monk and venerator of Amitabha Fazhao (died around 820) founded the monastery of Zhulin between 777 and 796, after he had 'seen' it in a vision he experienced at Foguang Si.[7] In the period between the vision and the start of construction Fazhao composed the melody of the five-part invocation of Amitabha, which can be heard in all monasteries of Jingtu. Zhulin

Si quickly established itself as one of the most important monasteries on Wutai Shan, because it was one of the three monasteries that had governmental approval to ordain monks and nuns.

With the exception of the five-storey pagoda with its octagonal plan, from the time of the Ming emperor Wanli (ruled 1573–1620), the Red Guards destroyed the entire complex during the Cultural Revolution. When I visited Zhulin Si at the end of 2006, I noticed to my astonishment that the Great Hall, which had been renovated after 1990, had been torn down again, supposedly to make room for a much larger structure. The lanky abbot and his few monks aimed to have built the largest monastery on all of Wutai Shan within ten years. Beside the stupa lay dozens of large tree trunks. Next to them stood two stone lions and, on wooden mounts, three buddha statues covered in transparent wrapping. During my next visit, six months later, work on the entrance gate was underway. The workers were using some old, already painted wooden beams in its construction. I was surprised that the monks had agreed to tear down the existing temple hall, which had attracted pilgrims and donations, thus cutting the monastery off from the streams of pilgrims.

Shiziwo Si 狮子窝寺 and Wanfo Ta 万佛塔

West of Zhulin Si the path rises in the direction of the central and western terraces to the monastery of Shiziwo, the 'lions' den'. This monastery from the Ming Dynasty (1368–1644) was also destroyed by the Red Guards. In autumn 2006 reconstruction of the octagonal, three-storey pagoda, as well as of three buildings, was complete. The exterior walls of the pagoda are decorated with some 10,000 majolica paintings, which portray the meditating Buddha. For this reason the stupa is called Wanfo Ta, which means 'pagoda of the

The Japanese pilgrim monk Ennin and Wutai Shan

Buddhism reached Japan presumably around the year 467 when, according to the Chronicle of the Liang, five monks from Gandhara travelled to a land called Fusang, which probably referred to Japan. Entirely certain, however, is the official introduction of the teachings of the Buddha in 552 when the South Korean kingdom of Baekje sent monks and scriptures to Nara in Japan. The Central Asian monk Marananta had brought Buddhism from China to Baekje in 384. Early Japanese Buddhism did not appeal much to the unlettered populace, however; the work of the scholarly monks consisted of praying for the ruling household and the state and conducting rituals. Only in the seventh century, thanks to the impetus of missionaries from China, did Buddhism begin to address the broad mass of people. In this way the most important schools of Chinese Buddhism gained a foothold in Japan, and it is worth noting that a few masters, such as the Japanese Saicho, shaped the establishment of more than one school.

The idealistic doctrine of the Weishi School reached Japan around 660, where it developed into the Hosso-Shu School. Between 736 and 740 the Kegon School arose from the teaching of Huayan. Then the blind Chinese monk and doctor Jianzhen (688–763) reached Japan on his sixth attempt and spread there both Chinese medicine and the emphasis, central to the Lü School, on monastic rules, out of which arose the school of Ritsu. Two schools of Japanese Buddhism trace back to the Japanese pilgrim monk Saicho (767–822), who studied in China in 804 and returned a year later: the school of Tendai, which corresponds to the Chinese Tiantai, and the school of Shingon of esoteric Buddhism, whose co-founder was the then-famous monk, poet, and calligrapher Kukai (775–835). The pilgrim monk Ennin (793–864), who is important in the context of Wutai Shan, not only deepened the teaching of the Tendai School as its third patriarch but also was the first to spread the practice, central to Jingtu, of the invocation of Amitabha, from with the Jodo School emerged in the twelfth century. Chan was also known in Japan, beginning in the eighth century, although the two leading schools of Zen formed only much later, Rinzai in the twelfth century and Soto in the thirteenth century.[8]

Ennin, who is also known in Japan under the posthumous name Jikaku Daishi, was born in 793. He became a student of Saicho at age 15. In 838 he travelled by ship as a member of an official Japanese delegation to China, in order to study there. He kept a detailed journal of his observations and experiences in China until his return nine years later. Ennin's journal is not only the earliest description of China by a foreigner, but Ennin also, in contrast to such European travellers as Rubruk or Marco Polo, learned Chinese and was Buddhist. Thus, he understood the Sino–Buddhist cultural world much better.

Ennin's journey was in many respects an adventure. The first two attempts to leave Japan, in 836 and 837, were thwarted by typhoons. When the delegation finally reached the Middle Kingdom

The Japanese pilgrim monk Ennin (793–864) visited Wutai Shan in 840 and kept a valuable journal. Idealised portrait from the twelfth century.

The pagoda of Linggong Ta
commemorates the general of the
Northern Song Dynasty, General
Yang Ye, who starved himself to
death after losing a battle to the
neighbouring Liao (907–1125).

in 838 they were received with hostility, and Ennin was forbidden from traveling on to Mount Tiantai, the stronghold of his school. When the delegation returned to Japan a year later, he bowed out and remained in China. He succeeded in obtaining a travel permit, whereupon he set out for Wutai Shan, which he reached in 840 and where he stayed for more than two months. He went first to the monastery of Zhulin Si, where his two students Isho and Igyo received monastic consecration on the ordination platform. In the same monastery he marvelled at a mural illustrating the first encounter of the Indian monk Buddhapala with Wenshu Pusa in the year 676. He then spent six weeks at Da Huayan Si, the present-day monastery of Xiantong, from which he visited four of the five terraces, as well as the Jingang Cave, in which Manjushri is said to have enclosed Buddhapala in 683. The Japanese monk was inspired by Wutai Shan and wrote,

> When one enters this region of His Holiness [Monju, that is Manjushri], if one sees a very lowly man, one does not dare to feel contemptuous, and if one meets a donkey, one wonders if it might be a manifestation of Monju. Everything before one's eyes raises thoughts of the manifestations of Monju. The holy land makes one have a spontaneous feeling of respect for the region.[9]

Ennin also visited, in the footsteps of his predecessor Ryosen, the monastery of Jinge Si. Ryosen, together with Ennin's teacher Saicho and with Kukai, travelled from Japan to China in 804. After years of translation work in the capital, he made a pilgrimage to Wutai Shan in 820 and settled at the monastery of Jinge Si. Here Ennin saw a then-famous relic of Ryosen, which was kept in a small bronze pagoda. He had tattooed a buddha on a 10 cm-long and 8 cm-wide section of the skin of his arm, then removed his skin and given it to the monastery of Jinge Si. A few years later, between 825 and 828, Ryosen was poisoned in the monastery of Lingjing Si, south of the Southern Terrace. This murder is perhaps connected with a vanished gift in the form of 100 gold coins, which Ryosen had received from the Japanese emperor in 825.[10]

But Ennin's pleasure at being able to visit the key sites of Buddhism in China was short-lived; with the ascension to power of Emperor Wuzong (ruled 840–46) a dark shadow fell over Buddhism and its adherents. As early as 841 Ennin requested permission to return to his homeland – without success. Thus he became a witness to the severe anti-Buddhist persecutions of 843–45 and their destructive fury. During this terrible time Ennin's elder student, Igyo, died. Between 841 and 845 he wrote over 100 petitions to the office responsible for religious affairs, without ever receiving an answer. Only when he asked in writing to return to the lay state did he receive permission to leave. Ennin's contemporary and compatriot Egaku, who collected money in Japan for the monasteries on Wutai Shan and who visited the Five Terrace Mountain in 842, was also forced to return to the lay state and expelled in 845. Still, he returned to Wutai Shan two years later.[11] How great the attraction of Wutai Shan remained in Japan even after the catastrophe of 843–45 is shown by the undiminished stream of Japanese pilgrim monks, above all those of the school of Tendai. Among them were the leading scholar-monk of the time Shuuei (808–84), who studied there in 863; the monk Chonen, who stayed on Wutai Shan in 982; and the scholar-monk Jojin (1011–81). Like his predecessor Ennin, Jojin left behind a journal, the *Report of a Pilgrimage to Tiantai and Wutai Shan*. As far as the school of Tiantai is concerned, the transmission of knowledge now flowed in reverse, from Japan to China. Jojin took from Japan to China more than 600 books, which he lent to the monks on Mount Tiantai for copying, and thus the Japanese Tendai School contributed to the survival of its Chinese mother school.[12]

The pagoda, built under Emperor Wanli (ruled 1573–1620), of Zhulin Si Monastery, founded at the end of the eighth century.

(Right) Ceramic relief sculpture of a heavenly guardian and seated buddhas, Wanfo Ta.

ten thousand Buddhas'. The uniformly shaped, ochre-coloured Buddhas wear green robes and sit against a blue background; they symbolise the protection of Buddha, which emanates in all directions. In front of the pagoda a white statue of Milefo sat on logs on the ground, substituting for the Tian Wang Hall, which did not yet exist.

Rizhao Si   日照寺

On an old Chinese map I had noticed that the monastery of Rizhao Si, the 'monastery of sunshine', lay a few kilometres southwest of Jinge Si, in a depression in the valley. At first no one knew of such a monastery, however – not a single monk at the ostensibly nearby Jinge Si. I decided to try to find it anyway and descended into the valley in order to make a systematic search. After a time I came to a small clearing on a steep slope, where I found a recently built wall foundation and a thick

retaining wall, which was supposed to prevent the collapse of the newly cleared slope. Beside the construction site stood a poor brick hut with three small, dirty rooms, one of which served as a prayer chapel. Surprisingly, no one in the nearby village on the valley floor knew of a monastery, and it took further effort for my translator to find an elderly woman who reluctantly supplied some rather confusing information. From this it emerged that a struggle had developed between the monks who worked there but were absent at the time and the village over ownership of the construction site, and the monks were thus unwelcome. She recalled that before the Cultural Revolution some ten monks of the Jingtu School had belonged to the monastery.

Jinge Si   金阁寺

Just under 15 km southwest of Taihuai, the Chan monastery of Jinge Si sits snugly up against the

Entrance gate, or pailou, at Jinge Si.

hill of the same name, shortly before the road passes by the modern western gate of Wutai Shan Park. The monastery was founded at the time of the Tang in 766, but restored in 1555. Its origin lies in a vision of the Chan monk Daoyi from the year 736. In the vision he saw Wenshu Pusa, who showed him a wonderful monastery made of golden buildings, reached by a golden bridge. The bodhisattva said to Daoyi, 'See, here stands the monastery of the golden pavilion' (Chinese: Jinge Si). The overwhelmed monk reported his vision to Emperor Xuanzong (ruled 712–56), who ordered that such a monastery be built, presumably according to a plan from Daoyi. Thirty years later Emperor Daizong (ruled 762–79) commanded the famous monk Amoghavajra (Chinese: Bukong Jingang, 705–74), who represented esoteric Buddhism and was close to the emperor, to complete the construction. Amoghavajra was appointed abbot of Jinge Si and swiftly completed the work. He elevated the monastery to a centre of esoteric Buddhism,

and strongly supported the cult of Manjushri, so that this deity rose from regional significance to become the national patron of China.[13]

Jinge Si also played a decisive role in the life of the pilgrim Zhang Shangying (1043–1122). Zhang was a high-ranking state official who served as prime minister of Northern Song from 1110 to 1111. During a period of neo-Confucianism he was a cosmopolitan personality and produced writings that were accepted into both the Chinese Buddhist canon of the Tripitaka and the Daoist canon. In 1087, when he was a judge in Kaifeng, he dreamed of the monastery of Jinge Si, which prompted him to undertake a pilgrimage to Wutai Shan the following year. First he had the region purged of the bandits loitering in the area, and then in the summer he set out on his pilgrimage. He reached the first monastery, Qingliang Si, on 18 July 1088 and then visited, among others, the monasteries of Jinge Si, Pusading Si, Louhuo Si, Shouning Si and Foguang Si, as well as all five terraces. In Foguang Si ten abbots of Wutai Shan asked Zhang to write down his visions and to help them get their illegally confiscated land back from the military, saying:

The clearing of fields and cutting of forests have exposed the dens of our dragon spirits, and eight or nine of every ten of our monastery buildings have been ruined, their communities of monks left destitute or scattered to the four directions. Thus have the teachings of our master Mañjuśrī come to the verge of extinction.[14]

He returned to Wutai Shan in 1089 and again the following year to ask Wenshu Pusa for rain for the province of Shanxi, which was experiencing a drought. In a memorandum to the emperor he maintained,

Recently, because of a drought in your minister's territory, he made a personal visit to Wu-t'ai Shan. Before the image of Mañjuśrī and the pool of the five dragons, he prayed for the blessing of rain. *The numinous radiances and precious blazes that followed day and night were so uncanny in form and strange in aspect, so gloriously bright and luminously shimmering, that none could put a name to their appearance. On that occasion a crowd of more than a thousand monks and laity from all about gathered together to worship and stare. Their cries of wonder shook the mountains and the valleys. Afterward, the rains poured down, inundating several districts. When your minister had first set out, the plants and trees were withered and exhausted, the farmers disconsolate. But when he returned, the trees, hemp, buckwheat, and pulse were all green and flourishing, and the villages and towns sang and danced in anticipation of an abundant harvest.*[15]

Whether the monasteries regained the land confiscated by the military is unknown. It is certain, however, that Zhang's *Report from Qingliang*, also known as the *Further Chronicles of Qingliang*, revived the ancient tradition of pilgrimage to Wutai Shan.

The Guanyin Hall of Jinge Si.

The 17.7 m-tall, 'thousand-armed' Qianshou Guanyin Pusa stands between his parents in the hall of the same name at Jinge Si. The statue, from the sixteenth century, actually has 42 arms.

The monastery of Qingliang Si (below) and the southern terrace (above). Southern section of the western wall of Cave 61, Mogao, late tenth century. Qingliang Si actually stands at the foot of the western terrace; because in the painting the five terraces, which are actually laid out in a semicircle, are shown in a horizontal line, the perspective is distorted.

A Burmese jade statue of Shijiafo (Shakyamuni) entering nirvana, below Qingliang Si. The statue lay for months unprotected in its broken case.

The hallmark of Jinge Si is the 17.7 m-tall standing statue of Guanyin Pusa, erected in 1588, in the hall of the same name. It portrays the thousand-armed Qianshou Guanyin (Sanskrit: Sahasrabhuja Avalokiteshvara), who is filled with universal compassion and helpfulness; the statue in fact has 'only' 42 arms, which reach well into the second storey. Each hand holds a different item that is meant to help suffering living beings. The first abbot of Jinge Si, Amoghavajra, translated the *Vajraskehara Sutra*, which provides each of these helpful instruments with a corresponding mantra.[16] The first figurative representation of a thousand-armed Guanyin bodhisattva comes from Amoghavajra's time; it is a 3.9 m-tall, painted sandstone statue in the rock temple of Zizhong, Sichuan Province.[17] Presumably the faithfuls used to gather at the foot of the statue of Qianshou Guanyin, in order to recite her dharanis aloud together.

The statue, crafted in the Sino-Tibetan style of the Ming Dynasty, is flanked by two garishly painted figures, typically Chinese in appearance, who are said to represent the parents of Guanyin Pusa. The mother wears a red robe, the father a green one. The body of the Guanyin statue is made of clay placed over a metal frame; the arms are made of wood. Despite its formidable dimensions, the figure appears harmonious and is of a high artistic standard. Small statues of the bodhisattvas Wenshu, Guanyin and Puxian Pusa are found in front of it in the centre of the altar; far to the right stands a statues of the model pilgrim Shancai, and to the left side one of the enlightened dragon maiden Lungnü. An octagonal, dome-shaped ceiling, divided into three crown-like levels that narrow as they rise, arches above the grouping of statues. From the highest, central section of the ceiling a red dragon gazes at the statues and observers. It felt to me as if I were standing in a gigantic, self-contained pagoda or in the sanctuary of a cathedral. Seen from the ground floor, the Guanyin statue appears sublime and awe-inspiring; seen from the first floor, it takes on a softer, friendlier aspect. Here on the first floor a statue of Wenshu Pusa on his blue lion stands to her left side and to the right, one of Puxian Pusa on his elephant.

Qingliang Si 清凉寺

This monastery lies west of the border of Wutai Shan Park, just under 20 km from Taihuai. It belongs among the few monasteries that go back to Emperor Xiaowendi (ruled 471–99) of the Northern Wei Dynasty, and it bears the same name that the Five Terrace Mountain was then called: Qingliang, meaning 'cool and clear' or 'chill clarity'.[18] Between 516 and 520 the famous scholar-monk Lingbian (477–522) wrote the first comprehensive commentary on the *Huayanjing* (*Avatamsaka Sutra*) in the monastery of Qingliang Si. This commentary in 100 volumes, called

Huayanjing Lun, had great influence not only in China during the Tang Dynasty (618–907) but also in Korea and Japan. At that time the administrative office of Wutai Shan, called Sengzhen Si, was housed in Qingliang Si.

In the seventeenth century the monastery achieved renewed fame when the rumour emerged that the first emperor of the Qing Dynasty, Shunzhi (ruled 1644–61), had not, as officially reported, died of smallpox but rather had feigned the illness in order to have himself ordained a monk. The death of Shunzhi's favourite concubine, Dong, had led him to take this unusual step. After his ordination the ex-emperor retreated as an ordinary monk to Qingliang, where he is said to have died in 1711. The monastery was completely destroyed during the Cultural Revolution and is under reconstruction today. It counts six monks of the Jingtu School.

During my visit in autumn 2006 the monastery made an ambivalent impression. On arrival, I was confronted with a shocking sight: a 4 m-long, reclining Buddha in the pose of entry into nirvana, made of white Burmese marble, lay unprotected in a weather-beaten wooden box out in the open. The semiprecious stones that had decorated the robe were missing, and moss had grown over it. This statue was the gift of a donor from Hong Kong and had lain on the roadside for many months, which hardly showed respect for either the donor or the Buddha. This unfavourable impression was reinforced in the first courtyard of the monastery, where six more marble statues had likewise stood exposed for a few weeks. Rubbish was piled up in a corner.

In the Tian Wang Hall, guarded by two stone lions, the big-bellied Milefo, made of gold-painted plastic, greets pilgrims; at his back stands the armoured General Weituo. Next follows the Great Hall, where white plastic statues of the Buddhas of the Three Times are enthroned; in front of them on the floor stand two stone statues of Wenshu

The future buddha Milefo (Maitreya) grants courage to visitors. Tian Wang Hall, Qingliang Si.

Jade statues from Burma of Wenshu Pusa, Amituofo, and Guanyin Pusa in the first inner courtyard of Qingliang Si.

and Puxian Pusa. Statuettes of the 500 luohans cling to the walls. In the second inner courtyard stands a great granite boulder, which is the subject of many legends. It is said that in ancient days it was unbearably hot on Wutai Shan in the summer, and strong winds raised much dust. Wenshu Pusa borrowed a magic stone from the dragon king of the Yellow Sea and brought it to Wutai Shan, where he dropped it. The stone had barely touched the ground when the weather turned sharply cooler and the winds ceased to blow. For this reason the region was called from then on 'clear and cool'. It is also said that the bodhisattva liked to meditate and pray on the rock.[19] Today pilgrims place small coins on the stone as offerings.

In the subsequent Manjushri Hall gold-painted plastic statues of the seated bodhisattvas Puxian, Wenshu and Guanyin are enthroned. In front of Wenshu Pusa stand two smaller figures of Shancai and Lungnü. Two impressive stone statues are found on the two side walls. One has four peaceful-looking heads and two arms; it is the transcendental Buddha Piluzhenafo (Sanskrit: Vairocana). Beside him yellow slips of paper with the names of deceased people are stuck to the wall. On the opposite side red slips of paper bearing the wishes of pilgrims are affixed beside the statue of the bodhisattva Wenshu Pusa, who has feminine facial features. In a side room decorated with golden yellow cloth a monk showed me the purported cell of Emperor Shunzhi.

The bodhisattvas Puxian,
Wenshu, and Guanyin
Pusa (from left to right);
in front of them stand the
enlightened dragon maiden
Lungnü (left) and the model
pilgrim Shancai (right).
Wenshu Hall, Qingliang Si.

Outlook on the future

Instead of worrying about life after death, it is much more worthwhile to tend to life before death.

—Chinese wisdom

My two research trips to Wutai Shan impressed me in many ways. I was stunned not only by the great number of monasteries and their artistic treasures but also by how perfectly they suited the landscape. Aside from the gigantic hall of the convent of Pushou, which was under construction, no monastery seemed to want to dominate its surroundings; each was integrated into the cityscape of Taihuai or the natural environment. I also found remarkable how well maintained most of the monasteries looked, in both the material and the figurative sense. A peaceful, focused spirit prevailed there, despite the great crush of pilgrims and visitors. It seemed that both the monasteries and the nuns and monks knew how to protect themselves without being abrasive.

I often compared Wutai Shan to the monastic republic of Athos and its 20 great monasteries, which also extend across a spectacular mountain landscape. A few additional parallels occurred to me: just as Wutai Shan was believed to have been inhabited by dragons in earlier days, it is said in Greek mythology that the wild giant Athos, during a battle with the gods, threw a huge stone at Poseidon, which fell into the sea and formed the peninsula. And as Wutai Shan is made holy by the presence of the bodhisattva Wenshu Pusa, Mount Athos is associated with the Virgin Mary. When she, together with John the Evangelist, sailed to Cyprus, their ship is said to have docked there. Moved by the beauty of the scenery, she asked her son if he would give her the peninsula as a garden. Thus both these blessed places developed in the fourth or fifth century into sacred sites, where monks settled and established first hermitages and later monasteries, which were financially supported by pious rulers. Finally, both places look back on a more than 1,000-year traditions of pilgrimages.

Just as obvious as the similarities, however, are the differences. Wutai Shan has always been open to all pious visitors, while at Athos the admittance of women is strictly forbidden and Orthodox pilgrims are preferred to visitors of other Christian confessions. Furthermore, the number of pilgrims is limited at Athos; Wutai Shan, by contrast, is practically swamped with pilgrims on certain holidays. The monasteries

Man using a cigarette to light a long, thin pipe, typical for China.

on Athos have also largely been spared wanton destruction; those on Wutai Shan have suffered terrible devastation, most recently only 40 years ago, after which tremendous efforts, lasting into the present day, have been necessary for reconstruction. Since many monks and nuns lost their lives during the Cultural Revolution, the monasteries had to reinvent themselves. This pioneering spirit, which strives to overcome even the greatest obstacles, can be felt in many monasteries on Wutai Shan. Another difference, less noticeable at first, concerns the question of ecumenism. The monasteries on Athos regard it and the reconciliation talks between the Orthodox patriarch of Constantinople, to whom they are subordinate, and the Roman Catholic Church with scepticism verging on hostility. On Wutai Shan, by contrast, the question of ecumenism is irrelevant, since relations between the individual schools and their monasteries are open and cordial.

Chinese Buddhism and with it the pilgrimage site of Wutai Shan defied the Communist ideology's hostility toward religion and emerged stronger from this conflict. After the state-ordered levelling of values, thoughts and lifestyles, Buddhism blossoms anew in China, since people can again live out their need for intellectual security, individual lifestyle choices and spirituality, albeit within relatively narrow bounds. In contrast to Tibet, however, where public confession of Tibetan Buddhism also includes a political-patriotic component, Chinese Buddhism is largely apolitical.

At the start of the twenty-first century Chinese Buddhism must confront the challenge of capitalism and its temptations. For one thing, the growing streams of pilgrims and visitors place great demands on the popular large monasteries. They feel obligated to let visitors in

and allow them to circulate quite freely. As several abbots and abbesses assured me, although the monasteries are to provide for monastic life, they must not close themselves off as an elite from the needs of simple believers. Every nun and every monk must live out the example of the merciful bodhisattvas who vowed to lead human beings out from universal suffering. One who wants to follow the example of the luohans, however, should seek an isolated mountain monastery.

On the other hand, it is vitally important for monks and nuns to separate themselves in order to devote themselves regularly to textual study and meditation. Monasteries are not tourist traps; they must not succumb to the temptation to sell as many entrance tickets, incense sticks or private rituals as possible. It seemed to me that the monasteries on Wutai Shan have thus far confidently resisted such temptations. At many monasteries the Great Halls close their doors for the daily communal devotions; stands selling devotional objects are also located outside the monastery walls, in contrast to many basilicas and cathedrals in Europe, where these are found within the Lord's house. The monasteries are immune to an additional temptation, that of the possession of great lands through donations and bequests, because land ownership is forbidden them by law.

The greatest challenge to Buddhism, however, lies in how flexibly it can respond to people's changing needs. Despite, or rather because of, its rapid economic development, huge social gaps have emerged in China, which could result in social strains and perhaps also indifference toward Buddhism. Finally, it is not known how the Chinese will react in the case of further government liberalisation of religious affairs and the Christian and Islamic missionary efforts that could be expected to follow.

The rebuilt pagoda of Wanfo Ta at the monastery of Shiziwo Si. The white statue of Milefo stands in place of the Tian Wang Hall, which has yet to be rebuilt.

Notes

I. Introduction

1. *The Vimalakirti Sutra*, translated by Burton Watson, 1997, p. 53.
2. On the Buddhist doctrine that all phenomena are empty and illusory, see pp. 95ff.
3. See pp. 109ff.
4. Tsukamoto Zenryu: *A History of Chinese Early Buddhism*, 1979, pp. 457ff.
5. Naqin Susan, Chün-fang Yü (ed.): *Pilgrims and Sacred Sites in China*, 1992, p. 11.
6. As described more fully in the third and fifth chapters, Chinese folk Buddhism adapted itself to Daoist-influenced ideas from traditional thought, while Daoism adopted important Buddhist content. Since the boundaries blurred further in the lived religion of the people, it is legitimate to speak in certain contexts of Dao-Buddhism.
7. Hu Cheng Xi: *A Guide to the Temples in the Wutai Mountains*, 1993, p. 4. Zhong Xin, Wei Lingwen: *Wu Tai Shan*, 1984, p. 94.
8. See p. 134.
9. Birnbaum, Raoul: *Studies on the Mysteries of Manjushri*, 1983, pp. 11ff.

10. Hu Cheng Xi: *A Guide*, p. 1. In this book temples and groups of temples are referred to as monasteries only if at least one monk or one nun lives there year-round.

II. The spiritual and historical context

1. Zheng Lixin: *Guide to Chinese Buddhism*, 2004, p. 4.
2. Wagner Mayke, Tarasov Pavel: *Das vergessene Reich der Jinsha*, 2007, pp. 96–103. Zhang Yuehui, Li Xiangpin: *The Sanxingdui Site: Mystical Mask on Ancient Shu Kingdom*, Beijing, 2006.
3. Haarmann Harald: *Universalgeschichte der Schrift*, 1991, pp. 106–10.
4. Sinor Denis (ed.): *The Cambridge History of Early Inner Asia*, 1990, p. 119. The Xiongnu are probably distantly related to the Huns.
5. On Legalism, see pp. 21ff.
6. Confucius, *The Analects*, trans. Arthur Waley, New York: Knopf, 2000: Book VI, 20.
7. Confucius, *The Analects*: Book XI, 11.
8. Confucius, *The Analects*: Book XV, 23. See also Book XII, 3, XIII, 6.
9. Confucius, *The Analects*: Book XII, 11.
10. Confucius, *The Analects*: Book XIII, 13.

11. Confucius, *The Analects*: Book XII, 19 and XIII, 6.

12. See pp. 67ff.

13. Schmidt-Glintzer Helwig (ed.): *Mo Ti. Gegen den Krieg*, 1975, p. 141.

14. Ibid., p. 95.

15. Bauer Wolfgang: *Geschichte der chinesischen Philosophie*, 2006, p. 113.

16. Watson Burton (trans.): *Records of the Grand Historian of China*, 1971, Vol. II, pp. 13, 24–27.

17. Naqin Susan, Chün-fang Yü (ed.): *Pilgrims and Sacred Sites in China*, 1992, p. 13.

18. Blofeld John: *The Wheel of Life: The Autobiography of a Western Buddhist*, 1972, p. 133.

19. Dschuang Dsi: *Das wahre Buch vom südlichen Blütenland*, 1994, p. 232.

20. Ibid., p. 84.

21. See pp. 34ff.

22. See pp. 35f.

23. See pp. 113ff.

24. Paludan Ann: *Chronicle of the Chinese Emperors*, 1998, p. 28.

25. Ibid., p. 33. Wright Arthur: *Buddhism in Chinese History*, 1965, p. 15. The five works attributed to Confucius are the Book of Changes, the Book of Odes, the Book of History, the Book of Rites, and the Spring and Autumn Annals.

26. Watson: *Records of the Grand Historian*, Vol. II, pp. 57–60.

27. A census in the year 2 CE recorded a population of 56 million. *Encyclopaedia Britannica*, 1998, Vol. 16, p. 79.

28. Wang Yi'e: *Daoism in China*, 2004, pp. 27ff.

29. A second Taiping rebellion convulsed China from 1850 to 1865, and its leader Hong Xiuquan (1813–64) combined Daoist and Christian ideas.

III. The spread of Buddhism to China

1. *Sutra in Forty-Two Sections*, 1977, pp. 3f.

2. See p. 45.

3. See pp. 98ff.

4. Sanskrit and Chinese sources refer to a second 'short' chronology, which dates Shakyamuni's nirvana to the year 368 BCE, while Hinayana texts give the year 543 BCE. See Ghose Rajeshwari (ed.): *In the Footsteps of the Buddha*, 1998, p. 8, and Notz Klaus-Josef: *Lexikon des Buddhismus*, 2002, p. 89.

5. Hu Cheng Xi: *A Guide to the Temples in the Wutai Mountains*, 1993, pp. 13f. The pagoda is the further development, widespread in East Asia, of the Indian stupa, which was originally a royal burial mound and later a Buddhist reliquary shrine. The term 'Dagoba', commonly used in China and Sri Lanka, comes from the Sanskrit word dhatugarbha, which means 'container of the elements'; that is, 'reliquary shrine'. The word 'pagoda' is a transposition of 'dagoba'.

6. Tsukamoto Zenryu: *A History of Chinese Early Buddhism*, 1979, pp. 57, 75.

7. Reichelt Karl Ludwig: *Truth and Tradition in Chinese Buddhism*, 2001, p. 203.

8. Hu Cheng Xi: *A Guide* , p. 57.

9. The Vimalakirti Sutra, 1997, p. 87.

10. Ibid., pp. 67, 95f.

11. Ibid., pp. 70 and 133.

12. See pp. 109ff.

13. Tsukamoto Zenryu: *A History*, pp. 51–60. Zürcher Emil: *The Buddhist Conquest of China*, 1972, pp. 19–24.

14. Hu Cheng Xi: *A Guide*, pp. 4, 7, 68. Zhong Xin, Wei Lingwen: *Wu Tai Shan*, 1984, p. 94.

15. Tsukamoto Zenryu: *A History*, pp. 60–63, 476.

16. Ch'en Kenneth: *Buddhism in China*, 1964, p. 41. Tsukamoto Zenryu: *A History of Chinese Early Buddhism*, 1979, pp. 73f. Zürcher Emil: *The Buddhist Conquest of China*, 1972, p. 28.

17. Tsukamoto Zenryu: *A History*, pp. 78–98. Zürcher: *The Buddhist Conquest*, pp. 30–36.

18. For the expansion of Buddhism in China, see the next chapter.

19. Reichelt Karl Ludwig: *Truth and Tradition in Chinese Buddhism*, 2001, p. 34.

20. Baumer Christoph: *Southern Silk Road*, 2000, pp. 110f.

21. Tsukamoto Zenryu: *A History* , pp. 109f, 138ff.

22. *The Lotus Sutra*, 1993, p. IX.

23. See p. 99.

24. *The Flower Ornament Scripture*, 1993, pp. 906, 1172.

25. See pp. 134f.

26. Tsukamoto Zenryu: *A History*, pp. 127, 133, 169, 175, 294.

27. Ch'en Kenneth: *Buddhism in China*, 1964, pp. 50ff, 184.

28. Ibid., p. 474.

29. Ibid., p. 425.

30. On Buddhist epistemology and ontology, see pp. 97f.

31. Ch'en Kenneth: *Buddhism in China*, pp. 8f.

32. See pp. 115ff.

33. See pp. 20f.

34. See pp. 250f.

35. Kasser Rodolphe: 'Saint Antoine et la naissance du monachisme', *Le Monde de la Bible*, No. 177, May–June 2007, p. 24.

36. See pp. 82f. and 109ff.

37. Tsukamoto Zenryu: *A History*, pp. 119ff.

38. Ch'en Kenneth: *Buddhism in China*, pp. 139ff, 207. Zürcher: *The Buddhist Conquest*, pp. 254–67.

39. Tsukamoto Zenryu: *A History*, pp. 156ff.

40. Zürcher: *The Buddhist Conquest*, SS. 259ff.

41. Benn James: *Burning for the Buddha*, 2007, pp. 33f. *Das Lotos-Sutra*, 2007, pp. 291–295. Prip-Møller Johannes: *Chinese Buddhist Monasteries*, 1982, p. 171. In the early twenty-first century, Tibetan monks also set fire to themselves out of despair. Hilmer Andreas: *Für Tibet und die Welt*, 2007, p. 151. See here p. 250.

42. See p. 75.

43. See p. 105.

44. See pp. 221f.

45. See p. 82.

46. Ch'en Kenneth: *Buddhism in China*, pp. 179, 208.

47. *The Buddha speaks the Ullambana Sutra*. The Buddhist Text Society. www.bttsonline.org, www.urbandharma.org/udharma4/ullambana.html.

IV. 'Barbarian Emperors' elevate Buddhism to the state religion

1. There were really only five dynasties, since the kingdom of Wu, traditionally included, fell in 280.

2. Tsukamoto Zenryu: *A History of Chinese Early Buddhism*, 1979, p. 406. Zürcher Emil: *The Buddhist Conquest of China*, 1972, p. 153.

3. Tsukamoto Zenryu: *A History*, p. 834.

4. Ibid., p. 261.

5. Rhie Marylin M.: *Early Buddhist Art of China & Central Asia*, 2002, pp. 254f.

6. Zürcher: *The Buddhist conquest*, p. 414.

7. Ch'en Kenneth: *Buddhism in China*, 1964, p. 150.

8. Li Hengsheng: *Les grottes de Yungang et la dynastie des Wei du Nord*, 2005, p. 14.

9. Rhie: *Early Buddhist Art*, p. 232.

10. Chin Connie: 'Monuments in the Desert', 2005, pp. 9f.

11. Baumer Christoph: *The Church of the East*, 2006, pp. 185f.

12. Since Wutai Shan was opened as a pilgrimage site under the Northern Wei and was interwoven with the Tang Dynasty, we conclude the historical overview here and will discuss the historical events relevant to Buddhism in the chapter on the monasteries of Wutai Shan.

13. See p. 44.

14. Baumer Christoph: *Southern Silk Road*, 2000. Rhie: *Early Buddhist Art*, p. 2002.

15. See pp. 51ff.

16. Ghose Rajeshwari (ed.): *In the Footsteps of the Buddha*, 1998, p. 117. Howard Angela Falco et al: *Chinese Sculpture*, 2006. pp. 102f, 203–6, 225. Lee Jung Hyo: 'Buddhist Imageries of China proper during the Han-Jin Period', 2006, pp. 174–80. Rhie: *Early Buddhist Art*, pp. 27–155.

17. Howard Angela Falco et al: *Chinese Sculpture*, p. 226.

18. Ibid., p. 228.

19. Alphen Jan Van (ed.): *The Buddha in the Dragon Gate*, 2001, p. 38.

20. Baumer Christoph: *Sogdian or Indian Iconography and religious influences in Dandan-Uiliq (Xinjiang, China)?*, 2007.

21. Sullivan Michael: *The Cave Temples of Maichishan*, 1969, pp. 2ff.

22. Siren Osvald: *Chinese Sculpture from the fifth to the fourteenth century*, 1998, Vol. I, pp. LI–LXXXV.

23. Alphen: *The Buddha in the Dragon Gate*, p. 44. Barrett T.H.: 'Climate Change and Religious Response', 2007, pp. 141ff.

24. Tsukamoto Zenryu: *A History*, pp. 753ff. Zürcher: *The Buddhist Conquest*, pp. 124, 198.

25. Tsukamoto Zenryu: *A History*, pp. 844ff, 854–58.
Zürcher: *The Buddhist Conquest*, pp. 124, 198, 219ff.

26. The full name of the sutra is Pratyutpannabuddhasam
mukhavasthitasamadhi-Sutra. Tsukamoto Zenryu: *A
History*, pp. 851, 867f.

27. See pp. 109ff.

28. Ch'en Kenneth: *Buddhism in China*, 1964, S. 172.

29. See pp. 95ff.

30. Tsukamoto Zenryu: *A History*, p. 458.

31. Ibid., pp. 457, 895.

32. Lusthaus Dan: *Chinese Buddhist Philosophy*, 1998, p. 5.

33. See pp. 16f.

34. Wu John C.H.: *The Golden Age of Zen*, 2003, pp. 74f.

V. The Ten Schools of Chinese Buddhism

1. Wu John C.H.: *The Golden Age of Zen*, 2003, p. 177.

2. For additional sources, see, *inter alia*, Bauer Wolfgang:
Geschichte der chinesischen Philosophie, 2006,
pp. 194–226. Chen Kenneth: *Buddhism in China*, 1964,
pp. 297–337. Hershock Peter: *Chan Buddhism*, 2005.
Sharf Robert: *Coming to terms with Chinese Buddhism*,
2002. Swanson Paul: *Foundations of T'ien-Tai philosophy*,
1989. Wu John C.H.: *The Golden Age*.

3. In this context the term 'zong' denotes a Buddhist
tradition that can be traced back to a founder, a 'first
patriarch', whose spiritual insights provide the basis for
the school and are further developed by his successors.

4. Ch'en Kenneth: *Buddhism in China*, p. 87.

5. See pp. 55ff.

6. Ch'en Kenneth: *Buddhism in China*, p. 310. Swanson:
Foundations, pp. 1–7.

7. Reiter Florian: *Religionen in China*, 2002, p. 171.

8. See pp. 328ff.

9. Howard Angela Falco et al. *Chinese Sculpture*, 2006,
p. 380.

10. Hu Cheng Xi: *A Guide to the Temples in the Wutai
Mountains*, 1993, pp. 66f.

11. Ch'en Kenneth: *Buddhism in China*, p. 321.

12. See p. 45.

13. See pp. 255f.

14. See pp. 113ff.

15. Alphen: *The Buddha in the Dragon Gate*, 2001, p. 48.
Paludan Ann: *Chronicle of the Chinese Emperors*, 1998,
p. 105.

16. Alphen: *The Buddha in the Dragon Gate*, p. 46.

17. See pp. 90ff.

18. Baumer Christoph, Weber Therese: *Eastern Tibet.
Bridging Tibet and China*, 2005, pp. 53f.

19. Paludan: *Chronicle of the Chinese Emperors*, p. 112.

20. See pp. 88ff.

21. Zheng Lixin: *Guide to Chinese Buddhism*, 2004, p. 62.

22. Howard Angela Falco et al. *Chinese Sculpture*, p. 380.

23. Faure Bernhard: *The Will to Orthodoxy*, 1997, p. 57.

24. Otto Franck: *Zen*, 2007, p. 77.

25. Eliade Mircea (ed.): *The Encyclopedia of Religion*, 1995,
p. 332.

26. Hershock: *Chan Buddhism*, p. 33.

27. Shibata M. & M.: *Les maîtres du Tch'an (Zen) en
Chine*, 1985, p. 36. Wu John C.H.: *The Golden Age of
Zen*, p. 67.

28. Ferguson Andy: *Zen's Chinese Heritage*, 2000, p. 158.
Gimello Robert: 'Chang Shang-ying on Wu-t'ai Shan',
1992, p. 119.

29. Weber: *The Language of Paper*, 2007, p. 75.

30. Hershock: *Chan Buddhism*, p. 75.

31. Wu John C.H.: *The Golden Age*, p. 172.

32. Bauer Wolfgang: *Geschichte der chinesischen
Philosophie*, 2006, p. 223.

33. Pine Red (ed. and trans.): *The Zen Teachings of
Bodhidharma*, 1989, pp. 15, 17, 25, 27, 73. Wu John
C.H.: *The Golden Age*, p. 225.

34. Lin Sen-shou: 'Hui Ke', 2004/1, p. 4.

35. Welter Albert: *Monks, Rulers and Literati*, 2006,
pp. 7f, 28f.

36. Ch'en Kenneth: *Buddhism in China*, pp. 355f.
Hershock: *Chan Buddhism*, pp. 97–101.

37. Ibid., p. 102.

38. Since the 'Platform Sutra', attributed to Huineng,
was composed long after his death, he should not be
understood as a historical personage but rather as an
idealised integrating figure.

39. Wu John C.H.: *The Golden Age*, p. 82.

40. Ibid., p. 74.

41. Ibid., p. 142.

42. In both India and early monasteries of China, monks and nuns were forbidden to work in the fields. Wu John C.H.: *The Golden Age*, p. 98.

43. Hershock: *Chan Buddhism*, p. 139.

44. Wu John C.H.: *The Golden Age*, p. 172.

45. *The Vimalakirti Sutra*, 1997, p. 70.

46. Brentjes Burchard: *Der Tierstil in Eurasien*, 1982, p. 30.

47. Siren Osvald: *The Chinese on art and painting*, 2005 pp. 105f.

VI. The nine sacred mountains of China and Mount Wutai Shan

1. *Flower Ornament Scripture*, 1993, p. 906.

2. See pp. 221f.

3. For pictures of the nine sacred mountains, see: Johaentges Karl, Franz Uli: *Chinas Heilige Berge*, 2005. Mullikin Maria Augusta, Hotchkis Anna: *The Nine Sacred Mountains of China*, 1973.

4. Other sources give 858 or 863.

5. Birnbaum Raoul: 'Thoughts on T'ang Buddhist mountain traditions and their context', 1984, pp. 17f. Cartelli Mary Anne: 'On a five-colored cloud: the Songs of Mount Wutai', 2004, p. 1. (*Journal of the American Oriental Society* 124 (2004): 737f.)

6. Gimello Robert: 'Chang Shang-ying on Wu-t'ai Shan', 1992, p. 99.

7. Birnbaum Raoul: *Studies on the Mysteries of Manjushri*, 1983, p. 11. 'The manifestation of a monastery', 1986, pp. 123ff. Cartelli: 'On a five-colored cloud', p. 2. Tribe Anthony: 'The cult of Manjusri', pp. 8f.

8. Eberhard Wolfram: *Lexikon chinesischer Symbole*, 1995, pp. 97f.

9. Cornu Philippe: *Dictionnaire encyclopédique du Bouddhisme*, 2001, p. 206.

10. Marchand Ernesta: *The Panorama of Wu-T'ai Shan as an Example of Tenth Century Cartography*, 1976, pp. 162, 173.

11. Jing Anning: *The Portraits of Kubilai Khan and Chabi by Anige*, 1994, p. 55.

12. Xu Xiake: *Randonnées aux sites sublimes*. Gallimard 1993, p. 240.

13. Jing Anning: *The Portraits*, p. 55

14. Regarding Manjushri: Cornu Philippe: *Dictionnaire encyclopédique du Bouddhisme*, 2001, pp. 351ff. Frédéric Louis: *Les Dieux du Bouddhisme*, 1992, pp. 182ff.

15. Cartelli: 'On a five-colored cloud', pp. 5f. *Surangama Samadhi Sutra*, 1998, pp. 79f.

16. *Flower Ornament Scripture*, 1993, pp. 1172f.

17. *The Lotus Sutra*, 1993, pp. 187ff.

18. Zhong Xin, Wei Lingwen: *Wu Tai Shan*, 1984, p. 93.

19. Birnbaum Raoul: 'The manifestation of a monastery', 1986, pp. 125f. Hu Cheng Xi: *A Guide to the Temples in the Wutai Mountains*, 1993, pp. 26f. Rhie Marylin M.: *The Fo-kuang ssu*, 1977, pp. 13f.

20. Birnbaum Raoul: *Studies on the Mysteries*, pp. 24ff, 32f.

21. Wong Dorothy: 'A Reassessment of the Representation of Mt. Wutai from Dunhuang Cave 61,' 1993, p. 39.

22. Marchand Ernesta: *The Panorama*, pp. 163, 165.

VII. Pilgrimage routes to the Five Terrace Mountain: The outer regions

1. Birnbaum Raoul: 'The manifestation of a monastery', 1986, p. 119. 'Li' is a measurement of length and corresponds to approximately 400 m. The expression 'ten thousand li' means a very long distance.

2. Hu Cheng Xi: *A Guide to the Temples in the Wutai Mountains*, 1993, p. 25.

3. Cui Zhengsen: *108 Temples of Mt. Wutai*, 2004, p. 118. Hu Cheng Xi: *A Guide*, p. 24.

4. Gimello Robert: 'Chang Shang-ying on Wu-t'ai Shan'. In: Naqin Susan, Chün-fang Yü (ed.): *Pilgrims and Sacred Sites in China*, 1992, pp. 109, 138. Rhie Marylin M.: *The Fo-kuang ssu*, 1977, pp. 13ff.

5. Hu Cheng Xi: *A Guide*, p. 27. Rhie: *The Fo-kuang ssu*, pp. 38–41.

6. Steinhardt Nancy: 'The Tang architectural icon and the politics of Chinese architectural history', 2004.

7. Under caesaropapism a head of state claims to be also head of a church. It is the opposite of theocracy, where the head of a church also controls the state.

8. Hu Cheng Xi: *A Guide*, p. 18. Prip-Møller Johannes: Chinese Buddhist Monasteries, 1982, pp. 30ff. Rousselle Erwin: *Vom Sinn der buddhistischen Bildwerke in China*, 1958, p. 39.

9. See pp. 26off.

10. Chandra Lokesh: *Dictionary of Buddhist Iconography*, Vol. 13, 2004, pp. 3749ff.

11. Halén Harry: *Mirrors of the Void*, 1987, p. 7.

12. Cornu Phillippe: *Dictionnaire encyclopédique du Bouddhisme*, 2001, p. 492. Fischer-Schreiber Ingrid et al.: *The Shambala Dictionary of Buddhism and Zen*, 1991, pp. 125f. Halén Harry: *Mirrors of the Void*, 1987, p. 84.

13. Howard Angela Falco et al.: *Chinese Sculpture*, 2006, p. 102.

14. Frédéric Louis: *Les Dieux du Bouddhisme*, 1992, pp. 110f.

15. Rupprecht, Crown Prince of Bavaria: *Reiseerinnerungen aus Ostasien*, 1923, pp. 215ff.

VIII. The five terraces and their monasteries

1. *The Surangama Samadhi Sutra*, 1998, pp. 79f.

2. Hu Cheng Xi: *A Guide to the Temples in the Wutai Mountains*, 1993, p. 62.

3. Reischauer Edwin: *Ennin's Travels in Tang China*, 1955, p. 205.

4. Ch'en Kenneth: *Buddhism in China*, 1964, p. 349.

5. Chandra Lokesh: *Dictionary of Buddhist Iconography*, 2003, p. 2425.

6. Giès Jacques: *Les arts de l'Asie centrale. La collection Paul Pelliot du musée national des arts asiatiques – Guimet*, 1996. Vol. 2, p. 284. Reischauer: *Ennin's Travels*, pp. 206f.

7. Birnbaum Raoul: 'The manifestation of a monastery', 1986, p. 120.

8. Chandra Lokesh: *Dictionary of Buddhist Iconography*, pp. 503f.

9. See pp. 250f. Benn James: *Burning for the Buddha*, 2007, pp. 135ff.

IX. The monastery city of Taihuai 台怀景区

1. See p. 51.

2. Birnbaum Raoul: 'The manifestation of a monastery', 1986, pp. 121, 125. Hu Cheng Xi: *A Guide to the Temples in the Wutai Mountains*, 1993, pp. 7, 66.

3. Ibid., p. 19.

4. Puay-Peng Ho: 'Building for Glitter and Eternity', 1996, p. 67.

5. Reischauer Edwin: *Ennin's Travels in Tang China*, 1955, pp. 199f.

6. Prip-Møller Johannes: *Chinese Buddhist Monasteries*, 1982, pp. 36, 40, 74. Rousselle Erwin: *Vom Sinn der buddhistischen Bildwerke in China*, 1958, p. 75.

7. Chandra Lokesh: *Dictionary of Buddhist Iconography*, 2003, Vol. 8, pp. 2239f.

8. Hu Cheng Xi: *A Guide to the Temples in the Wutai Mountains*, 1993, pp. 10, 53.

9. Prip-Møller: *Chinese Buddhist Monasteries*, p. 19. Rousselle: *Vom Sinn der buddhistischen Bildwerke*, p. 12.

10. Prip-Møller: *Chinese Buddhist Monasteries*, p. 21.

11. Ibid., pp. 15f.

12. Ibid., p. 40.

13. Jing Anning: *The Portraits of Kubilai Khan and Chabi by Anige (1245–1306), a Nepali Artist at the Yuan Court*, 1994, pp. 55f.

14. Hu Cheng Xi: *A Guide*, pp. 12–14.

15. Reichelt Karl Ludwig: *Truth and Tradition in Chinese Buddhism*, 2001, p. 214. Reischauer: *Ennin's Travels*, p. 196.

16. Prip-Møller: *Chinese Buddhist Monasteries*, p. 299.

17. Howard Angela Falco et al: *Chinese Sculpture*, 2006, p. 382.

18. See the following section on Tibetan Buddhism.

19. Tuttle Gray: *Tibetan Buddhists in the Making of Modern China*, 2005, p. 28.

20. Snelling John: *Buddhism in Russia*, 1993, pp. 28, 274.

21. Tuttle: *Tibetan Buddhists*, pp. 20–23.

22. Everding Karl-Heinz: *Die Präexistenzen der Lcan Skya Qutuqtus*, 1988, p. 205. Tuttle: *Tibetan Buddhists*, pp. 76, 260.

23. Henss Michael: *Rölpai Dorje – Teacher of the Empire*, 2005, pp. 1f, 9.

24. Tuttle: *Tibetan Buddhists*, pp. 20, 23, 76, 248.

25. Ibid., pp. 218f, 296f.

26. Wen-shing Chou: *Ineffable Paths. Mapping Wutaishan in Qing Dynasty*, China, n. 47.

27. Ferrari Alfonsa: *Mk'yen Brtse's Guide to the Holy Places of Central Tibet*, 1958, pp. 73, 166.

28. Tuttle: *Tibetan Buddhists*, pp. 97–102, 207, 216–19, 231.

29. Ibid., pp. 7, 12f, 55, 62, 69–73, 157f.

30. Cui Zhengsen: *108 Temples of Mt. Wutai*, 2004, p. 7. Hu Cheng Xi: *A Guide*, pp. 1, 63f.

31. Carpini Plano: *Kunde von den Mongolen*, 1997. P. 55. See also: Rubruk Wilhelm von: *Reisen zum Grosskhan der Mongolen*, 1984, p. 198.

32. www.savetibet.org, 22 June 2007.

33. Chin Hsiao (ed.): *A special exhibition of recently acquired gilt-bronze Buddhist images*, 1996, pp. 100f. Lee-Kalish Jeong-he (ed.): *Tibet Klöster öffnen ihre Schatzkammern*, 2006, pp. 401–408. Rhie Marylin M., Thurman Robert A.F.: *Wisdom and compassion*, 1991, pp. 280ff.

34. Tuttle Gray: *Tibetan Buddhism at Ri bo rtse Inga/Wutai Shan in Modern China*, 2006. (Internet publication without page numbers.)

35. Tuttle: *Tibetan Buddhists*, p. 27.

36. Wen-shing Chou: *Ineffable Paths. Mapping Wutaishan in Qing dynasty*, China, note 11.

37. Blofeld John: *The Wheel of Life*, 1972, p. 144.

38. Hu Cheng Xi. *A Guide*, p. 59.

39. Jing Anning: *The Portraits*, p. 55.

40. Benn James: *Burning for the Buddha*, 2007, pp. 4, 15, 25, 108.

41. Huo Xushu, Qi Xiaoshan: *The Buddhist Art in Xinjiang along the Silk Road*, 2006, p. 63.

42. *Das Lotos-Sutra*, translated by Max Deeg, 207, pp. 291–95. English text is from *The Lotus Sutra*, trans. Burton Watson, 1993, p. 285.

43. Benn: *Burning for the Buddha*, pp. 65–70, 130. Zürcher Emil: *The Buddhist Conquest of China*, 1972, p. 282.

44. Benn: *Burning for the Buddha*, pp. 65–70, 130. Zürcher: *The Buddhist Conquest*, pp. 33–45, 70–98.

45. Prip-Møller: *Chinese Buddhist Monasteries*, p. 181.

Reichelt Karl Ludwig: *Truth and Tradition in Chinese Buddhism*, 2001, pp. 287–292. Wieczorek Alfried, Tellenbach, Rosendahl Wilfried (ed.): *Mumien. Der Traum vom ewigen Leben*, 2007, pp. 141ff.

46. Ch'en Kenneth: *Buddhism in China*, pp. 280f.

47. Benn: *Burning for the Buddha*, pp. 139, 153.

48. Ibid., pp. 99f.

49. Prip-Møller: *Chinese Buddhist Monasteries*, p. 321.

50. Baumer Christoph: *The Church of the East*, 2006, pp. 111ff, 126ff.

X. The North

1. Gimello Robert: 'Chang Shang-ying on Wu-t'ai Shan, 1992, p. 130. Reischauer Edwin: *Ennin's Travels in Tang China*, 1955, pp. 195f. Wong Dorothy: 'A Reassessment of the Representation of Mt. Wutai from Dunhuang Cave 61', 1993, pp. 34–37.

2. Hu Cheng Xi: *A Guide to the Temples in the Wutai Mountains*, 1993, p. 56.

3. Maspéro Henri, *Mythologie de la Chine modern*, 2004, pp. 52f.

4. Frédéric Louis: *Les Dieux du Bouddhisme*, 1992, pp. 241ff. Hu Cheng Xi: *A Guide to the Temples in the Wutai Mountains*, 1993, p. 51.

5. Zhaoyuanwai Tang is the first of only two monasteries on Wutai Shan that the author did not visit, on account of heavy rain and landslides.

XI. The East

1. *The Vimalakirti Sutra*, 1997, p. 37. English text is from Watson's translation, 1997, p. 37.

2. The other site of this legendary discussion is Duitanshi on the western terrace. See p. 188.

3. Cui Zhengsen: *108 Temples of Mt. Wutai*, 2004, p. 39.

4. See p. 103.

5. See p. 36.

6. Brauen Martin (ed.): *Die Dalai Lamas*, 2005.

7. Mannerheim C.G.: *Across Asia from West to East*, 1940, pp. 685–95. Wimmel Kenneth: *William Woodville Rockhill*, 2003, pp. 167f.

XII. The South

1. Boerschmann Ernst: *Baukunst und Landschaft in China*, 1926, p. 70.

2. Cheng Manchao: *The Origin of Chinese Deities*, 1995, pp. 20–24.

3. Ibid., pp. 80–90.

4. Eberhard Wolfram: *Lexikon chinesischer Symbole*, 1995, pp. 96f. Williams C.A.S.: *Outline of Chinese Symbolism and Art Motives*, 1976, pp. 200ff.

5. Jing Anning: *The Portraits of Kubilai Khan and Chabi by Anige (1245–1306), a Nepali Artist at the Yuan Court*, 1994, pp. 54f.

6. Cui Zhengsen: *108 Temples of Mt. Wutai*, 2004, pp. 66–71. Hu Cheng Xi: *A Guide to the Temples in the Wutai Mountains*, 1993, pp. 31ff.

7. See pp. 167f.

8. Chandra Lokesh: *Dictionary of Buddhist Iconography*, 2005, Vol. 14, p. 4017.

9. Lingjing Si is the second of the two monasteries on Wutai Shan that the author did not visit on account of heavy rainfall and landslides. Information was obtained from the monks of the monasteries of Jinge Si and Puji Se as well as the pilgrim guide Cui Zhengsen: *108 Temples of Mt. Wutai*, 2004, p. 116.

10. Reischauer Edwin: *Ennin's Travels in Tang China*, 1995, pp. 158, 201ff.

11. Howard Angela Falco et al.: *Chinese Sculpture*, 2006, pp. 408.

12. Cheng Manchao: *The Origin of Chinese Deities*, 1995, pp. 53–58.

13. Cui Zhengsen: *108 Temples*, p. 127.

XIII. The West

1. English text from Reischauer Edwin: *Ennin's Travels in Tang China*, 1995, p. 196.

2. I thank Dr Veronika Veit of the University of Bonn for evidence of the identity of Prince Tsagaan Danjin. See Pelliot Paul: *Notes critiques d'histoire kalmouke*, pp. 19f., Plate II, no. 210.

3. Hu Cheng Xi: *A Guide to the Temples in the Wutai Mountains*, 1993, p. 58.

4. Tuttle Gray: *Tibetan Buddhism at Ri bo rtse Inga/Wutai Shan in Modern Times*, 2006. Part III, n. 29.

5. See p. 258.

6. Zheng Lixin: *Guide to Chinese Buddhism*, 2004, p. 70.

7. Hu Cheng Xi: *A Guide*, pp. 35, 65.

8. Cornu Philippe: *Dictionnaire encyclopédique du Bouddhisme*, 2001, pp. 265ff. Eliade Mircea (ed.): *The Encyclopedia of Religion*, 1995, Vol. 2, pp. 425–435. Tamura Yoshiro, Hunter Jeffrey: *Japanese Buddhism: A Cultural History*. 2000.

9. Reischauer: *Ennin's Travels*, p. 196.

10. Ibid., pp. 158, 201ff.

11. Ibid., pp. 208f.

12. Hu Cheng Xi: *A Guide*, pp. 73f.

13. Birnbaum Raoul: *Studies on the Mysteries of Manjushri*, 1983, pp. 15f, 30ff. Hu Cheng Xi: *A Guide*, pp. 34, 69f. Tribe Anthony: 'The cult of Manjusri', pp. 7, 10f.

14. Gimello Robert: 'Chang Shang-ying on Wu-t'ai Shan', 1992, p. 111.

15. Ibid., p. 114.

16. Chandra Lokesh: *Dictionary of Buddhist Iconography*, 2004, Vol. 10, p. 2971.

17. Howard Angela Falco et al. *Chinese Sculpture*, 2006, pp. 319, 324.

18. Gimello: 'Chang Shang-ying on Wu-t'ai Shan', p. 132.

19. Hu Cheng Xi: *A Guide*, p. 35.

Bibliography

Alphen, Jan Van (ed.): *The Buddha in the Dragon Gate*. Etnographisch Museum, Antwerpen 2001.

An, Jianhua: *Der Mönch von heiliger Loyalität* (Shengzhong Heshang). Xianggang Bihui Chubanshe), Hong Kong 2004.

Barrett, T.H.: 'Climate change and religious response: The case of early medieval China'. In: *Journal of the Royal Asiatic Society*, London. April 2007, pp. 139–56.

Bauer, Wolfgang: *Geschichte der chinesischen Philosophie*. Beck, München 2006.

Baumer, Christoph: *Southern Silk Road*. Orchid Press, Bangkok, 2000.

— *The Church of the East. An Illustrated History of Assyrian Christianity*. I.B.Tauris, London 2006.

— 'Sogdian or Indian iconography and religious influences in Dandan-Uiliq (Xinjiang, China)?' In: *Proceedings of the International Seminar on The Art of Central Asia and the Indian Sub-Continent in Cross-Cultural Perspective (1st–14th cent. AD)*. National Museum of New Delhi, March 2007.

Baumer, Christoph, Weber, Therese: *Eastern Tibet. Bridging Tibet and China*. Orchid Press, Bangkok, 2005.

Beckwith, Christopher: 'The Tibetans in the Ordos and North China: Considerations on the role of the Tibetan Empire in world history'. In: Beckwith Christopher (ed.): *Silver on Lapis: Tibetan Literary Culture and History*. Tibet Society, Bloomington 1987.

Bell, Charles: *Portrait of the Dalai Lama*. Collins, London 1946.

Benn, James: 'Where text meets flesh: burning the body as an apocryphal practice in Chinese Buddhism'. In: *History of Religions*, University of Chicago Press, Vol. 37, No. 4, May 1998, pp. 295–322.

— *Burning for the Buddha. Self-immolation in Chinese Buddhism*. University of Hawaii Press, Honolulu 2007.

Berger, Patricia: 'Miracles in Nanjing: An Imperial Record of the 5th Karmapa's visit to the Chinese capital'. In: Weidner, Marsha (ed.): *Cultural Intersections in Later Chinese Buddhism*. University of Hawaii Press, Honolulu 2001.

Berry, Scott: *Monks, Spies and a Soldier of Fortune. The Japanese in Tibet*. Athlone Press, London 1995.

Birnbaum, Raoul: *Studies on the mysteries of Manjushri*. Society for the Study of Chinese Religions, Boulder 1983.

— 'Thoughts on T'ang Buddhist mountain traditions and their context'. In: *T'ang Studies*, University of Wisconsin, Madison 1984.

Kungfutse: *Gespräche (Lun Yü)*. Diederichs, Düsseldorf, 1955.

Lee, Jung Hyo: 'Buddhist Imageries of China proper during the Han-Jin Period'. In: *Chinese Archaeology*; edited by Liu Qingzhu. China Social Sciences Press, Beijing, Vol. 6, 2006.

Lee-Kalish, Jeong-he (ed.): *Tibet Klöster öffnen ihre Schatzkammern*. Ausstellungskatalog. Kulturstiftung Ruhr, Essen u. Hirmer, München 2006.

Li, Hengsheng: *Les grottes de Yungang et la dynastie des Wei du Nord*. Editions des sciences et techniques du Shanxi, Taiyuan 2005.

Li, Yuming (ed.): *A Panorama of Ancient Chinese Architecture in Shanxi*. Shanxi People's Publishing House, Taiyuan 1986.

Lin, Chi: *The Zen Teachings of Master Lin-Chi*. Translated by Burton Watson. Columbia University Press, New York 1993.

Lin, Sen-shou: 'Hui Ke. China's Second Ch'an Patriarch'. In: *Tzu Chi Quarterly*, Taipei 2004/1. www.taipei. tzuchi.org.tw/tzquart/2004.

Ling, Haicheng: *Buddhism in China*. China Intercontinental Press, Beijing 2004.

Liu, Yan, Han Chunhong (ed.): *Scenic Beauty of Wutai Mountain*. China Photographic Publishing House, Beijing 2005.

Lusthaus, Dan: 'Chinese Buddhist philosophy'. In: Craig E. (ed.): *Routledge Encyclopedia of Philosophy*. Routledge, London 1998.

Mannerheim, C.G.: *Across Asia from West to East*. Suomalaisen Kirjallisuuden Seuran Kirjapainon Oy, Helsinki 1940.

Marchand, Ernesta: 'The Panorama of Wu-T'ai Shan as an example of tenth century cartography'. In: *Oriental Art*, Singapore XXII/2, 1976.

May, Reinhard: *Heidegger's Hidden Sources. East Asian Influences on his Work*. Routledge, London 1996.

Mullikin, Maria Augusta, Hotchkis, Anna: *The Nine Sacred Mountains of China. An Illustrated Record of Pilgrimages Made in the Years 1935–1936*. Vetch and Lee, Hong Kong 1973.

Naqin, Susan, Chün-fang, Yü (ed): *Pilgrims and Sacred Sites in China*. University of California Press, Berkeley 1992.

Notz, Klaus-Josef: *Lexikon des Buddhismus*. Fourier, Wiesbaden 2002.

Ollone, Vicomte de: *In Forbidden China. The D'Ollone Mission 1906–1908*. Fischer Unwin, London 1912.

Oort, H.A. van: *The Iconography of Chinese Buddhism in Traditional China*. E.J. Brill, Leiden 1986.

Otto, Franck: 'Zen'. In: *Der Buddhismus*. Geo Epoche. Gruner+Jahr, Hamburg, Nr. 26, 2007.

Overmyer, Daniel L.: 'Religion in China Today'. In: *The China Quarterly Special Issues*. New Series, No. 3. Cambridge University Press, Cambridge 2003.

Paludan, Ann: *Chronicle of the Chinese Emperors*. Thames & Hudson, London 1998.

Pelliot, Paul: *Notes critiques d'histoire kalmouke*. Œuvres posthumes, Bd. VI, Adrien-Maisonneuve, Paris 1960.

Peng, Xunhou: *China in the World Anti-Fascist War*. China Intercontinental Press, Beijing 2005.

Pi, Yuanping, Yang Chun'e: (eds): *Zu den Gipfeln des Wutai Shan*. Shanxi Guji Chubanshe, Taiyuan 2005.

Pine, Red (editor and translator): *The Zen Teachings of Bodhidharma*. North Point Press, New York 1989.

Pokotilow, D.: 'Der Wu Tai Shan und seine Klöster. Eine historisch-geographische Skizze und Schilderung der örtlichen Verhältnisse im Jahr 1889'. In: *Sinica-Sonderausgabe*. Jahrgang 1935, herausgegeben von Erwin Rouselle. China-Institut, J.W. Goethe-Universität, Frankfurt a.M.

Pratt, James: *The Pilgrimage of Buddhism*. Macmillan, New York 1928.

Prip-Møller, Johannes: *Chinese Buddhist Monasteries*. Hong Kong University Press, Hong Kong 1982.

Puay-Peng, Ho: 'Building for Glitter and Eternity: The works of the Late Ming Master Builder Miaofeng on Wutai Shan'. In: *Orientations*, Hong Kong May 1996.

Reichelt, Karl Ludwig: *Truth and Tradition in Chinese Buddhism*. Manoharlal Publ., New Delhi 2001.

Reischauer, Edwin: *Ennin's Travels in Tang China*. Ronald Press, New York 1955.

Reiter, Florian: *Religionen in China*. Beck, München 2002.

Rhie, Marylin M.: *The Fo-kuang ssu*. Garland Publishing, New York 1977.

Bibliography

Alphen, Jan Van (ed.): *The Buddha in the Dragon Gate.* Etnographisch Museum, Antwerpen 2001.

An, Jianhua: *Der Mönch von heiliger Loyalität* (Shengzhong Heshang). Xianggang Bihui Chubanshe), Hong Kong 2004.

Barrett, T.H.: 'Climate change and religious response: The case of early medieval China'. In: *Journal of the Royal Asiatic Society,* London. April 2007, pp. 139–56.

Bauer, Wolfgang: *Geschichte der chinesischen Philosophie.* Beck, München 2006.

Baumer, Christoph: *Southern Silk Road.* Orchid Press, Bangkok, 2000.

— *The Church of the East. An Illustrated History of Assyrian Christianity.* I.B.Tauris, London 2006.

— 'Sogdian or Indian iconography and religious influences in Dandan-Uiliq (Xinjiang, China)?' In: *Proceedings of the International Seminar on The Art of Central Asia and the Indian Sub-Continent in Cross-Cultural Perspective (1st–14th cent. AD).* National Museum of New Delhi, March 2007.

Baumer, Christoph, Weber, Therese: *Eastern Tibet. Bridging Tibet and China.* Orchid Press, Bangkok, 2005.

Beckwith, Christopher: 'The Tibetans in the Ordos and North China: Considerations on the role of the Tibetan Empire in world history'. In: Beckwith Christopher (ed.): *Silver on Lapis: Tibetan Literary Culture and History.* Tibet Society, Bloomington 1987.

Bell, Charles: *Portrait of the Dalai Lama.* Collins, London 1946.

Benn, James: 'Where text meets flesh: burning the body as an apocryphal practice in Chinese Buddhism'. In: *History of Religions,* University of Chicago Press, Vol. 37, No. 4, May 1998, pp. 295–322.

— *Burning for the Buddha. Self-immolation in Chinese Buddhism.* University of Hawaii Press, Honolulu 2007.

Berger, Patricia: 'Miracles in Nanjing: An Imperial Record of the 5th Karmapa's visit to the Chinese capital'. In: Weidner, Marsha (ed.): *Cultural Intersections in Later Chinese Buddhism.* University of Hawaii Press, Honolulu 2001.

Berry, Scott: *Monks, Spies and a Soldier of Fortune. The Japanese in Tibet.* Athlone Press, London 1995.

Birnbaum, Raoul: *Studies on the mysteries of Manjushri.* Society for the Study of Chinese Religions, Boulder 1983.

— 'Thoughts on T'ang Buddhist mountain traditions and their context'. In: *T'ang Studies,* University of Wisconsin, Madison 1984.

Christoph Baumer – a leading explorer of Central Asia, Tibet and China – has written several well-received books in the fields of history, religion, archaeology and travel. These include *The Church of the East: An Illustrated History of Assyrian Christianity* (2006) and *Traces in the*

Desert: Journeys of Discovery across Central Asia (2008), both published by I.B.Tauris. Dr Baumer is President of the Society for the Exploration of EurAsia and a member of the Explorers' Club, New York, and the Royal Asiatic Society and the Royal Geographical Society, London.

The author Christoph Baumer with the abbot of Shuxian Si Monastery, Sheng Zhong.

'This is a most informative and beautifully illustrated book about Mt Wutai, one of the four sacred Buddhist mountains dedicated to Manjushri (Wenshu), the Bodhisattva of Wisdom. It provides background information about the philosophical and religious heritage of China, the history of Buddhism, and major schools of Chinese Buddhism. Perhaps the most attractive feature of the book is its detailed description of the pilgrimage routes to the mountain and its five terraces together with more than sixty existing monasteries that the author visited personally. The reader is introduced to the history and legends of the monasteries and the resident monks and nuns. It is the next best thing to making the pilgrimage to the holy site oneself. I highly recommend the book to anyone interested in Buddhism, sacred geography, and pilgrimage.'

—**Chun-fang Yu,** Sheng Yen Professor of Chinese Buddhist Studies, Columbia University

'To enter the world of China's Holy Mountain is to follow in the footsteps of modern-day pilgrim and erudite explorer Christoph Baumer, who made his journey into one of China's most spiritual mountains: Mt Wutai in Shanxi Province. Richly illustrated and extremely readable, his book first sketches a background to China's religions then gives an eyewitness account of the author's visits to all the monasteries (primarily Buddhist) that still exist on the mountain. The record of his journey to Mt Wutai by Japanese Buddhist pilgrim Ennin (793–864) has left an indelible testimony of the sites and history of the mountain on the eve of the devastating mid-ninth century Buddhist persecution. Baumer's modern photo-journey similarly offers an up-to-date account of the religious institutions and practices of Mt Wutai in the early twenty-first century, including the prominence of Tibetan Buddhism since the late imperial period, in the aftermath of the Cultural Revolution, and during the throes of China's modernization. This remarkable book will be a valuable historical and ethnographical record for decades and perhaps centuries to come.'

—**Dorothy C. Wong,** Associate Professor of East Asian Art, University of Virginia

Index of names and places

Note: Page numbers in *italics* refer to photographs. An ampersand (&) in a page range indicates the passage is interrupted by two or more pages of photographs or other material.

Bibliography

Alphen, Jan Van (ed.): *The Buddha in the Dragon Gate.* Etnographisch Museum, Antwerpen 2001.

An, Jianhua: *Der Mönch von heiliger Loyalität* (Shengzhong Heshang). Xianggang Bihui Chubanshe), Hong Kong 2004.

Barrett, T.H.: 'Climate change and religious response: The case of early medieval China'. In: *Journal of the Royal Asiatic Society,* London. April 2007, pp. 139–56.

Bauer, Wolfgang: *Geschichte der chinesischen Philosophie.* Beck, München 2006.

Baumer, Christoph: *Southern Silk Road.* Orchid Press, Bangkok, 2000.

— *The Church of the East. An Illustrated History of Assyrian Christianity.* I.B.Tauris, London 2006.

— 'Sogdian or Indian iconography and religious influences in Dandan-Uiliq (Xinjiang, China)?' In: *Proceedings of the International Seminar on The Art of Central Asia and the Indian Sub-Continent in Cross-Cultural Perspective (1st–14th cent. AD).* National Museum of New Delhi, March 2007.

Baumer, Christoph, Weber, Therese: *Eastern Tibet. Bridging Tibet and China.* Orchid Press, Bangkok, 2005.

Beckwith, Christopher: 'The Tibetans in the Ordos and North China: Considerations on the role of the Tibetan Empire in world history'. In: Beckwith Christopher (ed.): *Silver on Lapis: Tibetan Literary Culture and History.* Tibet Society, Bloomington 1987.

Bell, Charles: *Portrait of the Dalai Lama.* Collins, London 1946.

Benn, James: 'Where text meets flesh: burning the body as an apocryphal practice in Chinese Buddhism'. In: *History of Religions,* University of Chicago Press, Vol. 37, No. 4, May 1998, pp. 295–322.

— *Burning for the Buddha. Self-immolation in Chinese Buddhism.* University of Hawaii Press, Honolulu 2007.

Berger, Patricia: 'Miracles in Nanjing: An Imperial Record of the 5th Karmapa's visit to the Chinese capital'. In: Weidner, Marsha (ed.): *Cultural Intersections in Later Chinese Buddhism.* University of Hawaii Press, Honolulu 2001.

Berry, Scott: *Monks, Spies and a Soldier of Fortune. The Japanese in Tibet.* Athlone Press, London 1995.

Birnbaum, Raoul: *Studies on the mysteries of Manjushri.* Society for the Study of Chinese Religions, Boulder 1983.

— 'Thoughts on T'ang Buddhist mountain traditions and their context'. In: *T'ang Studies,* University of Wisconsin, Madison 1984.

— 'The manifestation of a monastery: Shen-Ying's experiences on Mount Wu-T'ai in T'ang context'. In: *Journal of the American Oriental Society*, New Haven, Vol. 106.1, 1986.

Blofeld, John: *Rad des Lebens*. Rascher, Zürich 1961. *The Wheel of Life*, Shambala, Berkeley 1972.

Boerschmann, Ernst: *Baukunst und Landschaft in China*. Ernst Wasmuth, Berlin 1926.

Bonavia, David: *China's Warlords*. Oxford University Press, Hong Kong 1995.

Brauen, Martin (ed.): *Die Dalai Lamas*. Arnoldsche, Stuttgart 2005.

Brentjes, Burchard: *Der Tierstil in Eurasien*. Seemann, Leipzig 1982.

Bunce, Frederick W.: *An Encyclopaedia of Buddhist Deities, Demigods, Godlings, Saints and Demons*. D.K. Printworld, New Delhi 1994.

Carpini, Johannes von Plano: *Kunde von den Mongolen*. Thorbecke, Sigmaringen 1997.

Cartelli, Mary Anne: 'On a five-colored cloud: the Songs of Mount Wutai'. *The Journal of the American Oriental Society*. University of Michigan, Ann Arbor, Michigan January 2004.

Chandra, Lokesh: *Dictionary of Buddhist Iconography*, 15 vols. P.K. Goel, Delhi 1999-2005.

Chapin, Helen: *A Long Roll of Buddhist Images*. Artibus Asiae, Ascona 1972.

Ch'en, Kenneth: *Buddhism in China. A Historical Survey*. Princeton University Press 1964.

— *The Chinese Transformation of Buddhism*. Princeton University Press 1973.

Cheng, Manchao: *The Origin of Chinese Deities*. Foreign Languages Press, Beijing 1995.

Chin, Connie: 'Monuments in the Desert. A note on economic and social roots of the development of Buddhism along the Silk Road'. In: Waugh, Daniel C. (ed.): *The Silk Road. The Silkroad Foundation*, Saratoga, Vol. 3, No. 2, 2005, pp. 8–15.

Chin, Hsiao (ed.): *A Special Exhibition of Recently Acquired Gilt-Bronze Buddhist Images*. Ausstellungskatalog. National Palace Museum, Taipei, 1996.

Confucius: *The Analects*. Translated by Arthur Waley. Knopf, New York 2000.

Cornu, Philippe: *Dictionnaire encyclopédique du Bouddhisme*. Le Seuil, Paris 2001.

Cui, Zhengsen (ed.): *Mountain Wutai Temple*. Shanxi Renmin Chubanshe, Taiyuan 2002.

— *108 Temples of Mt. Wutai*. Shanxi Science and Technology Press, Taiyuan 2004.

— *Mountain Wutai*. Shanxi Renmin Chubanshe, Taiyuan 2005.

Denwood, Philip, Singer, Jane Casey (eds): *Tibetan Art. Towards a definition of style*. Laurence King Publishing, London 1997.

Dschuang, Dsi: *Das wahre Buch vom südlichen Blütenland*. Übersetzt von Richard Wilhelm. Diederichs, München 1994.

Dumonlin, Heinrich: *A History of Zen Buddhism*. Manohartal Publishers, New Delhi 2000.

Eberhard, Wolfram: *Lexikon chinesischer Symbole*. Ex Libris, Zürich 1995.

Eitel, Ernest: *Handbook of Chinese Buddhism being a Sanskrit–Chinese Dictionary*. Trubner, London 1888.

Eliade, Mircea (ed.): *The Encyclopedia of Religion*. Simon & Schuster, New York 1995.

Encyclopaedia Britannica. 32 + 1 vols. Chicago, 1998.

Everding, Karl-Heinz: *Die Präexistenzen der Lcan Skya Qutuqtus*. Harrassowitz, Wiesbaden 1988.

Faure, Bernhard: *The Will to Orthodoxy. A Critical Genealogy of Northern Chan Buddhism*. Stanford University Press, Stanford 1997.

Ferguson, Andy: *Zen's Chinese Heritage. The Masters and their Teachings*. Wisdom, Boston 2000.

Ferrari, Alfonsa: *Mk'yen Brtse's guide to the holy places of Central Tibet*. IsMEO, Rome 1958.

Fischer, Emil: *Travels through Japan, Korea and China*. Tientsin Press, Tientsin 1928.

Fischer-Schreiber, Ingrid et al.: *The Shambala Dictionary of Buddhism and Zen*. Shambala, Boston 1991.

Frédéric, Louis: *Les Dieux du Bouddhisme*. Flammarion, Paris 1992.

Getty, Alice: *The Gods of Northern Buddhism*. Dover Publications, New York 1988.

Ghose, Rajeshwari (ed.): *In the Footsteps of the Buddha. An Iconic Journey from India to China.* University of Hong Kong, 1998.

Giès, Jacques: *Les arts de l'Asie centrale. La collection Paul Pelliot du musée national des arts asiatiques – Guimet.* Réunion des Musées Nationaux, Paris 1996.

Gimello, Robert: 'Chang Shang-ying on Wu-t'ai Shan'. In: Naqin, Susan, Chün-fang Yü, (eds): *Pilgrims and Sacred Sites in China.* University of California Press, Berkeley 1992.

— *Environments Worldly and Other-wordly: Wutaishan and the Question of What makes a Buddhist Mountain Sacred.* www.hds.harward.edu, December 2006.

Gridley, Marilyn: *Chinese Buddhist Sculpture under the Liao.* Intl. Academy of Indian Culture and Aditya Prakashan, New Delhi 1993.

Gruschke, Andreas: *Grundlagen der Verbreitung des Lamaismus in China.* In: *Das neue China*, Berlin 27. Jg. March 2000.

— *The Cultural Monuments of Tibet's Outer Provinces.* Amdo. Vol. 2. White Lotus, Bangkok 2001.

Gundert, Wilhelm (editor and translator): *Bi-Yän-Lu. Meister Yüan-wu's Niederschrift von der Smaragdenen Felswand.* Carl Hanser Verlag, München 1967–77.

Guo, Zhicheng: 'Wutai Shan – A Museum of Chinese Temples'. In: *Orientations*, Hong Kong May 1996.

Haarmann, Harald: *Universalgeschichte der Schrift.* Campus, Frankfurt/Main, 1991.

Halén, Harry: *Mirrors of the Void. Buddhist Art in the National Museum of Finland.* Museovirasto, Helsinki 1987.

Henss, Michael: 'The Bodhisattva-Emperor: Tibeto-Chinese portraits of sacred and secular rule in the Qing Dynasty' (Two parts) In: *Oriental Art Magazine*, Singapore. Vol XLVII, No. 3 + 5, 2001.

— *Rölpai, Dorje* – 'Teacher of the Empire. A profile of the life and works of the Second Changya Huthugtu, 1717–1786'. In: *Chinese Imperial Patronage. Treasures from Temples and Palaces.* Asian Art Gallery, London 2005.

Hershock, Peter: *Chan Buddhism.* University of Hawaii Press, Honolulu 2005.

Higuchi, Takayasu (ed.): *The Silk Road and the World of Xuanzhang.* The Asahi Shimbun 120th Anniversary Commemorative Exhibition, Nara 1999.

Hilmer, Andreas: Für Tibet und die Welt; Interview mit dem XIV. Dalai Lama'. In: *Geo Epoche.* Gruner+Jahr, Hamburg, No. 26, 2007.

Howard, Angela Falco et al. *Chinese Sculpture.* Yale University Press, 2006.

Hsüan, Hua: *Pure Land Talks at Buddha Root Farm.* Buddhist Text Translation Society, Burlingame 2003.

Hu, Cheng Xi: *A Guide to the Temples in the Wutai Mountains.* Today China Publishing Company, Beijing 1993.

Huang, Po: *The Zen Teaching of Huang Po.* Translated by John Blofeld. Grove Press, New York 1958.

Hummel, Siegbert: Die Fußspur des Gautama-Buddha auf dem Wu-T'ai-Shan. Asiatische Studien. Lang, Bern, XXV, 1971.

Huo, Xushu, Qi Xiaoshan: *The Buddhist Art in Xinjiang along the Silk Road.* Xinjiang University Press, Urumqi 2006.

Jaini, Padmanabh: 'The story of Sudhana and Manohara: an analysis of the texts and the Borobudur reliefs'. In: *Bulletin of the School of Oriental and African Studies*, University of London. Vol. XXIX, part 3, 1966.

Jing, Anning: 'The portraits of Kubilai Khan and Chabi by Anige (1245–1306), a Nepali artist at the Yuan Court'. In: *Artibus Asiae*, Ascona, Vol. LIV, 1/2, 1994.

Johaentges, Karl, Franz, Uli: Chinas *Heilige Berge.* Frederking & Thaler, München 2005.

Kämpfe, Hans-Rainer (editor and translator): *Ni Ma'i, Od Zer/Naran-U Gerel. Die Biographie des 2. Pekinger lCan skya Qutuqtu Rol pa' rdo rje (1717–1786).* Monumenta Tibetica Historica, Section. II, vol. 1. VGH Wissenschaftsverlag St Augustin 1976.

Karetzky, Patricia Eichenbaum: 'The recently discovered Chin Dynasty murals illustrating the life of the Buddha at Yen-Shang-Ssu, Shansi'. In: *Artibus Asiae*, Ascona, Vol. XLII, No. 4, 1980.

Kasser, Rodolphe: 'Saint Antoine et la naissance du monachisme'. In: *Le Monde de la Bible.* Bayard, Paris, No. 177, May–June 2007.

Kungfutse: *Gespräche (Lun Yü)*. Diederichs, Düsseldorf, 1955.

Lee, Jung Hyo: 'Buddhist Imageries of China proper during the Han-Jin Period'. In: *Chinese Archaeology*; edited by Liu Qingzhu. China Social Sciences Press, Beijing, Vol. 6, 2006.

Lee-Kalish, Jeong-he (ed.): *Tibet Klöster öffnen ihre Schatzkammern*. Ausstellungskatalog. Kulturstiftung Ruhr, Essen u. Hirmer, München 2006.

Li, Hengsheng: *Les grottes de Yungang et la dynastie des Wei du Nord*. Editions des sciences et techniques du Shanxi, Taiyuan 2005.

Li, Yuming (ed.): *A Panorama of Ancient Chinese Architecture in Shanxi*. Shanxi People's Publishing House, Taiyuan 1986.

Lin, Chi: *The Zen Teachings of Master Lin-Chi*. Translated by Burton Watson. Columbia University Press, New York 1993.

Lin, Sen-shou: 'Hui Ke. China's Second Ch'an Patriarch'. In: *Tzu Chi Quarterly*, Taipei 2004/1. www.taipei. tzuchi.org.tw/tzquart/2004.

Ling, Haicheng: *Buddhism in China*. China Intercontinental Press, Beijing 2004.

Liu, Yan, Han Chunhong (ed.): *Scenic Beauty of Wutai Mountain*. China Photographic Publishing House, Beijing 2005.

Lusthaus, Dan: 'Chinese Buddhist philosophy'. In: Craig E. (ed.): *Routledge Encyclopedia of Philosophy*. Routledge, London 1998.

Mannerheim, C.G.: *Across Asia from West to East*. Suomalaisen Kirjallisuuden Seuran Kirjapainon Oy, Helsinki 1940.

Marchand, Ernesta: 'The Panorama of Wu-T'ai Shan as an example of tenth century cartography'. In: *Oriental Art*, Singapore XXII/2, 1976.

May, Reinhard: *Heidegger's Hidden Sources. East Asian Influences on his Work*. Routledge, London 1996.

Mullikin, Maria Augusta, Hotchkis, Anna: *The Nine Sacred Mountains of China. An Illustrated Record of Pilgrimages Made in the Years 1935–1936*. Vetch and Lee, Hong Kong 1973.

Naqin, Susan, Chün-fang, Yü (ed): *Pilgrims and Sacred Sites in China*. University of California Press, Berkeley 1992.

Notz, Klaus-Josef: *Lexikon des Buddhismus*. Fourier, Wiesbaden 2002.

Ollone, Vicomte de: *In Forbidden China. The D'Ollone Mission 1906–1908*. Fischer Unwin, London 1912.

Oort, H.A. van: *The Iconography of Chinese Buddhism in Traditional China*. E.J. Brill, Leiden 1986.

Otto, Franck: 'Zen'. In: *Der Buddhismus*. Geo Epoche. Gruner+Jahr, Hamburg, Nr. 26, 2007.

Overmyer, Daniel L.: 'Religion in China Today'. In: *The China Quarterly Special Issues*. New Series, No. 3. Cambridge University Press, Cambridge 2003.

Paludan, Ann: *Chronicle of the Chinese Emperors*. Thames & Hudson, London 1998.

Pelliot, Paul: *Notes critiques d'histoire kalmouke*. Œuvres posthumes, Bd. VI, Adrien-Maisonneuve, Paris 1960.

Peng, Xunhou: *China in the World Anti-Fascist War*. China Intercontinental Press, Beijing 2005.

Pi, Yuanping, Yang Chun'e: (eds): *Zu den Gipfeln des Wutai Shan*. Shanxi Guji Chubanshe, Taiyuan 2005.

Pine, Red (editor and translator): *The Zen Teachings of Bodhidharma*. North Point Press, New York 1989.

Pokotilow, D.: 'Der Wu Tai Shan und seine Klöster. Eine historisch-geographische Skizze und Schilderung der örtlichen Verhältnisse im Jahr 1889'. In: *Sinica-Sonderausgabe*. Jahrgang 1935, herausgegeben von Erwin Rouselle. China-Institut, J.W. Goethe-Universität, Frankfurt a.M.

Pratt, James: *The Pilgrimage of Buddhism*. Macmillan, New York 1928.

Prip-Møller, Johannes: *Chinese Buddhist Monasteries*. Hong Kong University Press, Hong Kong 1982.

Puay-Peng, Ho: 'Building for Glitter and Eternity: The works of the Late Ming Master Builder Miaofeng on Wutai Shan'. In: *Orientations*, Hong Kong May 1996.

Reichelt, Karl Ludwig: *Truth and Tradition in Chinese Buddhism*. Manoharlal Publ., New Delhi 2001.

Reischauer, Edwin: *Ennin's Travels in Tang China*. Ronald Press, New York 1955.

Reiter, Florian: *Religionen in China*. Beck, München 2002.

Rhie, Marylin M.: *The Fo-kuang ssu*. Garland Publishing, New York 1977.

— *Early Buddhist Art of China & Central Asia*. Brill, Leiden 1999, 2002.

Rhie, Marylin M., Thurman Robert A.F.: *Wisdom and Compassion. The Sacred Art of Tibet*. Catalogue. Abrams Inc. New York 1991.

Rousselle, Erwin: *Vom Sinn der buddhistischen Bildwerke in China*. Wissenschaftliche Buchgesellschaft, Darmstadt 1958.

Rubin, Museum New York: http://www.rmanyc.org/ education/resources/wutaishan/blockprint.

Rubruk, Wilhelm von: *Reisen zum Grosskhan der Mongolen*. Thienemann, Stuttgart 1984.

Rupprecht, Kronprinz von Bayern: *Reiseerinnerungen aus Ostasien*. Kösel & Pustet, München 1923.

Salzmann, Erich von: *Im Sattel durch Zentralasien*. Reimer, Berlin 1908.

Schmidt-Glinzer Helwig (ed.): *Mo Ti. Gegen den Krieg*. Diederichs, Düsseldorf 1975.

Schneider, Richard: *Un moine indien au Wou-T'ai Chan. Relation d'un pèlerinage*. In: Cahiers d'Extrême-Asie, section de Kyoto. Editor Jean-Pierre Drège. Ecole française d'Extrême-Orient, Paris 1987.

Schulemann, Günther: *Geschichte der Dalai-Lamas*. Harrassowitz, Leipzig 1958.

Schumann, Hans Wolfgang: *Buddhistische Bilderwelt. Ein ikonographisches Handbuch des Mahayana- und Tantrayana-Buddhismus.* Diederichs, München 1993.

Sharf, Robert: *Coming to Terms with Chinese Buddhism.* University of Hawaii Press, Honolulu 2002.

Shibata, M. & M.: *Les maîtres du Tch'an (Zen) en Chine.* Maisonneuve & Larose, Paris 1985.

Sinor, Denis (ed.): *The Cambridge History of Early Inner Asia*. Cambridge, 1990.

Siren, Osvald: *Chinese Sculpture from the Fifth to the Fourteenth Century*. Reprint SDI Publications, Bangkok 1998.

— *The Chinese on Art and Painting*. Reprint Dover Publications, Mineola 2005.

Snelling, John: *Buddhism in Russia. The Story of Agvan Dorzhiev, Lhasa's Emissary to the Tsar*. Element, Shaftesbury 1993.

Song, Bo: *Buddha Religion. Great Place Wutai Shan*. Huayi Chubanshe, Beijing 1998.

Stein, Rolf. A.: *Avalokiteshvara/Kouan-yin, un exemple de transformation d'un dieu en déesse*. In: Cahiers d'Extrême-Asie, section de Kyoto. Ecole française d'Extrême-Orient, Paris 1986.

Steinhardt, Nancy: 'The Tang architectural icon and the politics of Chinese architectural history'. In: *The Art Bulletin*, College Art Association, New York 2004.

Sullivan, Michael: *The Cave Temples of Maichishan*. Faber & Faber, London 1969.

Sutras:

The Flower Ornament Scripture. A Translation of the Avatamsaka Sutra, published by Thomas Cleary. Shambala, Boston 1993.

— *The Lotus Sutra*, translated by Burton Watson. Columbia University Press, New York 1993.

— *Das Lotos-Sutra*, übersetzt von Max Deeg, Wissenschaftliche Buchgesellschaft Darmstadt 2007.

— *Sutra in Forty-Two Sections*. A general explanation by Hsüan Hua. Dharma Realm Buddhas Association, San Francisco 1977.

— *The Platform Sutra of the Sixth Patriarch*. The text of the Tun-Huang manuscript, translated by P.B. Yampolsky. Columbia University Press, New York 1967.

— *The Pratyutpanna Samadhi Sutra*. Translated by Lokaksema and Paul Harrison. Numata Center for Buddhist Translation and Research, Berkeley 1998.

— *The Surangama Samadhi Sutra*. Translated by Kumarajiva and Paul Harrison. Numata Center for Buddhist Translation and Research, Berkeley 1998.

— *The Sutra of Queen Srimala of the Lion's Roar*. Translated by Diana Paul. Numata Center for Buddhist Translation and Research, Berkeley 2004.

— *The Ullambana Sutra*. The Buddhist Text Society. www. bttsonline.org, www.geocities.com/tokyo/pagoda/3570/ sutrao.

— *The Vimalakirti Sutra*, translated by Burton Watson. Columbia University Press, New York 1997.

Swanson, Paul: *Foundations of T'ien-Tai Philosophy. The Flowering of the Two Truths Theory in Chinese Buddhism*. Asian Humanities Press, California 1989.

Tamura, Yoshiro, Hunter Jeffrey: *Japanese Buddhism: A Cultural History*. Kosei, Tokyo 2000.

Tribe, Anthony: 'The cult of Manjusri'. In: *Western Buddhist Review*, Birmingham. Vol 1 (no date) www.westernbuddhistreview.com/vol.1.

Tsukamoto, Zenryu: *A History of Chinese Early Buddhism. From its Introduction to the Death of Hui-yüan*. Kodansha, Tokyo 1979.

Tuttle, Gray: *Tibetan Buddhists in the Making of Modern China*. Columbia University Press, New York 2005.

— *Tibetan Buddhism at Ri bo rtse Inga/Wutai Shan in Modern Times*. In: *Journal of the International Association of Tibetan Studies JIATS*. No. 2, August 2006.

Victoria, Brian Daizen: *Zen at War*. Rowman & Littlefield, Lanham 2006.

Wang Yi'e: *Daoism in China*. China Intercontinental Press, Beijing 2004.

Watson, Burton (editor and translator): *Records of the Grand Historian of China*. Translated from the Shih Chi of Ssu-Ma Ch'ien. Columbia University Press, New York 1971.

Weber, Therese: *The Language of Paper*. Orchid Press, Bangkok 2007.

Welter, Albert: *Monks, Rulers and Literati. The Political Ascendancy of Chan Buddhism*. Oxford University Press, Oxford 2006.

Wen-shing Chou: *Ineffable paths. Mapping Wutaishan in Qing dynasty, China*. The Art Bulletin, College Art Association, New York March 2007.

Whitfield, Roderick: *Dunhuang: Caves of the Singing Sands*. 2 vols. Textile and Art Pubs., London 1995.

Wieczorek, Alfried, Tellenbach, Rosendahl, Wilfried, Mumien (eds): *Der Traum vom ewigen Leben*. Philipp v. Zabern, Mainz 2007.

Williams, C.A.S.: *Outline of Chinese Symbolism and Art Motives*. Dover, New York 1976.

Williams, Paul: *Mahayana Buddhism. The doctrinal foundations*. Routledge, London 2005.

Wimmel, Kenneth: *William Woodville Rockhill. Scholar-Diplomat of the Tibetan Highlands*. Orchid Press, Bangkok 2003.

Wong, Dorothy: A Reassessment of the Representation of Mt. Wutai from Dunhuang Cave 61. In: Archives of Asian Art. The Asian Society, New York XLVI/1993.

Wright, Arthur: *Buddhism in Chinese History*. Atheneum, New York 1965.

Wu, Cheng-en: *Monkeys Pilgerfahrt. Die phantastische Reise des Affen Monkey – ein Buch aus den Essenzen des Himmels und der Erde*. Goldmann, München 1980.

Wu, John C.H.: *The Golden Age of Zen. Zen Masters of the Tang Dynasty*. World Wisdom, Bloomington 2003.

Xu, Xiake: *Randonnées aux sites sublimes*. Gallimard 1993.

Yu, Anthony C.: *State and Religion in China*. Open Court, Chicago 2005.

Zheng, Lixin: *Guide to Chinese Buddhism*. Foreign Languages Press, Beijing 2004.

Zhong, Xin, Wei, Lingwen: *Wu Tai Shan*. Cultural Relics Publishing House of Sanxi, Taiyuan 1984.

Zürcher, Emil: *The Buddhist Conquest of China*. E.J. Brill, Leiden 1972.

Acknowledgements

This book was produced only with the help of many people. A few preferred to remain anonymous; others are briefly acknowledged here, in alphabetical order.

Abbess Shi Chang Long of Baiyun Si Convent, who granted me two interviews and allowed me to photograph the birthday celebration for Shijiafo without restriction.
Abbot Fan of Xiantong Monastery, who kindly wrote the foreword.
Abbot Sheng Zhong of Shuxing Si Monastery, who granted me an extended interview.
All abbots and abbesses who permitted me to take photographs in their monasteries.
The monk **Xiang Xue**, vice president of the Buddhist Association of Beijing, for an informative conversation.
Helen Abbott of the Rubin Museum of Art, New York, who gave me the right to publish, free of charge, the colour map from *c.* 1846.
Maria-Antonia Fonseca, Moghegno, who read through the German manuscript critically.

Michael Henss, Zurich, who helped me countless times to identify photographed deities.
Professor Angela Howard, State University of New Jersey, who helped me to date the bronze figure of Maitreya at the Metropolitan Museum, New York.
Subhu Sengupta, Beijing and Zurich, who photographed Wutai Shan during a bitterly cold winter.
Grey Tuttle, Columbia University, who gave me valuable advice and arranged my contact with the Rubin Museum of Art, New York.
Professor Veronika Veit, University of Bonn, who provided advice regarding the identification of the pagoda of Ruiying Si.
Professor Therese Weber, Arlesheim, who accompanied me to Wutai Shan in the autumn of 2006 and took active part in the exploration of the monasteries and in many discussions.
Wei Zhang, Zurich, who identified some deities, translated names and inscriptions, and checked the pinyin transliteration.

About the maps and photo credits

Maps

Wutai Shan and its five terraces, (map drawn after GPS-data taken 2006 and 2007) pp. 178-79

The monastery city of Taihuai, (map drawn after GPS-data taken 2006 and 2007) pp. 208-09

Photo Credits

All photographs are by the author except for the following:

Boerschmann Ernst: pp. 175 bottom, 290
Finnland National Museum, Helsinki, © Osmo Thiel: pp. 47, 48
Gu Di/CTP/Redlink, Hong Kong: p. 160
Johaentges Karl, Hannover: pp. 26, 35, 116, 126

Liu Yang/CTP/Redlink, Hong Kong: p. 88
Musée Guimet, Paris-musée national des Arts asiatiques, © Photo RMN/©Richard Lambert: p. 61
Palace Museum of Beijing: p. 223
Shan Xiao Gang/CTP/Redlink, Hong Kong: p. 224 bottom
The Metropolitan Museum of Art, John Stewart Kennedy Fund, 1926 (26.123)
    Image © The Metropolitan Museum of Art: p. 40
The Rubin Museum of Art, New York: pp. 228–29, front- and endpapers
Tuttle Grey, Columbia University: pp. 141, 264
Wang Miao/CTP/Redlink, Hong Kong: pp. 146–47
Weber Therese: pp. 16, 28, 67, 144, 145, 182, 202 left, 227, 250, 251, 317 bottom, 325 all, 326, 340
Zhu Jian Quan/ CTP/Redlink, Hong Kong: p. 2, back jacket.

Christoph Baumer – a leading explorer of Central Asia, Tibet and China – has written several well-received books in the fields of history, religion, archaeology and travel. These include *The Church of the East: An Illustrated History of Assyrian Christianity* (2006) and *Traces in the Desert: Journeys of Discovery across Central Asia* (2008), both published by I.B.Tauris. Dr Baumer is President of the Society for the Exploration of EurAsia and a member of the Explorers' Club, New York, and the Royal Asiatic Society and the Royal Geographical Society, London.

The author Christoph Baumer with the abbot of Shuxian Si Monastery, Sheng Zhong.